The American Elections of 1980

Edited by Austin Ranney

American Enterprise Institute for Public Policy Research
Washington and London

Library of Congress Cataloging in Publication Data
Main entry under title:

The American elections of 1980.

  (AEI studies ; 327)
  Includes index.
   1. Presidents—United States—Election—1980—Addresses,
essays, lectures. 2. Carter, Jimmy, 1924- —
Addresses, essays, lectures. 3. Reagan, Ronald—
Addresses, essays, lectures. I. Ranney, Austin.
II. Series.
E875.A43   324.973'0926   81-7907
ISBN 0-8447-3447-0   AACR2
ISBN 0-8447-3448-9 (pbk.)

AEI Studies 327

Second printing, February 1982

Printed in the United States of America

030039

Contents

Preface

This book is the American Enterprise Institute's first analysis of an American election. Since it is intended to be the first of a continuing series, it seems appropriate to begin by saying something about the kind of book we have tried to produce.

The book will generally follow the leads of two well-known series on elections in other democratic countries. One is AEI's At the Polls series, directed by Howard R. Penniman, which includes books on at least two national elections in each of nineteen democratic countries on five continents, each written mainly by scholars from the particular countries concerned with occasional participation by American experts on the countries.[1] The other is the Nuffield studies—volumes on all British general elections from 1945 on, sponsored by Nuffield College, Oxford, with the distinguished British political scientist David Butler as the sole or senior author for every volume beginning with the one on the 1951 election.[2]

There is, however, one major difference between this book and most of the At the Polls volumes and all of the Nuffield studies: Each of those series focuses on a particular "general election"—that is, an election in which *all* of the seats in the dominant house of the national legislature are contested, and the party or coalition of parties that wins a majority of the seats not only controls the legislature but also determines who will be the executive head of government. In this sense, the United States does not have general elections. The elections held in "presidential years," such as 1980, come the closest, but even they are not full-fledged general elections. In 1980, for example, American voters in all fifty states and the District of Columbia voted

[1] As of April 1981 the series included books on elections in Australia, Canada, France, the Federal Republic of Germany, Great Britain, India, Ireland, Israel, Japan, New Zealand, Scandinavia, and Venezuela. AEI has also published a general comparative study of electoral institutions and processes in twenty-eight democratic countries: David Butler, Howard R. Penniman, and Austin Ranney, eds., *Democracy at the Polls* (Washington, D.C.: American Enterprise Institute, 1981).
[2] For a general review and evaluation of the Nuffield studies, see Austin Ranney, "Thirty Years of 'Psephology,'" *British Journal of Political Science*, vol. 6 (April 1976), pp. 217-30.

for president and vice-president; voters in each of the 435 congressional districts chose the district's member of the House of Representatives; but the staggered terms of senators meant that only thirty-four of the fifty states held senatorial elections.

There were also elections for some state offices in forty-five of the fifty states in 1980,[3] but in this book we will consider only the elections for national offices. Many books have been and continue to be written on American national elections in particular years, including 1980. They use a wide variety of approaches, ranging from the personal-observation-and-interpretation journalism of Theodore H. White, Elizabeth Drew, and Jules Witcover to Richard M. Scammon's authoritative biennial compilations of election returns. This book, however, will use an approach similar to that used in the At the Polls series and the Nuffield studies.

Since what happened in the 1980 presidential and congressional elections was in part a consequence of what had happened during the three-plus years of the Carter administration preceding them, we begin with my summary of the main events in that administration, particularly as they bore upon the ups and downs of President Carter's popularity, from its inauguration on January 20, 1977, to the formal opening of the 1980 campaign with the Iowa caucuses on January 21, 1980. We follow with chapters by Nelson W. Polsby, Charles O. Jones, and Michael J. Malbin on the preconvention contests for the two major parties' nominations and the main events of their conventions. All three authors attended the conventions they cover, and much of what they report is based on personal observation and interviews.

Next comes a chapter on the campaign and the issues by Albert R. Hunt, who traveled with the candidates and covered the day-by-day developments in the campaign for the *Wall Street Journal*. It is followed by Michael J. Robinson's chapter analyzing the content and impact of campaign coverage by the mass news media. William Schneider's chapter then examines the presidential election returns and public opinion polls to describe how and why the voters voted (or stayed home) as they did. This is followed by a chapter by Thomas E. Mann and Norman J. Ornstein describing what happened in the congressional elections, with special attention to the unexpectedly large Republican gains in the Senate.

---

[3] Thirteen states elected governors, and forty-four elected some legislators. The "off-years" (nonpresidential years) see substantially more state elections: In 1982, for example, thirty-six states will elect governors and forty-five will elect some legislators. Only five states—Kentucky, Louisiana, Mississippi, New Jersey, and Virginia—elect their governors and legislators in odd-numbered years.

The book closes with two chapters assessing what the election means for the future of the political system and public policy in the United States. Anthony King, an eminent British observer of American politics, points out the sharp differences between the way Americans choose their presidents and most other democracies choose their heads of government, and questions whether the American process is likely to produce the kinds of presidents the nation needs. Aaron Wildavsky, an eminent American analyst of public institutions and policies, concludes by assessing the possible consequences of the election for the future course of public policy under the Reagan administration.

In these ways we hope to emulate the At the Polls series and the Nuffield studies by providing, in our chapters and our appendixes, not only the analyses of our authors but also the basic facts any reader will need to make his or her own best analysis. We have a long way to go before we can parallel the accumulated contributions of the two established series, but we hope that this book is a good first step.

Austin Ranney
Washington, D.C.
April 1981

1
The Carter Administration

Austin Ranney

In the American presidential election of 1980 the Republican challenger, former governor Ronald Reagan of California, defeated the Democratic incumbent, President Jimmy Carter, with 43,899,248 popular votes (50.8 percent) to Carter's 35,481,435 votes (41.0 percent). Independent candidate John Anderson received 5,719,437 votes (6.6 percent), Libertarian party candidate Ed Clark received 920,859 votes (1.1 percent), and the remaining 474,699 votes (0.5 percent) were divided among seventeen other candidates.

Carter carried six states (Georgia, Hawaii, Maryland, Minnesota, Rhode Island, and West Virginia) and the District of Columbia, for a total of 49 electoral votes, and Reagan carried the other forty-four states, for a total of 489 electoral votes.[1]

The presidential results were especially noteworthy in several respects. For one, 1980 was the second straight election—but only the fourth in the twentieth century—in which an incumbent president was defeated for reelection (although Reagan's margin of 9.8 percentage points was considerably larger than the margin of 2.1 points by which Carter defeated Gerald Ford in 1976).[2] And for another, it continued to be the case that no president since Dwight D. Eisenhower (1953–1961) has served two full terms.

In the Senate the preelection party division was fifty-eight Democrats, forty-one Republicans, and one Independent. Thirty-four seats were up for election; the Republicans made a startling gain of twelve seats and took control of the Senate with fifty-three seats to the Democrats' forty-six—the first time the GOP had won control of either house of Congress since the elections of 1952.

[1] The election returns are given in detail in appendixes A and B.
[2] In fifteen of the twenty-one presidential elections held in the twentieth century, an incumbent president has run for reelection. The incumbents have won eleven times and have lost four times (Taft in 1912, Hoover in 1932, Ford in 1976, and Carter in 1980). Jimmy Carter has the distinction of being the first Democratic president since Grover Cleveland in 1888 to be defeated for reelection.

In the House of Representatives the preelection party division was 273 Democrats, 159 Republicans, and 3 vacancies. In the elections the Republicans won a net gain of 33 seats, and the Ninety-seventh Congress began with 243 Democrats and 192 Republicans.[3] This was the largest increase for the Republicans in any election since 1966, and their total of 192 seats restored them to about the level they had held from 1966 to the "Watergate election" of 1974.

For America-watchers, the most interesting question posed by these results is this: Was 1980 a true "realigning election," like that of 1932, signaling that the era of Democratic dominance that began in 1932 had now come to an end and that in the 1980s the Republicans would be the majority party in both presidential and congressional politics? Or was 1980, like 1952, a "deviating election" in which the voters' dissatisfactions with Jimmy Carter and a number of liberal Democratic senators precipitated a sharp but temporary setback for the Democrats—a setback from which they are likely to recover in the next election or two?

This book cannot offer definitive answers to these questions, if only because in the early 1980s it is too soon to tell. Massive party realignments do not take place in a single election; they take place over several elections. The 1932 election, for example, was a massive repudiation of Herbert Hoover and the Republicans because of their failure to cope with the Great Depression. Still, it took the activism of Franklin D. Roosevelt and his New Deal to make the Democrats into the majority party, and it was only after the Democrats' unprecedented gains in the 1934 congressional elections[4] and Roosevelt's landslide reelection in 1936 that the Democrats had clearly replaced the Republicans as the majority party.[5]

There is little doubt that the 1980 elections gave the Republicans a great opportunity to become again the nation's majority party. Whether or not they take advantage of that opportunity depends upon what the Reagan administration and the Republican Senate do with their power and upon how their uses of it are perceived by the voters. Hence what happens in the 1982 and 1984 elections will tell

---

[3] The congressional results are given in detail in appendix F.

[4] The 1934 elections remain the only midterm election since the Civil War in which the president's party has had a net gain of seats in both houses of Congress. For a review of this pattern and various explanations of it, see Austin Ranney, "The 1978 Congressional Elections: A Renaissance for Republicans?" *Public Opinion*, March/April 1978, pp. 17-20, and the studies cited therein.

[5] For a detailed study of the conditions producing this and earlier party realignments in American history, see James L. Sundquist, *Dynamics of the Party System* (Washington, D.C.: The Brookings Institution, 1973).

us a good deal more about whether 1980 was another 1932 or another 1952.

Nevertheless, the 1980 elections represented, at a minimum, a powerful reaction against the state of affairs under the Carter administration. Accordingly, it seems appropriate to begin this book with a review of the administration's course from the time of its inception to January 21, 1980, when the Iowa precinct caucuses officially opened the presidential selection process of 1980. That is the task of the present chapter.

Conception, Gestation, and Birth: 1974–1976

Perhaps the most remarkable thing about the Carter administration is that it existed at all—for Jimmy Carter won the 1976 presidential nomination of his party against greater odds than those overcome by any other major party nominee in history. When he began his campaign for the nomination in 1974, he was a one-term southern governor, and neither party had nominated a nonincumbent Southerner since the Civil War. He was almost entirely unknown to the national public and only slightly better known to the national and state leaders of his party. The first Gallup poll of Democratic voters in 1976 showed that only 4 percent favored Carter for the nomination, tying him with Edmund Muskie for last behind Edward Kennedy, Hubert Humphrey, George Wallace, Henry Jackson, Birch Bayh, and George McGovern.

Yet, against all the odds, Carter was nominated on the first ballot by the 1976 Democratic National Convention. The story of how he and his Georgia acolytes brought off this political miracle has been well told elsewhere and can only be outlined here.[6] Its essentials are that the new presidential nominating process created by the post-1969 reforms—especially the proliferation of presidential primaries and the allocation of delegates proportionally to the candidates' votes in the preference polls—made things much easier than ever before for a far-outsider like Carter. The "imperial presidencies" of Lyndon Johnson and Richard Nixon, with their attendant traumas of the Vietnam war and the Watergate scandal, made many Americans long for a decent man who had had no part in Washington's recent messes (even Gerald Ford had, after all, pardoned Nixon).

[6] The leading accounts include: Jules Witcover, *Marathon: The Pursuit of the Presidency, 1972-1976* (New York: New American Library, 1977); Martin Schram, *Running for President: A Journal of the Carter Campaign* (New York: Simon and Schuster, 1977); and Betty Glad, *Jimmy Carter: In Search of the Great White House* (New York: W. W. Norton, 1980) chaps. 11-20.

In November 1972 Hamilton Jordan wrote a long memorandum outlining the strategy by which Jimmy Carter could win the Democratic nomination in 1976, and his memorandum became the battle plan. It was a brilliant plan, based on a clear understanding that the new rules had created a new nominating game. Carter and his team executed the plan brilliantly and won. Their capture of the nomination was arguably the greatest feat in the entire history of presidential nominating politics.

The Carter team's performance in the 1976 general election contest was considerably less brilliant. Right after the Democratic convention, when Carter was safely nominated and Gerald Ford and Ronald Reagan were still locked in their bitter struggle for the Republican nomination, the Gallup poll gave Carter 62 percent to Ford's 29 percent—a 33-point lead. His lead shrank to 10 points just after the Republican convention, and in the November election he won by only 2.1 points (with 50.1 percent to Ford's 48.0 percent). Many observers believed this sharp drop in Carter's support was due to his poor campaign, whereas others put it down more to Ford's skill in capitalizing on the advantages of incumbency.

Yet the main significance of Carter's relatively poor performance in the general election campaign after his magnificent drive for the nomination strongly suggests that the new presidential selection process has separated nominating politics from electing politics and that a candidate and organization that are good at one may not be good at the other. (In this sense, at least, 1980 was a rerun of 1976: the Carter organization, with some help from the Ayatollah Khomeini and Leonid Brezhnev, handily turned back the Kennedy challenge, again locked up the nomination early—and again performed poorly in the campaign and election against the Republican candidate.)

Be that as it may, the inner circle of the Georgians in Carter's nomination campaign team—notably, Hamilton Jordan, Jody Powell, Charles Kirbo, Bert Lance, Gerald Rafshoon, Frank Moore, and Jack Watson—became and remained the inner circle of the Carter administration. And we have the testimony of James Fallows, Carter's chief speechwriter early in his administration, that the Georgians were acutely conscious that they had won the nomination where all the wiseacres in Washington had said it was impossible; it was the great experience of their lives, and it deeply colored their attitude toward the Washington establishment. In Fallows's words:

> At the start of the Administration, as in the general election campaign, Carter and his captains felt omniscient: they had done what no one else had been known to do. Why should

they take pains to listen to those who had designed the New Deal, the Fair Deal, the Great Society? The town was theirs for the taking; it would have required nothing more than allowing the old warriors a chance to help. But Powell and Jordan and Carter let these people know that they could go to hell. Where had they been, with all their sage advice, when the campaign was out of money and no one knew who Jimmy Carter was? What were they doing when Carter was drawing crowds of ten and twenty in tiny Iowa towns?[7]

Thus when the Carter administration found itself in major trouble in the next four years—as in the furor over Bert Lance's financial affairs in 1977, the "competency crisis" of April 1978, and the "crisis of confidence" of July 1979—they characteristically responded by turning to the inner circle of Georgians who had brought off the miracle of 1974–1976, not the Washington establishment that had doubted and opposed them.

The Game Plan

Every American administration begins with a version of what football coaches call the "game plan": a general strategy of action grounded in a certain basic conception of what the nation is like and what it needs and wants, and certain tactical notions of what kinds of people and policies will meet these needs and wants.

The core of the Carter game plan was the conviction that the American people were sick and tired of the Washington establishment and all of its products, especially those called "Vietnam," "Watergate," and "the imperial presidency." Again, the testimony of James Fallows:

It often seemed to me that "history," for Carter and those closest to him, consisted of Vietnam and Watergate; if they could avoid the errors, as commonly understood, of those two episodes, they would score well. No military intervention, no dirty tricks, no tape recorders on the premises, and no "isolation" of the President.[8]

This view led directly to certain approaches to making public policy but most of all to a strong emphasis on a new presidential style.

Style. When Jimmy Carter took the oath of office on January 20,

---

[7] James Fallows, "The Passionless Presidency," *Atlantic*, May 1979, pp. 33–46, at p. 46.
[8] Ibid., p. 38.

1977, he immediately sent out signals that his presidency would be the very opposite of the "imperial presidency" so discredited by the failures of Lyndon Johnson and Richard Nixon. Moreover, he and his advisers were well aware of how important symbols would be in carrying this message. As his private pollster and close adviser Patrick Caddell told him: "Too many good people have been defeated because they tried to substitute substance for style. They forgot to give the public the visible signals it needs to understand what is happening."[9]

So Carter appeared at the inauguration in an ordinary business suit, not the more formal dress worn by Ford before him and Reagan after him. When the presidential parade started for the White House from the Capitol, Carter did what no president had ever done before: hand in hand with his wife, he walked the mile and a half down Pennsylvania Avenue. Perhaps most important of all, he became the first president in history to choose as his official, bill-signing name the diminutive nickname "Jimmy Carter" rather than the name on his birth certificate, James Earl Carter, Jr., or even James E. Carter.[10] He announced that he did not want bands to play "Hail to the Chief" when he made an appearance anywhere. When he went on trips, whether to Camp David for a weekend or to a foreign capital for a summit conference, the television cameras showed him carrying his own suit bag aboard the planes. On the dozen or so occasions when he went to small towns for "town meetings" with their citizens, he stayed with a private family and made his own bed.

He had done similar things during his long and lonely campaign for the nomination, he was comfortable with them, and doing them was no mere cynical manipulation of symbols for political advantage. From his first campaign foray in 1974 to his "farewell address" on January 14, 1981, Carter deeply believed that he had a special relationship, direct and unmediated, with ordinary people, that he could learn from them and, like Antaeus touching the earth, renew his strength by communing with them face to face in small groups. That was far more important for true leadership than cajoling and stroking the leaders of the establishment. Carter put his core idea clearly in the early days of his administration when he addressed the office workers in the Department of Labor:

[9] Quoted in Haynes Johnson, *In the Absence of Power: Governing America* (New York: Viking, 1980), p. 142.
[10] Carter used "Jimmy" as his official name from his first entry into politics and continued it during his term as governor of Georgia: cf. Glad, *Jimmy Carter,* chaps. 5-10. One wonders about the symbolism of "Georgie Washington," "Tommy Jefferson," "Abie Lincoln," and "Frankie Roosevelt."

I am no better qualified than you are to address the problems of our country. We are partners in a process. . . . I also want us to realize that we are no better than anyone else. Just because I became president and because you work for the federal government or hold, even, an exalted job, doesn't make you any better than the unemployed American in Dallas, Texas, that you serve.

And to the workers in the Department of Commerce:

Arrogance is something that is a temptation for us all. I have tried to remove as much as I could the trappings of pomp and ceremony that has in the past followed presidents. I don't want ruffles and flourishes played when I walk into a group like this. I am just one of you.[11]

In his first "town meeting" at Clinton, Massachusetts, in March 1977, Carter urged everyone there and watching on television to write to him personally about their concerns and ideas for programs. "I'll tell my staff to bring these letters directly to me," he said. "You need not say that you were glad to have me with you and what a good job I did and so forth. Just say, 'This is what I think you ought to do to be a good president.' "[12]

They took him at his word: tens of thousands of letters flooded the White House, and the number of unopened letters soon exceeded 300,000. Moreover, between 20,000 and 30,000 telephone calls each day swamped the White House switchboard, and one of the results was that the White House staff, which Carter had promised to cut back severely as part of deimperializing the presidency, had to be increased substantially to handle the enormous increase in mail. Another result was that a good many calls from congressmen and other important political figures were lost in the flood and were not returned. For a time many of the leaders simply gave up trying to communicate with the president or his staff, and this state of affairs turned out to be all too typical of his relations with Congress.[13]

Relations with Congress and the Establishment. The reciprocal of having a direct and unmediated relationship with the people was needing to make no special effort to cultivate the Washington establishment, including the leaders and members of Congress. Indeed, it

---

[11] Both passages are quoted in Johnson, *In the Absence of Power*, pp. 148-49. Every Carter-watcher comments on how basic this view was to Carter's conception of the presidency: see, for example, Johnson, pp. 125, 142; and Glad, *Jimmy Carter*, pp. 409-11.

[12] Quoted in Johnson, *In the Absence of Power*, p. 153.

[13] Ibid.

would be better to keep them at arm's length to avoid the contagion of their narrow and distorted view of the world. As James Fallows puts it:

> Carter, who was able to learn from experience in a once-burned, twice-shy way, showed no inclination to prevent the burns by seeking associates who had been there before. Nowhere was he surer to need help than in his dealings with the Congress. His experience there was minimal, his campaign tone had been hostile, his skin crawled at the thought of the time-consuming consultations and persuasion that might be required to bring a legislator around. He did not know how congressmen talked, worked, and thought, how to pressure them without being a bully or flatter them without seeming a fool. He needed help from someone who knew all those things, who had spent time absorbing that culture. But for his congressional liaison, he chose a Georgian named Frank Moore, a man whose general aptitude was difficult for anyone outside the first circle to detect, and who had barely laid eyes upon the Capitol before Inauguration Day.[14]

Thus it is not surprising that Carter's early meetings with the leaders of Congress were more confrontational than cooperative. Though both sides were reasonably civil in expression, Carter typically opened the meetings by saying that the people demanded a particular policy—government reorganization or the energy package—and that Congress had better get to work on it. The congressional leaders—especially House Speaker "Tip" O'Neill and Senate majority leader Robert Byrd—would typically reply that Congress also had a mandate from the people—that, indeed, most congressmen had run well ahead of Carter in their districts—and that their responsibility was to use their own best judgment, not to take orders from the president.

One early episode typifies what many observers feel was wrong with Carter's legislative leadership throughout his administration. His first main policy initiative, as we shall see, was his energy program. He correctly identified our growing energy dependence as one of the nation's greatest problems, made a nationally televised speech about it on April 15, 1977, and on April 17 sent to the Congress a complex program developed in secret by the president and his advisers, especially James Schlesinger, without any consultation with congressional leaders. Nevertheless, the House passed the program substantially intact, largely because Speaker O'Neill made an all-out

---

14 Fallows, "The Passionless Presidency," p. 41.

effort for it. Parts of the program, however, then bogged down in the Senate, and other parts in a conference committee.

Carter had previously announced that his first major foreign tour, to seven nations on four continents, would begin on November 22. On November 7, however, he announced that he was postponing the trip to get his energy program moving, and on November 8 he gave another nationally televised speech urging its passage. Still, after that nothing much happened. During the rest of November and December Carter and his congressional liaison team made no special effort to break the conference committee's deadlock, and the great expectations created by the dramatic gestures of November 7–8 were soon swallowed up in the bustle and confusion of Washington's business-as-usual.

On November 29, with much of his energy program still in limbo, Carter announced that he now felt that things were well enough in hand that he could reschedule his trip for late December. On December 29, with the energy bill still deadlocked in the conference committee, he took off for Warsaw on the first leg of his tour.

The sharpest confrontation with Congress in the administration's early days came in February 1977. Just before the deadline for changing the fiscal year 1978 budget previously submitted by the Ford administration, Carter asked his cabinet members to suggest places to cut. Interior Secretary Cecil Andrus submitted a "hit list" of nineteen water projects in various states—exactly the kind of pork-barrel projects that congressmen count on to sweeten their states and districts and that executive budget analysts regard as the very quintessence of the "fat" and "waste" that should be cut out. When word of the elimination of these projects got out, there was a vituperative session between Carter and some powerful congressmen including the redoubtable Russell Long (Democrat, Louisiana), chairman of the Senate Finance Committee, in whose state five of the nineteen projects were located. The congressmen demanded that the projects be put back; Carter refused and threatened to take his case to the people. When the Senate, by a vote of 65 to 27, added the projects to a public works bill the administration needed, however, Carter did not veto the entire bill to get rid of the projects, and the whole episode was a legislative defeat for him that also left a considerable residue of resentment in Congress.

As his administration wore on, Carter made efforts to improve his relations with Congress and developed quite a cordial relationship with Speaker O'Neill and at least a speaking one with Senator Byrd. By 1979–1980 communications between the White House and the Hill were, on the whole, no worse (but no better) than the uneasy and changing mixture of cooperation and confrontation that had characterized most administrations and that seems inherent in the constitutional separation of powers. Jimmy Carter never abandoned his basic conception of himself as the "people's president" rather than the chief of the Washington governors, however, and that had a profound influence upon the substance as well as the style of his administration.

✓**Domestic Policies and Programs.** One of the most often heard criticisms of the Carter administration is that it had a long laundry list of domestic and foreign policies, but no program—that is, no clear sense or indication of priorities between what was more important and what was less important, what policies would be compromised or given up to ensure the adoption of what other policies. No administration can have all that it wants, however, and every administration finds itself putting more effort behind some programs than others. Judged by this standard, the Carter administration's most-wanted domestic programs were the following:

- *Energy conservation and production.* Carter, like Nixon before him, wanted "energy independence" for America—a situation in which the United States would no longer be dependent upon imported foreign oil as a significant source of energy. As Carter saw it, this involved a number of policies for conservation—for example, tax credits for home insulation, standby gasoline rationing powers, and the turning down of heating thermostats in the winter and the turning up of air-conditioning thermostats in the summer. It also involved the development of new energy sources, such as solar and geothermal power, and the expanded use of old sources, especially coal.

- *Government reorganization.* The rearrangement of executive branch agencies so that they would fit together more logically and complement, rather than compete with, one another for jurisdiction and personnel was modeled on what Carter had done when he was governor of Georgia.

- *Budgetary reform.* Reforms in this area were grounded in the concept of "zero-based budgeting"—the policy that no agency would get automatic increments every year, but every year each agency would have to justify its proposed activities and expenditures anew.

- *Tax reform.* The existing tax system, Carter said during the 1976 campaign, was "a disgrace to the human race," and although he was not very specific about what changes were needed, they were given a high priority in the administration's initial list of things to be done.

Other programs, such as Civil Service reform, deregulation and regulatory reforms, and a separate Department of Education, became important later in the administration, but the original game plan gave top priority to energy, reorganization, budgetary reform, and tax reform.

✓**Foreign Policies and Programs.** The Carter administration began with the strong conviction that the time had come to strike out in several new directions in American foreign policy. Most of them, and the world view underlying them, were outlined by Carter in a speech at the University of Notre Dame on May 22, 1977. In the section that attracted the most attention, Carter said, "Being confident of our own future, we are now free of that inordinate fear of Communism which once led us to embrace any dictator who joined us in our fear." Hence our foreign policy, he continued, should be based on five "cardinal premises": improved relationships with the Soviet Union and the People's Republic of China; a commitment to advance the cause of human rights; close cooperation with the other industrial democracies; an effort to reduce the chasm between the rich and the poor nations; and cooperation with all nations to solve the problems of the threat of nuclear war, racial hatred, the arms race, environmental damage, hunger, and disease. The first policies announced in furtherance of these principles were: reducing or ending aid to nations that violated human rights; concluding a treaty with Panama for the return of the Canal to Panamanian sovereignty; a new strategic arms limitation treaty with the Soviet Union (SALT II); and changing the concentration of previous administrations on East-West relations to a focus on "the North-South dialogue" culminating in improved relations between the United States and the nations of the "third world," especially in Africa.

That, in brief, was the Carter administration's game plan. The game began at noon on January 20, 1977, and the rest of this chapter will outline what happened from then until the Iowa precinct caucuses of January 21, 1980. The story is most succinctly told in table 1–1 and figure 1–1. Table 1–1 lists in chronological order the main events that took place between those two dates, and figure 1–1 traces the ups and downs of Carter's "presidential approval ratings" as measured by the percentage of people replying "approve" to the Gallup Poll's periodic question, "Do you approve or disapprove of the way Jimmy Carter is handling his job as president?"

As one tries to relate the ups and downs of the presidential approval values in figure 1–1 to the chronology of events listed in table 1–1, the Carter administration's story falls quite readily into

11

TABLE 1–1
CHRONOLOGY OF THE CARTER ADMINISTRATION

Date	Event
1976	
Nov. 2	Election results, presidential races Carter–Mondale: 40,830,763 popular votes (50.1%); 297 electoral votes Ford–Dole: 39,147,793 popular votes (48.0%); 240 electoral votes Other: 1,577,333 popular votes (1.9%); 1 electoral vote[a] Election results, congressional races[b] House: 292 Dems., 143 Reps. Senate: 61 Dems., 38 Reps.
Dec. 3	First cabinet appointments announced
Dec. 23	All cabinet appointments announced
1977	
Jan. 14	Bill Brock elected Republican national chairman in 5-man race requiring 3 ballots
Jan. 20	Jimmy Carter inaugurated 39th president
Jan. 21	Carter pardons all Vietnam War draft evaders; Kenneth M. Curtis chosen Democratic national chairman
Feb. 24	U.S. aid to Argentina, Ethiopia, and Uruguay reduced because of human rights violations
Mar. 5	Brazil rejects U.S. arms aid because of U.S. statements about human rights violations
Apr. 15	Carter makes television address on energy crisis, calling it "the moral equivalent of war"; outlines his program to combat inflation at news conference
Apr. 17	Carter energy program submitted to Congress
May 22	Carter speech on foreign policy at Notre Dame
June 30	Carter announces his decision not to build B–1 bomber
Aug. 4	Carter signs bill establishing Department of Energy and nominates James Schlesinger to be secretary
Sept. 7	Panama Canal treaties signed in Washington
Sept. 21	Bert Lance resigns as director of OMB
Nov. 7	Carter announces postponement of 4-continent foreign tour to get his energy program moving again
Nov. 8	Carter makes national television speech for his energy program

TABLE 1–1 (continued)

Date	Event
→ Nov. 15	Carter receives shah of Iran at White House, praises his rule; at press conference Carter promises a balanced budget by 1980
→ Nov. 19	Anwar el-Sadat begins his visit to Israel
Dec. 8	Kenneth Curtis resigns as Democratic national chairman
→ Dec. 20	Carter signs bill sharply increasing social security taxes
→ Dec. 29	Carter starts trip to Poland, Iran, India, Saudi Arabia, France, Belgium, and Egypt
1978	
Feb. 1	Administration decides to cut off aid to Anastasio Somoza in Nicaragua
Mar. 6	Carter invokes Taft-Hartley Act to end 91-day coal strike by United Mine Workers
Mar. 14	Coal strike settled
Mar. 16	Senate ratifies first Panama Canal treaty, 68–32
→ Apr. 7	Carter announces decision to defer production of neutron bomb
Apr. 15–17	Carter meets at Camp David with senior advisers and cabinet members to discuss ways to perform better and to improve declining presidential popularity
→ June 6	Proposition 13 passes in California
June 28	Supreme Court announces decision in Bakke case
July 1	Gerald Rafshoon joins White House senior staff
July 14	Dr. Peter Bourne resigns as presidential aide for health affairs after making out fictitious-name prescriptions for a controlled drug
Aug. 2	Congressman Philip M. Crane formally announces his candidacy for Republican presidential nomination—the earliest such announcement in history
→ Sept. 6	Camp David summit talks begin among Begin, Carter, and Sadat
→ Sept. 17	Camp David agreements signed in ceremonies in Washington, D.C.
Oct. 6	Congress votes to extend ratification time for ERA by 39 months to June 30, 1982
→ Oct. 13	Carter signs Civil Service Reform Act
Nov. 7	In congressional elections Republicans gain 13 seats in House, 3 seats in Senate. New lineup: House, Dems.–276, Reps.–157; Senate, Dems.–58, Reps.–41

(Table continues)

TABLE 1–1 (continued)

Date	Event
Nov. 29	Benjamin Fernandez announces his candidacy for the Republican presidential nomination
Dec. 8–10	Democratic midterm conference meets in Memphis with ovation for Kennedy speech and cool reception of Carter
1979	
Jan. 1	The United States and the People's Republic of China establish diplomatic relations; U.S. abrogates 1954 treaty with Nationalist Chinese government on Taiwan
Jan. 24	John Connally announces his candidacy for Republican presidential nomination
Jan. 28–Feb. 5	Deng Xiaoping visits U.S.
Feb. 8	United States breaks diplomatic relations with Somoza regime in Nicaragua
Mar. 12	Lowell P. Weicker, Jr., announces his candidacy for Republican presidential nomination (withdraws May 16)
Mar. 26	Israel-Egypt peace treaty signed in Washington, D.C.
Mar. 28	Accident happens at nuclear power plant at Three Mile Island, Pennsylvania
May 1	George Bush announces his candidacy for the Republican presidential nomination
May 14	Robert Dole announces his candidacy for the Republican presidential nomination
June 8	John Anderson announces his candidacy for the Republican presidential nomination
June 18	SALT II treaty signed in Vienna by Brezhnev and Carter
July 4	Carter cancels speech on energy; begins a series of talks at Camp David with various government and public leaders; talks end July 12
July 15	Carter delivers "crisis of confidence" speech on national television
July 19	Carter announces cabinet shakeup, with dismissal of Michael Blumenthal (Treasury), Joseph Califano (HEW), James Schlesinger (Energy), and Brock Adams (Transportation); Hamilton Jordan becomes president's chief of staff; Patricia Roberts Harris moves from HUD to HEW
Aug. 15	Andrew Young resigns as U.S. Ambassador to the United Nations after being censured for having an unauthorized meeting with a PLO representative
Sept. 25	Larry Pressler announces his candidacy for the Republican presidential nomination

TABLE 1–1 (continued)

Date	Event
Oct. 13	In Florida caucuses selecting delegates to a state Democratic convention at which a "straw vote" for presidential preference will be taken, Carter wins 522 delegates to 269 for Edward Kennedy
Oct. 17	Carter signs bill establishing Department of Education
Oct. 22	Shah of Iran flown from Mexico to New York City for medical treatment
Nov. 1	Howard H. Baker, Jr., announces his candidacy for the Republican presidential nomination
Nov. 4	Iranian students seize U.S. embassy in Teheran and take captive about 65 U.S. embassy personnel
Nov. 7	Edward M. Kennedy announces his candidacy for the Democratic presidential nomination
Nov. 8	Edmund G. Brown, Jr., announces his candidacy for the Democratic presidential nomination
Nov. 13	Ronald Reagan announces his candidacy for the Republican presidential nomination
Dec. 15	Shah leaves U.S. for Panama
Dec. 27	Soviet troops invade Afghanistan
Dec. 28	Carter withdraws from debate with Kennedy and Brown scheduled before Iowa caucuses
1980	
Jan. 4	Carter announces sharp curtailment of grain sales to Soviet Union and other measures in retaliation for invasion of Afghanistan
Jan. 5	Nationally televised debate held in Des Moines among Republican presidential aspirants Anderson, Baker, Bush, Connally, Crane, and Dole
Jan. 8	Larry Pressler withdraws from Republican race
Jan. 12	Mondale debates Kennedy and Brown in Waterloo, Iowa
Jan. 21	Iowa precinct caucuses are held

Notes: Dem. = Democrat. ERA = Equal Rights Amendment. HEW = Department of Health, Education, and Welfare. HUD = Department of Housing and Urban Development. OMB = Office of Management and Budget. PLO = Palestine Liberation Organization. Rep. = Republican. SALT = Strategic Arms Limitation Treaty.

a Reagan.

b Shown is the final composition of each house, by party affiliation.

Source: Author.

16

FIGURE 1-1

Carter's Approval Ratings, 1977–1980

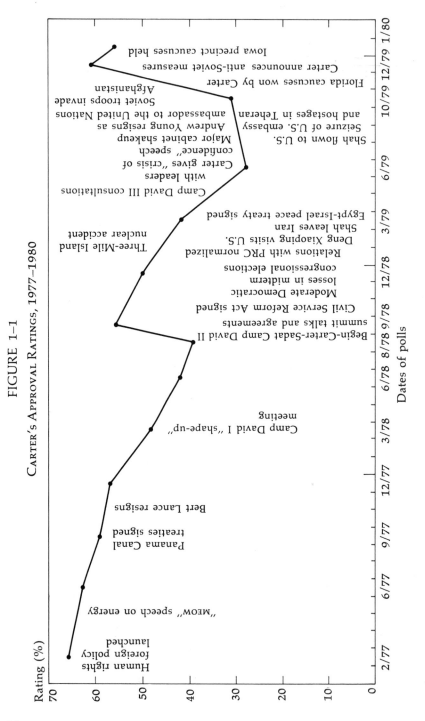

Rating (%)

Dates of polls

five periods, and I shall conclude by describing briefly the main developments in each of those periods.

The Honeymoon: January 20–August 31, 1977

About every month since World War II the Gallup poll has been asking national samples the presidential-approved question. Most presidents have begun their first terms with a high "approval rating" (percentage replying "approve" to Gallup's question), either as a carryover from their electoral success a few months earlier or as part of the rally-'round-the-new-president spirit that surges when a vice-president succeeds a fallen president. That initial high rating typically holds quite steady for the first six to twelve months.[15] This is also a period in which the news media generally report sympathetically on the new president's first initiatives, and congressmen of both parties are most disposed to give him what he wants because of his fresh popular mandate. Everyone understands, however, that sooner or later the new president's "free ride" must come to an end; so in a metaphor that also suggests something about American marriages, these opening months are generally called the new president's "honeymoon period."

Jimmy Carter had one, too. As the line in figure 1–1 shows, his initial approval ratings hovered around 70 percent, somewhat lower than the first ratings of the other Democratic presidents Harry Truman, John Kennedy, or Lyndon Johnson, but substantially higher than those of the Republicans Dwight Eisenhower, Richard Nixon, and Gerald Ford. Carter's initial rating reflected in part the widespread feeling that here was a truly different kind of president from whom, after the traumas of Vietnam and Watergate, the nation could expect great new things. Haynes Johnson of the *Washington Post* remembers the mood of the time very well:

> People saw—or wanted to see—something special in Jimmy Carter. Certainly they were ready for something different. They sensed integrity and simplicity. He was critical, but caring. He was competent. He seemed able to address the real questions troubling people—power and powerlessness, size and functioning of government, energy and environment, equity for the small as well as the large. (He makes his own bed, they said in surprise after he stayed at someone's home on an early New England trip. That these sym-

---

[15] For the ups and downs of the approval ratings of all presidents since World War II, see the chart in *Public Opinion*, March/April 1978, pp. 28-29.

bols of informality and unpretentiousness impressed people—and they did—showed possibly naivete, but also how desperate people were for a different presidential style.) And they also wanted to believe Carter was as capable a manager as his campaign made him out: zero-based budgeting (no one quite knew what it was, but supposedly it had worked in Georgia), make every program accountable, start fresh, shake things up, level with people, cut out the pomp and artificial trappings of power.[16]

In several respects conditions were very favorable. No great international crisis was brewing. No great domestic scandals had to be resolved. And the economy Carter inherited from Gerald Ford was in reasonably good condition: the annual inflation rate stood at 7.2 percent, and unemployment was at 8.1 percent. The prime interest rate was 6 percent, gold was selling at $133 per ounce, and the dollar was steady against the German mark and the Japanese yen despite a 1976 foreign trade deficit of $5.87 billion. There was the usual worry about what the Organization of Petroleum Exporting Countries (OPEC) might do to oil prices, but when Carter took office the world price was fifteen dollars per barrel.

From the day they were elected, Carter and his team intended to "hit the ground running" right after the inauguration, and they did, with a vengeance. On January 21 Carter pardoned all Vietnam war draft evaders, and on January 27 he sent to Congress a $31.2 billion package of proposed tax cuts, including a fifty-dollar rebate for individual taxpayers as well as tax relief for businessmen and investors. In the next six months he followed with the greatest outpouring of new proposals to Congress put forth by any first-term president in his first six months since Franklin D. Roosevelt in 1933.

- *February:* a request for congressional authorization to reorganize the executive branch; a major revision in the fiscal year 1978 budget left by Ford
- *March:* a new Department of Energy; a series of election law reforms, including universal voter registration, abolition of the electoral college, public financing of congressional election campaigns, revision of the Hatch Act to permit more political activity by civil servants, and revision of the Federal Election Campaign Finance Act; a major new foreign aid program
- *April:* a new inflation program, aiming to reduce the annual rate to 4 percent by 1979; major revisions in the food stamp program; establishment of a new consumer protection agency; measures to

16 Johnson, *In the Absence of Power*, p. 125.

contain hospital costs; a comprehensive energy program, including such conservation measures as a new gasoline tax, tax credits for home and factory insulation, price regulation of natural gas and electricity, and such production measures as increased use of coal, development of solar and geothermal energy, and slow deregulation of domestic natural gas and oil prices

- *May:* a new ethics-in-government law requiring full financial disclosure by all executive policy-making officers; a major increase in social security taxes
- *July:* a plan to reorganize the White House staff; labor law reform
- *August:* a program to deal with illegal aliens; comprehensive welfare reform, including new job training and placement programs, income maintenance payments, work benefits, income tax credits, and a $30.7 billion price tag.

Congress was swamped with these proposals: many of them had major tax features and clogged the procedures of the House Ways and Means Committee unmanageably. Many were highly controversial and required either a 1933-style sense of emergency or a devoted following in Congress in the style of Franklin D. Roosevelt, neither of which was present in Carter's "hundred days." Most damaging of all was the administration's failure to let Congress and its leaders know which items were urgent and which could be put on the back burner for a while. As far as Congress could tell, the administration thought *everything* was important, and Congress had better get moving on all of it.

The administration ultimately got most of these programs from Congress, some of them after long delays, many of them in substantially altered form, and almost all of them accompanied by a growing feeling in Congress that those Georgians simply did not know how things got done in Washington.

Undaunted, the new administration got off to an equally fast start on its symbolic program. On February 2 Carter gave his first nationally televised "fireside chat" from the White House, appearing in a cardigan sweater both to signal his own nonimperial manner and to underline his message that the nation needed to conserve energy even for heating homes. On March 5 he participated in a two-hour "phone-in" over CBS radio, with Walter Cronkite moderating the questions. CBS reported that over 9 million calls were placed, and Carter answered 42 of them on the air. On March 16 he traveled, carrying his own suit bag, to Clinton, Massachusetts, for his first "town meeting." He answered the questions of about 700 people gathered in a local auditorium, and stayed overnight in the guest room of a local beer distributor.

Another part of the fast start came on February 24 when the administration announced that U.S. aid would be curtailed to Argentina, Ethiopia, and Uruguay because of those countries' violations of their citizens' human rights (a week later Brazil announced that it would not accept *any* U.S. aid because of statements the Carter people had made about the state of human rights there). On March 17 Carter made his first address to the United Nations General Assembly and again emphasized the human rights theme of his foreign policy.

The first major warnings of trouble on the Hill were heard in March when Congress began to balk at various parts of the administration's tax package, especially the fifty-dollar-rebate proposal. Carter suddenly announced on April 14 that he no longer favored that proposal, but since he had neither consulted nor informed Democratic congressional leaders about the switch in signals, some began to say that honeymoons require consideration and communication by both partners, and perhaps this one was over already.

April 18 to 20 saw the major events of the honeymoon period. On the eighteenth he made a televised speech to the nation announced in advance as his most important pronouncement yet. The speech was devoted entirely to the nation's energy problems, especially its growing dependence on foreign oil. Conservation, he said, was one of the vital keys to solving the problem, and the American people needed to make a great national effort to meet the crisis. Indeed, he said, in a phrase he borrowed from William James, that effort should be the "moral equivalent of war."

On April 20 he presented to Congress his large and complex energy program, including measures for both conservation and production. He also recommended strong measures to maintain and extend regulations controlling strip mining, air and water pollution, and nuclear safety in the increased use of nuclear and coal-fired power plants.

The program received something short of universal applause. For one thing, many Republicans and spokesmen for the oil and gas industries said it put far too much emphasis on reducing consumption and far too little on developing incentives for more production. For another, many congressmen of both parties were greatly aroused by the fact that the program had been developed almost entirely in secret by James Schlesinger and his technocrats, without consulting with or even informing Congress about what to expect. For yet another, it would work great and unnecessary hardships on ordinary Americans.

Carter defended his program in an April 20 press conference. He abandoned the original speech's emphasis on the great national effort and stressed instead the immediate payoffs to most people: the proceeds from the gasoline tax would be rebated in the form of income tax credits, and the new energy production efforts would produce several hundred thousand new jobs. This sharp change in tone caused Russell Baker of the *New York Times* to comment wryly that the "moral equivalent of war" should be read as "MEOW"— and his quip appeared recurrently during Carter's remaining years in office as a symbol of the gap between the high rhetoric of his administration's initial presentations and the ineffectiveness of its subsequent follow-throughs.

Despite the energy program anticlimax, things continued to go reasonably smoothly for the next four months. On May 8 Carter made his first foreign trip, going to London to attend a summit meeting with the leaders of the governments of Great Britain, Canada, France, West Germany, Italy, and Japan. He got very good notices from the British and Western European press, and seems to have made a good impression on all his peers except perhaps Helmut Schmidt. He lost a good deal of this good impression in July when, after trying to persuade his colleagues in the North Atlantic Treaty Organization (NATO) not to oppose the deployment of the neutron bomb, he suddenly announced that he had decided not to deploy it after all.

His experiences with the Soviets took a different turn. Getting a new strategic arms limitation treaty (SALT II) with the Soviet Union was right at the top of Carter's foreign policy agenda, and in mid-March he sent Secretary of State Cyrus Vance to Moscow with a whole portfolio of new proposals. Soviet leader Leonid Brezhnev, however, showed no interest in any radical departures from previous agreements, the general atmosphere was cool because of the administration's talk about human rights, and Vance came home empty-handed. Things improved in May, when Vance and Soviet foreign minister Andrei Gromyko agreed in Geneva to resume the SALT negotiations on a more modest and incremental level.

By early August things were looking up a bit. On August 4 Carter signed the bill establishing the new Department of Energy and named Schlesinger as its secretary, and on August 5 the House of Representatives passed most of the administration's energy package— thanks largely to Speaker O'Neill's efforts on its behalf. In late

August, however, the Bert Lance affair brought the honeymoon period to an abrupt and permanent close.

The First Slump: September 1977 to September 1978

Figure 1–1 shows that Carter's approval rating held in the 63–70 percent range during the honeymoon period, and at the end of July 1977 it stood at 67 percent. By the end of September, however, it had dropped to 59 percent, and in the succeeding months it slumped steadily downward until, at the beginning of April 1978, it stood at 48 percent—the first of many negative ratings the administration was to receive. In part, no doubt, this slump was simply Carter's version of the post-honeymoon sag that seems to be part of every administration's life cycle. Still, in Carter's case it was earlier and steeper than most president's initial slumps, and there appear to have been several reasons for it.

First and most important was the Bert Lance affair. Lance was one of Carter's oldest and most trusted Georgia friends. He had served as highways director during Carter's period as governor, and he became Carter's handpicked candidate to succeed him as governor when Carter had to leave office in 1974. Lance ran well back in the 1974 Democratic primary and returned to his banking business while playing a major role in Carter's 1974–1976 drive for the presidency. His appointment as director of the Office of Management and Budget (OMB) was the first Carter announced after his election, and during the honeymoon period Lance was widely regarded as the second most powerful man in the new administration.

Lance's—and Carter's—troubles began on July 11, 1977, when Carter sent Abraham Ribicoff (Democrat, Connecticut), chairman of the Senate Government Affairs Committee, a request that the time be extended in which Lance, because of the new ethics rules, would be required to sell all his stock in the National Bank of Georgia in Atlanta, of which he had been president. The reason given was that the price of the stock had recently fallen, and an immediate forced sale would "place an undue financial burden on Mr. Lance." It all seemed very innocuous, but as Haynes Johnson observes:

> From these innocent beginnings . . . flowed events that shook the foundation of Carter's presidency, struck at the core of his pledges, raised questions about his judgment and standards, laid bare weaknesses in his inner circle of advisers, lowered his popularity, stirred partisan discord, aroused passions against the press, and shamed Senate and federal investigatory processes.[17]

[17] Ibid., p. 199.

22

It was revealed that since April 1975 the office of the comptroller of the currency (the agency that regulates national banks) had been investigating Lance's activities as president, first, of the National Bank in Calhoun, Georgia, and then as president of Atlanta's National Bank of Georgia. On August 18, 1977, the comptroller, John G. Heimann, issued his report, which said that although Lance was not guilty of any criminal wrongdoing, there were serious questions about the propriety of some of his actions in both banks—for example, allowing overdrafts amounting to $450,000 for himself and his wife and other large overdrafts for several of his friends.

The "Georgia Mafia," led by Hamilton Jordan and Jody Powell, immediately proclaimed their pleasure that the Heimann report had completely cleared Lance. Carter held a nationally televised press conference, with Lance at his side, in which he said that the report reconfirmed his faith in Lance's complete honesty, integrity, and good judgment, and at the end he turned and said directly to Lance, "Bert, I'm proud of you."

The press, however, scented a scandal. Led by William Safire of the *New York Times*, they continued to probe Lance's administration of the two banks and uncovered, one after another, more stories of large overdrafts, questionable loans from other banks, and a series of stories that revealed Lance as, at a minimum, a free-wheeling custodian of other people's money. The Lance affair came to resemble the Watergate affair in that it was "death by accumulation":[18] a new revelation would be made, some would say that's it, that's the whole story, then yet another revelation would be made, and people began to wonder if there was any end to it.

By September both houses of Congress and six other federal agencies were investigating Lance's banking affairs, and Sen. Charles Percy (Republican, Illinois) said the time had come to appoint a special federal prosecutor, as had been done in the Watergate case. Jody Powell, in angry retaliation, tried to plant with several newspapers the story that Percy, while president of the Bell and Howell camera firm, had used the company airplane for his own private affairs. The papers found out that Bell and Howell did not even have a company plane, however, and Powell had to make a public apology; but many observers felt the whole thing smacked of Nixon-like cover-ups and enemies lists.

On September 15 Lance appeared before the Ribicoff committee and made an adroit point-by-point defense of his banking affairs. Still,

[18] The phrase is Johnson's, *In the Absence of Power*, p. 213. Johnson, pp. 198–214, has the most complete account of the Lance affair.

too many people had come to feel that Lance, although probably not a criminal in the strict sense of the term, was not the kind of man who ought to be the president's chief financial adviser and in charge of the nation's budget. The inner circle of Georgians thought this was a grossly unfair attack on one of their own by the eastern establishment, but they saw that the game was up. At a televised press conference on September 21, Carter announced that he had accepted Lance's resignation as OMB director. Carter added that he still believed Lance was completely honest and trustworthy but suggested that perhaps the problem stemmed from "the extraordinary standards that we have tried to set in government and the expectations of the American people that was engendered during my own campaign and my inauguration statement." [19]

He may have been right. An administration that presents itself as a group of people who set above all other things the values of honesty, openness, and truthfulness is likely to be even more damaged by appearances of deceitfulness, cover-up, and steering close to the moral edge than one that accepts more of a wheeler-dealer, "old pol" image. The self-righteous, in short, not only had better behave with perfect propriety but also had better be universally *seen* as behaving so, and that was certainly not the case with Carter and his Georgians during the Lance affair. [20]

The next major development in this period was the signing and ratification of the Panama Canal treaties. They are often cited as major victories for the administration, but they did not seem to help its approval rating recover from the damage caused by the Lance affair. Carter's four predecessors, Kennedy, Johnson, Nixon, and Ford, had all recommended that the United States negotiate a treaty with Panama that would transfer ownership of the Panama Canal and sovereignty over the Canal Zone to Panama. For reasons that are not entirely clear, the Carter administration put getting such a treaty right at the top of its foreign policy agenda, along with negotiating a new SALT treaty with the Soviet Union.

Negotiations with Panama began immediately, and after seven months, two treaties were signed by Carter and General Omar Torrijos, the head of Panama's ruling junta. One treaty gave Panama

---

[19] Quoted in *Facts on File*, September 24, 1977, p. 718.

[20] In May 1979 Bert Lance and three associates were indicted by a federal grand jury in Atlanta on thirty-three counts of conspiracy to obtain $20 million in loans for their personal benefit from forty-one different banks between 1970 and 1978. The court later dropped all but twelve of the counts; in April 1980 the trial jury, after eight days of deliberation, acquitted Lance and his associates on nine of the counts, and a mistrial was declared on the other three because the jury could not agree on them. Eventually the judge dismissed the remaining charges.

possession of the canal and the zone after 1999, and the other guaranteed its neutrality thereafter. The treaty was signed at an elaborate televised ceremony in Washington on September 7 that was attended by the heads of seventeen different nations of the hemisphere.

The big party was followed immediately by a big fight. A number of prominent conservatives, led by Ronald Reagan and Senators Jesse Helms (Republican, North Carolina), Strom Thurmond (Republican, South Carolina), and Orrin Hatch (Republican, Utah), announced that they regarded the treaties as outrageous giveaways of vital American interests and they would fight hard to keep the treaty from being ratified by the Senate.

It is not easy to get the two-thirds vote needed to ratify a controversial treaty, and the administration made a far greater lobbying effort than any it had made before. It got endorsements from Gerald Ford and Henry Kissinger. Carter made a speech on national television plugging the treaty in February. As the vote on the first treaty neared, the administration made special concessions on both treaty language and benefits for their states to four undecided Democratic senators—Talmadge and Nunn of Georgia, Long of Louisiana, and especially DeConcini of Arizona—whose votes were expected to make or break the treaty.

The administration won the day on March 16 when the Senate voted 68–32 to ratify the first treaty, and on April 18 the second treaty was ratified, with all senators voting as they had on the first treaty. The ratifications constituted the first major success for the administration in the Senate, and some observers count it one of the administration's main achievements in its whole time in office.

Perhaps it was, but the cost was considerable. Not only did the administration hand out a large proportion of its limited number of political IOUs, but the affair also absorbed so much of its concern that other, perhaps more important questions did not get the attention—and certainly not the answers—they needed. For example, the energy program was far behind schedule and was making little progress. After its initial quick success in the House it was slowly but drastically being rewritten in the Senate. The original plan to decontrol domestic oil prices would have taxed the oil companies' windfall profits and would have rebated the additional costs of gasoline and heating oil to consumers, but this proposal was killed in Russell Long's Senate Finance Committee. The wrangle over the deregulation of natural gas prices continued to hold up the bill, and a filibuster by Senate liberals against deregulation was finally broken by some heavy-handed parliamentary rulings by Vice-President Mondale— an episode that outraged the liberals.

Despite these fireworks, however, the bill was still not moving, and well into 1978 there was no new energy policy in place. Media news commentators were increasingly prone to criticize Carter and his associates for weak leadership, both in their relations with Congress and in the tendency of cabinet officers to issue policy statements not in accord with what the White House was saying.

Worst of all, the economy continued to deteriorate. By mid-1978 the annual inflation rate had risen to 10.8 percent; not only was this a big increase over the 7.2 percent rate Carter had inherited from Ford, but it had crossed the line to "double-digit inflation"—a crossing of considerable symbolic as well as economic significance. Unemployment, to be sure, had dropped from 8.1 to 5.7 percent, but the polls showed that most people thought inflation, not unemployment, was the worst problem the nation faced. The dollar continued to slip against the German mark and the Japanese yen, and gold had gone from $133 to $202 per ounce.

Perhaps this explains why, despite the canal treaties victory, Carter's approval rating by April had fallen to 41 percent. It was evident that things were slipping badly, and Carter decided to do something about it: over the weekend of April 15–17 he staged what might be called "Camp David I," the first of three retreats at the presidential hideaway in the Catoctin Mountains in northern Maryland that were to highlight his presidency. In Camp David I he brought together his White House staff, his cabinet, and Charles Kirbo for three days of heart-to-heart talks about what all of them in the administration, from Carter down, had been doing wrong and how they might improve. They all, including Carter, confessed their errors and resolved to do better. It was agreed, among other things, that White House task forces would be appointed to oversee each of the administration's major programs and to follow each through Congress and the bureaucracy until it was firmly in place. It was also decided to bring Gerald Rafshoon back as a senior presidential adviser to make sure that the administration's case was presented more effectively and its achievements made better known to the public (he came on July 1, after putting his Atlanta public relations business in trust).

Camp David I helped very little, however. Regardless of how the administration's performance may or may not have improved, Carter's approval rating continued to sag. In August it fell to 39 percent—the lowest the Gallup poll had ever recorded for a president eighteen months after his inauguration. The administration desperately needed a major and highly visible success in *something*, they needed it soon—and in September they got it.

Camp David II, the Middle East Accords,
Renaissance in the Polls: September to December 1978

After the United States had finally withdrawn from the Vietnam war, the Arab-Israeli conflict in the Middle East became and remained the nation's prime concern in foreign affairs. There were many reasons. One was the strong support of Israel by Democratic and Republican administrations alike, another was the unremitting pressure by the American Jewish community to keep that support at maximum strength, a third was the nation's growing dependence upon oil imported from the Persian Gulf states, and finally there was the ever-present possibility of a direct and perhaps cataclysmic confrontation with the Soviet Union in the area.

The first great breakthrough came in late November 1977: Egyptian president Anwar el-Sadat said that he would go to Israel if he was invited, Israeli prime minister Menachem Begin issued the invitation, and Sadat made his historic visit to Jerusalem on November 19 . After that dramatic event, however, the negotiations between the two nations for a peace treaty dragged on, and nothing much happened. Both Sadat and Begin made several trips to Washington, with Carter trying to act as mediator. The discussions repeatedly broke down, however, because of apparently irreconcilable differences over the continued existence of the Israeli settlements in the territory captured from Egypt in the 1967 war. The direct talks between the two nations were broken off in January 1978 and were not resumed despite Carter's repeated pleas on their behalf.

In midsummer Carter resolved to make one last major effort. He invited Begin and Sadat to come to Camp David to resume their negotiations, with the understanding that he himself would actively participate. They accepted. The talks began on September 6, and after nearly two weeks of intensive bargaining between the two leaders, with Carter serving as an active mediator—and often messenger—between them, they finally arrived at a series of accords constituting a framework for an eventual peace treaty.

At a televised ceremony at the White House on September 17, Begin and Sadat signed the accords, and Carter signed as a witness. The next day Carter addressed Congress on the details, with Begin and Sadat in the gallery. Both leaders praised Carter's role, and for the first time in decades it looked as though there was real hope for peace in the Middle East, a hope that was the direct result of Jimmy Carter's determination, courage, and diplomatic skills.

That is evidently how the American people saw it: Gallup took a new poll right after Carter's address to Congress, and his approval rating shot up seventeen points to 56 percent—"the sharpest gain for a chief executive in four decades of Gallup Poll presidential popularity measurements." [21] It sagged a bit to the 50–52 percent range in the autumn and early winter, but it held steady through the November congressional elections. In those elections the Republicans had a net gain of thirteen seats in the House and three seats in the Senate. This was a shade better than the average loss of thirty seats in the House and three seats in the Senate for first-term presidents since Franklin Roosevelt—not as good as Kennedy's record in 1962 or Nixon's in 1970, but better than Truman's in 1946, Eisenhower's in 1954, Johnson's in 1966, and Ford's in 1974.

At the halfway point in Carter's administration, then, the polls and the midterm congressional election results taken together seemed to show that the great success of Camp David II had brought the administration back from the edge of disaster. If the reshuffling and high resolves of Camp David I were indeed to produce the hoped-for improved performance in the administration's second half, the prospects for Carter's renomination and reelection in 1980 should be excellent; but that is not how things turned out.

More Slump: January to November 1979

On December 8–10 the Democratic party held its second midterm conference in Memphis, Tennessee. On the few matters that came to a showdown the administration had the votes, but it was clear that the euphoria of Camp David II had evaporated. Carter's opening speech drew only polite applause, but on the next night Edward Kennedy's fiery (though indirect) attack on the administration's effort to reduce inflation by cutting government programs for the poor touched off a cheering, stamping ovation. A "dissident budget" maintaining the current levels of social expenditures was proposed by United Auto Workers president Douglas Fraser, and although it lost by 822 to 521, it was clear that the liberals were up in arms about what they regarded as the administration's conservative economic policies and that Carter's renomination would not go unchallenged in 1980.

The administration, however, had a far worse problem than the disgruntled liberals, and it lasted throughout 1979: the Carter anti-inflation program was not working, and the economy was performing worse all the time. By the end of 1979 the inflation rate stood at 13.3 percent—the highest since the Korean War and nearly double the

---

[21] Gallup poll, press release, September 28, 1978. This rise, as we shall see, was topped by Carter's rise in December 1979 after Iran took the American hostages.

7.2 percent rate Carter had inherited from Ford. Unemployment had dropped to 6.0 percent by the end of the year, down 2.1 points from what it was in January 1977, but even so Carter's "misery index" (the inflation and unemployment rates added together) was now 19.3, as compared with the 15.3 for which he had so sharply attacked Ford in the 1976 campaign. The prime lending rate had risen to 16 percent, the highest in many years. The dollar was getting weaker every day relative to the mark and the yen, and the price of gold per ounce skyrocketed from $202 in December 1978 to $800 in December 1979.

The greatest disasters, however, took place at the gasoline stations of the East and West coasts in midsummer. The Iranian revolution in January and February brought Iranian oil production nearly to a halt. The resulting shortages of crude oil soon resulted in a 10–15 percent drop in the supply of gasoline, and stations with Sorry, Out of Gas signs or long lines of cars waiting to be filled became increasingly common in March and April. In early May several counties in California adopted the "odd/even" system of gasoline rationing.[22] The shortage spread to the East Coast in June and grew to massive proportions in the densely populated Boston-Washington corridor. A number of eastern states adopted the odd/even system, and by early July most Americans, whose fondness for driving their cars has set the model for the world, were apprehensive, angry, and contemptuous of the administration's efforts to ease their deprivations.

As early as February 1979 Carter asked Congress for standby power to impose national gasoline rationing, but on May 10 the House voted it down by 246 to 159—one of the most humiliating defeats of the entire Carter administration. Carter repeatedly said that the oil shortage was real and beyond American control and that Americans would simply have to start using less gasoline. That, however, was not what most Americans believed or wanted to hear: an AP-NBC poll reported on May 4 that 54 percent of the people said the oil shortage was a hoax perpetrated by the big oil companies to boost prices, and only 32 percent believed Carter's message that the shortage was real and due mainly to foreign producers' failure to meet Americans' excessive demands. The Federal Trade Commission gave some credence to the popular view when it announced that it was investigating a possible hoax by the oil companies.

The shortages eased and the lines shortened in early September after most families ended their vacations, and by October the odd/even systems were lifted everywhere. Nevertheless the whole episode

---

[22] Lest we forget, this was a system in which cars whose last license plate number was odd could buy gas only on odd-numbered dates and those whose last number was even could buy only on even-numbered days.

did great damage to the administration's credibility and reputation for competence.

There were, to be sure, several developments in 1979 that the administration hailed as major successes. On January 1 the United States and the People's Republic of China resumed diplomatic relations by exchanging ambassadors. In late January the Chinese deputy premier, Deng Xiaoping, made a state visit to the United States. On March 26 Sadat and Begin signed the Egypt-Israel peace treaty at a televised ceremony in Washington, and both said it never would have been possible without Carter's intensive participation. On June 18 Carter and Leonid Brezhnev signed the SALT II treaty in Vienna and kissed each other on both cheeks to seal the bargain.

Regardless of whether these events were, on their merits, genuine administration triumphs, they did not help very much with the people in the gas lines, no matter how loudly Gerald Rafshoon hailed them. Carter's approval rating slipped from 50 percent in early January to 43 percent in February, to 38 percent in March, to 32 percent in May, and finally to 28 percent in mid-June. This was the lowest rating for any president since Gallup started polling in the 1930s, even lower than for Richard Nixon just before his resignation in 1974.

In late June, with the gas lines lengthening and his approval at an all-time low, Carter went to Tokyo for his third summit meeting with the leaders of seven Western nations. He planned to stop in Hawaii for a short vacation on his way back and then deliver yet another speech on energy, this one scheduled for July 5. His senior domestic affairs adviser, Stuart Eizenstat, however, sent Carter a long memorandum saying that the gasoline lines, the sharp rise in gasoline prices, and the uproar over the Department of Energy's allocation system were adding up to a political life-or-death crisis for the administration, so he had better skip his Hawaii vacation and come right back and do something about it.[23] What was needed was another Camp David—and Camp David III soon followed.

Carter went to the mountain retreat shortly after he returned to Washington on July 3. After reviewing the proposed text for the July 5 speech, he abruptly canceled it and decided to stay at Camp David to take stock of his administration and the country that held it in such low esteem. On July 5 his chief staff members joined him and hastily drew up a list of "key Americans" to invite for consultations. Each day from then until July 11 groups of consultants helicoptered to Camp David for conversations with Carter and his staff. All

[23] The Eizenstat memorandum is quoted at length in Johnson, *In the Absence of Power*, pp. 304-6.

told, he met with 134 persons chosen to represent what he and his staff regarded as the most important segments of the population: in addition to the inner circle of Georgians (but only 5 cabinet members), Carter talked with 16 senators (13 Democrats and 3 Republicans), 19 congressmen (all Democrats), 20 governors, 7 mayors, 6 state legislators, 9 clergymen, 8 businessmen, 8 labor leaders, 5 civil rights leaders, 3 college presidents, 4 college professors (no political scientists), and a few others.[24]

Camp David III reportedly consisted of broad-ranging conversations among consultants, president, and staff about many topics, including evaluations of Carter's leadership and speculations about what was wrong with the nation. On July 12, after the last group had left, the White House announced that the president would make a major televised address on July 15. When the night came, he had a much larger audience than he had been getting for his speeches for some time—the Camp David III buildup worked very well in at least this regard. His basic message, gained, he said, from the Camp David talks (but actually taken largely from a long memorandum his pollster, Pat Caddell, had presented to him on his return from Tokyo) was that the American people were deep in the throes of a spiritual "crisis of confidence":

> The symptoms of this crisis of the American spirit are all around us. For the first time in the history of our country a majority of our people believe that the next five years will be worse than the past five years. Two-thirds of our people do not even vote. The productivity of American workers is actually dropping and the willingness of Americans to save for the future has fallen below that of all other people in the Western world. As you know there is a growing disrespect for government and for churches and for schools, the news media and other institutions. This is not a message of happiness or reassurance, but it is the truth.[25]

The answer, Carter continued, is for Americans to snap out of it and meet the great challenges facing the nation. The greatest of these challenges was the energy problem, and the rest of the speech was a brief for his newly revised energy program.

Almost everyone agreed that Carter had delivered the speech much more forcefully than usual, but its content was generally praised by Democrats and belittled by Republicans. As one of the latter put it, "*His* polls are slipping, and the American *people* are sick?" Still,

[24] The guest list is given in the *National Journal*, July 21, 1979, pp. 1224-25.
[25] The text is given in *Facts on File*, July 20, 1979, pp. 533-34.

whatever the speech's merits, its effects were soon buried under the events of the "July massacre."

On July 17 Carter launched perhaps the most drastic presidential "purge" in history. He asked for the resignation of all his cabinet officers, and eighteen of his senior advisers offered theirs as well. He accepted those of Joseph Califano (Health, Education, and Welfare), Michael Blumenthal (Treasury), James Schlesinger (Energy), and Brock Adams (Transportation); and Griffin Bell (Justice), who had earlier given notice that he wanted to resign, was also allowed to go.

Carter also announced that he was dropping his longstanding objection to having a chief of staff (too reminiscent of Haldeman and Ehrlichman), and Hamilton Jordan would take up such a position immediately. Jordan then distributed thirty-item evaluation forms to all cabinet members to fill out about their top subordinates, asking such questions as, "On the average, when does this person arrive at work? Leave work?" and "How well does this person get along with (a) superiors, (b) peers, (c) subordinates, and (d) outsiders?"[26]

A few loyalists defended Carter's purge as evidence that he was "taking charge" and Jordan's appointment as a portent of the strong administration to come. Still, most commentators in America and abroad agreed with the sentiment, if not the rhetoric, of a remark made by Congressman Charles Wilson (Democrat, Texas): "Good grief! They're cutting down the biggest trees and keeping the monkeys!"[27]

For all their thunder and lightning, however, Camp David III and the July massacre did not help Carter's popular standing very much. His approval rating rose from 28 percent in July to 32 percent in August and stayed at 31 percent in mid-October. Moreover, all the polls showed that Edward Kennedy—who was sounding more every day like a man about to announce his candidacy—was running far ahead of Carter in the preferences of Democratic identifiers for the party's 1980 presidential nomination: a Gallup poll in early November, for example, reported 54 percent for Kennedy to 31 percent for Carter; and 58 percent said they hoped Carter would not run for reelection.[28]

By the beginning of November, a year before the 1980 election, things had not looked so dark politically for an incumbent president since modern scientific polling began, but everything changed on November 4, 1979.

[26] A copy of the questionnaire is reprinted in *Facts on File*, June 20, 1979, pp. 530-31.

[27] Quoted in *Time*, July 30, 1979, p. 11.

[28] *Public Opinion*, April/May 1980, p. 39.

Rallying around the President:
November 4, 1979, to January 21, 1980

On October 22, 1979, after a considerable behind-the-scenes debate about whether it should be allowed, the deposed shah of Iran flew from his home of exile in Mexico to New York City for medical treatment. On November 4 a mob of about 500 Iranian students seized the American embassy in Teheran and took 90 embassy personnel as prisoners, including an estimated 60 to 65 diplomats and military personnel. The captors, strongly backed by the Ayatollah Khomeini, declared that the hostages would not be released until the United States returned the shah to Iran to answer for the many crimes against the Iranian people with which he had been charged.

President Carter refused the demand, denouncing the hostage taking as a flagrant violation of international law, and emotions rose sharply in both nations. For many weeks thereafter almost every day thousands of Iranians paraded in front of the Teheran embassy shaking their fists and shouting demands that the hostages be tried as spies hired, in Khomeini's often-repeated phrase, by "America, the Great Satan." These scenes were shown nightly on American television, and American outrage rose accordingly: in many places all over the country there were protest marches and rallies against the Iranians and demands that strong measures be taken to force the hostages' release.

Carter took a series of actions. He first sent two mediators to Iran, but they were refused entry. On November 9, at American urging, the United Nations Security Council unanimously called for the release of the hostages (not even the Soviets or the Cubans voted no). On November 14 he ordered all Iranian assets in the United States frozen and banned the importation of Iranian oil and other products. On December 10 the U.S. attorney general filed a petition with the International Court of Justice in The Hague asking that the court order the Iranians to release the hostages, which it did on December 15 (the Iranians, of course, spurned all such resolutions and orders by international organizations). On December 12 Carter ordered most Iranian diplomats to leave the United States within five days. On December 10–11 Secretary of State Cyrus Vance went to Western Europe to enlist the support of the NATO countries for strong economic sanctions against Iran.

Events moved rapidly in Iran as well. Almost every day brought another denunciation by Khomeini of "the Great Satan" and Carter, its corrupt and lying leader, another march past the embassy by an Iranian mob, and another threat that the hostages would be tried as spies if the shah were not returned. On November 19–20 Khomeini ordered the release of five women and eight black hostages "in recognition of their oppression by American ruling circles." When the shah left Texas for Panama on December 15, the Iranians made new demands that the United States use its influence to see that he was sent back to Iran as the price of releasing the hostages, and again the administration refused.

On December 4 Carter formally announced his candidacy for renomination and reelection but said that he would engage in no active campaigning or other partisan activity until the hostage crisis was resolved. On December 28 he withdrew from a debate with Edward Kennedy and California governor Jerry Brown scheduled to be held in Iowa in January before the precinct caucuses. All of his campaigning, in Iowa and elsewhere, was done by surrogates, notably his wife Rosalynn and Vice-President Walter Mondale.

On December 29 the international situation became even more tense when 30,000 Soviet troops invaded Afghanistan just after a coup in which President Hafizullah Amin, considered shaky and unreliable by the Soviets, was deposed, killed, and replaced by the more reliable Babrak Karmal. Carter denounced the Soviet invasion as a total violation of international law, a serious blow to Soviet-American relations, and a grave threat to world peace. In a press conference on December 31 he said that as a result of the Soviet invasion, "my opinion of the Russians has changed more drastically in the last week than even the previous two and a half years."[29] On January 4, 1980, he sharply curtailed the sales to the Soviet Union of grain, high-technology equipment, and other strategic items, and added that the United States was seriously considering boycotting the summer Olympic Games scheduled for Moscow. On January 7 the United Nations Security Council voted 13 to 2 to condemn the Soviet invasion, but the resolution was nullified by the Soviet veto. On January 13 the Soviet Union vetoed another United States–sponsored resolution calling for economic sanctions against Iran until the hostages were released.

So the Carter administration entered 1980 deep in the two greatest foreign policy crises of its life. On many occasions in the past, international crises have generated strong rally-around-the-president moods,[30] but in this instance the mood was intensified by

[29] Quoted in *Facts on File*, December 31, 1979, p. 974.

[30] Karlyn Keene points out that many presidents have benefited from such a mood: Truman's approval rating rose from 37 to 46 percent after the Berlin airlift; Eisenhower's rose from 52 to 58 after the Marines' landing in Lebanon;

TABLE 1–2

Perceptions of Jimmy Carter, January 1980

Question: "Here is a list of terms—shown as pairs of opposites—that have been used to describe Jimmy Carter. For each pair of opposites, would you select the term which you feel best describes Carter?"

Description	Percentage Choosing
A man of high moral principles	78
A religious person	78
Takes moderate, middle-of-the-road positions	77
Displays good judgment in a crisis	74
A likable person	71
Puts country's interests ahead of politics	58
Sympathetic to problems of the poor	58
Says what he believes even if unpopular	57
A man you can believe in	50
Sides with the average citizen	49
Offers imaginative, innovative solutions to national problems	41
Decisive, sure of himself	39
You know where he stands on issues	38
Has strong leadership qualities	34
Has a well-defined program for moving the country ahead	31
A person of exceptional abilities	29

Source: Gallup poll, press release, January 27, 1980.

modern communications technology. As Haynes Johnson put it:

> The networks discovered [that] their Iranian broadcasts were attracting enormous new audiences. Iranian coverage, and competition for new angles of it, intensified. The political impact was immense. Attacks on Carter personally by Iranian leaders prominently reported via TV to Americans at home, gave the President a stature he had failed to achieve in three years in office. Carter became the personification of the nation, the symbol of American resolve, the rallying point for Americans at home to respond to insults from abroad.[31]

Kennedy's went from 78 to 83 after the Bay of Pigs and from 61 to 76 after the Cuban missile crisis; and Ford's went from 40 to 51 after the *Mayaguez* incident: *Public Opinion*, February/March 1980, pp. 28-29.

[31] Haynes Johnson, "Media," in Richard Harwood, ed., *The Pursuit of the Presidency* (New York: Berkley Books, 1980), pp. 43-44.

The effect showed itself, immediately and massively, in Carter's approval rating. It shot up from 32 percent just before the hostages were taken to 61 percent in early December—a truly vertiginous rise of twenty-nine points in just one month. His rating trailed off a bit to 57 percent in early January and 55 percent in early February, but it stayed far above the prehostage doldrums in which it had languished for so long.

On January 21 the 1980 presidential campaign officially began with the holding of the Iowa precinct caucuses. The story of the remaining months of the Carter administration is so intertwined with the stories of Carter's contests with Kennedy for the Democratic nomination and with Reagan for the election that I shall end my account here.

Since I have told so much of the Carter administration's story in terms of its ups and downs in the Gallup poll's presidential approval ratings, it seems fitting to end with Gallup's findings about how the people perceived Jimmy Carter's strengths and weaknesses in a poll taken in January 1980. The figures in table 1–2 tell volumes about what the American people thought about Jimmy Carter after three and a half years of his presidency. What future historians will think remains to be seen.

2

The Democratic Nomination

Nelson W. Polsby

The Democratic nomination of 1980 was won by the incumbent president, principally because he was the incumbent. Thus an explanation of the outcome entails two steps. First, we must discuss how incumbency came to overshadow all other effects in determining the 1980 nomination result. Second, we must take a backward glance at the processes which caused Jimmy Carter to be the 1980 incumbent and hence the beneficiary of the incumbency effect of that year.

Because the Democrats lost the 1980 presidential election, yielded their majority of nearly thirty years in the Senate to the Republicans, and gave up ground in the House of Representatives, it may constitute an appropriate preliminary to point out that the Democratic nomination for the presidency is nevertheless an immensely valuable prize. By far the largest number of Americans who claim a political party affiliation identify themselves as Democrats.[1] This has been true for decades, and it is nearly as true now as it ever has been. Americans likewise respond in public opinion surveys with predominant approval to a wide range of policy options associated with big government and with the national Democratic party.[2]

---

[1] A good summary of Gallup findings is contained in *Public Opinion* (February/March 1980), p. 34. Data for 1980 are from the Gallup poll, November 13, 1980.

Party Affiliation	Oct.-Dec. 1977	Oct.-Dec. 1978	Oct.-Dec. 1979	Nov. 1980
Democrats (%)	47	46	46	48
Republicans (%)	22	23	22	26
Independents (%)	31	31	32	26

A CBS News/*New York Times* poll conducted April 22-26, 1981, found the following figures, which are not exactly comparable to the Gallup figures given above: 49 percent said they were Democrats or Democratic-leaning independents, and 41 percent said they were Republicans or Republican-leaning independents (Adam Clymer, "Poll Finds Nation Is Becoming Increasingly Republican," *New York Times*, May 3, 1981).

[2] In his article "The Brittle Mandate," *Political Science Quarterly*, vol. 96

THE DEMOCRATIC NOMINATION

Indeed, in the first survey by Louis Harris and ABC News after President Reagan won the election, there were majorities for the anti-Reagan position on such social issues as abortion, affirmative action, handgun registration, and the Equal Rights Amendment.[3] The CBS/New York Times election day exit poll found that Reagan got many votes—38 percent of them—from people who could be interpreted as simply anti-Carter voters, giving as their strongest reason for voting Republican that it was "time for a change." Only one-third of this group called themselves conservative. An additional 15 percent of those questioned gave no reason for their Republican vote at all. By contrast, only 11 percent said they voted for Reagan because "he is a real conservative," and 12 percent gave party loyalty as their chief reason—as compared with 29 percent who said they stuck with Carter because he was their party's candidate.[4] And finally, in spite of the fact that in three of the last four presidential elections Republicans have won, voting for Democrats below the presidential level

(Spring 1981), Everett Carll Ladd gives findings from the National Opinion Research Center (NORC) 1980 General Social Survey on attitudes toward public spending. The table below shows majority views on U.S. spending.

	Too Little (%)	Too Little or About the Right Amount (%)	Too Much (%)
Halting crime	72	94	—
Drug addiction	65	92	—
Defense	60	88	—
Health	57	92	—
Education	55	89	—
The environment	51	84	—
Big cities	—	76	—
Blacks	—	74	—
Space exploration	—	57	—
Foreign aid	—	—	74
Welfare	—	—	59

This is not much of an endorsement for Republican frugality.

[3] Louis Harris, "No Mandate for a Switch on Social Questions Seen," *Washington Post*, December 4, 1980. The figures were 62/34 percent opposing a constitutional amendment that would ban abortion; 68/23 percent supporting "affirmative action programs in industry for blacks, provided there are no rigid quotas"; 67/32 percent favoring federal legislation requiring handgun registration; and a 52/46 percent majority favoring the passage of the Equal Rights Amendment. These results also square with the findings of the *Los Angeles Times* poll. See George Skelton, "Conservative Mandate for Reagan Contains Limits," *Los Angeles Times*, November 20, 1980.

[4] See Adam Clymer, "Displeasure with Carter Turned Many to Reagan," *New York Times*, November 9, 1980. See also *Public Opinion* (December/January 1981), p. 43. Respondents were allowed to check two reasons.

has remained strong. This year, as in the last fifteen congressional elections, more people voted for Democratic than for Republican House candidates.[5] Democrats control almost twice the number of state legislative houses nationwide (63/34), and far more Democrats than Republicans sit as members of state legislatures.[6]

Although it is true that many senior liberal Democrats lost their races for the U.S. Senate, a fair number of liberal Democrats—Cranston (California), Inouye (Hawaii), Hart (Colorado), Leahy (Vermont), Glenn (Ohio), Eagleton (Missouri)—bucked the tide and won. A great many liberal senators were exposed to the voters in 1980, far more than senators in any other category. As is true in many elections, senior senators did get knocked off by new faces. Hence, many of the losers were bound to be liberal. In two instances, however, where an open Senate seat provided a clear liberal-conservative choice, Connecticut and Illinois, the liberal Democrat won.[7] From all this I conclude it is not yet time to abandon the maxim that Republicans do not win presidential elections so much as Democrats occasionally lose them. This certainly seemed to be the case in 1980.

The Kennedy Challenge and the Hostage Crisis

In late 1979, casual observers could be pardoned for believing that the advantage of incumbency in presidential elections was overrated. For the great bulk of his presidency, Jimmy Carter had behaved as though the grand coalition of Democrats that elected him in 1976—a coalition quite similar in its membership to the coalition that had elected and reelected Franklin Roosevelt—was of no particular value.[8] He had more or less ignored the needs for recognition and participa-

---

[5] See *Public Opinion* (December/January 1981), p. 24. The popular vote for House candidates in 1980 was 51 percent Democratic, 48 percent Republican.

[6] The figures for 1980 are: Democratic members, 4,497; Republican members, 2,918. Over the last four years, Republicans have been gaining. *Public Opinion* (December/January 1981), p. 25.

[7] I am indebted to an unpublished paper by Norman Ornstein, "Political Prognosis for the 97th Congress," for reassurance on some of these matters.

[8] See Robert Axelrod's "1976 Update," *American Political Science Review*, vol. 72 (June 1978), pp. 622-24, to his valuable "Where the Votes Come From" series, which began in the *American Political Science Review*, vol. 66 (March 1972), pp. 11-20. Axelrod says (p. 622), "For the Democrats, the New Deal coalition made a comeback in 1976. . . . The Democrats got a majority of the votes from each of the six diverse minorities which make up their traditional coalition: the poor, blacks, union families, Catholics, southerners, and city dwellers."

tion in government of most of the major interest groups that make up the Democratic party—in particular, blue-collar labor unions and white ethnic groups.[9] His relations with a Congress overwhelmingly in the hands of moderate Democrats, like himself, were distant when they were not hostile.[10]

As the nomination and election season approached, however, President Carter appeared to modify his aloofness toward the Democratic party. Building upon relationships established by the White House office of liaison with states and municipalities, he reached out to make two mayors members of his cabinet: in the summer of 1979 Neil Goldschmidt of Portland, Oregon, and Moon Landrieu of New Orleans became secretaries of the Departments of Transportation and Housing and Urban Development (HUD). In November, a prominent leader in national Jewish organizations, Philip Klutznick, was appointed secretary of commerce.

It is arguable, however, that these sound and traditional political moves came too late. The Goldschmidt and Landrieu appointments came on the heels of the self-inflicted public relations disaster of the first magnitude, the flamboyant—and fake—sacking during the summer news doldrums of the entire cabinet and White House staff merely in order to dislodge Secretaries Joseph Califano and Michael Blumenthal from the Departments of Health, Education, and Welfare (HEW) and the Treasury, respectively.[11]

By October, despite his attempts at rapprochement with elements of the Democratic party whom he had earlier ignored, Jimmy Carter looked vulnerable. His approval ratings as president in the public opinion suriveys were extremely low, with roughly twice as many disapproving of the way he was handling his job as president as

[9] An early indication of this remarkable pattern of neglect was the design of the original Carter cabinet. See my "Presidential Cabinet Making: Lessons for the Political System," originally a paper prepared for the Poynter Center at Indiana University and later published in *Political Science Quarterly*, vol. 93 (Spring 1978), pp. 15-25.

[10] An excellent overview of Jimmy Carter's difficulties with the Washington community and especially Congress is Haynes Johnson's *In the Absence of Power* (New York: Viking, 1980). See also Betty Glad, *Jimmy Carter: In Search of the Great White House* (New York: Norton, 1980), for example, p. 420.

[11] There were, to be sure, other casualties: Energy Secretary James Schlesinger, who had about used up his political influence, Attorney General Griffin Bell, who wanted to leave anyway, and Transportation Secretary Brock Adams, a victim of his obvious distaste for the process by which President Carter went about the task of firing the others. By far the most thorough account of this curious series of events was Elizabeth Drew, "A Reporter at Large," *New Yorker*, August 27, 1979, pp. 45-73.

approved.[12] Among Democrats, as Everett Ladd points out, Carter's ratings were unprecedentedly bad in the summer of 1979 (34 percent approval). "This was the lowest proportion endorsing a President of their own party since Gallup began using this measure during the second term of Franklin Roosevelt."[13] In addition, severe inflation was eroding the traditional popular confidence in the Democratic party's capacity to maintain economic prosperity.[14]

Around Washington, Democratic elective officeholders were becoming restive. The prospect of facing the voters in 1980 with an unpopular, uncooperative president at the head of the ticket was discomfiting. Most likely alternative candidates were unavailable, however. The name of Walter Mondale, for example, was floated as a possible unity candidate, but he was locked into the vice-presidency and enjoyed one of the few satisfactory working relationships with President Carter that Carter had been able to establish with veteran members of the Washington community.[15]

[12] The *Gallup Opinion Index*, report no. 175 (February 1980), p. 13, summarized Carter's popularity in October 1979 as (in percent):

Poll Taken	Approve	Disapprove	No Opinion
October 5-8	29	58	13
October 12-15	31	55	14

See also "Presidential Popularity: A 43-Year Review," *Gallup Opinion Index*, report no. 182 (October/November 1980).

[13] See Ladd, "The Brittle Mandate." The lowest approval rating ever recorded among Democrats for Truman was 42 percent, Johnson 48 percent, Kennedy 71 percent, and Roosevelt 79 percent; among Republicans, Richard Nixon's lowest score was 51 percent, Ford's 60 percent, and Eisenhower's 80 percent.

[14] The economy had been the number one worry of the American people since 1974 according to the Gallup poll. See *National Journal*, October 20, 1979, p. 1730. The long-term advantage of the Democratic party on this issue is documented in the *Gallup Opinion Index* for April 1974 and November 1978 and is conveniently summarized in Nelson W. Polsby and Aaron Wildavsky, *Presidential Elections* (New York: Charles Scribner's Sons, 1980) p. 205. A narrow Republican lead on economic issues in late 1979 is shown in a survey reported in *Public Opinion* (February/March 1980), p. 35. Strong dissatisfaction with Carter's handling of the economy from September 1979 through September 1980 is shown in NBC/Associated Press (AP) polls reported in *Public Opinion* (December/January 1981), p. 27, along with a substantial Reagan lead over Carter on economic issues in September and October 1980 (ibid., p. 28). The figures for the October 22-24 poll have Reagan best at handling economic issues, 41 percent, Carter 22 percent.

[15] See Hedrick Smith, "Mondale Suggested as Possible Nominee," *New York Times*, September 6, 1979. Other stories about the same time suggesting unhappiness among Democratic leaders include Bill Peterson and Edward Walsh, "O'Neill Fuels Speculation on Kennedy," *Washington Post*, September 11, 1979; and Adam Clymer, "Move Grows at Capitol to Urge Carter to Shun Race," *New York Times*, September 13, 1979.

One possible alternative was the forty-one-year-old governor of California, Edmund G. Brown, Jr. Four years earlier, Brown had started late in the primary sweepstakes but had run successfully against Carter in the Maryland, Rhode Island, and New Jersey primaries, and so he certainly could not be automatically discounted. This year, however, his campaign was handicapped by a number of problems. There was the distraction of the Republican lieutenant governor of California, who threatened mischief whenever Brown left the state to campaign. The campaign itself, run under the slogan "protect the earth, serve the people, and explore the universe," encountered many difficulties. Much Brown newspaper coverage dwelt on such contretemps as his visit in April 1979 to New Hampshire to testify before the state legislature in favor of a constitutional convention to write a constitutional amendment requiring a balanced federal budget. After arriving in the state and being strongly and publicly advised to go home by local Democrats, he decided against testifying. Shortly thereafter he embarked on a quick trip to Africa with his friend, pop singer Linda Ronstadt, that reaped unfavorable press comment.

Adding to the appearance of disarray was a Hollywood flop multimedia publicity event that closed out an early primary campaign. In this event, broadcast throughout the state of Wisconsin, technical problems made it appear at one point as though the state capitol building were resting inside Brown's head and at another as though small people were walking on his collar.

There were, in consequence of these and other close encounters, repeated occasions when news commentators wrestled with the question whether Brown was a politician to be taken seriously or merely another rare and exotic and temporary phenomenon of popular culture from the ever-fertile West Coast. An adviser of Brown— Jacques Barzhagi, described in the press as a Parisian film maker— acknowledged the difficulty: "The snowflake thing was a problem. . . . Really, what's between Jerry Brown and the public was an image— and he's not that image. . . . I've never seen him meditate." In 1980 Brown spent $3 million, much of it raised through rock concerts, but after several months of campaigning managed to garner only a single delegate (David Clarenbach of Madison, Wisconsin).[16]

---

[16] Among useful news stories on the Brown candidacy, see T. R. Reid, "After 3,000 Mile Trip, Gov. Brown Cancels Speech," *Washington Post*, April 3, 1979; Richard Bergholz, "Brown Doesn't Get to Testify," *Los Angeles Times*, April 3, 1979; John J. Goldman, "Brown, Miss Ronstadt, Slip Quietly Out of New York," *Los Angeles Times*, April 7, 1979; "Brown, Miss Ronstadt on Trail of Wild Animals," *Los Angeles Times*, April 9, 1979; "Miss Ronstadt Denies She'll Marry

Brown's candidacy illustrated in an especially vivid way the problem all other possible alternatives to President Carter were having in dealing not only with Carter but also with Senator Edward Kennedy. Because of Kennedy's great popular visibility, it was generally conceded by everyone but Brown that no alternative to President Carter could succeed if Kennedy decided to make the race himself.

As T. R. Reid of the *Washington Post* wrote,

> President Jimmy Carter's political liabilities seemed so clear to so many leaders of his own party that Democratic VIP's from all over the country were literally lining up behind one another . . . outside [Kennedy's] office. Almost every day you could see two or three prominent Democrats there . . . waiting to ask him to . . . [become] the Democratic candidate for President.
>
> Among those making that plea . . . were Democratic Senators . . . facing reelection challenges in 1980 and all sorely worried about running on a ticket headed by Jimmy Carter. There were senior Democrats . . . who felt less personal jeopardy but feared a general Republic landslide. . . . There were state officials from the East . . . from the Midwest . . . and from the West. There were labor leaders . . . there were black leaders . . . and Jewish leaders and Greek-American leaders and feminist leaders. . . . In short representatives from nearly every traditional Democratic constituency.[17]

In all the Gallup polls from the fall of 1978 through most of 1979, Kennedy consistently beat Carter in trial heats among Democrats by a margin that hovered around two to one, as table 2–1 indicates.

Thus during the period of hesitancy before he decided to make the race, Kennedy effectively prevented anybody-but-Carter sentiment from coalescing around anybody else. Because anti-Carter sentiment within the Democratic party was strong, and because Carter looked so weak, the logic of the situation more or less propelled Kennedy into the race for the nomination.

---

on Trip," *Los Angeles Times,* April 12, 1979; Victoria Brittain, "The African Jaunt," *Washington Post,* April 16, 1979; Adam Clymer, "Brown Opens Drive in New Hampshire," *New York Times,* September 10, 1979; Rowland Evans and Robert Novak, "Brown Waits," *Washington Post,* September 12, 1979; Lou Cannon, "Brown's Damaged Campaign," *Washington Post,* January 4, 1980; and Wayne King, "Governor Brown, His Dream Ended, Returns to California," *New York Times,* April 3, 1980.

[17] T. R. Reid, "Kennedy," in Richard Harwood, ed., *The Pursuit of the Presidency* (New York: Berkley, 1981), pp. 65-66.

TABLE 2–1

PRESIDENTIAL PREFERENCES OF DEMOCRATS: CARTER OR KENNEDY
(percent)

Question asked of Democrats: "Suppose the choice for President in the Democratic Convention in 1980 narrows down to Jimmy Carter and Edward Kennedy. Which one would you prefer to have the Democratic Convention select?"

	Carter	Kennedy	Undecided
June 1978	31	55	14
November	32	58	10
February 1979	28	60	12
April	31	58	11
June 1–4	24	62	14
June 22–25	26	68	6
July	30	66	4
August	25	63	12
September	27	59	14
October	30	60	10
November 2–5	31	54	15

SOURCE: *Gallup Opinion Index*, December 1979, report no. 173, p. 4.

Circumstances also dictated the pace of events. A Kennedy aide told Hedrick Smith of the *New York Times*:

> Once there was a head fake from Kennedy, the Carter people had a massage parlor in one room and a rack in the other room to work on people they wanted to hold with the President. The Senator felt he just couldn't leave people out there alone to take that, not knowing for sure if he was running. He felt he had to go and go quickly.[18]

Kennedy announced his candidacy on November 6, 1979. By that time, something had happened that would drastically change the terrain over which the contest for the nomination would be fought: two days earlier Iranian extremists identified as students stormed the U.S. embassy in Teheran and took numerous Americans hostage.

The reaction of American public opinion was not instantaneous. The next Gallup poll, conducted between November 16 and 19,

[18] Hedrick Smith, "Price for Kennedy's Quick Entry into Campaign Was a Ragged Start," *New York Times*, November 15, 1979.

showed Kennedy ahead of Carter among Democratic voters by 55 to 36 percent, with 9 percent undecided. An unmistakable mobilization of public opinion, focused on the hostages, began to develop, however. In part this was stimulated by the television networks, but it was also orchestrated by President Carter, who chose to treat the matter in a highly public way—unlike, for example, the treatment of the capture of the *Pueblo* by the Johnson administration—and to emphasize that *Americans*, rather than *diplomats*, had been taken prisoner.[19] By December 1979, President Carter's approval rating had doubled, from the 30 percent range of a month earlier to 61 percent. This made Carter the recipient of the most dramatic rally-'round-the-flag effect ever recorded.[20]

It is reasonable to suppose that any incumbent president would have had the benefit of a similar effect. The phenomenon has now been charted through at least seven presidencies, and consists, simply, of an upwelling of support for incumbent presidents when some sort of crisis in foreign affairs occurs.[21] The key feature of the crisis is that it be a discrete set of events that momentarily has the power to arrest the attention of otherwise unfocused, casual, or episodic observers. If the element of danger is present and there is a specific foreign enemy involved, so much the better. It is not necessary that U.S. action be successful or, indeed, that the net effect of the events that are at the center of attention even be creditable to the United States. Indeed, famous fiascoes—the Bay of Pigs and Suez—have evoked the rally-'round-the-flag effect, as have such events as the Tonkin Gulf incident and *Mayaguez*.

Because the phenomenon arises from the focusing of the attention of ordinarily inattentive masses of people, the effect is normally subject to decay over time. How fast this decay takes place is in part dependent upon the way in which the news media choose to play the story. In the case of the Iranian hostages, the story was

[19] For a sharp criticism of President Carter's approach, see Michael Howard, "Return of the Cold War?" *Foreign Affairs*, vol. 59 (America and the World, 1980), pp. 461-62.

[20] "George Gallup described this turnabout as 'stunning' and called the overall jump in public approval of Carter's performance in office 'the largest increase in presidential popularity recorded in the four decades the Gallup Poll and the Gallup organization have made these measurements.'" Edward Walsh, "Rivals Doubt Carter Will Retain Poll Gains after Iran Crisis," *Washington Post*, December 17, 1979.

[21] An early discussion of this phenomenon is contained in Nelson W. Polsby, *Congress and the Presidency*, 3d ed. (Englewood Cliffs, N.J.: Prentice-Hall, 1975), p. 66. See also John E. Mueller, *War, Presidents, and Public Opinion* (New York: John Wiley, 1973), pp. 220-25.

unusually long-lived. Walter Cronkite made an editorial decision to mention the number of days the hostages had been held captive at the conclusion of each and every edition of his top-rated nightly news broadcast over the CBS television network. The ABC network inaugurated a nightly twenty-minute news broadcast that at its inception focused exclusively on the running story of the hostages.

President Carter swiftly converted this remarkable turn of events to his own political advantage. He immediately perceived that the hostage crisis provided an occasion to withdraw from ordinary political campaigning of the type that tends to put presidents on the same level as their competitors for the office. In particular the crisis was given as a reason not to accept the challenge of Edward Kennedy to debate in Iowa. This also hurt the candidacy of Jerry Brown, who was striving at that point for recognition as a serious candidate. Instead, Mr. Carter kept aloof and sent surrogates to campaign in his behalf, thus underscoring the special presidential responsibilities that were his to perform during the long-running crisis. "In times of crisis for our country," he said, "I believe it's very important for the President not to assume, in a public way, the role of a partisan campaigner in a political contest." [22] This tactic maximized the employment of the presidency in behalf of the incumbent's political interests and was intensely frustrating to Kennedy partisans, who undoubtedly would have acted the same way, given the chance.

Staying in the White House Rose Garden does not immobilize a president so much as it insulates him from the mass media and permits him to control what is said about him. A news article in early February noted:

> Last week he invited TV cameras and reporters into his office while he phoned to thank Canadian Prime Minister Joseph Clark for his help in securing the escape of six Americans from Iran. When one reporter sought to ask him a question, Mr. Carter declared, "I am not going to have a press conference." [23]

In many respects, Mr. Carter conducted politics as usual:

> He has been telephoning dozens of Democrats in the early primary and caucus states, seeking their support. He has met frequently in the Oval Office with Democratic officials

---

[22] Timothy D. Schellhardt, " 'Rose Garden' Tactic Keeps Carter Home, Leaves Kennedy Railing Out in the Cold," *Wall Street Journal*, February 7, 1980.
[23] Ibid.

who then announce their support for his renomination and reelection.

Meanwhile, hundreds of interest group leaders—ethnic leaders, women activists, religious officials, business execuitves—are ushered in the White House to meet Mr. Carter. . . .

Yesterday, in one half-hour period, Mr. Carter had separate meetings with a group of chaplains, the top two officials of the National Association of Manufacturers, a contingent of Boy Scouts, and the Mayor and city council of Hamtramck, Mich.[24]

The hostage crisis was the sheer gift of circumstances and could be exploited, though not anticipated, in the president's game plan. The plan itself, insofar as its contents leaked into the mass media, had only one novel feature. In recognition of the fact that the early results of primary elections and district and state caucuses tend to dominate disposition of the nomination, by acting as the most significant advertising that influences decisions made later on, the president's political managers prevailed upon several southern states to move the dates of their primaries to earlier periods.

As a memorandum from Carter's chief strategist Hamilton Jordan to the President put it:

It is absolutely essential that we win the early contests and establish momentum. . . . The easiest way . . . is to win southern delegates by encouraging southern states to hold early caucuses and primaries. . . . It is in our interest to have states that we are likely to win scheduled on the same day with states that we might do poorly in.[25]

The president's managers attempted, but failed, to move the Massachusetts primary from March 4, a week after the New Hampshire primary, to March 11, where it would be one among a number in southern states. They did get the Connecticut primary moved into April, however, and they finally succeeded in packaging Georgia and Alabama with Florida on March 11, for what they hoped would be an especially auspicious Tuesday for the president.

Jordan also attempted to move primaries in Alabama and then Tennessee to March 18 so as to minimize what he feared would be the adverse effect of Illinois. He also tinkered with April 22, the date of the Pennsylvania primary, attempting unsuccessfully to persuade

24 Ibid.
25 Martin Schram, "Carter's Campaign," *Washington Post*, June 8, 1980. See also Schram, "Carter," in Harwood, *Pursuit of the Presidency*, pp. 83-120.

TABLE 2–2
DELEGATES FOR CARTER, BY DATE ACHIEVED, 1976 AND 1980

	1976		1980	
	Cumulative number	As percentage of total needed to win[a]	Cumulative number	As percentage of total needed to win[b]
March				
1			10	0.6
6, 8	36	2.3	44	2.6
13, 15	70	4.6	225	13.5
20, 22	123	8.1	441	24.6
27, 29	167	11.0	552	33.1
April				
3, 5	167	11.0	623	37.3
10, 12	232	15.4	662	39.7
17, 19	258	17.1	706	42.3
24, 26	264	17.5	869	52.1
May				
1, 3	333	22.1	940	56.4
8, 10	552	36.6	1,120	67.2
15, 17	565	37.5	1,166	69.9
22, 24	717	47.6	1,223	73.4
29, 31	876	58.2	1,308	78.5
June				
5, 7	895	59.4	1,632	97.9
12, 14	1,115	74.0	1,644	98.6

[a] N = 1,505.
[b] N = 1,666
SOURCE: Delegate counts from *National Journal* from March 6 through June 12, 1976, and March 1 through June 28, 1981.

state party leaders to shift caucuses in Texas, Oklahoma, and Louisiana to that date. He succeeded in moving the Missouri caucus to offset what he assumed would be bad news in Pennsylvania.[26]

For whatever reasons, it took the president only a short period of time to establish a lead in the delegate count. By St. Patrick's Day, Carter had begun to pull sharply away from Kennedy. The rate of his progress toward the nomination in 1980 was much faster than in 1976, as table 2–2 and figure 2–1 indicate.

[26] Ibid.

FIGURE 2–1

PERCENTAGE OF DELEGATES CARTER NEEDED TO WIN, BY DATE ACHIEVED,
1976 AND 1980

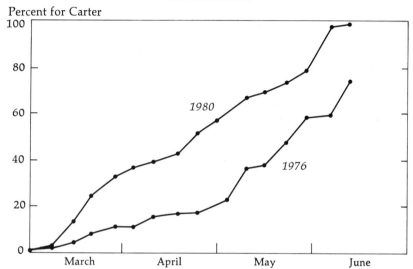

Percent for Carter

NOTE: 1976 N=1,505. 1980 N=1,666.

The Carter-Kennedy Campaign

Senator Kennedy persisted, however. Not only was the nomination period a time when his adversary, President Carter, was enjoying an extraordinary run of good luck; his own luck turned bad. Kennedys are used to getting something of a free ride from America's publicity machines, thanks to the skill and habit of cultivating journalists, now at least two generations old, among family members.[27] Moreover, Kennedys are undeniably good copy, attractive to newsstand purchasers of magazines, good looking, and, owing to the cruel vicissitudes of history, flamboyantly and publicly tragic. All this is charming to many journalists. Fatal flaws in other politicians become in the hands of Kennedy acolytes character-strengthening experiences for Kennedys.[28] This phenomenon has become so well known it has

[27] See, for example, Herbert S. Parmet, *Jack: The Struggles of John F. Kennedy* (New York: Dial, 1980); and especially Haynes Johnson's perceptive "On Arms-Length Coverage of the Kennedy Campaign," *Washington Post*, November 11, 1979.

[28] See, for example, the following extraordinary statement about the Chappaquiddick misfortune by Professor Arthur M. Schlesinger, Jr.: "The irony of it is that if Terry Kennedy were to run, it would make him a *better* President. Ever since Chappaquiddick, he has been spending his life trying to redeem himself for

begun to generate its own backlash among conscientious reporters. Members of the newest generation of boys on the bus have been known to take exception to the views of their elders that Kennedys are untouchable or that it is a lovably understandable foible of the press corps to give Kennedys special treatment.[29]

Something of these problems must have been on Roger Mudd's mind when he subjected Senator Edward Kennedy to an unusually stressful interview on the CBS special report that was aired on November 4, 1979—the same day the American embassy in Teheran was attacked. The senator must have been glad it ran against the first television screening of *Jaws*. Word got around, however.

A retrospective news story in the *Washington Post* characterized Kennedy's performance as "stuttering, vacuous . . . that portrayed a man who had no clear reason for running."[30] The interview touched, painfully, on his estrangement from his wife, who would later nonetheless be pressed into service as a campaigner in his behalf. And there was the matter of the decade-old incident at Chappaquiddick, an event which, as events of this character do in the United States, took on at least three layers of complexity.

At the first layer, for moralists concerned with the relations between men and women in American society, there were questions about what a married man was doing in the situation in which the Chappaquiddick incident discovered him. Kennedys traditionally draw much of their electoral strength in and around their home base from conventional members of the Catholic Church who do not like to hear of sexual hanky-panky.

Then there was the next layer of concern, about whether Senator Kennedy showed sufficient firmness of character in dealing with the fatal consequences of the accident itself, whether, for example, a person less concerned with his career and more for the life of the girl trapped in his car might have stopped for immediate help at the first lighted house along the road rather than delaying his approach to authorities and taking the convoluted path through the night that the senator described in his own defense.

Finally there was the issue of whether he was telling the truth about any or all of the above: about the occasion that brought him to

---

those hours of panic. He has become ever more serious, more senatorial, more devoted to the public good. I think this ceaseless effort at self-redemption may be for Teddy Kennedy what polio was for FDR." In Natalie Gittelson, "Chappaquiddick: The Verdict on Ted Kennedy," *McCalls*, August 1979, p. 146.

29 There is even a backlash against this backlash. See Tom Shales, "Petty for Teddy," *Washington Post*, January 30, 1980.

30 T. R. Reid, "Ill-Starred, Stumbling, Ever Gutsy," *Washington Post*, June 4, 1980.

the island; about the sources of the mistake that sent him, allegedly obliviously, down a dirt road at right angles to the asphalt road he said he thought he was taking; about what happened when his car went off the bridge and fell into the water; about what happened the rest of that night; and about what he has since said in connection with all of these events.

Kennedy's response to all this relied heavily on the findings of the Massachusetts magistrate, which largely exonerated him from wrongdoing at the time of the accident. The results of the Maine caucuses and the New Hampshire primary, however, suggested that this answer was not altogether convincing to the religiously observant residents of the three- and four-deck houses in the rundown mill-towns and cities of northern New England, people who had played such a significant role in establishing the Kennedys as unbeatable in New England.[31]

As the weeks rolled on, it became clear that the Kennedy effort would fail. Heavy spending in the senator's behalf at first soon gave way to a financial pinch.[32] President Carter, meanwhile, began to make effective use of the small change of presidential patronage. Joseph Kraft gave a few examples:

[31] Carter beat Kennedy 46.7 to 38.9 percent in the February 10 Maine caucuses and by 47.1 to 37.3 percent in the February 26 New Hampshire primary. See James M. Perry, "Many Democrats in Maine Oppose Ted Kennedy because of His 'Life Style' and Abortion Stance," *Wall Street Journal*, February 7, 1980. E. J. Dionne, Jr., "Chappaquiddick and its Devastating Political Effects," *New York Times*, March 22, 1980, reported: "The national NY Times-CBS poll released this week found that about a third of the nation's Democrats said that the way Mr. Kennedy handled the automobile accident at Chappaquiddick made them less likely to vote for him. . . . A quarter of the Democrats said they believed he had lied about the incident." See also E. J. Dionne, Jr., "Catholic Vote Hasn't Been Kennedy's for the Asking," *New York Times*, May 5, 1980. The *Washington Post* ran a series on Chappaquiddick that compactly summarizes the main issues: see George Lardner, Jr., "Chappaquiddick: Mystery Still Cloaks Tragedy of a Summer Night a Decade Ago," November 11, 1979; George Lardner, Jr., "Chappaquiddick: A Tale Time Has Not Resolved," November 12, 1979; and Martin Schram, "Chappaquiddick: Millstone of Uncertain Weight," November 13, 1979.

[32] When Kennedy's campaign began, the individual salaries of twelve aides were set at more than $42,000 a year. Contrary to the usual custom of maintaining modest office space, Kennedy headquarters in Chicago was the ninth floor of Water Tower Place, and Kennedy transportation consisted of a specially reconfigured, luxuriously appointed Boeing 727. The plane cost $5,000 a day sitting on the ground, unused, as it was for ten days while the senator took his Christmas vacation in Palm Beach. It was finally disposed of after the January 21 Iowa caucus. See Martin Schram, "Kennedy's Decision to Stay in the Race: After Iowa, the Agonizing Overhaul of a 'Cadillac' Campaign," *Washington Post*, February 5, 1980.

Governor Bob Graham of Florida, who is due to place the President's name in nomination, was given, from funds usually reserved for natural disasters, money to take care of the wave of Cuban refugees who came to Florida last winter. Lynn Cutler, a commissioner in Black Hawk County, who helped vitally in the Iowa caucuses, was given grants that enabled a meat-packing plant in Waterloo to stay open.[33]

The state of Maine received $75.2 million in federal grants during January, as compared with only $15 million in November and $23 million in December. Federal grants to New Hampshire doubled from December to January in preparation for its February delegate selections.[34] Stories abounded about HUD and Transportation grants won and lost by communities on the basis of whether prominent public officials endorsed the president or not. Los Angeles, where Mayor Tom Bradley backed the president, did well; Chicago, where the fickle Mayor Jane Byrne jumped to Senator Kennedy, was reported to be in trouble. East St. Louis, Illinois, where Mayor Carl Officer endorsed Carter, got a $7.8 million federal courthouse; Carbondale, Illinois, where Congressman Paul Simon endorsed Kennedy, unexpectedly lost a HUD grant.[35]

None of this was coincidental, as journalists discovered when they inquired of federal officials. Hedrick Smith reported in the *New York Times*:

The Carter administration is boldly working the politics of incumbency this fall by directing federal aid to its political allies and timing aid announcements for maximum political impact on states involved in the early stages of the 1980 campaign.

The Florida caucuses last weekend produced a gush of federal aid into Florida, but they were only the first stream of what White House officials candidly acknowledge is a much broader Niagara of federal aid being steered toward Iowa, New Hampshire, Illinois, New York, Massachusetts, North Carolina, and Minnesota.[36]

[33] Joseph Kraft, "The Carter Machine," *Washington Post*, August 12, 1980.

[34] Timothy B. Clark, "As Long As Carter's Up He'll Get You a Grant," *New York Times*, April 21, 1980; and Clark, "Carter Plays Santa Claus for His Reelection Campaign," *National Journal*, April 5, 1980, pp. 548-53.

[35] Timothy D. Schellhardt, "Carter, Who Railed against Pork-Barrel Politics in 1976, Now Exploits Them for Illinois Primary," *Wall Street Journal*, March 6, 1980.

[36] Hedrick Smith, "White House Using Grants to Woo States in Campaign,"

Nobody knows how effective any of this was in mobilizing voters or in persuading them to vote for President Carter. Perhaps more important were Carter's efforts to maintain the saliency of the Iranian situation. Just before the Wisconsin primary election, for example, President Carter was able to announce hopeful news about Iran from his sanctuary in the White House Rose Garden.[37] After a while, as President Carter's lead piled up, observers had difficulty explaining to themselves why Kennedy persisted at all, and as the press entourage covering the senator shrank in size, the remaining group began to redefine the story as a chronicle of gallant idealism, an attempt to rally Democrats to the old-time religion of high government expenditures and concern for the poor, in the face of inflationary pressures that clearly perturbed the great mass of Democratic voters far more.

In the end, Jimmy Carter received 50 percent of all votes cast in the Democratic primaries of 1980; Kennedy received 38 percent. Kennedy entered all thirty-four primaries and lost twenty-four; he contested all twenty-five state and territorial caucuses and lost twenty. He was, as T. R. Reid said, "the year's champion loser."

The human story is that he was a gutsy and gracious loser.

The enduring irony of the 1980 Kennedy camapign was that the candidate who lost for lack of character demonstrated a rare degree of tenacity, decency and inner strength. He showed himself, in short, to be a man of considerable character.

Through all the reverses he experienced, Kennedy abso-

New York Times, October 17, 1979. See also David S. Broder, "President Finally Putting the Perks of Office to Political Use," *Washington Post*, September 12, 1979; Walter S. Mossberg and Timothy D. Schellhardt, "Carter Plans a Gift for New Englanders—at Primary Time," *Wall Street Journal*, September 17, 1979; Frank Lynn, "Some Democrats Say Carter Offers Census Jobs to Allies," *New York Times*, September 24, 1979; Fred Barbash and David S. Broder, "Politics and Pettiness: Carter vs. Kennedy in Florida," *Washington Post*, October 13, 1979; and John J. Goldman, "New York Gets the Carter Touch," *Los Angeles Times*, January 31, 1980.

[37] The president's news conference on the subject took place at 7 A.M. on the day of the primary vote. According to the CBS/*New York Times* exit poll of Wisconsin voters, most of those who cited Iran as having an effect on their vote went for Mr. Carter. The NBC/AP poll found that the president received the vote of 48 percent of those who made up their minds on election day as compared with 28 percent for Senator Kennedy. E. J. Dionne, Jr., "Iran and Wisconsin Primary," *New York Times*, April 3, 1980. See also Bernard Gwertzman, "Carter Is Delaying Sanctions As Iran Makes Hostage Bid," *New York Times*, April 2, 1980.

lutely refused to cry or complain; he kept plugging reso-
lutely away.[38]

The question remains, however, why he continued to the end. A
number of reasons were given by Kennedy and his aides, among
them that the selection process provided a forum for the senator to
promote his views of the issues and that remaining in the race would
make him the party nominee if for any reason President Carter
faltered or became unavailable.[39] There were other possible reasons:
loyalty to his followers, enjoyment of the publicity, or because he
could exact concessions on the platform in return for a display of
party loyalty at the convention. Although it appeared he could not
possibly win the nomination, he could certainly jeopardize Jimmy
Carter's chances for reelection. Kennedy supporters, though fewer
than Carter supporters, were far more enthusiastic for their man.
Conceivably this enthusiasm would be worth something at the convention or during the election campaign, or even during a Carter
second term.

The Drive for an Open Convention

Jimmy Carter had long since sewn up the Democratic nomination
by the time his rally-'round-the-flag effect had begun to fade and his
prior unpopularity with the voters had begun to reassert itself. By
late July, only 21 percent of all voters approved of his conduct of the
presidency, an all-time low for this particular Gallup measurement.[40]
In early August the *New York Times* reported:

> One poll taker who surveyed 18 closely contested Congres-
> sional districts around the country, and averaged the re-
> sults, found that Mr. Carter was running third, with 23%
> of the vote. Mr. Reagan had 34% and John B. Anderson . . .
> had 25%. Another survey of 16 districts found Mr. Carter
> running third in nine of them.[41]

This tallied with information released by the liberal House Democratic
Study Group, from

---

[38] Reid, "Kennedy," pp. 68, 73-74.

[39] See Walter S. Mossberg, "Figures Indicate Kennedy's Bid Is Futile, He
Persists They Can Be Made to Add Up," *Wall Street Journal*, May 12, 1980.

[40] "Presidental Popularity: A 43-Year Review," *Gallup Opinion Index*, report
no. 182 (October/November, 1980), p. 13.

[41] Steven V. Roberts, "Democrats in Congress Fear Carter May Hurt the
Ticket," *New York Times*, August 9, 1980.

a series of polls showing Mr. Carter running far behind Mr. Reagan in many districts now held by Democrats. . . . The President was running first in only 10 of 50 districts surveyed and his level of support had dropped by 30% in three months.[42]

Some Democratic congressmen from shaky seats watched this turn of events with dismay, as they realized that soon they would face the electorate with a weak and unpopular president at the head of their ticket. From an ad hoc association of such congressmen, some allied with the Kennedy candidacy, some not, came a short-lived campaign for an "open convention," in which delegates would be freed from their obligation to vote for the candidate in whose name they were selected.

The issue arose formally in connection with the proposal in the call to the convention to include in the procedural rules of the convention a rule on voting—rule F(3)(c)—that read as follows:

All delegates to the National Convention shall be bound to vote for the presidential candidate whom they were elected to support for at least the first Convention ballot, unless released in writing by the presidential candidate. Delegates who seek to violate this rule may be replaced with an alternate of the same presidential preference by the presidential candidate or that candidate's authorized representative(s) at any time up to and including the presidential balloting at the National Convention.[43]

Since conventions, being the sovereign entities of their political parties, must adopt their own rules, a fight over adoption of this rule provided the occasion of a battle between those who supported President Carter and those who preferred any other nominee.

Much high-minded rhetoric was heard on this issue. Anti-Carter people won the battle of nomenclature by proclaiming their side the one in favor of "openness." They argued against "a convention in

---

[42] Ibid.

[43] Democratic National Committee, *Final Call: The Democratic National Convention* (Washington, D.C., 1979), p. 17. Among the useful news stories on this issue were Adam Clymer, "Disquiet among Democrats," *New York Times*, May 8, 1980; T. R. Reid and Bill Peterson, "House Group Seeks 'Open Convention,'" *Washington Post*, July 29, 1980; Hedrick Smith, "Carter Camp to Insist on Discipline on First Ballot Vote," *New York Times*, July 30, 1980; A. O. Sulzberger, Jr., "Democrats Weigh Rule Binding Delegates," *New York Times*, July 31, 1980; and Martin Plissner, "The Open Convention: A Kennedy Scenario," *Atlantic*, August 1980, pp. 4-8.

which courage and conscience would be replaced by computer-like control."[44] As attorney Edward Bennett Williams put it: "Nineteen million Democrats never voted for Rule F(3) (c). They voted instead for men and women of conscience and character.[45]

Carter people piously deplored the open convention on the grounds that this would lead to the return of a brokered convention, that odious institution presumably banished by the party reforms of 1968–1972. Meanwhile, backstage, Carter and his representatives busily dealt away their positions on several key platform planks in return for a show of party unity by the Kennedy forces. More relevantly, Carter managers pointed out that Kennedy and his allies were asking that delegates now break faith with the thousands of voters in primary elections who had years ago been put in the saddle by reforms advocated by the liberal—now Kennedy—wing of the party.

In fact, the open convention was nonsense from the start. The point of the eight-year-old reforms had been to take power from state party leaders, and delegations no longer fairly represented the sentiments of state parties, nor did they pretend to do so. Delegations had been packed by interest groups—the Machinists Union and the National Education Association, for example—whose delegates' organizational loyalties lay with them, not with state party leaders. Even more to the point, in the overwhelming majority of state primaries delegates had not even been elected by name: "delegates *for*" the various presidential candidates, who were named on the ballot, were what voters voted for. After the results of primary elections were known, candidate agents within each state selected delegates to represent the candidate in the numbers to which the primary results entitled them, and according to complex demographic quotas fastened upon them by national party rules. These delegates, the vast majority of all those present at the convention, sat in the convention solely by virtue of their selection by the candidate whom open-convention advocates wished them to repudiate. They had no other legitimate cause to be in Madison Square Garden at all.

Thus the idea of an open convention was entirely incoherent, given the process that selected delegates. Of course under some other selection scheme, one, for example, in which delegates represented something other than the candidate who chose them, an openly

[44] Edward Bennett Williams, "The Rule's a Bummer," *Washington Post*, August 7, 1980.

[45] Ibid. See also Hugh L. Carey, "An Open Convention," *New York Times*, May 21, 1980. For counterarguments, see Don Fowler, "The Kennedy Flip on Party Rules," *Washington Post*, July 6, 1980.

deliberative convention could be seen to make sense. Indeed, until the reforms of 1968–1972 entirely preempted the work of the national party convention, representatives of state parties, members of Congress, and other leaders were ordinarily present in adequate numbers to conduct a peer review of prospective candidates and exercise judgment that had some legitimate claim to be the authentic result of a process of party selection.[46] Unknown, anonymously selected delegates, representing nothing and nobody except the presidential candidate who appointed them, no matter how laden with conscience, how infused with character, could claim no such thing.

Theology aside, the politics of the situation were quite straightforward: anti-Carter forces operating outside the convention never had the votes to overturn the results of the primaries and caucuses that elected pro-Carter delegates to the convention, no matter how unenthusiastic these delegates might have been. Democratic governors, meeting at the National Governors Conference in early August, declined to join the movement in a body. Few of them were themselves up for reelection. Many of them, Carter supporters included, conceded that Democrats were in for a tough year in their states. And one or two—notably Carter supporter Ella Grasso of Connecticut—called for the president to withdraw his support from rule F(3)(c) on the quite reasonable supposition that the vast bulk of his delegates would vote for him anyway.[47]

Carter people, in no mood to take chances, declined this advice. As soon as the vote on the rules, which Carter won 1,936.4 to 1,390.6,

---

[46] This Democratic convention upheld the postreform trend away from participation in the convention by senators and congressmen. (See Polsby and Wildavsky, *Presidential Elections*, p. 110.) Only 41 of 275 Democratic U.S. representatives were delegates or alternates; only eight of fifty-eight Democratic senators were delegates or alternates. The record is nearly as bad for mayors. Of the mayors of the fifty largest cities with Democratic mayors, only fourteen were delegates or alternates according to my count from the published official roster. My list of Democratic mayors comes from page 3 of the Democratic National Committee publication *The Democrats: 1980 Democratic National Convention* (Washington, D.C., 1980). The fourteen I could discover in attendance as delegates or alternates were (in order of the populations of their communities) Ed Koch of New York, William Green of Philadelphia, Coleman Young of Detroit, Marion Barry of Washington, D.C., Diane Feinstein of San Francisco, Janet Gray Hayes of San Jose, Ernest Morial of New Orleans, Richard Caliguiri of Pittsburgh, Maynard Jackson of Atlanta, James Griffin of Buffalo, Don Fraser of Minneapolis, Maurice Ferre of Miami, Richard Arrington of Birmingham, and Philip Isenberg of Sacramento.

[47] Dennis Farney, "Democratic Governors, at Denver Meeting, Refuse to Join Drive to 'Open' Convention," *Wall Street Journal*, August 5, 1980; and Joyce Purnick, "Movement to 'Open' Convention Wins the Support of Gov. Grasso," *New York Times*, July 30, 1980.

was concluded, Kennedy went on television to withdraw his name from further consideration for the presidential nomination.

The rest of the convention consisted mostly in waiting, by delegates and observers alike, to see whether Senator Kennedy would embrace the ticket and how happily and whether he would agree to campaign in the fall. Carter strategists offered concessions on the platform, agreeing to Kennedy-inspired planks providing $12 billion for a job program and giving a high priority to fighting unemployment. Carter refused to yield on Kennedy demands for wage and price controls. These three planks were gaveled through the convention by Chairman Thomas P. O'Neill on voice votes—at least one of which clearly went the other way.[48]

Kennedy and his enthusiasts did not seem to be mollified, however. Although his name was never placed in nomination, Kennedy received nearly all the votes on the first ballot that had been pledged to him. After Jimmy Carter was securely nominated and it was time for symbolic gestures of unity, Kennedy delayed his appearance on the platform. When he arrived, he shook Carter's hand with no show of warmth, stayed the minimum length of time, and departed.

The 1980 Nomination as a Consequence of the 1976 Nomination

As more and more Democrats faced their own dissatisfactions with the results of the 1980 selection process—a process that yielded a 25 percent defection rate of Democratic voters in the general election[49]—calls for reconsideration of the reforms of 1968–1972 began to be heard. Democrats were far from unanimous in their diagnoses of what went wrong, however. It was, for example, implausible to think that a set of party rules resembling those replaced in the reforms of 1968–1972 would have failed in 1980 to renominate a sitting incumbent. Indeed, the reforms had made incumbents more vulnerable, not less, as Gerald Ford's experience in 1976 could also testify.

Thus the roots of the difficulty had to be traced back at least four years. In 1980, Jimmy Carter won a renomination that would

---

[48] In addition, women delegates succeeded in securing the adoption of minority platform planks denying the financial support of the national Democratic party to party candidates who failed to espouse the Equal Rights Amendment and favoring government aid for abortions for poor women.

[49] This is the defection rate according to the CBS/*New York Times* exit poll on November 4, 1980. See Adam Clymer, "The Democrats Look for New Ideas, and Jobs," *New York Times*, November 9, 1980.

undoubtedly have been his under nearly any realistic circumstances, by virtue of his incumbency. It was the events of 1976, however, that made him the beneficiary of the advantages of incumbency in 1980, and so it is necessary to understand the processes that gained him the 1976 nomination.

It should be stated at once that Jimmy Carter won the 1976 Democratic nomination fair and square. There was, however, a profound difficulty that was lodged within the process through which he won. Under the rules and regulations that came into being in the national Democratic party in time for the 1972 nomination, the balance of advantage in the nomination process had shifted sharply away from candidates who could assemble a broad coalition of consenting politicians to their nomination and toward candidates who could successfully mobilize a narrow but loyal faction of supporters.[50]

That faction could be mobilized by any number of means: passionate feelings over one or a few issues, ideology, or sectional loyalty. The key to success, however, was clear: as the delegate selection process became ever more exclusively dependent upon primary elections with a few state caucuses thrown in, what was required above all was not that candidates organize a majority coalition but rather that candidates come out high in rank order in a field of alternatives that could resemble the starting line of an Oklahoma land rush—preferably first. Being first in a crowded field—and early in each election year the field is usually fairly crowded with prospective candidates—entails primarily mobilizing your own supporters to vote. Through a series of such trial heats Jimmy Carter emerged in early 1976: in the Iowa caucuses, where he had spent nearly a year in intensive cultivation of a following; in New Hampshire, where he was the only centrist candidate pitted against a flock of left-leaning hopefuls; and in Florida, where he billed himself as the local, respectable alternative to George Wallace.

By the end of the arduous struggle, Jimmy Carter could truthfully say he owed his nomination to no one—except possibly to Andrew Young. He had identified clearly and early what part of the market he intended to make his own, and he succeeded. Neither peer review nor deliberation on the part of party leaders played a major part in his success. He was required to make his peace with few state party leaders, and senators and representatives in Congress,

---

[50] For an elaborated discussion of this trend, see Nelson W. Polsby, "Coalition and Faction in American Politics: An Institutional View," in S. M. Lipset, ed., *Emerging Coalitions in American Politics* (San Francisco: Institute for Contemporary Studies, 1978), pp. 103-23.

with whom a president must collaborate in the business of governing, had by 1972 all but disappeared from the presidential selection process.

It was surely not required that Jimmy Carter behave as president in such a way as to maximize the impact of the defects in the process that nominated him. By coincidence, however, he did so, inferring quite erroneously that whatever breadth of political support was necessary to achieve the nomination was adequate to sustain a president who is trying to govern. Thus he more or less dismissed that major part of the grand coalition of Democrats that had not assisted in his nomination but had elected him, and it was not until far too late in his term of office that he was willing to attend to the damage that this severely parochial view caused his reelection chances.

The nub of the difficulty was that this view was neither confronted nor rebutted by the nomination process itself, and so in 1976 the Democratic party, by all reasonable measures the long-term majority party of the United States, nominated for the presidency—and elected—a candidate who defined himself as, and was, the candidate of a narrow faction within the broad Democratic spectrum. And so he remained as president. Thus he was a far more equal opponent in 1980 to the authentic tribune of the much more narrowly based Republican party than any Democrat needs to be. In 1976 the Democratic coalition held, and it delivered a victory to the candidate who emerged first in rank order from among the factional candidates in the primary elections of that year. In 1980 their candidate, though the incumbent, was still at best a factional leader and had only grudgingly edged away from political attitudes appropriate to an unreconstructed factionalist in his perspective toward the rest of the Democratic party. This time the underappreciated legions of the broad Democratic coalition could not deliver for Jimmy Carter.

3

Nominating "Carter's Favorite Opponent": The Republicans in 1980

Charles O. Jones

March 19, 1980: the results were in from the Illinois presidential primary, and Ronald Reagan was a big winner over both John Anderson and George Bush. The Illinois primary was only the ninth in a long series, but Reagan won seven of the first nine. Further, Gerald Ford announced on March 15 that he would not enter the race. Thus on March 19—just three weeks after the New Hampshire primary—the pundits declared that Ronald Reagan had won the Republican nomination for president. President Jimmy Carter's equally impressive victory over Sen. Edward Kennedy in Illinois was also viewed as settling matters on the Democratic side.

Having declared the nominations ended, press attention naturally turned to the general election. How might a Carter-Reagan contest turn out? Anthony Lewis of the *New York Times* warned that "after Illinois, the Democrats had better think again" about how easy it would be to defeat Reagan in November.[1] An English reporter, Douglas Ramsey, advised Western foreign policy pundits to "start thinking the unthinkable: within months, Ronald Reagan may be President."[2] Nevertheless, James Reston, the respected columnist for the *New York Times*, judged that the Republicans had played directly into Carter's hands. He guessed that the Republican nomination process was "being run by the Democratic National Committee." The Democrats were presumably very worried about Gerald Ford and concerned about John Connally, Howard Baker, George Bush, and John Anderson. "A Ford-Anderson ticket would have given him [Carter] fits."

[1] Anthony Lewis, "The Reagan Prospect," *New York Times*, March 20, 1980, p. A-27.
[2] Douglas Ramsey, "Reagan as President," *New York Times*, April 3, 1980, p. A-23.

> But now Carter is left with Reagan alone, and if Jimmy and the Georgians and the Democratic National Committee could have planned the whole thing, this is precisely how they would have worked it out.
>
> They were really scared at the beginning of this year. With interest rates and prices up almost 20 percent, with the Soviets in Afghanistan and the hostages in Iran, and the allies running for cover, Jimmy Carter was in the deepest economic trouble since Herbert Hoover, and in the worst political trouble in his own party since George McGovern.
>
> But Republicans are compassionate people. . . . They know Mr. Carter didn't invent inflation or mean to get into all this trouble at home or abroad, so they are giving Carter, as they gave Lyndon Johnson in 1964, their favorite candidate, and *Carter's favorite opponent—Ronald Reagan.*
>
> Seldom in the history of American politics has a party out of power shown so much generosity to a President in such deep difficulty.[3]

Mr. Reston need not assume full responsibility for the view that the Republicans were again courting electoral disaster by nominating Ronald Reagan for president. I heard it expressed many times during the campaign: "Why didn't the Republicans nominate a winner?" "If the Republicans had only nominated Ford, or Bush, or Baker—any one of them would have been a shoo-in." I might point out that I heard these views expressed rather late in the campaign—no doubt, long after Reston and President Carter had changed their minds about favorite opponents.

What was the basis for the judgment that Reagan would be a pushover for the president? How soon we forget, once a candidate has demonstrated the capacity to win. First and foremost Ronald Reagan is a conservative from the West. Recalling the Goldwater precedent, most pundits were convinced that a candidate so solidly identified with the Republican right could not win a national election—a minority within a minority and all that. Second is the matter of Reagan's age. If elected he would be the oldest person ever to take the oath. President Eisenhower was seventy when he left office; President Reagan reached seventy shortly after taking office. Then there is the fact that Reagan has had no Washington-based political experience. How could he claim to right those many wrongs of the present administration that were attributable to Carter's misunderstanding of politics in the nation's capital? Further, though Reagan

---

[3]James Reston, "Carter's Secret Weapon," *New York Times*, March 21, 1980, p. A-27. Emphasis added.

did serve two terms as governor of the largest state in the nation, he had held no elected position at all for six years. It did seem that Ronald Reagan was an unlikely candidate for leading the Republicans to victory over an incumbent president.

Yet there were other puzzling features of the pending election. The many reforms in the process of selecting delegates to the Democratic National Convention have had their effect on the Republican nominating process, too. The American way of nominating has changed rather dramatically in recent years, and many people believe that it now provides us with candidates who are not qualified to serve in the White House. Former undersecretary of state George W. Ball expressed these worries as follows:

> Our foreign friends see no hope from the U.S. elections. Though the prospect of four more years of Carter depresses Europeans, the thought of Ronald Reagan as president terrifies them.
>
> "How can it happen," a thoughtful French friend asked, "that out of a nation of 220 million of the world's ablest, best educated and often brilliant people, your leader must be chosen between Carter and Reagan? Your electoral system must be badly out of alignment!" I could not answer him.[4]

Here, then, are two important questions to guide the description and analysis of the 1980 Republican nominating process: (1) What has happened to the presidential nominating process? (2) How and why did Ronald Reagan win the nomination? I will present evidence that bears on these questions and return to consider them more directly in the conclusion. For now, let me state simply that Ronald Reagan won the Republican nomination in large part because he (and, by implication, his managers) understood what was required to win under the new system. He conducted a *trifocal* campaign for the nomination, concentrating on creating party unity and winning the general election while seeking to become the Republican candidate. Trifocal campaigns are not common. Indeed, among Republicans, they are particularly rare, since emphasizing party unity has been thought to detract from winning Democratic votes. In addition, the new nominating system presumably deemphasizes political party, perhaps even actively encourages separation between the candidate and the party. Still, the Reagan organization plotted a trifocal campaign from the start. We turn now to consider how and why all of that happened—starting with a review of the nominating process.

[4] George W. Ball, "Carter's Policies Stun Allies," *Pittsburgh Press*, March 23, 1980, p. B-2.

The American Way of Nominating Presidents

In the last edition of his classic work on political parties and interest groups (1964), V. O. Key, Jr., stressed the political party functions served by the presidential nominating process.

> The process of nomination of a presidential candidate begins long before the convention, in campaigns to sell a potential candidate *to the party.* . . .
>
> The character of the preconvention campaign to round up support for aspirants for the nomination . . . becomes a function of the tensions and cleavages within the party. Durable bases for conflict exist within each party.[5]

Key then proceeded to describe a nomination process we would hardly recognize today. He speaks of favorite-son candidates, negotiating with party leaders, "enlisting the support of state and local leaders," and strategic decisions about "whether to enter the presidential primaries."[6]

In his careful study *Presidential Selection,* published in 1979, James W. Ceaser describes quite a different system.

> Over the past fifteen years the nominating process has . . . been transformed from a mixed system, in which control over the nomination was shared by the people and the party organizations, to what can be termed a plebiscitary system in which the key actors are the people and the individual aspirants. Along with the emergence of this new institutional form has come a new method of generating support in presidential campaigns: "popular leadership," or the attempt by individual aspirants to carve out a personal mass constituency by their own programmatic and personality appeals and by the use of large personal campaign organizations of their own creation. At the nomination stage, this form of leadership takes place entirely without the filter of traditonal partisan appeals, *as the nomination race is in effect a national nonpartisan contest.*[7]

On October 18, 1979, a most enlightening debate was held on presidential nominating politics between Richard Scammon, director, Elections Research Center; Ken Bode, political correspondent for NBC News and formerly on the staff of Democratic party reform com-

[5] V. O. Key, Jr., *Politics, Parties, and Pressure Groups* (New York: Thomas Y. Crowell, 1964), p. 399. Emphasis added.

[6] Key, *Politics,* pp. 399-405.

[7] James W. Ceaser, *Presidential Selection: Theory and Development* (Princeton, N.J.: Princeton University Press, 1979), p. 5. Emphasis added.

missions; Austin Ranney, resident scholar at the American Enterprise Institute and a member of Democratic party reform commissions; and David Broder, political correspondent for the *Washington Post*. The group was sharply divided in its analysis of the extent to which the many reforms enacted by the Democrats have affected the nominating process in both parties. Ranney and Broder argued that the reforms have hurt the political parties and are bound to produce weak presidents. Scammon and Bode were unwilling to attribute events to the reforms, nor were they prepared to believe that the outcomes of the nominating process have been so bad. In addition, Scammon expressed faith in participation, regardless of the outcome. "Forget whether the reforms are good or bad; if they produce an exercise of popular will greater than we see anywhere else in the world, then I am impressed."[8] Austin Ranney referred to this as the virtue-is its own-reward school of thought.[9]

My own view is an amalgam of these positions. I believe, with Ranney and Broder, that the reforms have had an effect. I also agree, however, with a portion of the Scammon-Bode position, that is, the reforms derive from other events, and we must consider the whole set of social/political changes that led to specific reforms of the nominating process. In turn, there is no single explanation for the type of candidate that emerges as our presidential choice from this process.

What are the changes that help us to understand the new system and what it produces? I suggest two types of developments: first, broad, contextual changes having to do with government itself; second, specific changes in the means by which we nominate presidential candidates. Included among the broad, contextual changes are the following:

1. increased public cynicism about government, politics, and politicians
2. increased attention and scrutiny by the media of the personal and public lives of all elected officials
3. exponential growth in government programs to treat domestic issues, with little apparent effect in resolving these issues and growing public doubt as a consequence (see 1 above)
4. little or no control of the budget by elected decision makers because of obligations associated with entitlement programs, indexing, military spending, and a gigantic debt

[8] *Choosing Presidential Candidates: How Good Is the New Way?* (Washington, D.C.: American Enterprise Institute, 1980), p. 7.

[9] *Choosing*, p. 5.

5. a shift from expansive to consolidative issues in government—from formulating new programs to controlling and managing what is already on the books.[10]

This first set of changes may help George Ball explain to his "thoughtful French friend" why it is hard to get the best candidates. One has to have special motivation to get involved in politics today. As we will see, it helps to be out of a job. Faced with public cynicism, press criticism, ineffectiveness of existing programs, limited capacity to make things better, and a high probability that things will get worse, it is no wonder that those with intelligence, drive, creativity, and their integrity still intact busy themselves elsewhere.

Yet there is more. David Broder observes:

> In the old way, whoever wanted to run for president of the United States took a couple of months off from public office in the year of the presidential election and presented his credentials to the leaders of his party, who were elected officials, party officials, leaders of allied interest groups, and bosses in some cases. These people had known the candidate over a period of time and had carefully examined his work.
>
> In the new way, the first thing a candidate does is to get out of public office so he has nothing to do for two, three, four, or, in some cases, six years, except run for president of the United States. The candidate takes his case not to the professionals who know him or to his political peers, but to the amateurs who meet him only briefly in their living room or in the town hall [or on a television set] and have very little basis on which to make that screening. . . .
>
> The significance of the difference for the presidency is that in one case, a man, if he is elected, comes with the alliances that make it possible for him to organize the coalitions and support necessary to lead a government.[11]

Thus there are also changes in the precise method of choosing nominees that surely have had an effect on who runs and how they run. Most of these changes are traceable to recommendations by Democratic party reform commissions after the tumultuous Democratic convention in 1968. These reforms sought to democratize the

[10] For particularly thoughtful discussions of these and related developments, see Anthony King, ed., *The New American Political System* (Washington, D.C.: American Enterprise Institute, 1978), and James L. Sundquist, "The Crisis of Competence in Government," in Joseph A. Pechman, ed., *Setting National Priorities: Agenda for the 1980's* (Washington, D.C.: The Brookings Institution, 1980).

[11] *Choosing*, pp. 2-3, 7.

nominating process by broadening representation among delegates (establishing quotas, according to some), by expanding the participation in delegate selection, by providing delegates to a candidate in proportion to votes received in a primary, by limiting participation to Democrats only (no open primaries except in Wisconsin), and by virtually eliminating elected officials from serving as delegates. The Republicans followed with their own reform commissions but did not implement such sweeping reforms. In general, "the Republican party emphasized the exclusively federal nature of the party system." The changes tended to be advisory to state parties, not obligatory.

> Authority over state matters such as delegate selection standards resided at the lower levels. This emphasis did not prohibit a strong national headquarters staff from emerging, but it did require that the national party assure a basically supportive and supplemental posture to state party actions. Non-interference was emphasized. Power, if not always political resources, remained at the state level. Within this framework, any reform recommendations that impinged on what were considered state processes, even if adopted by the national convention, were accepted only as suggestions. The differences between the two national parties in approaching this issue were fundamentally and diametrically opposed.[12]

Inevitably, however, the changes in the majority party had their effect on the overall nominating system for both parties. Here are some of the more important developments:

1. *a significant increase in the number of presidential primaries* (before 1972, typically fewer than twenty states; 1976, thirty states; 1980, thirty-five states plus the District of Columbia and Puerto Rico)
2. *an increase in the number of primaries relying on proportional representation or a district system for awarding delegates* (for the Democrats, twenty-nine and two; for the Republicans, fifteen and seven)
3. *a weekly schedule of primaries from late February to early June, relieved only by an Easter break*
4. *an increase in the number of binding primaries* (for the Democrats, twenty-eight states; for the Republicans, twenty-six states)

12 William J. Crotty, *Political Reform and the American Experiment* (New York: Thomas Y. Crowell, 1977), p. 256.

5. *more minority and women delegates at both conventions, but fewer public officials; more delegates attending their first conventions*
6. *public financing of presidential candidate campaigns under specified conditions.*

These several important changes appear to have had a significant effect on who runs and how. The change to a greater number of primaries occurring in rapid succession encourages candidates to announce early and tends to favor those with nothing else to do, at least those not holding major public office. The proportional delegate-allocation systems encourage candidates to enter as many primaries as possible (consistent with their particular winning strategy). The binding preference vote makes the late entrant or dark-horse strategy extremely difficult to manage. Quotas and other mechanisms to deprofessionalize the party convention tend to reduce any possible contact and communication between the working government and the presidential nominating process. Public financing reduces party contact with and control over presidential candidates. Finally, several characteristics of the new system encourage challenges to an incumbent president. As Austin Ranney observes: "The whole purpose of the rules is to make it easy to challenge an incumbent president. Henceforth, no incumbent president . . . will ever again have an absolute certainty of being renominated."[13]

In summary, changes in public attitudes, government programs, and authority of elected decision makers appear to have influenced who runs for the presidency. And specific reforms in the nominating process tend to favor certain types of candidates—those with the time and resources to start early and organize efforts in the first caucuses and primaries. Both types of changes introduce greater uncertainty than in the past and therefore encourage media speculation about probable outcomes. As will be discussed below, this speculation over the long period of campaigning tends to become an important factor in and of itself. As Donald R. Matthews puts it:

> The news media are the main way the actors in this dispersed and prolonged drama communicate with one another and with those who prefer to stand aside and watch. A struggle over the content of political news has become the core of presidential nominating politics.[14]

[13] *Choosing*, p. 16.
[14] Donald R. Matthews, "Winnowing: The News Media and the 1976 Presidential Nominations," in James David Barber, ed., *Race for the Presidency: The Media and the Nominating Process* (Englewood Cliffs, N.J.: Prentice-Hall, 1978), p. 55.

The Nomination of Ronald Reagan

All scholars of presidential selection politics naturally stress the variation in campaign situations. We need not review all of the possibilities here. Suffice it to say that in 1980 the Republicans had a competitive, no-incumbent, multicandidate type of campaign. We now know that it got settled rather quickly. Still, a great deal of speculation in the early stages of the campaign stressed the possibility of a deadlocked convention, with Gerald Ford possibly emerging as the compromise candidate. Even so experienced a politician as Melvin Laird (former Representative from Wisconsin and secretary of defense) developed a scenario in October 1979 by which no candidate would get to Detroit with more than 35 percent of the delegates—thus favoring a Ford nomination.[15]

A reading of a scholarly paper by John H. Aldrich, prepared for the spring 1979 meeting of the Midwest Political Science Association, would have raised serious doubts about any such scenario. Aldrich concluded that even in a field of several candidates (eight, ten, or even more), the preconvention campaign is likely to be decisive in determining the candidate.

> Contrary to conventional wisdom, the prospects of a "deadlocked convention" need not be great. Obviously, the propositions produced here do not guarantee the emergence of precisely *one candidate* before the convention, but they do imply a rapid narrowing of the field. If the field is narrowed to, say, exactly two candidates quickly enough, then ... the pre-convention campaign will be decisive.[16]

Aldrich points out that the reforms have had the desired effect of allowing the public, through the primaries, to play a major role in choosing nominees. Clearly his analysis suggests probable failure of the "inactive but available" candidacies of a Humphrey in 1976 or a Ford in 1980.

Thus we begin this review of the 1980 Republican nomination with the knowledge that a competitive, multicandidate race with no incumbent running may very well get settled well in advance of the convention. How does any one candidate ensure that he (all were men in 1980) survives the winnowing process? No formula can

[15] As reported in a column by J. F. terHorst, *Pittsburgh Press*, October 19, 1979.
[16] John A. Aldrich, "A Dynamic Model of Presidential Nomination Campaigns," *American Political Science Review*, September 1980, p. 663. See also Steven J. Brams, *The Presidential Election Game* (New Haven, Conn.: Yale University Press, 1978), chap. 1.

guarantee success. Still, John Kessel is surely correct in asserting that "success in nomination politics does depend on both the strategy that is followed and on the structure of competition."[17] The structure of competition is a given, only marginally under the control of any one candidate at the start. The strategy to be followed is very much under the control of the candidate, however, and is itself subject to the resources available—including money raised, status in the polls, capable staff, effective organization, and relationships with the media. Still, none of these advantages will help if the candidate loses control of the expectations surrounding his effort. Matthews points out:

> Who wins—or loses—a presidential primary is frequently unclear. . . . More often than not, winning a presidential primary means doing better than expected; losing means disappointing expectations.[18]

Aldrich agrees with this analysis but also believes that the expectations are shaped primarily by the candidates and the media. Further, he describes a progression of expectations from one primary to the next.

> Expectations are "forecasts" of likely results determined no later than shortly after the preceding primary. This assumption allows candidates to modify their campaign strategy after any or all earlier events, and thus potentially to modify the difference between actual and expected results. . . .
> Deviations from expectations . . . yield changes in the competitive standings of the candidates and, hence, in the probability of their nomination.[19]

To recapitulate, this Aldrich-Matthews-Kessel image of a multi-candidate campaign has us watching to see how candidates collect and use resources for the strategic management of expectations about their campaigns. Our analysis of each candidate and the progress of the campaign, therefore, will be directed by the changes in competitive standing, first in the public opinion polls preceding the primaries, then in the primaries themselves. With this framework in mind, we turn next to the flow of the campaign itself.

---

[17] John Kessel, *Presidential Campaign Politics: Coalition Strategies and Citizen Response* (Homewood, Ill.: Dorsey Press, 1980), p. 33.

[18] Matthews, "Winnowing," p. 63.

[19] Aldrich, "A Dynamic Model," p. 653.

The Candidates and Why They Ran

Jimmy Carter's surprising success in capturing the 1976 Democratic nomination certainly influenced Republican nomination politics in 1980. If a political unknown from Georgia can do it, "why not me?" Unfortunately, many prospective candidates misunderstood the special circumstances surrounding the Carter nomination. For one thing, there was no obvious Democratic front-runner in 1976; for another, Carter had one important resource for the new plebiscitary system— he had time to devote exclusively to the task at hand.

Finer points aside, the fact that Carter had gone all the way was sufficiently motivating for many Republican public figures to contemplate seeking the presidential nomination in 1980. Eventually a field of eleven candidates actually announced. Two of these— Benjamin Fernandez and Harold Stassen—were never recognized as important in the campaign and will not be considered further. Two others—Sens. Lowell Weicker (Connecticut) and Larry Pressler (South Dakota)—were in and out of the race so fast that they hardly had a chance to know what it was like (see figure 3–1). Weicker pulled out after just two months, citing a presidential preference poll that showed him running third in his own state. Pressler's campaign lasted just over three months. He was not invited to the Iowa debate and failed to get on the New Hampshire ballot.

The other seven candidates launched visible campaigns. In addition, Gerald Ford was a presence throughout—an unannounced candidate who "would be a candidate if my political party wanted it,"[20] would respond "if there was a deadlocked convention, and if some support developed for me."[21] The strengths and weaknesses of the seven candidates plus one are summarized in table 3–1. I identify four types of candidates: front-runner, statesman-in-waiting, serious challengers, and also-rans. Why did they run (or, in Ford's case, indicate availability)? For some the reasons are obvious from a review of their strengths and weaknesses. Reagan was established by the press and the polls as the front-runner rather early. He led Ford in the Gallup poll throughout the latter months of 1978 and all of 1979. Therefore, one need hardly probe why he ran—the nation would have been stunned had he decided against running. His front-runner status permitted him to wait until last to announce. The obviousness of his candidacy permitted him to concentrate on issues

[20] Hedrick Smith, "Ford Seems to Soften His Stand against a 1980 Race," *New York Times*, November 20, 1979, p. B-12.
[21] "An Ex-President Is Available," *Time*, February 18, 1980, p. 27.

FIGURE 3–1

THE REPUBLICAN CANDIDATES' CALENDAR, ANNOUNCEMENT AND
WITHDRAWAL DATES

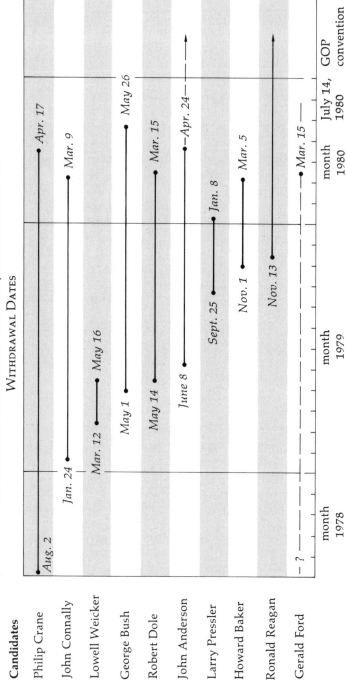

Candidates

Philip Crane

John Connally

Lowell Weicker

George Bush

Robert Dole

John Anderson

Larry Pressler

Howard Baker

Ronald Reagan

Gerald Ford

SOURCE: Author.

TABLE 3–1

Strengths and Weaknesses of the Republican Candidates

Candidate	Major Strengths	Major Weaknesses
1. Front-runner: Ronald Reagan (governor of California, 1967–75)	Status in polls, firm base of support, access to money, organization, campaign experience	Age, lack of Washington experience, no recent public office, association with the right
2. Statesman-in-waiting: Gerald Ford (representative from Michigan, 1949–73; vice-president, 1973–74; president 1974–77)	Status in polls, access to money, former president, broad-based support, campaign experience	Defeated by Carter in 1976, lack of organization, problem in becoming an active candidate
3. Serious challengers: John Anderson (representative from Illinois, 1961–81)	Media attention, forthright positions on issues	Limited organization and funds, association as liberal, status in polls
Howard Baker (senator from Tennessee, 1967–present)	Senate Republican leader, political moderate, role in Watergate	Limited organization and funds, Senate record
George Bush (representative from Texas, 1967–71; ambassador to U.N., 1971–73; Republican national chairman, 1973–74; head of U.S. liaison in China, 1974–75; CIA director, 1976–77)	Washington experience, organization, access to money, personality	Status in polls, previous electoral defeats
John Connally (secretary of the navy, 1961; governor of Texas, 1963–69; secretary of the treasury, 1971–72)	Washington experience, access to money	Former Democrat, status in polls, controversial stands on issues

(Table continues)

TABLE 3–1   (continued)

Candidate	Major Strengths	Major Weaknesses
4. Also-rans:		
Philip Crane (representative from Illinois, 1969– present)	Early announcement	Status in polls, organizational problems, association with the right
Robert Dole (representative from Kansas, 1961–69; senator from Kansas, 1969–present; Republican national chairman, 1971–73; vice-presidential candidate, 1976)	Campaign experience, Washington experience, wit	Status in polls, lack of organization and funding, negative response to vice-presidential campaign

SOURCE: Compiled from information in Congressional Quarterly, *Candidates '80.*

in his statement, as well as to begin moderating his image with the media and the American people. Thus, for example, the *New York Times* report on his announcement observed that "his words tonight appeared less dogmatic" than in the past. "The more moderate tone apparently reflected the efforts of some of his advisers to give Mr. Reagan a more moderate image and to make him more attractive to middle-of-the-road voters."[22]

Gerald Ford's involvement is likewise simple to explain. As a former president and defeated presidential candidate (by the narrowest of margins), he was naturally considered a potential nominee in 1980. At the same time, however, the costs of becoming an active candidate were great. He would have had to start early in order to ensure sufficient organizational and financial support, he could not avoid the primaries, since the choice is really made there, and he would have faced serious problems in winning support from the political right. Thus his role was more or less defined for him—statesman-in-waiting, available should the other candidates fail to command sufficient support to win the nomination.

The "serious challengers" varied considerably in their motivations. Certainly the most interesting candidate in this group was John

[22] Adam Clymer, "The 1980 Model Reagan: Strident Campaign Tone Is Gone," *New York Times*, November 14, 1979, p. A-25.

Anderson, a little-known Republican representative from upstate Illinois. Anderson appeared to be moved by genuine concern about social and political developments in the United States.[23] He also seemed impatient with his increasing isolation from his House Republican colleagues (despite his leadership position as chairman of the House Republican Conference) and possibly even bored with legislative service. A forceful and articulate speaker, Anderson soon carved out a role for himself as critic of both Reagan and Carter. As intellectual gadfly he was bound to attract media attention, as well as develop a small but bipartisan following.[24] The expectations associated with his candidacy are particularly interesting and will be discussed below. Suffice it for now to state that he was influenced by what was being said about him, and eventually he tried to become an image of himself.

There is legitimate doubt about how motivated Howard Baker (Tennessee) was in becoming a presidential candidate. His name had been frequently mentioned following his role in the Senate Watergate investigations and his apparent near miss in being selected as Ford's running mate in 1976. He also rated relatively high in the early polls—behind Reagan and Ford. Still, he also received high marks as Senate minority leader, apparently liked the job, and was forced to make difficult political choices in supporting the Panama Canal treaties. He was the last candidate but one to announce, and he was the first of the major candidates to pull out (see figure 3–1). In his announcement on November 1, 1979, Baker stressed his experience, noting that he "knows Washington well enough to change Washington."[25]

No one doubted George Bush's enthusiasm for the race—he was the classic self-starter. His wide-ranging experience in Washington had convinced him that he was prepared for the White House. Bush was never shy about citing that experience—either in his announcement or later on the campaign trail. Though he lost twice in efforts to win a Senate seat in Texas, Bush was convinced that he could launch an effective national campaign for the presidency.

The earliest major challenger to announce was John Connally,

[23] For example, see James Reston's column on Anderson, *New York Times*, April 18, 1980, p. A-31.

[24] Anderson received a higher percentage of "good press" than any other candidate in either party, January 1-March 1, according to a study by Michael Robinson, "The Media at Mid-Year: A Bad Year for McLuhanites?" *Public Opinion*, June/July, 1980, pp. 41-45.

[25] Adam Clymer, "Baker Joins Campaign for Presidential Nomination," *New York Times*, November 2, 1979, p. A-1.

former Democratic governor of Texas. No doubt encouraged by early indications of support from many Republicans, Connally appeared to represent a formidable challenge to Reagan. He also was able to raise large sums of money. Still, a poll conducted by the *New York Times* and CBS in fall 1979 showed that Connally evoked nearly as much unfavorable as favorable comment from voters.[26] As one account put it: "Connally has had a long time to build up legions of friends and enemies."[27]

Finally the also-rans deserve brief mention. Two factors appeared to influence the candidacy of Representative Philip Crane: Jimmy Carter's early start in winning the Democratic nomination in 1976 and Ronald Reagan's age. He announced his drive for the presidency more than two years before the 1980 general election and stressed his image as a young Ronald Reagan. Senator Robert Dole was obviously encouraged by his national campaign as Ford's running mate to try for the presidency. His 1976 campaign did not receive rave reviews, however, and his 1980 campaign never got off the ground.

To summarize, the motivations for running among the active candidates include positive assessments of political strength (Reagan), expectations associated with present position (Baker), self-confidence (Anderson, Bush, Connally), and wishful thinking (Crane, Dole). We turn next to how well they fared.

The Candidates and How They Ran

John Kessel speaks of four stages of nomination politics: early days, between the midterm election and when the first delegates are chosen; initial contests, those much-heralded early caucuses and primaries; mist-clearing, the crucial period in which the issue is typically resolved; and the convention, that marvelous rally that confirms the nomination and marks the beginning of the fall campaign. There are useful measures in each stage to indicate "how they ran." The polls are relied on heavily in the early days; the primaries serve to show progress during the second and third stages; and media coverage and analysis, as well as postconvention polls, tell us something about success at the convention.

The labels I attached to each of the candidates suggest a set of expectations one might reasonably have about their campaigns. The

---

[26] Adam Clymer, "Poll Finds Reagan Keeping Lead; More Democrats Back Kennedy," *New York Times*, November 6, 1979, p. A-1.

[27] Congressional Quarterly, *Candidates '80* (Washington, D.C.: Congressional Quarterly, 1980), p. 40.

FIGURE 3–2

PUBLIC PREFERENCE FOR REPUBLICAN CANDIDATES:
THE EARLY DAYS

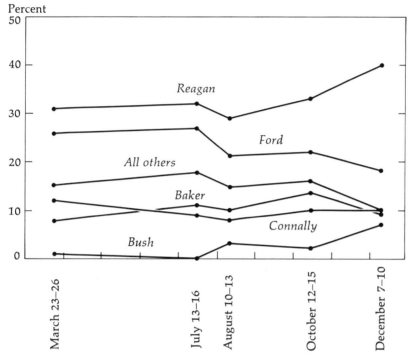

NOTE: Persons expressing no opinion were 7 percent on March 23-26; 3 percent on July 13-16; 14 percent on August 10-13; 3 percent on October 12-15; and 6 percent on December 7-10.
SOURCE: *Gallup Opinion Index*, Report Nos. 165, 168, 170, 172, 173 (1979).

greatest expectations for success are naturally associated with the front-runner. In the early days, Ronald Reagan had to maintain his lead in the polls and hope that no active candidate pulled away from the pack to mount a serious challenge to his front-runner status. Figure 3–2 shows that he was successful in this regard. He did drop in the polls during August, but so did the others (except for Bush). And by year's end Reagan had put real distance between himself and the other candidates.

The Ford candidacy is particularly interesting for what it contributed to Reagan. There was, of course, always the possibility that Ford might become an active candidate, in which case the Reagan campaign for the nomination would have been seriously threatened (not to mention the party's chances in the fall). Until that actually

FIGURE 3–3

FORD AND REAGAN VERSUS CARTER: THE EARLY DAYS

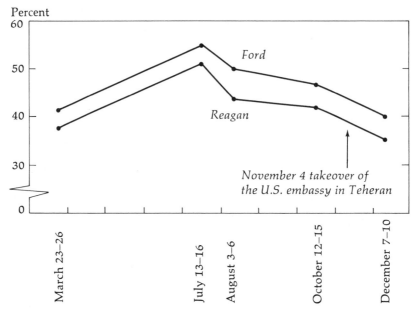

SOURCE: *Gallup Opinion Index*, Report Nos. 171, 174 (1979).

happened, however, a passive Ford candidacy performed the important function for Reagan of preventing other challengers from gaining strength. Thus in those early days, before the primaries settled the issue, media attention was focused on Ford as the credible alternative to Reagan. The rest of the candidates had to split the leftover conservative support (presumably going to Connally and Crane) or the leftover moderate support (presumably going to Baker and Bush). The credibility of Ford's "competitive standing" during this period is shown in figure 3–3. Note that whereas Reagan consistently ran ahead of Ford as the preferred Republican candidate, Ford consistently ran better than Reagan when matched against Carter. Thus quite unintentionally Ford performed the nice service of blocking up the middle for Reagan. Ford later made other contributions to the Reagan campaign.

The remaining candidates can be conveniently divided into two groups for analyzing the early expectations associated with their competitive standing. First are those candidates sufficiently well known to have attracted public and media attention before their announcements—John Connally, Howard Baker, and Robert Dole.

TABLE 3–2

EXPECTATIONS AND RESOURCES OF MAJOR CANDIDATES:
ENTERING INITIAL CONTESTS

Candidates	Expectations[a]	Resources[b]
Ronald Reagan	High	Ample
Gerald Ford	High	Potentially Ample
John Anderson	Low	Limited
Howard Baker	Moderately High	Limited
George Bush	Low	Substantial
John Connally	Moderately High	Ample
Philip Crane	Low	Substantial
Robert Dole	Moderate	Limited

[a] Those expectations others had about the candidacy based on notoriety, poll status, and public record of the candidate.
[b] Gross estimate of the availability of money, organization, and capable staff.
SOURCE: Author.

Connally was a Reagan stand-in, Baker a Ford stand-in. It was not clear whom Dole might replace—which was part of the problem with his candidacy—but his vice-presidential campaign in 1976 resulted in frequent mention of his name. These candidates were faced with the difficult problem of capturing ground already occupied by Reagan and Ford. Since neither of these favorites in the polls and media was willing to retreat, Connally, Baker, and Dole were never able to gain control of their own campaigns. Ironically, their own prominence cost them competitive standing in this particular situation.

Second are those candidates who had little or no public recognition—Philip Crane, George Bush, and John Anderson. They all had the Carter advantage of being unknown and therefore of producing a "surprisingly good showing." Crane, however, had the disadvantage of being a Reagan or Connally stand-in, and neither was likely to pull out before the primaries. Anderson and Bush at least had the potential of picking up Ford supporters in the primaries. And as compared with Baker, the early expectations of their candidacies were so low that victory in defeat was possible.

Thus, entering the "initial contests" the candidates demonstrated a wide range of expectations and resources. Table 3–2 shows the range. The media are always hungry for the first contest and therefore focused a great deal of attention on a straw vote at the state Republican convention in Florida on November 17, 1979. Connally campaigned heavily for support but lost to Reagan, who came to the state just once. George Bush surprisingly finished a strong third.[28] Ford was not entered.

The Florida vote had no effect on delegate selection and provided little more evidence in the early days than that available in the polls. The Iowa precinct caucuses on January 26, 1980, constituted the first major confrontation between the candidates. All of the candidates but Reagan participated in a well-publicized debate on January 5 sponsored by the *Des Moines Register*. Reagan's trifocal strategy was the public reason for his passing up the debate. He argued that the debate might adversely affect party harmony. As it turned out, however, the debate got high marks from the media. A *New York Times* editorial called it "surprisingly interesting and revealing" and said "it conveyed an overriding sense of earnest, ordered democracy."[29] The event was "civil"—not conflictive, as Reagan had predicted. The winner was difficult to pick, since all candidates were judged to have performed well. Yet Ronald Reagan was uniformly cited as the loser for not showing up. A statewide poll showed that he dropped from 50 percent support in December 1979 to 26 percent support after the debate.

The Iowa caucus straw polls offer a superb illustration of the effect of precontest expectations. The front-runner lost, and a major challenger was created. George Bush won 31.5 percent of the straw vote, Reagan 29.4 percent. Baker, Connally, Crane, Anderson, and Dole finished in that order. "As Iowa showed, this is a year to expect the unexpected," according to David Broder.[30] How did the candidates view the results? Bush was elated with the increase in his competitive standing. As one account put it, however: "Now the standards change. From now until Bush either is elected president or falls from contention, he will be treated to the same intense scrutiny as candidates like Reagan and Sen. Edward Kennedy."[31] A Harris poll taken the day after the Iowa caucuses showed that Bush had drawn even with Reagan among Republican and independent voters surveyed.

After the Iowa results, the Reagan forces announced that they were reconsidering the decision not to enter debates with Republican

---

[28] Rhodes Cook, "Carter, Reagan Win Florida Convention Tests," *Congressional Quarterly Weekly Report*, November 24, 1979, p. 2662.

[29] "Beyond Debate in Iowa," *New York Times*, January 7, 1980, p. A-18.

[30] David Broder, "Iowa Vote: What Happened and Why," *Washington Post*, January 23, 1980, p. A-1.

[31] James Herzog, "Iowa Caucus Puts Bush in Serious Contenders' League," *Pittsburgh Press*, January 23, 1980, p. A-6.

rivals. Reagan was quoted as saying: "I can't be the only one concerned with unity. . . . I'm going to have to think of self-survival." In making the announcement, however, Reagan observed that in the past, debates led to schisms in the party, with the result that some Republicans "would rather win the convention than an election."[32] Thus the trifocal campaign strategy cost Reagan dearly in the first encounter, but he was determined not to stumble again.

Connally judged his results in Iowa to be a "blessing in disguise," since Reagan's problems were assumed to be his profit. Senator Baker ran third but observed Bush capturing the largest share of the moderate, or Ford, vote. Of the other candidates, only John Anderson could be at all encouraged. He received favorable press response for his performance in the debates and ran respectably, despite his limited campaign in the state.

What was begun in Iowa was completed in New Hampshire, South Carolina, and Illinois. The initial contests also cleared away the mist, and so Kessel's second and third stages more or less merged into one in 1980. The initial month of primaries dealt successive blows to the Bush, Connally, and Anderson challenges to Reagan's front-runner status. The final pocket of mist was dissipated when Gerald Ford announced on March 15, 1980, that he would not be a candidate.

Table 3–3 shows the results of the thirty-four Republican primaries. I have divided them into three groups—early, middle, and late. The first nine were the most crucial. Reagan had to win in New Hampshire and Illinois, avoid disastrous defeat in Massachusetts, and demonstrate expected strength in the South. Bush had to win the New England primaries, do better than expected in the South, and do respectably in Illinois. Connally judged that his prospects rested with demonstrating an ability to defeat Reagan in South Carolina—thereby triggering a move to him among conservatives. And the rest of the candidates had to show some strength in the initial New England primaries or withdraw.

Only Reagan was able to meet the expectations associated with his campaign. He won where he had to win, ran neck-and-neck with Bush and Anderson in Massachusetts, and unexpectedly won in Vermont. Reagan participated in two debates in New Hampshire— appearing with all other candidates on one occasion and with Bush alone on another. The second debate may have seriously hurt Bush's chances in New Hampshire. Reagan invited all other candidates to

---

[32] Both quotations from "Reagan to Reconsider His Decision Not to Debate with G.O.P. Rivals," New York Times, January 23, 1980, p. A-16.

TABLE 3–3
Republican Presidential Primary Results, 1980

Primaries	Candidates (percent of vote)				Total Vote
	Anderson	Bush	Reagan	Others[a]	
Early (Feb. 17–Mar. 18)					
Puerto Rico (Feb. 17)	—	60.1	—	39.9	186,371
New Hampshire (Feb. 26)	9.8	22.7	49.6	17.9	147,157
Massachusetts (Mar. 4)	30.7	31.0	28.8	9.5	400,826
Vermont (Mar. 4)	29.0	21.7	30.1	19.2	65,611
South Carolina (Mar. 8)	—	14.8	54.7	30.5	145,501
Alabama (Mar. 11)	—	25.9	69.7	4.4	211,353
Florida (Mar. 11)	9.2	30.2	56.2	4.4	614,995
Georgia (Mar. 11)	8.4	12.6	73.2	5.8	200,171
Illinois (Mar. 18)	36.7	11.0	48.4	3.9	1,130,081
Average[b]	20.6	25.6	51.3	15.1	—[c]
Middle (Mar. 25–May 20)					
Connecticut (Mar. 25)	22.1	38.6	33.9	5.4	182,284
Kansas (Apr. 1)	18.2	12.6	63.0	6.2	285,398
Wisconsin (Apr. 1)	27.4	30.4	40.2	2.0	907,853
Louisiana (Apr. 5)	—	18.8	74.9	6.3	41,683
Pennsylvania (Apr. 22)	2.1	50.5	42.5	4.9	1,241,002
Texas (May 3)	—	47.4	51.0	1.6	526,769

TABLE 3-3 (continued)

Primaries	Candidates (percent of vote)				Total Vote
	Anderson	Bush	Reagan	Others[a]	
District of Columbia (May 6)	26.9	66.1	—	7.0	7,529
Indiana (May 6)	9.9	16.4	73.7	—	568,315
North Carolina (May 6)	5.1	21.8	67.6	5.5	168,391
Tennessee (May 6)	4.5	18.1	74.1	3.3	195,210
Maryland (May 13)	9.7	40.9	48.2	1.2	167,303
Nebraska (May 13)	5.8	15.3	76.0	2.9	205,203
Michigan (May 20)	8.2	57.5	31.8	2.5	595,176
Oregon (May 20)	10.1	34.7	54.5	0.7	304,647
Average[b]	12.5	33.5	56.3	3.8	—[d]
Late (May 27–June 3)					
Idaho (May 27)	9.7	4.0	82.9	3.4	134,879
Kentucky (May 27)	5.1	7.2	82.4	5.3	94,795
Nevada (May 27)	—	6.5	83.0	10.5	47,395
California (June 3)	13.6	4.9	80.2	1.3	2,512,994
Montana (June 3)	—	9.7	87.3	3.0	76,716
New Jersey (June 3)	—	17.1	81.3	1.6	277,977
New Mexico (June 3)	12.1	9.9	63.7	14.3	59,101
Ohio (June 3)	—	19.2	80.8	—	854,967

(Table continues)

TABLE 3–3   (continued)

Primaries	Candidates (percent of vote)				Total Vote
	Anderson	Bush	Reagan	Others[a]	
Rhode Island (June 3)	—	18.6	*72.0*	9.4	5,335
South Dakota (June 3)	6.3	4.2	*82.1*	7.4	88,325
West Virginia (June 3)	—	14.4	*85.6*	—	133,871
Average[b]	9.4	10.5	*80.1*	6.2	—[e]
Total, all primaries	—	—	—	—	12,785,184

NOTE: Italics indicate the largest percentage in each row.

[a] The "others " category includes individuals expressing no preference.

[b] Total percentage (for the period) divided by the number of primaries the candidate entered.

[c] 3,102,066, or 24.3 percent of the total for all primaries (all periods).

[d] 5,396,763, or 42.2 percent of the total for all primaries (all periods).

[e] 4,286,355, or 33.5 percent of the total for all primaries (all periods).

SOURCE: Compiled from data in *Congressional Quarterly Weekly Report*, July 5, 1980, pp. 1870-71.

participate and was successful in conveying the impression that Bush was responsible for denying them the right to appear. The four candidates—Anderson, Baker, Crane, and Dole (Connally did not accept the invitation)—stood by sheepishly on the stage as Reagan forcefully pressed for their inclusion.

> "I am paying for this microphone," Mr. Reagan declared with a glare of fury that brought cheers from the crowd. [Reagan agreed to pay the $3,500 required to rent the hall].
> "I realize some effort has been made to embarrass them," he said apologetically to the four, who could only shrug and wait and gesture supplicatingly to the crowd.[33]

The moderator, Jon Breen, executive editor of the *Nashua Telegraph*, nevertheless refused to permit the four to participate. Bush waited with no solution in sight and eventually the four stalked off.[34] In-

[33] Francis X. Clines, "A Reporter's Notebook: Grand Old Pandemonium," *New York Times*, February 25, 1980, p. A-18.

[34] Clines "A Reporter's Notebook," *New York Times*, February 25, 1980, p. A-18.

terestingly, in this case, Reagan argued for broad participation as contributing to party unity, and he was successful in having Bush criticized by the other candidates as hurting the party. At one time it was estimated that Bush led Reagan in New Hampshire. On election day he lost by more than two to one.

Thus the Reagan campaign was back on track, and the Bush effort would never recover from this defeat. Baker ran a weak third in the New Hampshire primary and subsequently withdrew (see figure 3–1). Connally was concentrating on South Carolina and thus could argue that his candidacy was not on the line in New Hampshire. Anderson was satisfied with his showing and continued to receive favorable media coverage. The other candidates delayed withdrawal statements but were finished.

The Massachusetts and Vermont primaries were reported as triumphs for John Anderson. Declared "Underdog of the Week" by the *New York Times,* Anderson ran second in both elections.[35] His strong support among independents probably marked the first step in his independent candidacy, launched in April. Just as important, however, was the strong showing of Reagan (winning in Vermont, running just 2.2 percent behind Bush in Massachusetts) and the relatively unimpressive totals for Bush. Anderson's healthy vote totals had important effects: encouraging his own ambitions, drawing support from the faltering Bush campaign, and, therefore, permitting Reagan to survive the New England primaries unscathed.

Bush must have felt totally boxed in during the New England primary campaign period. Anderson and Baker got support he might otherwise have claimed. One can appreciate his frustration in watching moderates split the vote. If Bush had received the Anderson and Baker vote in New Hampshire, Reagan would still have won, but by just 4 percent. With the Anderson and Baker votes, Bush would have won by margins of approximately 38 percent in Massachusetts and 33 percent in Vermont. These results surely would have changed the competitive standing of both Bush and Reagan.

Ford caused further pain to the Bush campaign. When Reagan recovered with an impressive win in New Hampshire, the pundits turned to Ford as the only viable alternative to Reagan. The press was full of "Ford rumblings" after New Hampshire—a second contribution of the former president to Reagan's fortunes. Thus Bush found himself fighting an Anderson candidacy ironically headed for an independent campaign, a revitalized Reagan organization, and a passive but strong candidacy by a former president. To compound

[35] "The Anderson Underdog Paradox," *New York Times,* March 6, 1980, p. A-22.

his problems, John Connally was running an anti-Bush campaign in South Carolina, determined not to let his fellow Texan gain support from conservatives that might otherwise go to him (Connally). Bush's room for maneuvering was getting smaller all the time. Lee Atwater, Reagan's South Carolina campaign coordinator, summarized it accurately when he said about Bush: "He's been slowly melting since New Hampshire."[36]

As is clear from table 3–3, the Connally candidacy was terminated by the South Carolina primary. Not even support from South Carolina senator Strom Thurmond could save it. Reagan won by nearly a two-to-one margin, and Connally withdrew (reportedly having spent $11.5 million in his long campaign to win one delegate). He later endorsed Reagan.

As expected, Reagan continued his sweep of the South (see table 3–3). The next major contest for him was on March 18 in Illinois, where he faced a challenge from John Anderson. At one point Anderson was reportedly ahead in the state polls. Anthony Lewis wrote:

> On top of his strong showing in New England, he has a real chance of winning the Illinois primary next Tuesday. George Bush is fading. Depending on what Gerald Ford does, we could wake up next week and find that Anderson is the only live Republican alternative to Ronald Reagan.[37]

Anderson himself was quoted as saying: "I'm going to be the Republican nominee."[38] Much was written during the period before the Illinois primary about a new coalition politics, led by John Anderson and including elements of both parties, plus a new force of independents.

The media's emphasis on Anderson's prospects was fortunate for Reagan, since it once again permitted him (Reagan) to exceed expectations. Iowa created Bush for Reagan to defeat in New England, Connally offered himself in South Carolina, and New England produced Anderson as an Illinois sacrifice. The media (including the polls) played the important role in each case of advertising the potential strength of Reagan's opponents. There were two important consequences of these developments: (1) the margin of victory for Reagan

---

[36] James P. Herzog, "Reagan Win Expected in South Carolina," *Pittsburgh Press*, March 6, 1980, p. A-8.

[37] Anthony Lewis, "Anderson in Illinois," *New York Times*, March 13, 1980, p. A-23.

[38] Tom Wicker, "Getting Down to Cases," *New York Times*, March 16, 1980, p. E-19.

was always "surprising," and (2) the cumulative effect of the surprises was to convince the pundits that Reagan was invincible. He had developed what John Aldrich refers to as a "positive spiral" and what others simply call momentum.[39] Whatever the label, it was certain after the March 18 Illinois primary that Ronald Reagan would be the Republican nominee for president. The account of that event by Ted Knap was typical.

> After winning big in the Illinois Primary [Reagan received 48.4 percent of the vote—see table 3–3], Republican Ronald Reagan and President Carter are almost certain to face each other in the fall election.
> It will take a monumental goof by either to lose their nominations.
> Reagan has won seven of the nine primaries, including the last five. The former governor of California has won in the East, the South and the Midwest, and the West is acknowledged to be his strongest territory.[40]

The mist had thus cleared by March 18. Yet there were still twenty-five primaries to go. Bush won four of these—Connecticut (a state his father once represented in the United States Senate), Pennsylvania, the District of Columbia (not contested by Reagan), and Michigan. He ran well in Wisconsin, Texas (his home state), Maryland, and Oregon. Anderson also continued his campaign but failed to receive even 30 percent in any of the remaining primaries. Bush might well have quit earlier, but he had the money and the organization to continue, plus the encouragement of possible wins in big states (Pennsylvania, Texas, and Michigan). On May 26 he did finally concede, noting: "I am an optimist. But I also know how to count to 998 [the number of delegates needed to nominate]."[41]

The Bush concession completed the winnowing process. One by one the candidates withdrew from the race, and all but Anderson fell in behind Reagan. Reagan had moved steadily through the largest number of Republican primaries in history—winning twenty-nine, losing just six (all to Bush). With the nomination firmly in hand, he could now remove one lens and focus on uniting the party and winning the general election.

---

[39] Aldrich, "A Dynamic Model," p. 652.

[40] Ted Knap, "Reagan, Carter Win Big in Illinois," *Pittsburgh Press*, March 19, 1980, p. A-1.

[41] Douglas E. Kneeland, "Bush Says He'll Quit Active Campaigning," *New York Times*, May 27, 1980, p. A-1.

Candidate Reagan and Party Unity

On July 17 Ronald Reagan accepted the nomination of his party for the presidency. He then turned immediately to party unity—a theme that had been evident throughout his campaign.

> I am very proud of our party tonight. This convention has shown to all America a party united, with positive programs for solving the nation's problems; a party ready to build a new consensus with all those across the land who share a community of values embodied in these words: family, work, neighborhood, peace and freedom.
>
> I know we have had a quarrel or two, but only as to the method of attaining a goal. There was no argument about the goal.[42]

Reagan has often been compared with Barry Goldwater, and one can understand why. Both western conservatives, they each had a vision of building a new political coalition so as to win the presidency. Still, Goldwater's strategy differed markedly from Reagan's. He sought bipartisan conservative support and thus was not moved to seek harmony with moderate Republicans. His acceptance speech in 1964 was different in message and tone from Reagan's in 1980. Following a reference to the "strained, discordant, and even hostile elements" of the convention week, he said:

> Anyone who joins us in all sincerity we welcome. Those who do not care for our cause, we don't expect to enter our ranks in any case. And let our Republicanism so focused and so dedicated not be made fuzzy and futile by unthinking and stupid labels.
>
> I would remind you that extremism in the defense of liberty is no vice.
>
> And let me remind you also that moderation in the pursuit of justice is no virtue![43]

No doubt Reagan's strategy was influenced by the utter failure of Goldwater's efforts. Still, it was apparent at the convention, and before, that Reagan intended to rely on a united Republican party as a base for a winning coalition in November. A Reagan aide cited the following organizational goals for the convention:

---

[42] "Reagan: 'Time to Recapture Our Destiny,'" *Congressional Quarterly Weekly Report*, July 19, 1980, p. 2063.

[43] "Text of Goldwater Speech Accepting GOP Nomination," *Congressional Quarterly Weekly Report*, July 17, 1964, p. 1529.

We want to look good on television. We want things to run on time so as to contrast with earlier Democratic conventions. We want to minimize conflict, show the party in harmony. And we want to set some themes for the fall campaign—stressing the aura of Reagan himself and "coming together for a new beginning." We are seen as responsible for the convention and we are in charge. Everything is cleared through us.[44]

I have suggested that party unity was a serious concern of the Reagan organization from the very start. The candidate wanted to emerge from the primaries without having alienated the moderate wing of the party. Two events in particular tested Reagan's patience in this regard. Ford's refusal to take himself out of the race until mid-March was disconcerting. Even more distressing, however, was his statement on March 1 that he found "growing sentiment that Governor Reagan cannot win the election" because of his conservatism. Reagan responded by inviting the former president to "pack his long johns and come out here on the primary trail."[45] He conceded in answer to a reporter's question that Ford's comment strained the Republican Eleventh Commandment: Thou Shalt Not Speak Ill of Other Republicans. Still, Reagan's response was basically moderate. One might have argued that Ford had a right to cause at least one problem, given what his passive candidacy had contributed to the Reagan campaign.

The second event was more in the manner of a nonevent: George Bush's failure to withdraw from the campaign after the Illinois primary, or at least after the Texas primary. The Reagan organization was anxious to get on with unifying the party for the fall campaign, but it could not afford to let up in securing the nomination. Reagan's campaign manager was quoted as saying: "Bush is a drain on our time and attention."[46] Yet Reagan refused to put pressure on Bush to withdraw, citing the importance of party unity in the fall.

"The wheels are going to fly off this Republican unity, this shotgun wedding."[47] National party chairmen are supposed to make statements of this sort, and John C. White, Democratic National Committee head, did not disappoint. Still, White was wrong. The Reagan organization worked hard at promoting party unity in the period

---

[44] Personal interview, July 14, 1980.

[45] Both quotations from Wayne King, "Reagan Challenges Ford to Join Him on Primary Trail," New York Times, March 3, 1980, p. D-9.

[46] "The End Game for Reagan," Time, May 19, 1980, p. 26.

[47] Adam Clymer, "GOP Hopes Breed Unity—And Save Brock," New York Times, June 15, 1980, p. E-5.

between Bush's withdrawal and the convention and then used the convention itself to display its achievement. Here is a sample of the work that was accomplished in the preconvention period:

1. *Retention of Bill Brock as national party chairman.* Despite pressures to remove Brock, Reagan decided that he should stay. Conservatives were anxious to take charge of the party headquarters, but Reagan and Brock worked out an agreement that included appointing a Reagan staff person—Drew Lewis—as deputy chairman of the Republican National Committee.

2. *Expansion of the Reagan staff.* Old-line Reagan supporters from California were eventually joined by persons who had supported other candidates—notably William E. Timmons, former legislative aide to President Ford, and James Baker III, campaign manager for George Bush.

3. *Public displays of unity.* At a highly-publicized fund-raising dinner on June 13, six losing candidates joined Reagan in an extraordinary demonstration of preconvention support. The purpose of the dinner was to raise money to pay off the debts of the losing candidates.

4. *Meetings with candidates and party leaders.* Reagan met with Republican members of Congress at the Capitol and with the Republican governors and spoke at large rallies in New York and Chicago.

These efforts were remarkably successful. The Republican party was as united as it had ever been following an open contest for the nomination. Not everything had gone as smoothly as might have been desired, of course. Distressed at the party platform statement on women's rights, the co-chairman of the national committee, Mary Crisp, blasted the party as "suffering from serious internal sickness."[48] She did not attend the convention itself. Preconvention work on the platform evidenced division over support for the Equal Rights Amendment (ERA). Furthermore, the far right was by no means pleased with conciliatory moves by Reagan toward the Ford-Baker-Bush wing of the party. Still, press coverage of this period tended overwhelmingly to stress harmony within the party, not division, and the polls registered a steady increase for Reagan in a race against Carter. By the opening of the convention, Reagan had overtaken Carter in the Gallup Poll (see figure 3–4). His lead in other polls was even greater. Thus by these measures, Reagan's preconvention strategy was working.

---

[48] Bill Peterson, "In Her Farewell, Mary Crisp Blasts GOP 'Sickness,' " *Washington Post*, July 10, 1980, p. A-1.

FIGURE 3–4

CARTER VERSUS REAGAN VERSUS ANDERSON: THE GALLUP POLL

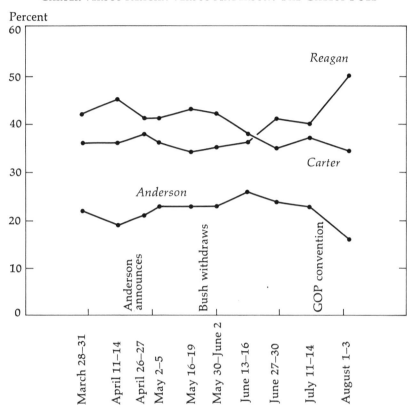

NOTE: The dates span the primaries, the preconvention period, the convention, and the postconvention period.

SOURCE: Taken from "Opinion Roundup," *Public Opinion*, vol. 3 (August/September 1980), p. 24.

Preserving the Peace in Detroit

A Republican convention in Detroit? The Michigan city seemed an odd choice; but primarily because of its image as a "crime-ridden, no-hope city,"[49] local officials were determined to put on a good show. The results were outstanding. The thousands of delegates, alternates, media representatives, and visitors were overwhelmed by the hospitality they experienced.

[49] Mayor Coleman Young so characterized the Detroit image, as quoted in "A Grand Old Party for the G.O.P.," *Time*, July 28, 1980, p. 24.

Democratic Mayor Coleman Young was successful in achieving his goal of preserving the peace outside the convention hall. Presidential candidate Ronald Reagan was faced with the challenge of preserving the peace inside the hall. Nelson W. Polsby and Aaron Wildavsky point out: "One of the lessons of recent presidential elections is that national conventions are declining in importance as decision-making bodies."[50] They are undoubtedly correct as regards the choice of the presidential nominee. In fact, only four conventions since 1928, two for each party, have required more than one ballot to make that important decision. Yet conventions are important for other reasons. Even though Reagan had the nomination locked up, he had at least three major tasks to accomplish in Detroit. The platform had to be written in such a way as to prevent a floor battle; the daily management of the convention had to project efficiency and effectiveness; and a vice-presidential nominee had to be selected who would maintain party unity.

The Platform. Work on the platform began months before the convention as hearings were held in several cities. Most of the drafting was completed by the time the Committee on Resolutions (the platform committee) first met on July 7. Senator John Tower (Texas) chaired the full committee, and members of Congress chaired all but one of the seven subcommittees. The platform document is lengthy (seventy-five printed pages of text), and very little of it stirred much controversy.

The two sections that resulted in the most debate and division were those devoted to women's rights and abortion. On the first issue, the staff-prepared draft read as follows:

> We reaffirm our party's historic commitment to equal rights and equal opportunity for women, a commitment which made us the first national party to endorse the Equal Rights Amendment. We are proud of our pioneering role and do not renounce our stand.[51]

The draft then expressed dismay at several problems and pressures associated with the ERA movement. Conservatives were not happy with this language, and their preferences prevailed. As finally adopted, the section on women's rights essentially assumed a states' rights position as regards the ERA, stating that "ratification . . . is now in the

---

[50] Nelson W. Polsby and Aaron Wildavsky, *Presidential Elections* (New York: Charles Scribner's Sons, 1980), p. 148.

[51] Warren Weaver, Jr., "Equal Rights Plan Splits Republicans Drafting Platform," *New York Times*, July 8, 1980, p. A-1.

hands of state legislatures."[52] Supporters of a stronger ERA position were not even able to muster sufficient votes to file a minority report so as to bring the issue to a vote on the convention floor.

A more conservative plank on abortion was also written by the Subcommittee on Human Resources. As finally adopted, the language affirmed "support of a constitutional amendment to restore protection of the right to life for unborn children."[53] Language was also added to the section on the judiciary that Republicans would "work for the appointment of judges at all levels . . . who respect traditional family values and the sanctity of innocent human life."[54] Again, opponents were unable to muster support to bring the issue to the floor.

On July 15, the platform was read by a seemingly endless number of committee members before a bored convention—all according to plan. The delegates shouted their approval.

Convention Proceedings. The Reagan organization was anxious to keep to the schedule on the convention floor so as to present an efficient image on national television. Tuesday evening turned out to be somewhat of a disaster in this regard. Twelve speakers (many with long-winded introductions) were scheduled (including the keynote speaker), along with the reading of the platform. In addition Benjamin Hooks, executive director of the National Association for the Advancement of Colored People (NAACP), was invited to address the convention.[55] Since the meeting went beyond midnight, the keynote address by Representative Guy Vander Jagt (Michigan) was postponed until the following evening. As convention chairman John Rhodes (Arizona) explained: "It was wisely said . . . that you don't save many souls after midnight."[56]

Efficiency was one goal, but the Reagan group also wanted to use the proceedings in an effective way so as to promote party unity. The last-minute invitation to Hooks was such a move, a response by Reagan to the National Black Republican Council. The podium was also used, however, to parade before the convention party leaders,

---

[52] Committee on Resolutions, Republican National Convention, *Republican Platform*, July 14, 1980, p. 10.

[53] Ibid., p. 13.

[54] Ibid., p. 48.

[55] In part the invitation to Hooks was to repair damage done to the Reagan campaign when the candidate turned down an invitation in late June to address the NAACP convention. Reagan had planned a holiday in Mexico during that time.

[56] "Win One for the Party, GOP Tells Reagan Tonight," *Pittsburgh Press*, July 16, 1980, p. A-1.

defeated candidates, prominent women and leaders of minority groups, and potential vice-presidential candidates. Of Reagan's opponents in the primaries, only Philip Crane did not appear on the podium in some capacity. Ford gave a rousing speech on the first evening, stimulating some talk among the delegates that he should be the running mate. Even former secretary of state Henry Kissinger—so hated by many conservative Republicans—addressed the convention. The most prominent Republican name missing from the proceedings was that of former president Richard M. Nixon.

Reagan was also very active during the week in meeting with special groups—particularly those dissatisfied with parts of the platform. He met with a delegation of women and promised to consider appointing a woman to the Supreme Court. He met with a group of unemployed workers and with several representatives of the Black Republican Council (the latter meeting resulting in an invitation to Benjamin Hooks to address the convention). In addition, he consulted with party leaders from throughout the country in making his choice for vice-president and sent special teams to meet with state delegations (policy advisers or staff personnel). Clearly the Reagan forces were not content to let party unity happen on its own; they actively—even aggressively—pursued that goal throughout the convention.

Selecting a Running Mate. The only real suspense in the modern nominating convention is that associated with selecting a vice-presidential candidate. A candidate who must fight for the nomination right through to the convention, as Gerald Ford had to in 1976, has little time to devote to screening candidates in advance. Still, Ronald Reagan had the nomination locked up weeks in advance. Thus his organization was able to conduct careful analyses of all potential running mates and even float a few trial balloons. The list of candidates was long and included primary opponents like Baker and Bush, long-time Reagan confidant Senator Paul Laxalt (Nevada), prominent Republican representatives and senators such as Jack Kemp (New York), Guy Vander Jagt (Michigan), Richard Lugar (Indiana), and former cabinet officials like Donald Rumsfeld (former secretary of defense) and William Simon (former secretary of the treasury). Senator Jesse Helms (North Carolina), a leader among southern Republicans, also proposed that he might run for the nomination if Reagan did not choose someone to his (Helms's) liking. The decision had to be made carefully, since both wings of the party were watching. All of the painstaking work to build party unity could go for nought if the wrong choice was made.

One name seldom included in the list but in the back of many minds was that of the former president, Gerald Ford. If he were willing to run, he would solve many problems. He was unquestionably popular, reportedly running eleven points ahead of other candidates in polls.[57] He was not associated with either the eastern establishment or the southern or western brand of conservatism. Furthermore, he would bring experience and stability to the ticket. Senator Laxalt called it "a political marriage made in heaven."[58]

The Ford flurry has been described and analyzed in detail—it made the week for most of the media. The discussion of arrangements by which Ford would play a key role in presidential decision making was particularly intriguing to observers. Having been in Detroit myself, I want to add my own special interpretation of its importance. Bearing in mind the significance of the choice for Reagan's goal of a unified party, the Ford negotiations constituted the former president's third important contribution to Reagan's success. In the first place, a potential Ford candidacy diverted everyone's attention from the other choices. It was a spectacular news event and was so treated by all television networks. Those supporting other candidates were thrown off track by the surprising interview of Ford by Walter Cronkite on CBS News. The point is that this event made Reagan's choice of George Bush more acceptable to those supporting other candidates, since Bush was not Reagan's first choice (nor, in a sense, was Bush selected in competition with the other candidates— particularly those supported by conservative Republicans).

Still, many conservatives were incensed over the choice of Bush, whom they identified with eastern Republicanism, despite his residence in Texas. Thrown off stride by the Ford announcement, however, they were unable to mount a campaign for a candidate more to their liking. Caucuses were held on Thursday morning to discuss what might be done. I attended one in which delegates from Texas and Louisiana expressed outrage and demanded to be heard on the convention floor. The Reagan staff worked throughout the day to prevent an embarrassing scene on the convention floor. Since most of the press was spending Thursday reconstructing the Ford nondecision, reporters missed covering the fence-mending efforts by the Reagan organization. Thus the Ford diversion had a second beneficial effect for the new nominee of the party, that is, failure by most of the

---

[57] At least according to Reagan pollsters Robert Teeter and Tully Plesser. "Inside the Jerry Ford Drama," *Time*, July 28, 1980, pp. 17-18.
[58] "The G.O.P. Gets Its Act Together," *Time*, July 28, 1980, p. 12.

national media to focus on the problems caused by the Bush selection among Reagan's long-time supporters.[59]

Concluding Comments

In an article published shortly after the completion of the Republican convention, David Cohen, president of Common Cause, spoke for many of us in lamenting the decline of American political parties.

> In the past, successful political parties mobilized the electorate and in doing so wove together disparate elements in the country and produced a governing coalition to advocate, defend, and build a concept of the public good. It was a means of resolving cleavages and differences in America. Parties have abandoned or neglected that function with the end result that interest groups of all kinds are the centers of action in American politics.[60]

I noted earlier that a part of this breakdown is associated by many with reforms of the nominating process. As James Ceaser observes: "The nomination race is in effect a national nonpartisan contest."[61] Certainly few would deny that the changes set in place after the 1968 Democratic convention gave us a new and different presidential nominating system. Thus, for example, in the debate mentioned earlier ("Choosing Presidential Candidates") Ken Bode stated that he believed "the impact of the reforms" on state parties "has been vastly overstated." He then pointed out that

> what the reforms have done is said simply that delegate status to a nominating convention can no longer be considered a legitimate patronage function of the party; that the people, the rank-and-file party voters, have to have some say. Delegate slots cannot simply be passed out to the party jobbers and envelope lickers and fat cats.[62]

One is led to wonder how fundamental a reform has to be to have "impact" in Mr. Bode's eyes. He concludes that the changes have

---

[59] I should point out that most of the press analysis of the Ford incident was unflattering to Reagan. David Broder referred to it as a "fiasco" and stated that Reagan "did enough to damage himself to make Mr. Carter seem smart to have left Mr. Reagan onstage alone." David Broder, "How Reagan's Bungling Helps Carter," *Pittsburgh Press*, July 19, 1980, p. B-2.

[60] David Cohen, "Three Steps to Invigorate Political Parties," *Christian Science Monitor*, July 25, 1980, p. 22.

[61] Ceaser, *Presidential Selection*, p. 5.

[62] *Choosing*, p. 9.

"simply" removed the power of political parties to determine who goes to their conventions. Most of the rest of the world's politicians and political analysts view our efforts to substitute nomination decisions by "the people" for those by party leaders as curious and not a little naive.

Still, there is no denying the tendency of American political reformers toward plebiscitary over party-responsibility solutions when they are faced with a new set of issues. Weak as political parties have always been in the United States, they still take it "on the chin" when things go wrong. However much one may wish it were not so, there is no denying this tendency. Thus it was perfectly consistent and highly predictable that so important a process as that for nominating presidential candidates would also be subject to the cry of "all the power to the people."

Now that the changes have been made and we do have a new American way of nominating, we also observe that the party has not disappeared. It is at this point that there is a convergence in the treatment of the two major questions for this essay: What has happened to the presidential nominating process? How and why did Ronald Reagan win the nomination? The changes in the presidential nominating process have unquestionably created a new context within which political parties must operate. That is saying something quite different from what Ceaser or Bode has said. It is not correct to say that the race is nonpartisan—that overgeneralizes from the Carter case—nor is it correct to argue that the reforms have had only limited impact on the parties. We do have a new system, and political parties have survived. In fact, they are slowly making accommodations to these new methods for encouraging greater participation in nominating presidential candidates. The measured pace of adjustment should not surprise the experienced student of political parties. Actually, the weakness of parties may be their strength when they are faced with radical reform. That is, a more hierarchical structure might be rational enough to be truly insulted and powerful enough within itself to disband.[63]

Accepting the altered context of greater public participation in the nominating process, the Reagan organization demonstrated the capacity to accomplish much of what David Cohen viewed as party success in the past. It is my interpretation that Ronald Reagan ran

[63] Before proceeding, I hasten to introduce the caveat that in writing more from the Republican party perspective, I may well be accused of understating the reform effects on the Democrats. Since most analyses tend to generalize about the process almost entirely from what happened to the Democrats, however, perhaps counterbalance is in order.

the most party-oriented nomination campaign in recent decades, a particularly significant development within the minority party, since its candidates are often tempted to deemphasize party (even conservative candidates like Goldwater). One bright young Reagan aide said that he and his colleagues viewed "the party as a house ready to move into for the candidate's organization."[64] He made this observation as though it were commonplace analysis. Yet in fact few presidential candidates in recent years have viewed the party in this way. It should also be noted that the impressive work of Bill Brock as national party chairman made the Republican house well worth moving into. Thomas E. Patterson is undoubtedly correct in his statement that "today's presidential campaign is essentially a mass media campaign."[65] There is nothing in Patterson's statement to suggest that political parties must disappear because of the importance of the mass media. Rather he has described a changing context to which the modern party must adjust if it is to survive. Both Brock and Reagan appear to have understood the importance of encouraging the political party to take advantage of the mass media rather than permitting the mass media to take advantage of the party.

In my judgment, Reagan's trifocal campaign was a major political event in 1980. I have tried not to overdo the analysis on this point— thus, for example, I have noted that many mistakes were made along the way and that the Reagan forces were just plain lucky on occasion (as are all those who win the nomination). In the end, however, the strategy worked. A nomination was won under the new system not only without sacrificing party connections but by positively emphasizing party unity. It is, of course, too early to tell whether this technique will be adopted and further developed by others in the future. It is enough for now to record what happened and to recommend that those interested in viable political parties study the 1980 Republican nominating process.

As it turned out, James Reston was at least half-correct in his analysis, quoted at the beginning of this chapter. Although there are serious doubts about whether Ronald Reagan was, in the end, "Carter's favorite opponent," by the time it was all over, no one doubted that the Republicans gave Carter "their favorite candidate."

[64] Personal interview, July 14, 1980.
[65] Thomas E. Patterson, *The Mass Media Election: How Americans Choose Their President* (New York: Praeger, 1980), p. 3.

4

The Conventions, Platforms, and Issue Activists

Michael J. Malbin

Ronald Reagan and Jimmy Carter had very different tasks ahead of them as they prepared for their national conventions. Reagan, like Carter four years earlier, could approach his convention with no doubts about his nomination. Therefore, like the 1976 Democratic nominee, Reagan could concentrate on using his convention to reassure the elements of his party that still were wary of him while broadening his appeal to the general voting public.

Carter's 1980 chore was more difficult. Like Gerald Ford in 1976 and George McGovern in 1972, Carter's nomination was not assured until a vote on the rules at the convention itself. Once that key battle was over, Carter then, with much less time than his opponent had available, had to focus on exactly the same matters that had preoccupied Reagan—uniting the party and kicking off the fall campaign.

Using a modern convention to achieve these objectives requires a great deal of political skill. Over the past decade, conventions of both parties increasingly have become filled with interest groups and issue activists. Issue groups have become vital to winning nominations since the proliferation of primaries and the postreform delegate-selection rules. In addition, the campaign finance law's spending limits for the presidential race inflate the importance of volunteers and organizational networks for the general election. The activists' support, however, can bring costs along with their benefits. Their single-

I should like to thank the many people who read and commented on this chapter when it was in draft form. Except for John Kessel and Byron Shafer, however, the readers were participants, and some of them asked to remain anonymous. Rather than name some of these readers without others, it seemed better to leave them all unnamed. They know who they are, and I acknowledge my debt to them. Any errors in fact or judgment that remain are, of course, my own responsibility.

minded preoccupation with issues can cause serious problems for the candidate as he tries to use the convention to broaden his base. These problems were exposed repeatedly as Republicans and Democrats worked to put together their 1980 platforms. How Carter and Reagan dealt with them tells a great deal about their respective political positions as they made their transitions from the nomination to the general election.

The Republicans

Ronald Reagan had three strategic goals for the Republican convention that was held in Detroit on July 14–17. He wanted to maintain the enthusiasm of the conservative supporters who won him the nomination. He wanted to reach out to centrist and moderate Republicans, particularly to white-collar suburbanites who might be thinking about voting for independent candidate John Anderson.[1] Finally, he wanted to build on his appeal to normally Democratic blue-collar workers.

To reach blue-collar workers, Reagan decided to emphasize economic and foreign policy issues, instead of the divisive social and racial issues that Richard Nixon and Spiro Agnew had used to win the "hard hat vote" in 1968 and 1972. By concentrating on these themes, which the polls showed dominating public concern throughout the year, Reagan was able to serve several political objectives at once. His economic themes appealed simultaneously to middle-class blue-collar workers, who normally vote Democratic, and to potential Republican defectors to Anderson, who might be turned away from Reagan by social issues. For the longer term, by focusing on a positive economic message, Reagan was following the strategy that was most likely to encourage the basic political realignment whose possibility Republican pollsters sensed they saw in their data.[2]

It always helps a presidential candidate to have his party behind him, but Ronald Reagan had some new incentives in 1980 for presenting himself as a centrist Republican at the head of the unified ticket. The Republican National Committee (RNC) had been running advertisements all year criticizing the Democratic party on economic issues.[3]

---

[1] For a summary of the steps Reagan took at the convention to reach out to centrist and moderate Republicans, see Charles O. Jones, "Nominating 'Carter's Favorite Opponent': The Republicans in 1980," this volume, chap. 3.

[2] M. Malbin, "The Republican Revival," *Fortune*, August 25, 1980, p. 86.

[3] For a discussion about the financial resources the RNC had available to help Reagan and Republican congressional candidates, see Thomas E. Mann and Norman J. Ornstein, "The Republican Surge in Congress," this volume, chap. 8.

The advertisements were to continue through the fall and were to be supplemented by an $8 million effort run through state party organizations that got 800,000 unpaid volunteers working in the field to push slates of GOP candidates.[4]

These resources would have helped any Republican candidate, but Reagan had another reason for wanting to tie himself closely to the party. Reagan's biggest potential weakness as a candidate was the public perception of him as a person who was loose with the facts and generally unfamiliar with national policy. He was able to counter this by relying on a series of policy networks centered in Washington that the RNC under its innovative chairman, Bill Brock, had worked to put together since 1977. At Brock's insistence, these networks had ignored the social issues that tended to divide Republicans in favor of economic and foreign policy themes on which the party was broadly united. The political question for Reagan was whether he could do the same without dampening the enthusiasm of his vast army of potential volunteers. The platform would be his first major test.

The Republican Platform Process. The process of putting together a GOP platform formally began on January 14, 1980, with the first of ten hearings scheduled to be held around the country. This formal beginning, however, had little to do with the real job of drafting a platform. Since platform committee members were not chosen until after most of the hearings were finished, the hearings were largely designed to gain some publicity for the party and to give interested people a chance to put their views on the record.

While the hearings were droning on in public, more significant developments were taking place behind the scenes. Bill Brock had chosen Senator John Tower of Texas to chair the platform committee and had named Representative Trent Lott of Mississippi and Governor Otis Bowen of Indiana to serve as vice-chairmen. By his selections, Brock was signaling that the party's platform was going to be drafted by people from Congress and from the Washington issue networks. This seems to be a common pattern for the party out of power. The Republicans followed it in 1968, as did the Democrats in 1976. According to Representative Michael Barnes (Democrat, Maryland), who was executive director of the 1976 Democratic platform committee, the platform that year "was basically written by congressional staff. Obviously, the Carter campaign was very important to us, as

[4] M. Malbin, "How Many Go to the Polls Could Settle the Election," *National Journal*, November 1, 1980, p. 1840.

were the various leaders of the Democratic coalition. The Carter people pushed on maybe two or three things, but it was not basically a Carter document."[5] The Republicans in 1980 worked much the same way.

The top staff choices for the committee confirmed this basic direction. Roger D. Semerad was named executive director. Before that, he had been executive director of the RNC advisory councils, the working units Brock had developed to formulate party positions on policy. Made up of some five hundred members of Congress, former cabinet and subcabinet officials, people active in past presidential campaigns (including some leading people from the 1976 and 1980 Reagan campaigns), state and local party leaders and legislators, these bodies worked together to thrash out about two dozen position papers in foreign, economic, and urban policy. Many of their recommendations entered the mainstream of party thinking. Semerad's appointment as the platform committee's executive director and Michael E. Baroody's as its editor in chief ensured that they would also work their way into the 1980 platform.[6] (Baroody, the RNC's director of communications, had edited the advisory council reports.) Two of the other early top staff appointments reaffirmed Congress's importance to the process—Richard Thompson, from Tower's Senate Republican Policy Committee, and David Hoppe, from Lott's House Republican Research Committee. Still, Semerad said, one side effect of the councils was that "the Hill staff had to contend with the RNC."

The staff early on set up a series of task forces including representatives from each of the Republican presidential candidates. Reagan's representatives were Richard Allen for foreign policy and Martin Anderson for domestic policy. One luncheon meeting between Semerad, Anderson, and Allen was held shortly after the March 18 Illinois primary, when it became clear that Reagan would be the Republican nominee. According to Semerad: "They told me that Reagan was not going to have a platform that would be stuffed down the throat of the convention. That made me feel very good. It made me feel that we were not going through a foolish exercise."

[5] The quotation comes from an interview with the author. For the remainder of the chapter, quotations without footnotes come from such interviews or from one of the many ephemeral, unpublished typescripts that appear during conventions and disappear thereafter. (The text makes clear which is which.)

[6] For example, an advisory council committee chaired by former secretary of housing and urban development Carla Hills recommended creation of tax-sheltered savings accounts for down payments on houses, similar to individual retirement accounts. It also recommended reverse-annuity mortgages, under which homeowners could use their equity to supplement their retirement income. Both proposals were included in the 1980 Republican platform.

By late May, the drafting process was well under way. Tower had appointed his six subcommittee chairmen, all members of Congress: Senator Robert Dole of Kansas for agriculture, Representative David Stockman of Michigan for energy, Representative Jack Kemp of New York for foreign policy and defense, Senator William Roth of Delaware for fiscal and monetary affairs, Representative Robert Michel of Illinois for human resources, Representative Margaret Heckler of Massachusetts for housing and urban affairs, and Representative Mickey Edwards of Oklahoma for government regulations. The subcommittees all were staffed by this time as well, generally with congressional staff aides.

The drafting process involved a series of staff drafts that were written under Baroody's direction and then reviewed by an executive committee that included Tower, Lott, Bowen, the subcommittee chairmen and staffs, Allen, and Anderson. Although the executive committee reviewed the drafts extensively, the platform remained a party statement that Anderson and Allen cleared, as opposed to a Reagan document.

One issue that caused a great deal of trouble in drafting was the Equal Rights Amendment (ERA). The party had endorsed an ERA for forty years, but the 1976 endorsement came only after Betty Ford's personal intercession and only by a four-vote margin. Everyone on the executive committee knew the issue would again be divisive and that most Reagan delegates did not like the amendment. After a lot of wrangling, the group came up with an attempted fudge:

> We reaffirm our Party's historic commitment to equal rights and equal opportunity for women, a commitment which made us the first national party to endorse the Equal Rights Amendment. We are proud of our pioneering role and do not renounce our stand.

This language, cleared by Anderson, was drafted by Stockman, who was probably the most active executive committee member throughout the long hours of rewriting. (He was seen banging away on the preamble at a typewriter in Detroit at 3 o'clock one morning.) His efforts reflected his belief that control over the rhetorical terms of debate is a vital element of politics whose importance generally is underestimated. (He learned this in part from one of his teachers at Harvard, Daniel Patrick Moynihan.) Stockman's efforts meshed with those of Baroody, who can claim much of the credit for making the draft a thematic document instead of the more normal grab bag of programs and unrelated issues.

The Draft. The importance of executive committee advance drafts to the GOP platform process generally has been overlooked. Copies are not widely distributed, and press coverage focuses on platform committee changes and additions. Until recently, in fact, most platform committee members did not even get to see copies of the draft in advance.[7] This changed in 1976, when platform committee members supporting Reagan asked to see copies so they could work on amendments. The new procedure was followed again in 1980. In both years, despite hundreds of amendments, the bulk of the final platform could be found in the advance draft.

The 1980 draft was organized as a series of concentric circles—individual, family, neighborhood, work, peace, and freedom. These topics had been used by Reagan as the basic, although often unexpressed, organizational themes of his speeches since 1978, and they were repeated by him at the beginning and end of his convention acceptance speech. The message implied by the structure was that the Republicans wanted to broaden public discussion to include a concern for the importance of institutions that stand between government and the individual. Although the platform had any number of phrases that looked on the surface as if they represented a rejection of the New Deal, a more careful reading showed that the party was trying to restructure, and not simply reject, the role of government.

Perhaps the most remarkable of the platform's sections rhetorically were the ones on economics. The programs in the platform had to do with cutting taxes, regulation, and government spending—standard GOP fare in recent years. The rhetoric, however, was not standard. "It is important to develop a growing constituency which recognizes its direct relationship to the health and success of free enterprise," the platform said.[8] To this end, it abandoned its past rhetorical focus on higher productivity and business profits and concentrated instead on the jobs that supposedly will result from them. The platform's structure made Reagan's political aim clear: to present Republican "supply side" economics in terms that would appeal beyond the board rooms to the concerns of the urban working class. Still unknown was whether the committee would let the platform, and thus the proceedings of convention week, retain so clear a focus.

---

[7] See Nelson W. Polsby and Aaron Wildavsky, *Presidential Elections: Strategies of American Politics*, 5th ed. (New York: Charles Scribner's Sons, 1980), p. 99.
[8] "1980 Republican Platform Text," *Congressional Quarterly Weekly Report*, July 19, 1980, p. 2403.

Getting Ready for Detroit. The platform committee's structure was not conducive to helping Reagan achieve his political objectives. Platform committees in both parties are chosen from those convention delegates who are willing to put in long hours of hard work for at least a week, at their own expense. Such people tend to take their work seriously. Although some politicians may be willing to take on the responsibilities—and, for some reason, more Republicans do so than Democrats—the process tends to produce a higher percentage of uncompromising issue activists on both parties' platform committees than at their conventions, let alone among the voters.[9]

The process also tends to make subcommittees more extreme than the full committee. Traditionally, both parties let platform committee members pick their subcommittees. Any attempt to assign members might well provoke rebellion, but self-selection introduces predictable distortions. In general, the subcommittees handling divisive issues on both parties' platform committees were stacked with the delegates who cared the most about the issues involved. The effect on the Republicans' debates over ERA and abortion was palpable.

To understand the way these debates developed, it helps to have a sense of how outside groups helped structure the basic framework. The main organizations active on abortion were the Pro-Life Impact Committee on one side and the National Women's Political Caucus (NWPC) on the other. Marlene Elwell of Farmington Hills, Michigan, chaired the pro-life group, which was a decentralized collection of local pro-life organizations whose convention activities were coordinated by people living in or near the host city. In an interview Elwell described how her group prepared for the convention:

> In March, we put together an incorporated group for the purpose of impacting the Republican platform. We began by assigning one person from Michigan to each state and to the territories. We were a small group; we had one staff director and fifty-four troops. We got the state delegation lists as the delegations were appointed. Once the lists of delegates were made known, we contacted one person in each state, and we did two mailings to every convention delegate. Once that was done, we identified the two platform committee delegates and we polled them. Then we waited for the subcommittees to be named. We did not work at the state level to get people appointed to the platform committee, but some of our local groups did. They knew their people and in some states they did have the equivalent of a veto, but I won't say which ones. Once the delegates to the platform

[9] See footnote 33, below.

committee were selected, we individually lobbied people and encouraged them to go on the human resources subcommittee. I don't think we have a similar proportion of pro-life people on the full platform committee. The pro-life people are more likely to be on this subcommittee than elsewhere.

Stop-ERA was similar to the pro-life group in structure—decentralized, with convention operations organized by a Detroit-based committee. Unlike the pro-life group, Stop-ERA did have a highly visible national media "star" to promote its cause, Phyllis Schlafly. The organizational work, however, was done by a small group of local activists chaired by Elaine Donnelly of Livonia, Michigan. Donnelly said that her group "started organizing almost from the day we knew that the convention would be in Detroit." Schlafly said that their group did not try to persuade delegates to join the subcommittee, but Donnelly said that once the delegates were chosen, "we set out to find out how many friends we had. We talked to everyone on the platform committee personally."

The National Women's Political Caucus might have been willing to try a similar approach, but it did not have much support among the delegates. The feminist group lost on abortion in 1976, but their lobbying was crucial to the party's narrow endorsement of ERA that year. In 1980, Kathy Wilson, NWPC's Republican vice-chairwoman, and Pamela Curtis of the NWPC's Republican Women's Task Force, attended the platform committee meetings to lobby delegates and speak with the press. That did not make a lot of difference, however. "We tried to get people on the platform committee in states where we had control," Curtis said, "but we did not have control in a lot of states. Reagan won, so Reagan's people chose."

Curtis's statement may help explain why the antiabortion group had to work to get people on the human resources subcommittee whereas Stop-ERA could let things develop naturally. Although both organizations describe themselves as single-issue groups, most of the people active in Stop-ERA are suspicious of governmental action in general and of the courts in particular. Their supporters, on the whole, would be conservative Republicans even without the ERA issue. The antiabortion group was more diverse. Some were opposed to ERA. Some were associated with the Moral Majority and endorsed the full panoply of conservative "pro-family" positions. Others had little but abortion in common with other Reagan delegates. According to Elwell, a former Democrat:

> We're strictly one-issue people. I don't think there's a single
> issue on which we are united except abortion. If we get a

court reversal, there would be a splintering. We have many people who would never vote for Ronald Reagan except for this issue. For example, many of our grass-roots people are against capital punishment.

Kathleen Edwards, a Missourian who chaired the 1976 pro-life impact committee and attended the 1980 platform committee meetings, pointed out some of the occasional tensions between the pro-life and Stop-ERA groups:

> The right-to-life voters Reagan has attracted include many moderate to liberal Democrats, but the anti-ERA voters are mostly conservative Republicans. We have found that they will try to hold you on a lot of issues. On some things, our people just went along. They stayed quiet because the right-to-life issue was so important.

So, partly through interest-group efforts and partly through the natural inclinations of the delegates, antiabortion and anti-ERA delegates found their way in disproportionate numbers to the human resources panel. About 80 percent of the requests for subcommittee slots were said to have come from people who wanted that subcommittee. (Most people apparently did not specify a subcommittee.)

Tower exacerbated the effects of the laissez-faire selection process by trying to return to pre-1976 procedures. Before 1976, meetings of the platform committee were closed to the public. The meetings were opened that year at the insistence of Reagan delegates but over little opposition from Ford delegates. Tower wanted closed meetings in 1980, but the delegates again voted to open them. Then, once the panels were open, Semerad, acting on Tower's behalf, refused to distribute copies of the staff draft to the press. Since most of the panels' work consisted of line-by-line amendments to the draft, this meant the press could not follow the proceedings unless someone explained the language being discussed. Incredibly, the staff on some subcommittees were even told not to answer reporters' questions about what amendments were adopted by their panels. The human resources panel was about the only place where journalists could figure out what was happening. (Lobbyists were freely passing out the draft language and typed amendments.) The result was predictable. Although there was no way to avoid the press's heavy concentration on abortion and ERA, Tower's decisions ensured that the press could not have covered anything else if it had wanted to. Thus, Tower's worst fears were realized: days of negative headlines about the big fights over two issues, with almost no coverage of the bulk of the document.

Abortion and ERA in Subcommittee. The fireworks began quickly on the human resources subcommittee. Immediately after the reading of the staff draft on equal rights, Donald E. White of Alaska moved that the subcommittee consider the paragraphs on women's rights first. John Leopold, Hawaii's 1978 gubernatorial candidate, tried to substitute the 1976 language endorsing the ERA, but was defeated 4–11. Marilyn Thayer of Louisiana next proposed the staff draft's first sentence, reaffirming the party's "historic commitment to equal rights and equality for women" without the rest of the draft language, which said that the party did "not renounce" its past endorsement of the amendment. Thayer's amendment also said:

> We support equal rights and equal opportunities for women, without taking away traditional rights of women such as exemption from the military draft. We support the enforcement of all equal opportunity laws and urge the elimination of discrimination against women. We oppose any move which would give the federal government more power over families.
>
> Ratification of the Equal Rights Amendment is now in the hands of state legislatures, and the issues of the time extension and rescission are in the courts. The states have a constitutional right to accept or reject a constitutional amendment without federal interference or pressure. At the direction of the White House, federal departments launched pressure against states which refused to ratify ERA. Regardless of one's position on ERA, we demand that this practice cease.

Glenda Mattoon, a fiery delegate from Oklahoma who said she would "do anything" to keep George Bush from gaining the vice-presidential nomination because of his views on ERA and abortion, moved to insert language explicitly repudiating the ERA. At this point, Trent Lott called a five-minute recess. Lott, who was chairing the subcommittee in place of the absent Michel, was acting as members of Congress usually do in Republican platform meetings. He suspected the votes were there for Mattoon's motion and he wanted to cool things off. Mattoon, in an interview, said that she agreed during the recess to withdraw her amendment on the understanding that she would offer it in full committee if anyone there pushed for a vote to endorse the ERA. "We cut a deal," Mattoon said. Mattoon insisted she could have won in subcommittee, and she probably was right. Her victory, however, would not have been as large as the 14–1 vote for Thayer's position.

Betty Rendell of Indiana next offered a long "bill of rights" for women that contained a detailed set of legislative and administrative proposals to eliminate discrimination against women. The bill of rights was adopted whole, except for the first paragraphs, which were made redundant by the prior adoption of Thayer's language. What never came out at the platform committee was that the superseded paragraphs had been endorsed explicitly by Reagan.

The bill of rights was written by the National Federation of Republican Women. Betty Heitman, president of the federation from 1978 until she became co-chairman of the RNC after the convention, had been moving the federation toward more active involvement in women's issues. In June 1979, she put together an advisory council of Republican women in Washington, most of whom had high-level experience in government.

Nancy M. Chotiner, the council's chairwoman, began pulling together material on issues in early 1980. When it became apparent that Reagan would be the nominee, Chotiner said she began working "to head off what happened." Chotiner's old friend from California, Lorelei Kinder, was the Reagan campaign staff aide designated to track ERA and other human resources issues on the platform committee. Suggesting that the issues Chotiner had been preparing for the federation be called a bill of rights, she took them to California to show Reagan.

Although the bill of rights waffled on the ERA in much the same way as the RNC staff draft did, it contained specific recommendations relating to pay, child care, small business, credit, career counseling, social security, and taxes. Reagan agreed with everything in the federation plank, asking only that language be added pledging enforcement of statutes already on the books and repeal of statutes that promote discrimination against women. The language to which Reagan agreed was then left with the RNC. For some reason, apparently accidental, it was not put into the staff's draft platform. The general understanding, however, was that it would almost surely be adopted without much change by the committee.

These expectations were thrown awry when White changed the order of business and then Leopold and Thayer seized the initiative with their opposing amendments, preempting the federation's position from either side. Although the federation's specific proposals were adopted, the subcommittee thus swept aside Reagan's commitments to enforce existing antidiscrimination laws and to repeal remaining laws that discriminate. His interest in making these commitments was never brought out, in keeping with a strategic decision to limit the candidate's personal exposure on platform issues. Although Reagan's staff did work in private with the delegates on some issues, notably on foreign policy, it made little sense politically for his name to become involved in a public dispute over specific language that would indicate his support for equal rights without an amendment. Once the opportunity slipped by in subcommittee, it seemed more politic to let Reagan describe his own position later.

In its other actions, the subcommittee showed that its commitment to the new right's agenda extended across the board. The staff draft had tried to straddle the abortion issue by simply describing it as a "difficult and controversial" one on which Republicans disagree. Guy Farley of Virginia offered a substitute plank endorsing a constitutional amendment "to restore protection of the right to life for unborn children" and supporting "congressional efforts to restrict the use of taxpayers' dollars for abortion." Farley's plank also pledged "the appointment of new justices on the Supreme Court who respect traditional family values and the sanctity of all human life." Lott ruled this last provision out of order for the section of the platform dealing with individual rights; so the subcommittee promptly tacked it onto the section on the judiciary. The rest of the antiabortion plank carried, 11–4.

The platform plank on families that was drafted by the staff contained nothing objectionable to the social conservatives on human resources. The draft supported voluntary, nondenominational school prayers and tuition tax credits for private nonprofit elementary and secondary schools, and it opposed forced school busing to achieve racial integration. This was not enough for the subcommittee, however. Don White of Alaska, who identified himself as a supporter of the Reverend Jerry Falwell's Moral Majority, successfully sponsored a plank supporting "legislation protecting and defending the traditional American family against the ongoing erosion of its base in our society." He told the subcommittee that this plank was intended as an endorsement of Senator Paul Laxalt's family protection bill, which Lott then characterized as "a good bill." Laxalt's bill would, among other things, withhold federal funds from any school whose program "may, directly or indirectly, inculcate values or modes of behavior which contradict the beliefs and values of the community, as demonstrated by parents, representatives of parents, and recognized religious groups" or from any school board that purchased any material that tended "to denigrate, diminish, or deny the role differences between the sexes as they have been understood historically in the United States."

Other Subcommittees. While public attention was focused on human resources, a great deal was also happening in the other subcommittees. On most, individual delegates pushed their own ideas, encountering no serious resistance. For example, Senator Dole's agriculture subcommittee tripled the length of its section of the platform. The ranking Republican on the Senate Finance Committee (and its chairman in 1981) operated true to his committee's practices, gaining unanimous support by letting everyone add something. (Iowa's Marjorie Askew, for example, pushed for a specific reference to gasohol in the energy plank on "alternative fuels," and Oregon's John K. Gram made sure the timber industry was not overlooked.) On the government regulation subcommittee, Representative Mickey Edwards of Oklahoma added one of his major congressional concerns, revision of the Administrative Procedures Act. Representatives Stockman and Heckler essentially redrafted their subcommittees' planks on energy and urban affairs to reflect their work in Congress. On Senator Roth's panel on fiscal and monetary affairs, Freda J. Poundstone of Colorado inserted a provision on estate and gift taxes to help family farms. She also offered a completely rewritten plank on inflation that she said she had done at the staff's request. Although the staff worked out the language in advance with the Reagan staff, Poundstone said that there was no visible evidence of Reagan staff people in the subcommittee during its deliberations. This observation, echoed by people on most of the other subcommittees except human resources and foreign affairs, contrasts sharply with both the Democratic experience of 1980, when candidate staffs stood around the room signaling thumbs up or down on every vote, or the Republican experience of 1976, when electronically wired aides from both the Reagan and Ford camps monitored developments constantly. Even on the human resources and foreign affairs panels, the staff presence was relatively low key. With the nomination settled, the costs of constant monitoring, which would have belittled the independent importance of the issue activists, far outweighed the benefits.

The staff was very concerned about foreign affairs, however. Richard Allen, Reagan's principal foreign policy adviser, underlined this by testifying in person as the leadoff witness before the subcommittee. (Most subcommittees took no direct testimony.) The main source of Allen's concern was Senator Jesse Helms, who, as in 1976, came armed with a series of amendments he considered matters of principle. For example, the draft pledged to develop a long list of weapons President Carter had either delayed or opposed. The purpose, the draft said, was to "build toward a sustained defense expenditure sufficient to close the gap with the Soviets." To this phrase, Helms added: "and ultimately reach the position of military superiority that the American people demand." A "capability to oversee our internal security efforts" was added to the section on terrorism, as was a paragraph deploring "the Marxist Sandinista takeover of Nicaragua" in the section on the Americas. The paragraph on Nicaragua also rejected U.S. assistance "to any Marxist government in this hemisphere." On the other hand, Helms, a senator, did not act simply as an independent issue activist. He withdrew at least two of his proposed amendments, one condemning the Panama Canal treaty and the other demanding renewed governmental relations with Taiwan, in the face of arguments that they could be damaging politically.

Full Committee. The interplay between issue activists and political professionals continued through the full committee markup of the draft. Mary Dent Crisp of Arizona, co-chairman of the RNC through the convention, used her last appearance as co-chairman to give a speech blasting the platform committee's position on the ERA and abortion. Crisp's speech, which got extensive television coverage, was given on July 9, just before the first full committee markup, in a context in which many women long active in the GOP were telling the press that the ERA plank could well mean a loss of votes to John Anderson. (Crisp eventually joined the Anderson campaign.) In the time between the two meetings, the Reagan staff, after repeated failures during the night, finally was able to arrange a compromise that gave Republican feminists some sense that they were not being read out of the party. The compromise, which was introduced by Farley and seconded by Mattoon, added this sentence before the subcommittee language on ERA: "We acknowledge the legitimate efforts of those who support or oppose ratification of the Equal Rights Amendment." This obviously did not satisfy ERA supporters, but it gave them some leverage to use in negotiations that were to continue throughout convention week.

Much of the remaining debate in full committee involved members of Congress trying to restrain their fellow committee members. The congressional representatives won some points and lost others, but their presence introduced an element of moderation that was missing from the Democratic committee, whose few senators and representatives generally were absent.

For example, Representatives Michel, Kemp, and Stockman noticed that the platform contained no separate plank for black Americans and drafted one that was added in full committee. Senator Dole drafted similar planks for Hispanics and for the handicapped. Michel successfully urged the deletion of a sentence endorsing "full voting rights" for the Virgin Islands and Guam because it would give those territories more power than the District of Columbia. He also successfully opposed an amendment that would have made men eligible for social security at sixty, citing the costs. Stockman and Senator Malcolm Wallop of Wyoming defeated an amendment that would have given states veto power over new federal wilderness designations, and Wallop spoke against a "sagebrush rebellion" proposal to return federal land to the states.

The members of Congress, however, were not always successful. The delegates refused to accept Michel's argument on the Department of Education—that the department was a bad idea but abolishing it might be costly and the president should be allowed some flexibility. They also refused, 43–44, to accept a clause supporting federal funding for research conducted by the National Institutes of Health. (The delegates were upset aboout research on test-tube fertilization.) When Faith Whittlesey of Pennsylvania wanted to add a second policy test ("belief in the decentralization of the federal government") to the antiabortion test already applied to prospective federal judges, Lott's and Wallop's counterarguments proved unsuccessful.

In a few cases, the members of Congress divided. For example, Representative Bud Shuster of Pennsylvania, the ranking Republican on the House Surface Transportation Subcommittee, defended the 55-mile-per-hour speed limit on grounds of safety, but Stockman joined the critics and prevailed. Shuster's intercession was more significant on other issues. He had come to the platform committee with a series of transportation planks on mass transit, highways, and regulation. His attempt to change the plank on "urban transportation" to one on "public transportation" that included both urban and rural transit failed when Kemp and Stockman insisted on the rhetorical need to have the word "urban" appear in the table of contents. Shuster had no trouble, however, getting a separate plank on rural transportation and substituting his own plank on transportation regulation for the one reported by the subcommittee. Originally, the regulation plank spoke of the benefit deregulation would mean for consumers. Shuster's more traditional plank called not for deregulation but for an end to the excessive regulation that was hurting business profits.

A similar clash between the old and new Republican economic rhetoric involved Senator Dole. Republicans seized every available opportunity during platform week to use Detroit's high unemployment to their political advantage. For example, a meeting between leading

113

Republicans and officials of the United Automobile Workers Union (UAW) stimulated a comment from the UAW president, Malcolm Fraser, that Reagan might well win a large number of his workers' votes. Dole tried to follow this up in committee by offering a tax credit for buyers of American cars. Kemp, Roth, and Stockman could barely restrain themselves. They were concerned that all the funds for the general tax cut they favored would be frittered away in special interest tax breaks. Eventually they prevailed, and Dole's tax credit was watered down to a statement of concern for unemployed auto workers.

The final sections of the platform, on foreign policy and national security, were given special treatment by the full committee. Until then, planks were read aloud one at a time and then opened for amendment. Every time a delegate would ask for unanimous consent to dispense with the reading, another would object that the press had no copies. Before beginning on foreign policy, Tower asked the delegates to keep their amendments to a minimum. "In the area of foreign policy and defense we should be in lock step with our presidential candidate," he said. Lott made sure the press was given copies of the draft, and a motion again was made asking unanimous consent to do away with the reading. One delegate objected, saying "a large number of us have spent a great deal of time and money to come here"; so the request was put as a motion to suspend the rules and was carried 52–26, exactly the required two-thirds margin. Virtually no amendments were offered—a stark contrast to the previous day and a half spent on domestic policy. One important exception was a series of amendments drafted by the Reagan staff and offered by Kemp in a block as a series of supposedly technical amendments, although several clearly were not technical. One, for example, said that the establishment of a Palestinian state on the West Bank of the Jordan River would be destabilizing and harmful to the peace process. Another added a sentence to Helms's paragraph on Nicaragua that Allen, in an interview, said was designed to preserve the possibility of offering that country foreign aid. Both issues obviously had been cleared with the interested parties. No dissent was heard.

Convention Week. The special treatment given foreign policy by the platform committee and the defeat of Dole's special interest tax credits helped Reagan maintain the thrust of the platform's basic campaign messages. Still, much remained to be done if the messages were to have a chance of dominating the public's perception. ERA and abortion remained the biggest burrs under Reagan's saddle. Satisfying conservative activists on these issues had always been fairly easy: he opposed ERA and abortion; so did they. The difference was that the activists thought nothing was as important as their issues, while Regan was quite willing in the fall campaign and during the early stages of his presidency, for substantive as well as tactical reasons, to subordinate social issues to economics and foreign policy. Reagan was not about to spell this difference out too clearly, however, since doing so might make him appear hypocritical to, and lose the support of, his primary constituency. Yet he had to do something to mollify the feminists. Failure to do so could cause the party to appear divided and hurt his election prospects over an issue that was not central to him.

The feminists were not going to let Reagan off the hook with the single compromise sentence on ERA that was added in full committee. A mass street rally for ERA was planned for the convention's first day (Monday, July 14), when the light schedule ensured good television coverage. At the same time, party moderates were gearing up for a floor fight on Tuesday, when the convention was to vote on the platform. The floor challenge was to center on the antiabortion litmus test for appointing federal judges. Senator Charles H. Percy of Illinois called the judicial selection test "the worst plank I have ever seen in any platform by the Republican party," and Senators Charles McC. Mathias of Maryland and Jacob K. Javits of New York were similarly outspoken in their reservations.

To defuse the concern feminists had over how Reagan planned to implement equal rights without an amendment, Lorelei Kinder had been working to set up a meeting with Reagan requested by ERA supporters on the platform committee. The meeting was held the morning of July 15. (The platform was presented to the convention that evening.) Attending were Mary Louise Smith, the chairman of the RNC before Brock; Helen Milliken, president of ERAmerica and wife of the governor of Michigan; Betty Southard Murphy, former chairman of the National Labor Relations Board; Carla Hills, former secretary of housing and urban development; Senator Nancy Kassebaum of Kansas; Representative Margaret Heckler; Maureen Reagan, the nominee's daughter and an active campaigner for the amendment; Betty Heitman; Pamela Curtis; Lorelei Kinder; and seven others. At a press briefing afterward, Smith described the meeting as "positive" and "productive." Similarly peaceful statements from the other participants, widely reported in Detroit, calmed the atmosphere in time for the platform's presentation to the convention.

Opponents of the ERA and abortion planks had been searching on July 14 and 15 for ways to open the platform to a televised floor debate. Although there were not enough votes to force a vote on any minority planks under the rules, a motion to suspend the rules could be brought by a majority of the delegates from six states. Delegates from New York, Illinois, and several other states voted on the morning of the fifteenth, before Reagan's meeting, to refuse support for such a motion. Despite this, Hawaii's John Leopold sought recognition on the convention floor, shortly before the final vote on the platform, for a motion to suspend the rules. When no other state supported Leopold, the platform was adopted by voice vote.

Wednesday, July 16, was the day of the convoluted negotiations over the vice-presidency. As has been mentioned elsewhere in this volume, George Bush's selection helped appease party moderates, and the prolonged discussions concerning former president Gerald R. Ford diverted attention away from the social conservatives' unhappiness with Bush.[10]

One piece of business remained. As he had promised the people at the Tuesday meeting, Reagan inserted a paragraph on discrimination against women at the beginning of his acceptance speech:

> I know we have had a quarrel or two, but only as to the method of attaining a goal. There was no argument about the goal. As president, I will establish a liaison with the 50 governors to encourage them to eliminate, wherever it exists, discrimination against women. I will monitor federal laws to insure their implementation and to add statutes if needed.[11]

With this public affirmation of the principles he had endorsed in the ill-fated federation plank, Reagan was free to put his stress where he wanted it: on economics, foreign policy, and the fall campaign.

The Democrats

Jimmy Carter's political problems going into his convention made Reagan's look easy by comparison. The president's renomination was not assured until he had won a fight on the rule binding the delegates' votes on the nomination.[12] Although the president's victory was never seriously in doubt, the fight took up most of his own and his

---

[10] For more on this, see Jones, "Nominating 'Carter's Favorite Opponent.'"

[11] "Convention Texts, Acceptance Speeches, Reagan: 'Time to Recapture Our Destiny,'" *Congressional Quarterly Weekly Report*, July 19, 1980, p. 2063.

[12] For more on the rules fight, see Nelson W. Polsby, "The Democratic Nomination," this volume, chap. 2.

staff's time until the vote was safely out of the way on August 11, the first night of the convention. To make matters worse for Carter, supporters of the "open convention" had been filling the press with statements criticizing his performance as president. This came at the same time as public revelations about White House and Justice Department efforts to get the president's brother, Billy Carter, to register as a foreign agent for Libya. When combined with the normal postconvention halo effect benefiting Reagan, the public opinion polls before the Democratic convention showed Carter trailing by anywhere from thirteen to twenty-eight percentage points. (See figure 4–1.)

If Carter was to overcome his low standing in the polls, he desperately needed to use the convention to make party activists want to work for him. He owed his 1976 election to the wholehearted efforts of organized labor and other interest groups, and he would need similar efforts to stand a chance in 1980.[13] Carter, however, simply did not have a reservoir of enthusiastic supporters. Many Kennedy supporters were overtly antipathetic toward Carter, and many of the president's own convention delegates were there less out of commitment than because the groups they represented thought supporting Carter served their interests. This meant that Carter had to tread carefully if he was to achieve his objectives. For enthusiasm, he would rely on their fears of Reagan. This enthusiasm could quickly be dampened, however, if he failed to satisfy the economic and ideological interests that brought the delegates into the process. Therefore, after using all his resources to win the rules vote, there were limits to how much he could afford to fight over the platform. Knowing this, groups felt encouraged to ask for a lot and to refuse any compromises. The result was a series of symbolic victories for the groups that might well have meant little to government policy if Carter had been reelected but that temporarily served the groups' own needs while causing the president some political embarrassments.

White House Draft. Although the Democrats more than made up for it later, the early stages of their platform process were more straightforward than those of the Republicans. Elaine C. Kamarck, executive director of the platform committee, worked with David Rubenstein (Stuart Eizenstat's deputy assistant to the president for domestic affairs and policy) and David Aaron (Zbigniew Brzezinski's deputy

---

[13] See, for example, M. Malbin, "Labor, Business, and Money—A Post-Election Analysis," *National Journal*, March 19, 1977, pp. 412-17; and Malbin, "How Many Go to the Polls," pp. 1840-42.

assistant to the president for national security affairs) to produce a draft platform that was essentially a White House document. The early stages of the process therefore looked more like those of the Democratic party in 1964 or the Republican party in 1972 than like those of the out-party Democrats in either 1972 or 1976.[14]

As a White House document, the draft essentially was a defense of the administration. Policy successes were detailed, failures were laid primarily at the feet of the Nixon and Ford administrations, and commitments for future action generally reiterated legislative or foreign policy initiatives already begun. The document was longer than that of the Republicans (114 pages in final form versus 75), more detailed on programs, and less thematic. Where policies worked to the benefit of specific groups, the benefits were spelled out clearly. For example:

> More women, blacks and Hispanics have been appointed to federal judgeships during the Carter Administration than during all previous Administrations in history.[15]

And:

> In the past four years federal aid to education has increased by 73 percent—the greatest income increase in such a short period in our history. . . . We favor a steady increase in federal support.[16]

These reminders to women, minorities, and teachers barely scratched the surface of the platform's commitments. Public interest lawyers were promised funding for advocating their positions before government agencies.[17] While one section of the platform gave the administration credit for "the most sweeping deregulation in history," feminist organizations were pleased with another that called for "equal pay for work of comparable value," with value to be determined by governmental job classification.[18] The draft went on, offering future programs or reminders of past favors to all of the party's constituency groups.

---

[14] Major differences were to show up later in the process. In 1964 the White House draft essentially was the final document. In 1972 the Republican platform committee made dozens of changes to the draft, but none over the White House's strong objection.

[15] "1980 Democratic Platform Text," *Congressional Quarterly Weekly Report*, August 16, 1980, p. 2405.

[16] Ibid., p. 2399.

[17] Ibid., p. 2394.

[18] Ibid., pp. 2406, 2394.

Two basic reasons explain why the Democratic platform contained more specific promises to identifiable constituency groups than the Republican platform. First, Democrats, at least until 1980, generally were more willing than Republicans to use governmental programs to gain the support of such groups. (In this respect, Senator Dole's desire to use tax credits to gain auto workers' support represents a more "Democratic" approach to politics than that of most of his colleagues in Detroit.) Second, President Carter needed to use specific promises, even more than most Democrats, to get people and groups that felt no deep enthusiasm for his administration to work for his reelection.

The Preconvention Platform Process. Almost all of the major platform developments after the staff draft were shaped decisively by Senator Kennedy's decision to continue contesting the nomination after the primaries had all but sealed his defeat. Kennedy repeatedly justified his decision to remain a candidate by referring to his differences with the administration over domestic policy priorities. Kennedy wanted a commitment to fight unemployment with federal programs, whatever the cost; Carter opposed Kennedy's approach as inflationary and knew that if he gave in, he would face a Republican party that was united in making its approach to inflation a major campaign theme. Kennedy wanted to fight inflation with continued oil and gas price regulations and with wage-price controls; Carter opposed both. Kennedy wanted immediate, comprehensive national health insurance; Carter wanted to phase in a program as the federal budget permitted it.

The first stages of the platform confrontation between Carter and Kennedy took place within weeks of the last primaries. Unlike the Republicans, Democrats schedule their platform committee deliberations during June—after the final primaries but well before the convention. The scheduling stems from the experience of 1972, when party officials felt George McGovern was damaged by the issues debated in platform committee meetings the week before the national convention. (The Nixon-Agnew campaign referred to them as the three A's—acid, amnesty, and abortion.) Because of that experience, Democrats decided to separate the committee's work from the publicity glare surrounding the convention. The tactic was only partly successful. The party succeeded in keeping the 1980 platform committee off the front pages of most newspapers. As a result, some potentially embarrassing issues never were aired during the televised convention coverage. The tactic could not by itself, however, stifle the ongoing battle between Kennedy and Carter. Moreover, groups whose issues transcended that battle learned that if they kept pressing their demands beyond a point that Carter could accept, they could still gain the national convention exposure for themselves that the tactic was meant to prevent.

Because the June meetings were not well publicized, they had little direct effect on the election. They were important primarily for the way they set the stage for the floor fights of August. There is little need, therefore, for us to recount them in the kind of detail given earlier for the Republican platform committee meetings.

The June meetings, held between the seventeenth and twenty-fourth, involved three different sets of working units. First came the drafting subcommittee, which was made up of nine who supported Carter, five who supported Kennedy, and one who was uncommitted, Senator Daniel P. Moynihan of New York. When it finished, the full platform committee was divided into task forces on the economy, energy, human needs, foreign policy, and government operation and reform. Third came the full platform committee.

The drafting subcommittee essentially followed the preliminary draft, but incorporated numerous amendments that were not contested by either candidate. Most prominent among these were dozens of labor amendments offered by John Lyons of the American Federation of Labor–Congress of Industrial Organizations (AFL-CIO), through whose efforts were adopted all of the amendments on which labor could agree. Labor, however, was itself divided on the issues that divided the candidates. All such issues were decided in Carter's favor.

The overriding importance of the Kennedy-Carter split to the platform committee was publicly obvious during the task force and full committee meetings, as White House and campaign committee staff people stationed themselves around the room to give "thumbs up" or "thumbs down" signs before contested votes. On most issues, voting discipline held, and Carter won by votes of between 80 and 90 to about 55. The lines held firm on economic issues. The most serious Carter defections on foreign policy came over an amendment offered by Carter delegate Joe Smith from Oregon, who opposed the administration's decision to deploy the MX missile. Smith's amendment was rejected 69–76.5, but Carter prevailed easily on most other foreign policy issues.

On two task forces, energy and human needs, a number of the Carter delegates acted as issue activists first and as Carter delegates second. The Democrats, like the Republicans, had permitted people to select their own task forces. The results were similar. Feminists and gay activists packed the human needs task force, and those who were most upset about nuclear power gravitated toward energy. Scores of amendments were added without opposition on human needs, but the issues of gay rights and nuclear power were contested by Carter. In both cases, the concessions won by the activists resulted from well-planned, "outsider" lobbying campaigns.

Antinuclear and Gay Activists. Although they might not like to hear it, the antinuclear and gay groups lobbying the Democratic platform committee were remarkably similar in structure and tactics to the antiabortion and Stop-ERA groups at the Republican convention. Their issues differed, but the delegate-selection processes and the strategic needs of the candidates provided all four with opportunities not available to similar groups under older delegate-selection rules.

The Campaign for Safe Energy ran the antinuclear lobbying campaign on a total budget that one group spokesman put at only $100,000. The Boston-based group, run by Douglas Phelps, was an offshoot of the Massachusetts Public Interest Research Group, an organization in the Ralph Nader network of public interest groups. The group began by confronting candidates in the New Hampshire primary at citizen forums around the state. Then, according to Larry Magid, the group's press spokesman:

> After New Hampshire, we made the critical decision to go national. We started with the same kind of candidate encounters in Massachusetts and then followed the primaries, keeping that kind of pressure on the candidates. For example, when George Bush came to Sarasota, Florida, to speak to potential voters, he was greeted by a group from the Campaign for Safe Energy that asked him some follow-up questions to ones that were asked him the week before in Massachusetts. . . . We just kept the pressure up.

Once it became clear that Carter and Reagan would be the nominees, the group turned its attention to the platform. Local supporters showed up at every regional meeting of the platform committee. As delegates to the committee were chosen, group supporters began calling them up, finding out their positions, and sending them material. Since Kennedy supported their position, the effort concentrated on gaining support from Carter delegates. By June, the group had succeeded in persuading some to put the issue ahead of their loyalty to the president.

121

Largely because of the Campaign for Safe Energy's lobbying and the task forces' self-selection process, the energy task force voted 17–11 to overturn the draft platform's support of nuclear power. Replacing it was a call for a moratorium on all new nuclear power plants and "an orderly phase-out" of existing plants "as alternatives are phased in." The 17 votes in the majority included 5 Carter delegates.

Carrie Wasley, a Carter delegate from Minnesota, led the anti-nuclear forces. When she was asked whether she might unknowingly be helping Kennedy, she denied it, saying: "I'm just against nuclear power. Now I can go back to my liberal friends in Minnesota and tell them that the platform really stands for something." [19] Jan Robertson of Mississippi, another antinuclear Carter delegate, took a similar position:

> I guess you could say I am an ideologue. I am interested in ideas and principles and that is why I'm in the Democratic party. That's why I wanted to be on the platform committee. I worked very hard for Jimmy Carter as a field coordinator, but the issue is more important than any candidate.

On the day the issue reached the full platform committee, June 23, President Carter was attending an international energy conference in Venice, where the heads of state issued a joint communiqué endorsing the continued development of nuclear power. Had members of Congress played a role on the Democratic platform committee, they surely would have tried to use their influence to preserve the president's flexibility and save him from a direct embarrassment while he was abroad. There were only four members of Congress on the full committee, however, and even they stayed away most of the time. (The Republicans, in contrast, had eleven senators and representatives serving as chairmen and vice-chairmen of the committee and subcommittees and another nine as regular members. Almost all were active.) Of course, the Democratic members of Congress might not have got very far if they had tried. The odds are so stacked against them in their party's platform process that most see only risks and no gains in extended participation.

Most observers at the meetings expected a closer vote in the full committee on nuclear power than the 17–11 task force margin. Carter might have won, but a victory would have permitted the opposition to file a minority report on an issue that would split

---

[19] "Platform Unit Rejects Carter Plank in Urging Nuclear Phaseout," *Washington Star*, June 23, 1980.

Carter forces in the convention. Although Carter's staff was willing to take that risk on the MX missile, it was not willing on nuclear power. Instead, it agreed to a compromise that called for a moratorium on new plants until questions of safety are resolved. The compromise also committed the party to "retire nuclear power plants in an orderly manner" as renewable sources of energy become available.

Antinuclear delegates hailed the compromise as a victory, but Stuart Eizenstat said the platform would not bind the administration. "We are not writing administration policy here," he said. "The administration's policy is that nuclear power is part of our future. It was the best language we could get."

The platform victory did not satisfy the antinuclear activists. In Magid's eyes, "The platform is only a piece of paper. It is only as valuable as the public discussion it develops." The problem, Magid said, was how to get public discussion and exposure after winning in committee.

> When we went to the platform committee, our expectation was to win a minority report. We didn't think we would win a compromise version of our actual plank. So we came out faced with an interesting dilemma. We were pretty happy with the wording, but were disappointed that the issue didn't come before the convention.

Still hoping for some television coverage, the safe energy group threw its weight behind a minority report on solar power. (See table 4–1, no. 16.) Robert Chlopak, a Campaign for Safe Energy lobbyist in Washington, moved into the office of the Solar Lobby to call delegates and to prepare for a street demonstration slated for August 10, the day before the convention. As in the platform committee, lobbying focused on Carter delegates. By August 10, the groups claimed to have support from more than 1,700 of the convention's 3,331 delegates. Once again, the Carter forces backed off. At a press conference held August 10, Eizenstat said he would support the solar plank.

That still left the groups without a television forum. They asked the Carter staff to permit Representative Edward Markey of Massachusetts, a nuclear power opponent, to address the convention. When the convention managers refused, the safe energy campaign and solar lobby gathered 645 signatures on a petition to nominate Markey as vice-president—almost double the 332 signatures needed. Markey intended to speak about nuclear power and withdraw his name. Once the signatures were obtained, the convention managers decided to let

TABLE 4–1
Democratic Platform: Minority Planks and Their Disposition

1. (K) Kennedy's general economic plank, including wage-price controls and the items in numbers 2, 3, and 4 below. *Rejected, voice vote.*
2. (K) The government will take no fiscal, monetary, or budgetary actions that will have the effect of increasing unemployment. *Adopted, voice vote.*
3. (K) $12 billion antirecession jobs program. *Adopted, voice vote.*
4. (K) The Democratic party will not pursue a policy of high interest rates and unemployment as the means to fight inflation. Preconvention agreement resulted in compromise language *adopted by voice vote.*
5. (K) Opposition to reductions in funding for federal programs whose purpose is to serve "the basic human needs of the most needy." *Accepted by Carter* before convention.
6. (K) Commitment to a single, comprehensive national health insurance bill, instead of the administration's piecemeal approach. *Rejected 1,349–1,573.*
7. Pledge to oppose any change in cost-of-living formulas for social security and other indexed benefits. *Accepted by Carter* before convention.
8. (K) Pledge to introduce legislation next year federalizing welfare costs. *Accepted by Carter* before convention.
9. (K) Guarantee of a job for every American able to work stated as "our single highest domestic priority." *Adopted 1,790.6–1,392.8.*
10. The Democratic party shall withhold financial assistance to candidates who do not support the ERA. Carter opposed. No Kennedy preconvention position. *Adopted, voice vote.*
11. Federal funding for Medicaid abortions. Carter opposed. No Kennedy preconvention position. *Adopted 2,005.2–956.3.*
12. (K) Opposition to giving any federal agency (such as Carter's proposed Energy Mobilization Board) the power to override state or federal environmental, health, or safety laws. *Accepted by Carter* before convention.
13. (K) Repeal of $5.2 billion in various oil industry tax deductions. *Rejected 1,166.2–1,520.3.*
14. (K) Pledge to oppose use of gasoline taxes or oil import fees. *Rejected, voice vote.*
15. (K) Pledge to introduce legislation to reimpose price controls on domestic oil. *Withdrawn* by preconvention agreement.
16. Commitment to spend more money on solar and other renewable forms of energy than on synthetic fuels. Sponsored by the Solar Lobby and Campaign for Safe Energy. *Accepted by Carter* before convention.
17. (K) Moratorium on acquisition by oil companies of coal and solar energy companies. *Rejected, voice vote.*

TABLE 4–1 (continued)

18. (K) Pledge to introduce legislation to give states and Indian tribes the power to veto nuclear waste disposal sites. *Accepted by Carter before convention.*

19. Federal chartering of oil companies. Carter opposed. Not on Kennedy's list of amendments but sponsored by some Kennedy delegates. *Rejected, voice vote.*

20. Opposition to deployment of the MX missile. Sponsored by Carter delegate Joe Smith of Oregon. Carter opposed. No Kennedy position. *Rejected 1,276.6–1,873.9.*

21. Immediate freeze on further testing, deployment, and development of all nuclear weapons during negotiations on strategic arms limitations. Sponsored by Kennedy delegate Theodore Sorensen of New York. Carter opposed. No Kennedy position. *Rejected, voice vote.*

22. (K) Opposition to peacetime registration for the draft. *Preconvention compromise language* retains president's authority to register.

23. (K) Opposition to accelerated development of a land-based MX missile system. *Withdrawn.*

NOTE: (K) indicates minority reports sponsored by Senator Edward Kennedy.
SOURCE: Author.

Markey speak before names were put in nomination. He did, but the speech was ignored.

The story of Gay Vote '80, an organization of gay activists, directly parallels the one just told. Led by Tom Bastow and Mary Spottswood Pou, the organization worked out of Washington, D.C., with a budget of about $100,000. The group worked in four stages: first, to get gays around the country politically involved in the delegate-selection process; second, to raise the issue at candidate forums; third, to make sure gays became delegates; fourth, to lobby the candidates to put gays on the platform committee. Although only four 1976 Democratic delegates and alternates were openly gay, seventy-seven were in 1980. Even more remarkable, six of the seventy-seven ended up on the platform committee.

At the platform committee, gay delegates, like their antinuclear counterparts, were able to work toward a majority by building on solid support from the Kennedy camp and chipping away at Carter supporters. Carter had agreed shortly before the drafting subcommittee began meeting to add the phrase "sexual orientation" to the civil rights plank.[20] The question was whether the gays could also

[20] Statement by President Carter to the Democratic Platform Committee, June 12, 1980, p. 54. Compare "1980 Democratic Platform Text," p. 2404.

win a plank calling for specific legislation and executive orders affecting their position.

Such a plank lost by only four votes in the human needs task force. The stage seemed set for a confrontation in full committee that would permit a minority plank to go forward to the convention. Carter aides offered a compromise that called for "appropriate legislative and Administrative actions" without specifying what they would be.[21] Several of the gay delegates wanted to continue fighting. They, and several top Carter staffers, thought they had the votes either to win or to come close. When they were faced with several strong hints of retaliation by the White House staff, however, a majority of the gay delegates decided to withdraw their proposal without a vote. It was enough for them to have won the first plank in history affirming gay rights. Since the absence of a vote meant there would be no minority report, however, the gays were left without a forum for airing their views on television at the convention. Like the anti–nuclear power people, they tried to gather enough signatures to put up a vice-presidential candidate, but the effort fell short. By any standards, however, Gay Vote '80 won some remarkable victories in the Democratic platform. Its low-budget efforts, and those of the Campaign for Safe Energy, demonstrated the permeability of the process in the clearest possible terms.

Carter-Kennedy Negotiations between June and August. The nuclear power and gay rights issues are useful for illuminating the platform process, but they were essentially sideshows to the main event—the ongoing struggle between Kennedy and Carter. Twenty-three minority reports were filed to the report of the platform committee. Of these, seventeen were Kennedy planks that had produced straight Kennedy-Carter votes in committee. Included were minority planks relating to jobs, wage-price controls, national health insurance, and energy. The six remaining minority reports included ones on solar power, the MX missile, public funding for Medicaid abortions, and a cutoff of party aid to candidates who do not support ERA. (See table 4–1 for a list of the minority reports.)

With twenty-three planks in dispute, the sponsors of the minority reports probably could have extended the convention by several days if they had insisted on roll-call votes for every item. Such delaying tactics also would have improved whatever slight chance Kennedy had to win the nomination. The most favorable convention

21 "1980 Democratic Platform Text," p. 2404.

program for Kennedy would have put the rules vote after the plat-form, which in turn would have been delayed as long as possible to give Kennedy supporters time to lobby. Well aware of this, the pro-Carter convention managers wanted to schedule the rules vote for Monday, the first day of the convention.

Negotiations over scheduling continued until the day before the convention. Kennedy finally accepted a Monday vote on the rules and agreed to hold down the number of platform roll calls. In return, Carter agreed to hold debate on the major economic con-troversies (1–4) during prime time on Tuesday and to let Kennedy address the convention during that debate. Carter also agreed to accept six minority reports without a fight (5, 7, 8, 12, 16, and 18), including ones on solar power and on the proposed Energy Mobiliza-tion Board (12 and 16) that were critical of administration policy. Kennedy withdrew one amendment before the convention (15), with-drew one at the convention after defeat was certain (23), and agreed to language on a third (22) that was consistent with administration policy. Carter also agreed to a rule requiring candidates to issue written statements indicating their reservations to the platform before the convention voted on the nomination. Kennedy wanted the rule because he thought it would help him win over Carter delegates; Carter agreed to it because it could be turned to his advantage after he won the rules fight.

Carter's strategy was made clear by his concessions before and during the convention. Televised floor fights were to be held to a minimum, voice-vote defeats were to be preferred to roll-call defeats, and peace gestures were to be made to Kennedy delegates and dis-gruntled Carter issue activists after the vote on the binding rule. Kennedy's platform strategy was equally clear. Once he lost his bid to put the platform debate before the rules vote, Kennedy knew he had little chance of winning. Moreover, putting the rules vote first meant that it made little sense to prolong the platform debate with endless roll calls. Still, Kennedy was fighting for something more than this one nomination. He genuinely wanted to influence the party's future policies. He also wanted to restore himself as a possible future contender. Both ends were served by his preconvention agreements.

The Floor Fights. As in the platform committee, the major convention floor fights involved interest groups chipping away at Carter dele-gates to form majorities on specific issues. This time, however, the interest groups were some of the biggest in the Democratic party— each one large enough to have its own, independent whip system on the convention floor.[22] The three most important were the AFL-CIO, which had 405 convention delegates (600, according to one labor source, if one counted spouses and close "friends"); the National Education Association (NEA), with 302 delegates, most of whom were among Carter's 1,900; and the National Organization for Women (NOW), which claimed 200 members as delegates and alternates. Added to these were undetermined numbers of union members associated with non-AFL-CIO unions (such as the United Auto Workers or United Mine Workers) and women who identified with the National Women's Political Caucus or other feminist groups without belonging to NOW.[23]

All of Carter's floor defeats came on Tuesday, August 12, the first of two days the platform was before the convention. By prior agreement, Kennedy's major economic planks (minority reports 1–4) were to be presented in a block during prime time. In the afternoon session, minority reports 5, 7, and 8 were accepted by acclamation, and Kennedy's national health insurance plank (no. 6) was defeated in a straightforward vote that saw few Carter defections.

Then came minority report number 9, the general job plank that was seen widely as a test vote for the evening. The AFL-CIO

[22] Convention floors are so confusing, and so filled with rumor and misinformation, that it is impossible to operate effectively on them without both elaborate advance planning and the kinds of connections among delegates, convention floor managers, and candidates that generate floor passes for whips.

[23] Black and Hispanic caucuses also met frequently during the convention but did not play as important a role as they have in the recent past. It was probably a measure of their success that most blacks at the convention acted first as Carter or Kennedy delegates and not as blacks. For the role of minority and other caucuses in recent Democratic party conventions, see Denis G. Sullivan, Jeffrey L. Pressman, Benjamin I. Page, and John L. Lyons, *The Politics of Representation: The Democratic Convention of 1972* (New York: St. Martin's Press, 1979), chap. 3; Denis G. Sullivan, Jeffrey L. Pressman, and F. Christopher Arterton, *Explorations in Convention Decision Making: The Democratic Party in the 1970's* (San Francisco: W. H. Freeman and Co., 1976), chap. 4; and Denis G. Sullivan, Jeffrey L. Pressman, F. Christopher Arterton, Robert Nakamura, and Martha Weinberg, "Candidates, Caucuses, and Issues: The Democratic Convention of 1976" (Paper presented at the 1976 annual meeting of the American Political Science Association), pp. 15-32. For a contrast showing the relatively less important role played by caucuses in the Republican party and the more important role of state delegations, see Denis G. Sullivan, Robert Nakamura, Martha Weinberg, F. Christopher Arterton, and Jeffrey L. Pressman, "Exploring the 1976 Republican Convention: Five Perspectives," *Political Science Quarterly*, vol. 92 (Winter 1977-78), pp. 633-82, esp. pp. 673-82. For the role of the black and Hispanic caucuses in the 1980 Democratic convention, see Ronald Smothers, "Minority Delegates Debate the Uses of the Newly Increased Influence," *New York Times*, August 12, 1980; and Herbert H. Denton, "For Blacks at the Convention, Growing Strength, Less Unity," *Washington Post*, August 13, 1980.

had been split during the year between unions supporting Carter and unions supporting Kennedy. AFL-CIO president Lane Kirkland was determined to show labor's strength at the convention on at least one issue that united all of the federation's unions. He sent notices to all delegates asking them to support the broad jobs plank. Labor's position spurred enough Carter defections to carry the minority report by a 400-vote margin. After the vote, negotiations on the first four Kennedy economic planks moved off stage, and the abortion and ERA planks moved on.

Even before the Democrats reached New York, their platform contained provisions of interest to feminists that were not in the Republican platform. They included support for the Equal Rights Amendment, opposition to state reversals of past ratifications of the ERA, a pledge not to hold any national or regional party meetings in states that have not ratified the amendment, support for similar boycotts by other national organizations, endorsement of the 1973 Supreme Court abortion decision, support for increased federal funds for child-care programs, and a commitment to the principle of equal pay for work of comparable value.

Although leaders of most feminist organizations were pleased with the Democratic platform, they were determined to use the party rules giving men and women equal representation at the convention to push for more. Specifically, they wanted planks supporting Medicaid funds for abortions and withholding party funds and technical campaign assistance from candidates who do not support the ERA. President Carter opposed both.

Despite Carter's opposition, a coalition of feminist organizations lobbied hard for both planks. Eleanor Smeal, president of the National Organization for Women, called them "bottom line" issues for women and warned that if they lost, feminists might sit out the presidential election and support independent John B. Anderson. "We do not feel the commitment level of the past three and a half years has been strong enough to guarantee our support," Smeal said at a press conference.

As late as one day before the convention was to vote on the planks, their supporters did not know whether the Carter forces would fight to hold their delegates on the two issues. Sarah R. Weddington, the White House assistant for women's issues, met with Smeal, Betty Friedan, the NWPC's Iris Mitgang, and others until 4 A.M. in an attempt to persuade them to accept a compromise on party funds. Supporters of the plank were unmoved.

By early afternoon, as it became clear that the NEA was going to urge its Carter delegates to support the minority plank on abortion funds, Carter aides decided not to try to hold their delegates on that issue, but to keep them in line on the party-aid plank. At about the time that word of this decision was reaching the floor, former representative Bella S. Abzug of New York, one of NOW's floor whips, was telling delegates that Kennedy whips had just been told to help them on the party-assistance plank and that many would also help on abortion funding.

Shortly before the vote, NOW vice-president Jane Wells-Schooley of Pennsylvania said that all of the California and New Jersey delegates, more than 90 percent of the Michigan delegates, and more than 75 percent of Pennsylvania's would support the ERA plank, even if Carter held firm in his opposition.

These numbers were known to both sides. Shortly before the vote, the Carter forces decided to accept defeat. "It is obviously difficult to lose on any issue," Weddington said, but when Hamilton Jordan and Tom Donilon, Carter's chief convention strategists, were advised that "it was getting very bitter on the floor, with a lot of divisiveness between people who normally work together," they gave the order to call off the whips.

In his statement of reservations to the platform the next day, Carter reiterated his personal opposition to federal funds for abortions but said nothing about the ERA plank. When asked about this silence at a briefing, Eizenstat said the president felt the matter was within the jurisdiction of the Democratic National Committee (DNC).

While the convention was voting on ERA and abortion, negotiations were moving ahead on the economics planks. As debate on the four planks began, NEA executive director Terry E. Herndon met with Alexander E. Barkan, director of the AFL-CIO's Committee on Political Education, and William D. Ford of Michigan, chairman of the House Education and Labor Subcommittee on Postsecondary Education. At that meeting, which took place in Barkan's sky suite at Madison Square Garden, Herndon agreed to release NEA's 302 delegates on the $12 billion jobs program vote. With several large state delegations already nearly unanimous on the issue, the NEA's decision was enough to put the plank over the top.

After Kennedy's electrifying speech to the convention on the minority planks, the Carter forces bowed to the inevitable. On the advice of House Speaker Thomas P. O'Neill, Jr., of Massachusetts, the convention chairman, they did not insist on roll calls and accepted voice-vote defeats on both the jobs program and a related plank in return for a win on wage and price controls.

That was not the end of the story, however, because of the rule requiring Carter to distribute a statement to the convention about the platform. In his statement, Carter said, "I accept and support the intent" of the amended jobs plank, and added that he would "soon announce an economic program compatible with those aims."[24] Carter again refused, however, to specify a dollar figure or to rely on public service jobs. Instead, he said, his program would involve tax incentives, "public investment programs," and other targeted incentives as well as countercyclical assistance to high-unemployment states. Carter's statement also rejected the view that jobs should "take precedence" over inflation, calling both important.

Lane Kirkland, president of the AFL-CIO, called Carter's statement acceptable, but Jerry Wurf, president of the American Federation of State, County and Municipal Employees (AFL-CIO); William W. Winpisinger, president of the International Association of Machinists (AFL-CIO); and some other key Kennedy delegates said it was not. Carter obviously still had many fences to mend before the fall campaign.

Carter was able to reassert his control over the convention on Wednesday, August 13. Although he had given up a great deal in private negotiations, he lost no votes on the second day of platform debates. All stops were pulled out on the MX missile: Carter sent every delegate a letter pleading his case,[25] and Secretary of Defense Harold Brown led a lobbying effort that included Secretary of State Edmund Muskie and national security adviser Zbigniew Brzezinski. (This was the first time a defense secretary had attended a national convention since 1956.)[26] Kennedy delegates were not impressed, but most Carter delegates were. Joe Smith's minority report failed by 600 votes.

The rest of the convention, from renomination to Carter's wooden acceptance speech, seemed devoted to getting Senator Kennedy to show signs of support for the ticket. Carter's speech was noticeable less for its content than for its plea for Kennedy's support and for its flubs—including a reference to "Hubert Horatio Hornblower, uh, Humphrey" and two sets of boos from the delegates when Brzezinski's name and draft registration were mentioned. About twenty minutes after the acceptance speech, Kennedy finally appeared

---

24 "Carter Supports Minority Plank Ideals," *Congressional Quarterly Weekly Report*, August 16, 1980, p. 2421.

25 See Helen Dewar, "Heavy Lobbying Overwhelms Foes," *Washington Post*, August 14, 1980.

26 Jim Klurfeld, "Mobilizing for the MX," *Newsday*, August 14, 1980, p. 26.

FIGURE 4–1

REAGAN'S LEAD OVER CARTER IN PRECONVENTION AND
POSTCONVENTION POLLS

(in percentage points)

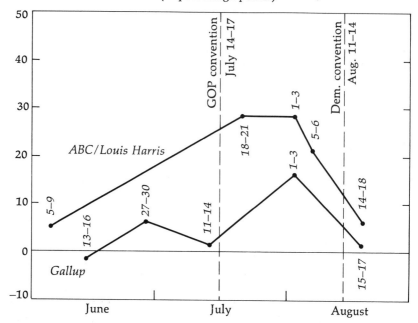

on the podium, shook Carter's hand coolly, and avoided the president's efforts to get him to join in a hands-above-the-head victory photograph.

To almost every neutral observer in New York's Madison Square Garden, the convention had caused Carter as many problems as it had solved. Some Kennedy supporters, far from being mollified, seemed almost contemptuous of the president. Moreover, the president's speech had failed to state a positive theme around which supporters could build up some enthusiasm. He mentioned dozens of specific programs, but the only convention speech with a broad, positive theme was Kennedy's. The observers who were there, however, must either have missed things that came across on the television or paid too much attention to things that did not. Public opinion polls taken immediately afterward showed Carter recouping most of the ground he had lost to Reagan over the summer (see figure 4–1). The constant criticism of Reagan in the speeches by Carter, Kennedy, keynote speaker Morris Udall, and Vice President Walter Mondale clearly had a cumulative impact that had little to do with the subtle tealeaf variations observed by professional convention watchers. Both candidates had weaknesses; the polls put them even. The fall campaign was ready to begin.

Afterthoughts

If we try to step outside the 1980 context to think about platform politics more generally, three lines of inquiry suggest themselves: (1) the effect of the reformed delegate-selection process on the platform, (2) the effect of platform politics on the fall campaign, and (3) the effect of the platform on government policy. Although more work needs to be done on each of them, some preliminary observations seem in order.

Delegate Selection and the Platform Process. Betty Heitman, co-chairman of the Republican National Committee, vented her frustration at the platform committee's handling of the women's rights plank by referring to some of its members in an interview as people "who come in off the streets." [27] Heitman was referring to the difference between the elected officials and state party leaders who used to dominate national conventions and the activists of today.[28] It certainly is important to point out the declining role of elected officials

---

[27] Heitman's full statement, given in an interview with the author, was as follows: "How are you going to end up with good results if you take people who come in off the streets? The people are going to be angry with the Republican party leadership, and we had no control at all. It's an insane process."

[28] Fred Greenstein felt comfortable, as late as 1970, referring to convention delegates as "accredited representatives of the state parties." See F. Greenstein, *The American Party System and the American People*, 2d ed. (Englewood Cliffs, N.J.: Prentice-Hall, 1970), p. 91. Greenstein's assessment has been challenged, however, even as applied to the 1950s and 1960s. According to John Kessel, one of the major differences between primary and caucus states, at least as far back as 1952, was that primary states gave outsider candidates and issue activists a better chance than caucus states to defeat state party leaders. Kessel sees what happened between 1952 and 1976 as more a change in degree than in kind. In 1952, 39 percent of both parties' delegates were chosen in primaries. The percentages "remained fairly stable through 1968. But the Democratic percentage jumped to 65 percent in 1972 and 76 percent in 1976, while the Republican proportion rose to 57 percent in 1972 and 71 percent in 1976." See J. Kessel, *Presidential Campaign Politics: Coalition Strategies and Citizen Response* (Homewood, Ill.: Dorsey Press, 1980), p. 252. Still, this change in degree does seem to amount to a change in kind. The selection process has moved from a system in which activists and candidate enthusiasts once had a chance, through primaries, to become a minority of the delegates to a system in which most delegates are chosen in primaries, caucuses have become wide open and permeable, and these kinds of delegates numerically dominate the conventions.

in postreform conventions, particularly in the Democratic party.[29] It goes too far, however, to refer to the new breed of delegates as people who come in off the streets. Austin Ranney's more precise description is that they are "candidate and issue enthusiasts." [30] Some of the delegates are primarily candidate enthusiasts, some are primarily issue enthusiasts (or interest group representatives), and some are a little of both.[31]

One convention floor whip for Carter made this point succinctly when he was asked to compare the behavior of the delegates on the platform votes with their behavior the previous night on the open-convention rule:

> Last night they were Carter delegates pure and simple. To-day they are Carter delegates who are labor delegates . . . , who are women delegates . . . , who are teacher delegates. It's just not possible for a Carter whip to walk up and down the aisle and say "thumbs up," "thumbs down." [32]

Of course, interest group representatives are nothing new to convention politics. What is new is that their numbers have gone up, and the groups they represent have become more varied as the role of

[29] According to figures compiled by the DNC's Elaine Kamarck, the percentage of elected senators, representatives, and governors attending Democratic national conventions as delegates or alternates has been declining steadily since the McGovern-Fraser Commission.

	Senators (%)	Representatives (%)	Governors (%)
1956	90	33	100
1960	68	45	85
1964	72	46	61
1968	68	39	83
1972	36	15	80
1976	18	15	47
1980	14	15	76

The increase in the percentage of governors at the 1980 convention reflects some modest efforts by a party commission in 1978 to urge states to assign additional at-large seats to elected officials, but most of these were used by party officers instead of elected officials. See M. Malbin, "Democratic Party Rules Are Made to Be Broken," *National Journal*, August 23, 1981, p. 1388.

[30] Austin Ranney, *Curing the Mischiefs of Faction: Party Reform in America* (Berkeley, Calif.: University of California Press, 1975), pp. 152-60; and A. Ranney, "The Political Parties: Reform and Decline," in Anthony King, ed., *The New American Political System* (Washington, D.C.: American Enterprise Institute, 1978), p. 234.

[31] One implication of this for the future is that the present delegate-selection process would be at least as likely in a multiballot convention, where binding rules do not apply, to produce brokering among interest groups as among candidates.

[32] Christopher Buchanan, "Loser Kennedy Leaves Imprint on 1980 Platform," *Congressional Quarterly Weekly Report*, August 16, 1980, p. 2363.

elected officials has declined. Once a minority, the activists now seem to dominate the conventions. Once limited to the major economic and social issues, groups now come to conventions to press virtually every divisive issue on the government's potential agenda. Indeed, the rise of activists and decline of elected officials go hand in hand. Candidates depend on local activist groups and reward the groups by making members convention delegates, precisely because state and local elected officials cannot deliver the vote in a primary.

With the changing composition of the convention comes a new attitude on the part of the delegates toward the platform. Most state or local elected officials who come to conventions do so for reasons that relate primarily to state and local politics and only tangentially to national policy. Most members of Congress are deeply interested in the policies in the platform, but their role as legislators trains them to think in terms of compromising with the person who may be their president.

Interest or issue group representatives are different from both state officials and members of Congress. Unlike state officials, they become delegates precisely because they want something from federal policy. Unlike members of Congress, however, the internal needs of their organizations, as well as their own individual wishes, lead them to ask for as much as they can get. To them, the platform is not a document for winning votes in the fall, but a bargaining chip to be used in future policy negotiations. When looked at in this way, it seems logical to expect that whatever they win, they should push for more. If they ask for more than they can get, no harm is done. Economic groups can always pull back to consolidate their position, as the AFL-CIO did on jobs after Carter's statement on the platform. The social issue groups have even less reason to be concerned. These groups depend on publicity to help build up their constituencies. Unless faced with a direct threat of retaliation, as the gays were in the Democratic platform committee, it may well be better for them to be defeated on national television than to accept a compromise quietly.

These dynamics should help explain why Stuart Eizenstat, in a speech before the National Press Club on December 4, 1980, called the platform "the sum total of the maximum demands of every group." There can be no doubt that the nomination process and rules affect who becomes a delegate, the nature of the delegates affects the platform process, and the process affects the substance. To put it bluntly, the delegate-selection process puts issue groups in a position to win concessions that alter the platform by making it both more

135

explicit and more extreme. To some extent, there is nothing new about the observation that convention delegates may be more extreme on the issues than the voters to whom candidates and party leaders would like the platform to appeal.[33] What is new is the extent to which the activists seem able to determine the convention's issue agenda. The result is a platform that may be far removed from the one on which the candidate ideally would like to run. The question is, What difference does this make to the fall campaign and to policy?

The Platform and the Fall Campaign. The fact that issue groups can win concessions candidates do not like does not settle what the effect of the platform may be. Politically, the concessions are a two-edged sword. The campaign finance law's limitations on general election spending by presidential candidates increase the importance of the groups' organizational and political resources for the fall. To the extent, therefore, that a candidate depends on the groups for grass-roots volunteer campaigning, the concessions they win may help the campaign indirectly by motivating volunteers.[34]

---

[33] Herbert McCloskey et al. showed in 1960 that convention delegates were more polarized on the issues than voters. See Herbert McCloskey, Paul J. Hoffman, and Rosemary O'Hara, "Issue Conflict and Consensus among Party Leaders and Followers," *American Political Science Review*, vol. 54 (June 1960), pp. 406-29. Jeane J. Kirkpatrick made a similar point in her survey of the 1972 Democratic and Republican conventions, in which she found the opinions of Democratic voters to be closer to those of Republican than of Democratic delegates on several key issues. See J. Kirkpatrick, *The New Presidential Elite* (New York: Basic Books, 1976), pp. 281-347, and "Representation in American Conventions," *British Journal of Political Science*, vol. 5, no. 3 (1975), pp. 265-322. Everett Carll Ladd, Jr., reports on similar research for 1976 in *Where Have All the Voters Gone? The Fracturing of America's Political Parties* (New York: Norton, 1978), p. 65.

[34] Whether the groups prove helpful in fact may be another question. NOW and the Campaign for Safe Energy did little for Carter in the fall, but the Gay Activist Alliance was of some help. Labor, which spent an estimated $11 million in unreported "soft money" on Carter's behalf in 1976, matched that effort financially in 1980 but was unable to match its 1976 enthusiasm. (For labor in 1976, see Malbin, "Labor, Business, and Money," pp. 412-17. For labor in 1980, see James W. Singer, "Unions Hard at Work for Carter's Reelection," *National Journal*, November 1, 1980, pp. 1836-39.

The Republican party was able to liberate itself somewhat in 1980 from depending on issue groups for volunteers. At the joint request of DNC chairman John White and RNC chairman Bill Brock, Congress amended the campaign finance laws in 1979 to permit state and local parties to raise and spend unlimited amounts, as long as they went toward using volunteers to promote slates of candidates. The Republicans managed to raise about $8 million and use about 800,000 volunteers under this provision in 1980. The Democrats, in contrast, spent virtually nothing on these activities and could barely raise the $4.6 million the law allowed the DNC to spend directly on President Carter's

On the other hand, the same concessions may well be counter-productive to the candidate's efforts to win support from undecided voters, ticket splitters, or independents. In 1980, as Carter and Reagan both knew, these people were worried about inflation and were willing to control public spending to fight it. In other words, they would have rejected the Kennedy jobs plank.[35] At the same time, they rejected the extreme positions taken by the groups on both left and right on social issues.[36] Thus, Betty Heitman's frustration

---

behalf. See Malbin, "How Many Go to the Polls," p. 1840; and Malbin, "The Republican Revival," pp. 85-88.

[35] The opinions of the voters on the relative importance given to jobs and inflation showed up repeatedly in 1980 surveys. For example, the CBS News/ New York Times poll of September 10-14 showed that 61 percent of all probable voters nationally ranked inflation as a more important problem than unemployment, whereas only 24 percent said the reverse. CBS News and the New York Times found similar results in exit polls of Democratic primary voters. For example, in June 3 surveys, 40 percent of New Jersey Democrats ranked inflation as the top issue; 30 percent said jobs. For Ohio, the numbers were 39 percent inflation, 39 percent jobs. For California, 47 per cent inflation, 26 percent jobs. Thus, even Democratic primary voters in states with high unemployment were unwilling to rank jobs ahead of inflation, as the convention delegates did when they adopted the general jobs plank (table 4-1, no. 9).

[36] On the Equal Rights Amendment, a CBS News/New York Times survey of August 2-7 found 48 percent of all registered voters in favor of ERA and 42 percent opposed. Registered Republican voters split 36 percent in favor and 55 percent against, whereas a July CBS News/New York Times poll of the Republican delegates showed only 28 percent support for the amendment. Registered Democrats favored the amendment 55 to 36 percent. No poll data are available on Democratic convention delegates' opinions on ERA, but this observer would be surprised if support fell below 95 percent.

On abortion, the Republican platform committee's strong support of a constitutional amendment prohibiting abortions conflicted with the position not only of registered Republican voters, but of Republican convention delegates. According to a CBS News/New York Times poll, 36 percent of the male Republican delegates favored an amendment while 49 percent opposed; women were 29 to 56 percent against. See Warren J. Mitofsky and Martin Plissner, "The Making of the Delegates, 1968-1980," Public Opinion (October/November 1980), pp. 37-43.

Opinions of the general public on abortion have proved difficult to tap. A CBS News/New York Times survey on August 2-7 discovered that percentages varied with the wording of the question. Asked whether there should be an amendment prohibiting abortions, 30 percent of registered Republicans said yes, and 61 percent said no. Democrats answered 33 percent yes and 62 percent no. All registered voters split 30-62 percent. When asked whether there should be an amendment protecting the life of the unborn child, however, registered Republicans split 44-44 percent, Democrats were in favor 54-37 percent, and all registered voters were in favor 48-41 percent.

According to these results, Democrats seem more antiabortion than Republicans, particularly with the pro-life wording of the question. This reverses the positions of the convention delegates. Moreover, although the GOP delegates were more pro-life than GOP voters, even they did not seem to favor the

with the platform process was the expression of a political professional who saw that it favored positions that would be viewed skeptically by the swing voters who decide elections. The obvious logical strategy for candidates in the fall, therefore, is to go back to the basic themes they had hoped the platform would stress, while keeping silent in public about the planks that please the activist volunteers.

John Kessel's research on the 1972 platform indicates that this is exactly what happens. According to Kessel, platforms and convention acceptance speeches more closely resemble inaugural addresses and State of the Union messages in content than fall campaign speeches.[37] He explains this by differentiating the nomination and general election "seasons" and describing the platform as a product of nomination politics. Our analysis suggests a different explanation. The platform seems to be made up of a draft that is written with an eye toward the general election but that gets amended by constituencies vital to the nomination. Both parts, the draft and the amendments, are important to the general election. The original draft suggests themes that will be distilled in simplified form in campaign speeches. The amendments are not in the campaign speeches because they are not the candidate's own themes and because they may cause problems with undecided voters. They may nonetheless be useful to the fall volunteer effort.

Whether draft or amendment, the disparity between the platform and campaign speeches may have as much to do with the audience as with any difference between the nomination and election "seasons." Platforms are concerned with the kind of specific policy details that the Washington issue networks know and care about. To the extent these networks matter for the fall, the platform matters. Since most voters, however, operate on a broader level,[38] it does not seem sur-

---

amendment that was overwhelmingily endorsed by the platform committee.

No comparable figures on abortion are available for Democratic convention delegates. Suffice it to say that pro-life Democrats were a small minority at the convention, nowhere near the 33 percent or 54 percent figures suggested for registered Democrats by the CBS News/New York Times questions. The issue the convention actually faced was public funding of abortion. More than two-thirds of the delegates favored public funding, whereas a July 8-9 NBC/Associated Press poll showed all likely voters opposed by 43-47 percent.

[37] John H. Kessel, "The Seasons of Presidential Politics," *Social Science Quarterly*, vol. 58 (December 1977), pp. 418-35.

[38] The CBS News/New York Times poll of August 2-7 asked people to identify the Republican platform's position on the ERA. Despite all the publicity, only 1 percent of the registered voters and 2 percent of the Republicans gave the right answer, that it took no position. Nineteen percent of the registered voters thought the platform favored ERA, 43 percent thought it was opposed, and 37 percent said they did not know.

prising to find campaign speeches, in both the primaries and the general election, pitched more to that level than to one more appropriate for Washington.

Platform and Public Policy. Although Kessel's attempt to remove the platform from the fall campaign seems unpersuasive, the connection he found between platforms and the early speeches of a presidential term are important. The conventional writing on the subject compares platforms to European party manifestoes and tends to dismiss platforms as meaningless documents.[39] Kessel's research, on the other hand, confirms Gerald Pomper's, which shows that most platform pledges are indeed fulfilled.[40]

The fact that people fight over platforms and that their pledges generally are fulfilled should be enough to dispel the myth that they are unimportant. Still, that does not tell us *how* the pledges become policy. When conventions were dominated by elected officials, perhaps promises made by elected officials to each other created presumptions of future action, particularly since these promises tended to build on the officials' past behavior in office. But how and why does the process continue to work in a postreform era?

The answer seems straightforward when the platform is an incumbent's. Despite the many amendments forced by issue activists, the bulk of the platform remains a presidential document, involving promises made by a president who is building incrementally on actions he took during his first term.

What about the out-party? Here we begin to see the importance of the generally overlooked role of Congress and the Washington issue networks in formulating the original draft. Republicans rely heavily on members of Congress and their staffs; Democrats draw just as heavily on congressional staff, but without the members. In both cases, the platform drafts are essentially congressional docu-

[39] See, for example, P. Herring, *The Politics of Democracy*, 2d ed. (New York: Norton, 1965), p. 230; M. Ostrogorski, *Democracy and the Organization of Political Parties*, vol. 2 (Garden City, N.Y.: Doubleday, 1964), pp. 138-39; David Truman, *The Governmental Process* (New York: Knopf, 1951), pp. 282-83; American Political Science Association, Committee on Political Parties, "Toward a More Responsible Two-Party System," *American Political Science Review*, vol. 44 (September 1950), supplement. The view of platforms expressed in these works is not far removed from the view held by Democrats today who favor midterm party conferences and the rule requiring candidates to state their views on the platform before the convention votes on the nomination.

[40] Gerald M. Pomper with Susan S. Lederman, *Elections in America: Control and Influence in Democratic Politics*, 2d ed. (New York: Longmans, 1980), chap. 8.

ments, supplemented by other elements of the quasi-permanent Washington issue networks.[41]

The importance of Congress to the process was well understood in the 1950s and 1960s, when senators were the most likely nominees. Congress remained just as central in 1976 and 1980, however, when the out-party nominated Washington outsiders. In both years, the outsiders were weak on specifics and had to rely on the networks that wrote the platform to fill them in.

The issue networks' and Congress's "education" of the candidate through the platform process may also be crucial to the president's subsequent administration. We know from Paul Light's work that a president's first year is decisively important to any policy successes he may achieve in subsequent years.[42] Any president who wants to get much out of Congress has to "hit the ground running." About the only way he can do that, particularly if he is an outsider, is to turn to the same networks that helped develop his platform. Some congressional staff aides who worked on the draft will be brought into the administration, and the ideas of others will be adopted by the administration more indirectly. Outside appointees will bring ideas of their own, of course, but the commitments worked out six months before will not be forgotten. If they look as if they may be, the same networks that developed them will be around to remind people.

These observations help explain why groups are willing to fight for platform planks opposed by the candidate. Having such planks can help a group achieve its policy objectives in at least two different ways. If the group's presence at a convention, and therefore its ability to win concessions, is based on its campaign activities, those same activities in the fall may result in some administration appointments. If the candidate's reluctance to endorse the group's plank is based on electoral tactics rather than substance, an appointment might settle the issue. If the group fails to gain such power through appointments, however, or if the president remains dubious for substantive reasons, the platform's promises still retain some influence. Virtually every group able to win a plank will have con-

---

[41] For the importance of technically competent, specialized issue networks to policy formation, see Hugh Heclo, "Issue Networks and the Executive Establishment," in King, New American Political System, pp. 87-124. For the role of congressional staffs within these networks, see M. Malbin, Unelected Representatives: Congressional Staff and the Future of Representative Government (New York: Basic Books, 1980).

[42] Paul Light, "The President's Agenda: Notes on the Timing of Domestic Choice," Presidential Studies Quarterly, vol. 11. no. 1 (Winter 1981), pp. 67-81.

gressional allies. Presidents may choose not to honor a pledge, but doing so will mean alienating somebody in Congress. Presidents may decide to go back on the pledge anyway, but the cost is real, even when small. To give just one example, Senator Moynihan's 1980 decision to remain uncommitted was connected in part to what he saw as Carter's failure to live up to platform pledges on foreign policy, welfare reform, and tuition tax credits.

Platforms thus are a good deal more than empty rhetorical straws tossed out randomly to catch the currents of a passing political wind. They are part of an ongoing process of government. The delegate-selection rules may well make them permeable to influence by fringe groups, but so, to a lesser degree, is Congress. Making members of Congress even more prominent may well decrease the fringe groups' role, and for that reason politicians may well want to change delegate-selection rules accordingly.[43] Whatever they may decide, we must conclude that Congress's present role has been underestimated and misunderstood. If Congress and the issue networks are truly crucial to the platform, the platform crucial to a new administration's first year, and the first year crucial to what follows, then despite all of the well-known signs of disunity and fractionalization that need not be recounted here, the parties may nonetheless remain more important across the branches than most people realize.

---

[43] For some arguments in favor of increasing the role of elected officials at conventions, see Jeane J. Kirkpatrick, Michael J. Malbin, Thomas E. Mann, Howard R. Penniman, and Austin Ranney, *The Presidential Nominating Process: Can It Be Improved?* (Washington, D.C.: American Enterprise Institute, 1980), pp. 15-27.

5

The Campaign and the Issues

Albert R. Hunt

The Beginning: Opportunities, Problems, and Strategies

Labor Day, 1980: Ronald Reagan addresses a working-class crowd in Hudson County, New Jersey, and then goes to Detroit to see some unemployed workers. Jimmy Carter starts at a Tuscumbia, Alabama, picnic and then comes back to the White House for a bash with labor leaders. For the past four months, it has been clear that President Carter will be the Democratic presidential nominee and Ronald Reagan will be his Republican opponent. They both have campaigned for months with an eye to the November election.

Still, if Labor Day is not the de facto kickoff of the general election, it is when the contest starts to take focus. Circumstances will cause strategic adjustments over the next nine weeks, but the preliminary skirmishing is over. On September 1, both candidates emphasize the economy. That is a natural Labor Day message; with unemployment at 7.5 percent and double-digit inflation and interest rates, it is also an unavoidable one. Still, their respective launching pads are revealing. Jimmy Carter, the first authentic southern president in more than one hundred years, is back home fighting to protect his base. Ronald Reagan, the champion of right-wing Republicanism for the past fourteen years, is reaching out to blue-collar Democrats. More than any polls or political experts, this juxtaposition underscores the challenger's early edge.

The Republicans are unified, the Democrats divided. Reagan has a solid base—ideologically among conservatives, geographically in the West. Carter's base is weaker than that of any incumbent president since Herbert Hoover in 1932. Economic hardship at home and the perceived loss of U.S. prestige abroad are fueling a growing conservatism, or at least a hankering for change. Yet on Labor Day, the moods of the two camps, curiously, do not mirror this political picture. The Carter high command is confident, even smug and boastful; campaign chairman Robert Strauss and Patrick Caddell, the president's

142

omnipresent poll taker, are eager to bet "serious money" on Carter's reelection. On the other side, the Reaganites are visibly nervous.

Until the last few weeks, the Republicans were brimming with optimism. Reagan has spent months successfully mending fences with party moderates. The GOP nominee weathered an ill-advised attempt to pick former president Gerald Ford as his running mate at the July convention and won plaudits for selecting former Central Intelligence Agency director George Bush instead. The convention was a tour de force for Reagan, as he overcame divisive struggles over the Equal Rights Amendment and abortion with an eloquent acceptance speech that touched all the right political bases. The Reagan-Bush ticket enjoyed a massive lead in the midsummer polls.

Although this huge bulge was artificial, the Reagan strategists nevertheless felt they were in excellent shape. In terms of electoral votes, they felt assured of more than half the 270 needed to win even before the campaign began. This base included almost all of the West plus such GOP strongholds as Indiana and New Hampshire. Further, they saw appealing opportunities in the industrial heartland, with states such as Ohio and Michigan suffering an economic depression. The main focus of the campaign would be the industrial belt, starting in New Jersey and Pennsylvania and going to Illinois. Jimmy Carter's South looked promising, too. In August, the Reagan command was confident it could keep Virginia in the GOP column and pick up Texas and Mississippi and perhaps Florida and Louisiana as well.

Reagan had no intention of emulating the right-wing strategy embraced by his original political mentor, Senator Barry Goldwater, in 1964. In a private memorandum to the candidate months earlier, Richard Wirthlin, the campaign's pollster and chief strategist, warned: "We can expect Ronald Reagan to be pictured as a simplistic and untried lightweight (dumb), a person who consciously misuses facts to overblow his own record (deceptive) and, if president, one who would be too anxious to engage our country in a nuclear holocaust (dangerous)." Wirthlin then also warned about the "extreme right" among Reagan backers, which, he said, was becoming "more shrill and more visible," and laid out a plan to expand the candidate's base and largely to ignore these elements.

Accordingly, at the convention the campaign launched the "Great American Team," consisting of well-known Republican leaders such as Gerald Ford and Henry Kissinger plus scores of governors, senators, congressmen, and other GOP establishment leaders. This silly-sounding concept was aimed at enhancing the candidate's credibility and stature, especially in foreign affairs, and at providing a vehicle for tough surrogate attacks on the Carter presidency. William Timmons, the campaign's political director, told the *Wall Street Journal*, "We will charge the Carter administration is dumb, dangerous and deceitful," in a deliberate counter to the anticipated Carter charges. Carter's record, particularly on the economy, would clearly be the focus of this effort.[1] "The failed presidency and President Carter's lack of leadership will be the major theme of the campaign," Reagan staff chief Edwin Meese told the *Washington Post*.[2]

Soon, however, Reagan discovered the difference between a primary aspirant and a presidential candidate in the general election. It is like the difference between Broadway and New Haven or between the Boston Red Sox and the Winston-Salem (North Carolina) Red Sox. In primaries, a minor gaffe or careless statement usually merits only a paragraph or two in news accounts and maybe a passing reference on television; a major mistake is usually only a one- or two-day story. Yet the general election candidate faces intense scrutiny. Every speech is examined for nuances; contradiction and conflicts are magnified, and mistakes or misstatements can plague a candidate for days, even weeks.

Reagan Gaffes. Reagan's introduction to the *Realpolitik* of the general election began with the decision to send running mate George Bush to China. Campaign chairman William Casey thought this would underscore the foreign policy credentials of Bush, a former envoy to China, and dilute Reagan's longstanding pro-Taiwan and anti-China position. On August 16, however, as Reagan sent Bush off, the former California governor reiterated his intention to reestablish official governmental relations with Taiwan. The upshot: the Bush trip was an unmitigated disaster because of an especially frosty Chinese reception. Reagan spent much of the next week backing and filling and coming across as inept and inexperienced.

Next, in a speech to the Veterans of Foreign Wars, Reagan himself overshadowed the strong defense message he had hoped to convey when, in passing, he called the Vietnam war a noble cause. Reagan was stepping on his own themes with such deeds, a common, though politically painful, affliction of new presidential candidates.

By now the Republican contender was reeling. On August 20, Lou Cannon began his dispatch in the *Washington Post*: "Ronald Rea-

---

[1] James M. Perry and Albert R. Hunt, "Reagan Plan Is to Make Carter the Issue, Stress Large Industrial States," *Wall Street Journal*, July 14, 1980.

[2] Lou Cannon and David S. Broder, "Reagan to Attack 'Failed Presidency,'" *Washington Post*, July 19, 1980.

gan campaigned today in gloomy weather, which matched some of the omens for his candidacy."[3] Cannon is the most experienced Reagan-watcher in the press corps; he has covered Reagan since 1966, has written one of the best books on the Californian, and has superb sources within the Reagan inner circle. Thus when Lou Cannon says the campaign is in trouble, other members of the media—most important the powerful television networks—often follow his lead.

A week later in the *Washington Post*, Robert Kaiser, who presented the most innovative and thorough analysis of media coverage of the campaign, noted the negative press for Reagan. "The consequences of those rocky 10 days could be devastating for Reagan or they could disappear entirely before November," Kaiser wrote. "All that can be said with confidence now is that Reagan squandered the initiative and revived the one issue that probably can hurt him most—his own plausibility as a president—during the opening days of the campaign season."[4]

Other apparent blunders followed. After Reagan charged that the Carter administration had plunged the country into a "severe depression," an adviser later admitted that the economy was really only in a recession. John Chancellor started the NBC "Nightly News" that evening with talk of another Reagan gaffe.[5] Then at a press conference before an address to religious fundamentalists in Dallas, Reagan acknowledged that he had doubts about the theory of evolution. (This prompted one Democrat to suggest that they grew out of Reagan's experience costarring with a chimpanzee in *Bedtime for Bonzo*.) Thus it was not surprising when on September 1 pollster Louis Harris reported that his latest survey indicated "worry about Reagan's extemporaneous remarks increasing." Reagan insiders attributed most of this to the "shakedown cruise." Early appearances before right-wing groups, they claimed, would not be repeated. "We want to offer a healthy dose of reaffirmation early on to our base constituency," said James Brady, the Reagan research director. "This will make it easier to spend the rest of the campaign reaching out to labor and others without offending this base."

Over the Labor Day weekend, though, top Reagan strategists were apprehensive. Top officials gathered with the candidate at his temporary Virginia home to evaluate the inauspicious start. It wasn't a very productive session, and some top aides left discouraged.

[3] Lou Cannon, "A Day of Gloomy Omens," *Washington Post*, August 20, 1980.
[4] Robert Kaiser, "Reagan's First 10 Days: A Rocky Lesson in the Mass Media," *Washington Post*, August 28, 1980.
[5] John Chancellor, NBC "Nightly News," August 27, 1980.

"I have this terrible feeling we're about to snatch defeat right from the jaws of victory," lamented one.

The Summer: The Democrats. This was the view from the Carter camp, too. "We'll win because Jimmy Carter is the luckiest politician in America," ventured Carter media consultant Greg Schneiders during the president's political doldrums that summer. This notion—that luck was essential—was an article of faith among the Carterites; after all, they had watched the obscure Georgia governor startle the political experts four years earlier and defy the conventional wisdom again in 1980 by turning back the challenge of Senator Edward M. Kennedy (Democrat, Massachusetts).

To be sure, Carter needed lots of luck this time. The primary fight with Kennedy was bitterly divisive. The public, which had rallied to the Carter cause after the illegal seizure of fifty-two Americans in Iran (actually sixty-six hostages were initially seized, but fourteen were released), was growing impatient as the crisis reached its tenth month without resolution. Billy Carter's questionable dealings with the radical anti-Israeli Libyan regime commanded headlines over the summer. Most important, the economic issue, which the Democrats had dominated since the depression of the early 1930s, was cutting against the incumbent; Jimmy Carter was the first Democratic president in this century to seek reelection in the midst of a recession produced in his own administration. These problems affected all the major elements of the Democrats' constituency: labor, liberals, Jews, and minorities. Even where Carter was much preferred, such as among blacks, there was little enthusiasm.

Yet top Carter aides remained optimistic. Before the Democratic convention, Pat Caddell outlined how Carter would win reelection: "For one, never underestimate the powers of incumbency," he mused over a long summer lunch. "We learned in 1976 that the incumbency is like an 800-pound gorilla, and we'll use it better than Ford did." He acknowledged Carter's problems were severe but maintained that there were as many political pluses: "He still scores pretty well on trust and nobody believes Jimmy Carter is going to blow up the world. The economy is a problem but our data show people believe the economy is getting better. If that perception holds, we'll be in good shape."

Caddell also speculated that Jimmy Carter himself believed the timing of the economic conditions would prove propitious. "He thinks inflation, which was dominant in the primaries, was better to have up front running against Kennedy, who had weaknesses on that score," Caddell said, recalling a conversation with the president a few days earlier. "Now with unemployment rising, Reagan is less able than Kennedy to capitalize on that." Moreover, the president's pollster argued, the press was "enormously overstating Reagan's draw with blue-collar Democrats. It didn't show up in the primaries like Illinois and Wisconsin and we don't see it in our surveys." Caddell believed that working-class suburban Catholics probably held the key to the election and that most of them would stick with their Democratic leanings.[6]

Although some presidential aides talked about a positive pitch, the Carter effort would mainly be a negative, anti-Reagan campaign. One top White House aide suggested the campaign message would be: "Why throw this bum out who has some experience for a bum with no experience?" And playing on Carter's 1976 autobiography, *Why Not the Best?*, another strategist said this year's theme would be, "At least he's not the worst." At the Democratic convention, Carter's media specialist, Gerald Rafshoon, plastered the anticipated themes on his hotel room wall. Under the rubric "anti-Reagan spots" these slogans included: "He's not acting, he means it," "Empty Oval Office," and "Places he would attack." Separately, Caddell was reassuring nervous Democratic politicians that Reagan's lead in the polls was deceptive because the GOP candidate's "acceptability threshold" —which purports to measure how the public envisions Reagan as president—was very negative. "After doing a lot of in-depth work on Reagan, I feel much better running against him," Caddell said. "There's so much to work with, when you look at the data you just salivate."[7]

The particulars spanned Reagan's opposition to Medicare fifteen years earlier, his age-old reservations about social security and criticism of the minimum wage, his ties to fat-cat businessmen, and, most of all, the charge that he was a dangerous warmonger whose frequent calls for U.S. intervention (such as his proposal months ago to blockade Cuba in retaliation for the Soviet invasion of Afghanistan) would be perilous in the nuclear age.

Given a mercurial and cynical electorate, the Carter aides contended, it was not unusual for the incumbent to trail badly in early polls. On the state level during the past few years, they noted, Democratic governors Brendan Byrne of New Jersey, Hugh Carey of

[6] Personal interview. Where not otherwise documented, the direct quotations given in the text are taken from interviews given to the author during the campaign.
[7] James M. Perry and Albert R. Hunt, "Carter Plans to Win by Depicting Reagan as Shallow, Dangerous," *Wall Street Journal*, August 14, 1980.

New York, and Jerry Brown of California had all come from behind to win decisive reelections when the focus shifted to the challenger. They also saw a parallel to 1976, when Jerry Ford almost overcame a massive deficit to overtake Jimmy Carter. "We have a better candidate than Ford," argued Rafshoon. "That's the extra three points we need to win."[8]

To understand Reagan better, campaign chief Hamilton Jordan met, over the summer, with two veteran California Democrats: state treasurer Jesse Unruh, who lost the 1970 gubernatorial race to Reagan, and Bob Morretti, the Democratic assembly leader during the second Reagan term. They warned Jordan not to underestimate Reagan, that he possessed a unique talent for understanding and appealing to the public mood even if he did seem schmaltzy to politicians. Similar advice came from Les Francis, who a few months later became the campaign's political director. Francis, a Californian who knew Reagan's appeal firsthand, in a private memo to Jordan cautioned: "While Reagan may be vulnerable on some points . . . and negative media may have some limited value . . . , for us to assume that an anti-Reagan campaign . . . will win this election is—I believe—totally in error. Most of the people around Reagan are competent and tough. He (Reagan) may not be an intellectual, but he is no dummy."

Although the quartet of top Carter aides—Jordan, Caddell, Rafshoon, and press secretary Jody Powell—listened to such advice, they were never really able to accept it. They simply could not imagine that the voters would elect Ronald Reagan as president of the United States.

In terms of electoral votes, the Carter strategy was clear. Despite the sour economy, they felt they could win most of the major industrial states Carter carried in 1976, although Ohio would be tough. They expected some defections in the South—Texas and Florida, the two biggest states in the region, were particularly worrisome—but Jordan repeatedly claimed that that region would not turn its back on its first native-son president in this century. Still, to offset a few likely defections from the 1976 column, they needed to win a handful of states that Ford had carried four years earlier. Three big states—Michigan, New Jersey, and Illinois—were rated possibilities, as were a handful of smaller states in New England (Maine and Connecticut) and the Northwest (Oregon and Washington).

There was some disagreement over how actively the president should campaign. "We can't have him running around the country

---

[8] Ibid.

looking like a candidate for sheriff," argued proponents of a more "presidential" look. Others, however, worried that after Carter's refusal to campaign in the primaries, using the hostages as an excuse, a "Rose Garden" strategy would look too calculated. Thus they settled on a mix: in the early stages Carter would make frequent "presidential forays" around the country for "town meetings," a format in which he excelled, and symbolic bill-signing ceremonies but would still spend most of his time at the White House in hopes of appearing "presidential."

The Anderson Factor. At this stage, independent candidate John Anderson was a major worry for the White House. One on one, Caddell argued over the summer, Carter led Reagan in electoral votes about 2½ to 1, but "when you toss Anderson in, the picture totally flip-flops. In almost all the major states Anderson hurts us more than Reagan." By late summer it was plain that Anderson would not simply disappear, as the White House had earlier dreamed.

Still, Hamilton Jordan argued, Anderson would follow the fate of most third-party candidates and would plummet to 6 to 8 percent in the public opinion polls—down from 15 to 20 percent—by mid-September. Thus at the August Democratic convention, Anderson was never mentioned, and Carter, in his acceptance speech, directed all his fire at Reagan. By Labor Day the Carter camp claimed its polls showed that Anderson was "dropping like a rock."

The Campaign's First Phase

The Klan Flap. That day Reagan gave the White House even more cause for confidence. The GOP nominee was off to a good start; with the Statue of Liberty as a backdrop, the Hudson County speech was a natural for the evening television news. In Michigan, he was accompanied enthusiastically by that state's popular moderate governor, William Milliken, with unemployed steel and auto workers at a backyard barbecue and at the Michigan state fair in the evening. At the fair, however, Reagan spotted a heckler wearing a Carter mask. He immediately contrasted his appearance in the heavily Democratic areas of Michigan with that of the president who, he charged, was "opening his campaign in the city [Tuscumbia, Alabama] that gave birth to and is the parent body of the Ku Klux Klan." Although this was too late to make the nightly TV newscasts, the crowd instantly gasped at the remark, and reporters peppered defensive Reagan aides with questions.

The backdrop was that Reagan was smarting over a recent effort by Carter's secretary of health and human resources, Patricia Harris, to link the GOP nominee with the Klan. One branch of the Klan had endorsed the Republican party platform, but Reagan immediately disavowed any support from this white-supremacist organization, and it was generally agreed that Harris's comments were a cheap shot. Moreover, Tuscumbia was neither the birthplace nor the main head-quarters of the Klan.

The next day, campaigning in Missouri, Carter seized on this latest Reagan mishap. Encouraging reporters to ask about the incident, the president was righteously indignant: "Anybody who resorts to slurs and innuendoes against a whole region of the country based on a false statement and a false premise isn't doing the South or our nation a good service."

In Detroit the same day Reagan and top aides huddled for hours to mend the damage. Finally, they released a two-and-a-half page statement expressing "regret" over any unintended slurs but then accusing the Democrats of having raised the Klan issue first. It was clumsy and counterproductive. The incident hurt Reagan especially in the South; for instance, it ended private negotiations to win the endorsement of Alabama's Democratic governor Fob James. In general, it furthered the candidate's shoot-from-the-hip image.

The Klan flap also overshadowed positive signs that week for the Republican contender. The day after Labor Day, he toured a Chrysler plant and demonstrated anew his flexibility, reversing earlier opposition to federal aid for the ailing auto concern and sympathizing with cutting back on Japanese auto imports. Then he scored a big hit later in the week while campaigning in Florida and Louisiana. Going on the offensive, he accused the Carter administration of compromising national security by leaking, for political purposes, information about development of a supersecret "stealth" aircraft that could reportedly evade radar detection.

On Thursday of that week an important development occurred on the campaign plane when political strategist Stuart Spencer started traveling with the candidate. Reagan aides knew some added political expertise was necessary after the early mistakes, and political director Bill Timmons argued that Spencer was the perfect person to bring experience and sensitivity to the entourage. Still, Spencer, who directed Reagan's initial 1966 gubernatorial victory, had fallen out with the Reagans; in 1976 he masterminded Jerry Ford's primary wins over the Californian, and Reagan insiders, including the candidate's wife, Nancy, remained bitter. Thus there was fear that the inner circle would try to freeze Spencer out. Reagan realized the need for a broader appeal, however, and Spencer would fit in comfortably; almost immediately the traveling operation functioned more smoothly.

Early on, Carter zeroed in on the war/peace issue. In Harry Truman's home town of Independence, Missouri, he warned that Ronald Reagan would set off a "massive nuclear arms race" that could lead to war with the Soviet Union. The presidential choice, he told the town meeting, provided the "sharpest difference" between the major party contenders of any choice in his lifetime. The Carter scare tactics had begun in earnest.

Political Ads. The two campaigns also started their advertising campaigns in early September, though the Reagan side would squirrel away some $7 million for the last two weeks of the campaign. Of the $29.4 million each candidate received in federal funds, about 60 percent would be spent on media. Both sides started with a more positive pitch—Carter's stressing a hard-working man who kept the nation at peace and Reagan's dwelling on his dreams of peace and prosperity and a "documentary" on his record as governor of California. The negative stuff would follow shortly, however.

Not many political commercials would pass a truth-in-packaging test, and these were no exceptions. One Carter ad claimed the president won support from Congress for 80 percent of his legislative aims; actually this was based on a *Congressional Quarterly* statistic that measures support only for issues on which the president takes a "clear-cut" position, not distinguishing minor from major measures. Even here, Carter never achieved 80 percent support, and his congressional relations were notoriously poor. The Reagan commercials stressed the tax rebates he handed back as California governor and implied that he was a big tax-cutting chief executive. They neglected to point out that taxes had increased $21.3 billion during the Reagan years and the rebates had totaled less than $6 billion.

Anderson Gains. The most important development in early September was the gains scored by John Anderson. Ever since launching his independent bid in April, Anderson had two major worries: one was to raise sufficient funds for him to be treated as a serious presidential contender, and the other was to be included in any presidential campaign debates. During the summer, the ten-term Illinois congressman kept a low profile. Campaign planners, principally New York media expert David Garth and campaign manager Michael MacLeod, decided to devote their scarce resources to the painstakingly difficult task of getting on the ballots in most states. "We know we're going to pay a price in visibility, but it's the only way to be a credible alternative in the fall," argued MacLeod. By early September, it was apparent that this strategy had paid off; despite efforts by the Democrats to block him, Anderson probably would be on all fifty-one ballots, an impressive achievement.

Did Anderson really think he could win? Privately, top aides admitted it was a long shot. Still, as a moderate Republican, Anderson had long been contemptuous of Reagan, and the more he campaigned, first in the GOP primaries and then as an independent aspirant, the more he grew to dislike Carter. At first, he worried that his effort would only serve to elect Reagan; later, he convinced himself that both candidates were so bad that it made little difference. In late August, when he persuaded Kennedy Democrat Patrick Lucey, the former governor of Wisconsin, to be his running mate (after feelers to several more prominent Democrats had failed), the fifty-eight-year-old lifelong Republican told intimates that he could envision Carter and Reagan destroying themselves and that he had a serious chance of winning.

It was never easy to understand how. Anderson was strong in about a half-dozen states in New England (Massachusetts and Connecticut), the upper Great Lakes (Wisconsin and Michigan), and the Pacific Northwest (Oregon and Washington). When he won the New York Liberal party endorsement in early September—the first time the Liberals had shunned a Democratic presidential contender—David Garth thought that the Empire State was winnable, and Anderson felt California was also a possibility. The independent contender never had any support in the South, however, and only lukewarm backing in the industrial areas.

Money was also a problem. Unlike the two major-party contenders, he would not get any federal funds before the election but was still limited by the $1,000 contribution ceiling. He got a break on September 4, however, when the Federal Election Commission ruled that the Anderson candidacy should be treated as a third-party effort: if the independent candidate received at least 5 percent of the vote on election day, he would qualify for postelection federal funds. This would be anywhere from $3 million to the full $29.4 million, depending on his share of the vote. The significance of this ruling, the Anderson forces felt, was that it might enable them to borrow money using the expected postelection funds as collateral. Coupled with the $10 million the campaign planned to raise privately, this would permit the major media effort necessary to a national campaign.

The Anderson-Reagan Debate. Anderson's other major concern was that he be included in any presidential debates. The League of Women

Voters had conducted the 1976 Ford-Carter debates and became the self-appointed orchestrators for the 1980 debates. Over the summer the league decided basically that a candidate would qualify if he was drawing 15 percent in the public opinion polls.

Despite the slump after the conventions, Anderson was meeting that test in early September. A *Los Angeles Times* poll (September 2 to 7) put Reagan at 37 percent, Carter at 36 percent, and Anderson at 18 percent. The September 3 to 7 Louis Harris poll reported Reagan at 41 percent; Carter, 37 percent; and Anderson, 17 percent. Thus on September 9 the league invited Anderson to join Reagan and Carter in a debate in Baltimore in the next two weeks.[9]

The Reagan camp accepted, and so, of course, did Anderson. The Republicans were not sure if Carter was bluffing in indicating that he would not debate Anderson. He wasn't. Top strategists, particularly Jordan, felt that Anderson was hurting Carter and that it would only add to his credibility to appear on the same stage with the president. They also reasoned that they had weathered well their refusal to debate Kennedy in the primaries and that there would be other opportunities to debate.

Accordingly, under the pretense of insisting on a head-to-head encounter with Reagan, the White House turned down the league's invitation. The debate was then slated for September 21, and NBC and CBS decided to televise it live; ABC chose to carry a movie instead. This would be critical for Anderson. "The debate is one of the seminal events of this campaign," claimed Tom Matthews, Anderson's press secretary.

During the one-hour debate both men pointedly criticized the president's absence. Otherwise, their responses and charges were pretty uneventful, with both mainly reiterating campaign rhetoric. The most emotional clash in the generally civil exchange was in response to the final question on abortion. Anderson, with some passion, called for "freedom of choice" for pregnant women; Reagan countered: "There's one individual who isn't considered at all. That's the one who is being aborted." In their closing statements, Anderson was punchy and full of facts, whereas Reagan ended with a patriotic flourish on the destiny of America. Neither man made any costly mistake, and the stilted format precluded a real give-and-take. A few postdebate polls gave Anderson a slight edge, but it seemed that the independent candidate had not scored any major breakthrough. Reagan held steady in the next round of preferential polls, whereas both Carter and Anderson slipped slightly.

[9] League of Women Voters, press release, September 9, 1980.

Midcampaign

The campaign trail had become considerably smoother for the Republican challenger by now. He was carefully shielded from reporters to avoid any impromptu verbal miscues. Substantively, the focus was almost entirely on the economy. Reagan outlined his economic program in consultation with the pillars of the GOP economic establishment: Arthur Burns, former Federal Reserve Board chairman; Alan Greenspan, chairman of the Council of Economic Advisers under President Ford; and former Republican treasury secretaries George Shultz and William Simon. This was intended to counter any notion that Reagan was irresponsible or a radical right-winger.

The Reagan Economics Issue. Reagan stuck with his call for a 30 percent across-the-board individual tax cut spread over three years, as well as other business tax reductions. Defense spending would be increased 5 percent a year, after adjusting for inflation, under the Reagan plan, but overall spending would be sliced by 7 percent of the figure projected earlier for 1985. The Reagan economic targets, by the end of his first term, were modest: inflation at a 7.5 percent annual rate and unemployment down only to 6.5 percent.

Although the GOP nominee was focusing on the economy and a tougher defense posture, he was conspicuously staying away from the "hot" social issues such as abortion and the Equal Rights Amendment. "We knew we had those votes [antiabortion and anti-ERA] and we didn't want to antagonize moderate Republicans and independents who disagreed with the governor on those issues," said top Reagan aide Drew Lewis. Similarly, when former Philadelphia Democratic mayor Frank Rizzo sent out feelers that he wanted to endorse Reagan, Lewis, also a leading Pennsylvania politician, vetoed the suggestion. Rizzo, he reasoned, was popular with blue-collar Democrats but remained anathema to blacks and many suburban whites. (While ignoring abortion Reagan did frequently advocate tuition tax credits, a popular proposal in Catholic communities but not one that triggered emotional negatives.)

If the campaign was going more smoothly for Reagan, however, it wasn't for Carter. A few weeks into the fall campaign, the Carterites were frustrated that assaults on Reagan's record and rhetoric from Vice-President Mondale and cabinet officers were not receiving much attention. Thus some aides felt Carter himself had to hit harder at his Republican rival.

The Carter "Meanness" Issue. Tough, even mean, political rhetoric has been a trademark of the born-again Baptist president; privately, Carter personalizes politics more than most national politicians and is not reticent about venting those feelings when it might be advantageous. In 1970, he waged a vicious campaign against former Georgia governor Carl Sanders. In 1976, when Hubert Humphrey was considering another run for the presidency, Carter suggested that he was a washed-up hack. In 1980, Carter sanctioned his campaign's thinly veiled charges in television commercials that Edward Kennedy was personally immoral.

On September 16, 1980, addressing a black audience at the church of the late Martin Luther King's father, Ebenezer Baptist Church in Atlanta, Carter let loose. "You've seen in this campaign the stirrings of hate and the rebirth of code words like 'states' rights' in a speech in Mississippi, in a campaign reference to the Ku Klux Klan, relating to the South," he declared. "That is the message that creates a cloud on the political horizon. Hatred has no place in this country. Racism has no place in this country."

A week later, before a labor crowd in Los Angeles, the president solemnly intoned: "Six weeks from now, the American people will make a very profound choice—a choice not just between two men but between two futures. And what you decide on that day, you and those who listen to your voice, will determine the kind of life you and your family will have, whether this nation will make progress or go backward and *whether* we have war or peace." Two weeks later, in Chicago, he said that the election would determine whether "America will be unified or, if I lose the election, whether Americans might be separated, black from white, Jew from Christian, North from South, rural from urban." The message was not subtle: the election of Ronald Reagan might breed war and racial and religious strife.

In each instance, Carter tried to backtrack or deny that he was leveling charges against Reagan. Privately, however, aides admitted that this was a calculated effort; the day after the war/peace remark, while Carter was insisting he was not accusing Reagan of warmongering, press secretary Jody Powell distributed a prepared memorandum listing old Reagan statements calling for U.S. military intervention around the world. Caddell brushed off suggestions that this tough rhetoric could be counterproductive. "All elections involve a certain amount of seeding and that's what Carter is doing now," the poll taker said privately. "He is planting doubts and concerns about Reagan. Sometimes the message is obscured some because of the filter [the news media], but we're basically pleased." Still, ever since 1976 many political journalists have felt that there was a petty, mean streak to Carter that was frequently at odds with his intelligent, moral side.

This time the press seized on Carter's meanness, including critical editorials in such un-Republican papers as the *Washington Post*. In the liberal *Boston Globe*, longtime Carter-watcher Curtis Wilkie wrote: "Just as surely as the werewolf grows long fangs and facial hair on a full moon, the darker side of President Carter emerges in election years." The Carter campaign, Wilkie charged, is "the symbol of gracelessness under pressure."[10] The cartoonists were even harsher. Oliphant, in the *Washington Star*, compared Carter's tactics with Nixon's, and Herblock, in the *Washington Post*, drew a smallish Jimmy Carter wallowing in slime with a paint brush poised to smear again.

By early October, some Carter aides knew they were in trouble on this score. Vice-President Mondale had privately voiced concern about the get-tough strategy for weeks. Eventually the campaign decided that the president should use an October 8 interview with ABC's Barbara Walters to promise that he would refrain from any more mudslinging.

Later some Carter advisers admitted that the meanness issue had taken an unexpected toll. "We really overestimated Carter's nice guy, decent image and didn't realize it was slipping away," recalled Greg Schneiders. "The continuous charges of meanness and pettiness had an effect; people vote on character and that was supposed to be our issue."

Factors in the Campaign. As the campaign entered the final four weeks, it was clear that Anderson had slipped significantly and that the only questions were whether he would get 5 percent of the vote (to qualify for postelection funds, though he had been unable to secure any bank loans using this possibility) and which other candidate he would hurt most. The consensus in both camps was that Anderson was still taking more votes from Carter. The Reagan-Carter race, at this stage, remained uncertain, as there were some unusual currents and contradictions. These included:

Issues. Both sides agreed that the economy and the war/peace issue were dominant in voters' minds. Other issues clearly were

[10] Curtis Wilkie, "Old Tricks of the Trail for Carter," *Boston Globe*, September 21, 1980.

secondary. Yet on the two main issues, the parties' historical strengths seemed reversed in 1980.

The economy was undoubtedly helping Reagan. An October 8–10 NBC/Associated Press (AP) poll of 1,548 likely voters asked which candidate would do the best job in solving the nation's economic problems. The results: Reagan an easy first with 43 percent, followed by Carter with 17 percent and Anderson with 8 percent, whereas 32 percent either said it made no difference or were unsure. Louis Harris found similar results, noting, "[This] marks the first time in modern politics that a Republican has moved ahead of a Democrat on how he would handle the economy."

Yet the same NBC/AP poll asked which candidate "would do the best job in keeping the United States out of war." Here, 40 percent said Carter, and only 14 percent said Reagan. By 44 percent to 24 percent a late September Gallup poll preferred the Democrats as "better for peace" than the Republicans; Gallup said this was the Democrats' most decisive edge on this question in years.

The same conclusion was evident in a series of focus group interviews conducted around the country for the *Wall Street Journal* by Washington pollster Peter Hart. These were small sessions of about a dozen citizens and were aimed not at predicting the election outcome but at probing, in depth, the evolving attitudes of voters as they struggled to make up their minds.

Many of these voters praised Reagan for being more forceful on foreign affairs than Carter and expressed concern that the United States was too weak militarily. Still, they also were very worried about the GOP nominee's inexperience in foreign affairs and a feeling that he might be too reckless. "I think he [Reagan] would like to carry a big stick, but I'm not sure he knows what to do with it," said J. William Datz, a fifty-year-old Glassboro, New Jersey, school administrator and a political independent. The sentiment changed, however, when the economy became the topic. "I'd rather take a chance on what Reagan might do than sit and do nothing for the next four years," declared Mary Interthal, a thirty-year-old housewife whose husband makes about $20,000 a year in McKees Rock, Pennsylvania (a working-class Pittsburgh suburb).[11]

Yet these sessions also indicated a notable negativism about both candidates. Although voters were fearful of Reagan on foreign policy, they criticized Carter as weak and vacillating; frustration over his in-

[11] Timothy D. Schellhardt, "Cool to All Candidates, Most Voters on a Panel Will Just Wait and See," *Wall Street Journal*, September 18, 1980. See also Albert R. Hunt, "Carter and Reagan Get Bad Economic Grades from Two Panels of Voters," *Wall Street Journal*, October 17, 1980.

ability to secure release of the Iranian hostages was growing. And although the president was given almost universally bad marks on the economy, voters were overwhelmingly skeptical of Reagan's promises to increase defense spending, balance the budget, curb inflation, and cut taxes by 30 percent at the same time.

Still, understandably, Reagan wanted to focus the campaign on the economy, and Carter on war and peace. The Republicans were encouraged when the October NBC/AP poll found that only 24 percent of the public thought their family finances would be better off during the next years. And the Democrats thought the outbreak of war between Iran and Iraq would raise voters' concerns about how a President Reagan would respond to such a situation.

Constituencies. Both sides were worried about protecting parts of what should be their natural base: for Reagan, suburbanites; for Carter, blue-collar democrats.

Although the suburbs are not a homogeneous vote—ranging from the rich country-club set to ethnic working-class neighborhoods —Republicans usually count on these areas to offset Democratic margins in the large cities in presidential contests. In 1980 some Republican planners worried that the war/peace issue and social and cultural divisions on social issues such as ERA and abortion might hurt Reagan in some key suburban areas. This was the one area where Anderson might take more votes from Reagan than from Carter. Conversely, the White House thought losses elsewhere might be offset by improved showings in suburbs in such key states as Illinois, Pennsylvania, Ohio, and Michigan.

The situation was reversed in blue-collar areas. Reagan, recalling his success with union rank-and-file voters in California, thought this was fertile territory. The campaign widely distributed a brochure stressing the candidate's background as president of the Screen Actors Guild twenty-five years earlier. "Elect a former Union President, President," it declared, and Reagan frequently mentioned his union background. He also reversed several earlier positions to enhance his appeal to labor union members. Now he was promising that he wouldn't seek to extend antitrust laws to unions or repeal the Occupational Safety and Health Act (OSHA) or the Davis-Bacon Act, which artificially boosts construction workers' wages, or eliminate the minimum wage or seek a national right-to-work law. The campaign also searched for visual ways to dramatize an affinity with workers. In economically devastated Youngstown, Ohio, for instance, Reagan toured a huge abandoned steel plant, making for ideal television pictures that evening.

With unemployment nationally at 7.5 percent and ranging between 13 percent and 20 percent in Democratic strongholds such as Youngstown and Flint, Michigan, the White House knew the labor vote was a serious problem. They were relying heavily on individual labor unions to deliver for them, but the labor leaders knew that the only way to do this was to raise fears about Reagan. Steve Schlossberg, the general counsel for the politically potent United Auto Workers, admitted their only hope was to scare their members. Throughout the campaign, though, many of these labor leaders were dubious that this scare strategy would work.

Another key battleground was the Jewish vote. Jews make up less than 5 percent of the electorate but are disproportionately influential in several big states, principally New York (where they constitute close to 20 percent of the vote), Florida, New Jersey, Pennsylvania, and California. In 1976, Carter won an estimated 70 percent of the Jewish vote, providing the margin of victory in a few critical states.

In 1980 Jewish antipathy to Carter, mainly over what was perceived as insufficient support for Israel, was extraordinary, if somewhat irrational. Many Jews gave the president little credit for what was probably the most impressive achievement of his term: the Camp David summit. Lieutenant Governor Mario Cuomo of New York urged Carter to "do a Houston" with Jewish voters—drawing a parallel with John F. Kennedy's celebrated 1960 confrontation with Protestant ministers in Houston to address apprenhension about his Roman Catholic religion. Carter did stage a miniconfrontation at a Jewish community center in New York in mid-October, but there never was a dramatic encounter. Still, the president made other moves with an eye to the Jewish vote: he announced, with great fanfare, that the United States would not sell parts to Saudi Arabia for the war planes the United States had sold the Arabs earlier, and in late October former Israeli defense minister Ezer Weizman was conspicuously present on the president's campaign plane.

Reagan, a longtime supporter of Israel, also made a big effort with the Jewish vote; his Mideast policies were decidedly pro-Israel, and in New York, his campaign chief, Roger Stone, was constantly wooing Jewish constituencies. Still, there were problems here: Reagan's social conservatism turned off some Jews, and his October appearance with Jerry Falwell, the fundamentalist Christian Moral Majority leader, positively scared many Jewish voters.

There was also a struggle for the Hispanic-American vote, especially in Texas, where Mexican-Americans constituted close to 10 percent of the vote. The Carter campaign sent their old foe Ted Kennedy to Texas in hopes that the Kennedy name, still magic among Chicanos, would turn out a big Democratic vote. In hopes of reducing Carter's margin with this vote, Reagan relied heavily on Texas's Republican governor, William Clements. "Every time our polls show Carter gaining in South Texas, Clements appoints another Mexican-American judge," chortled Reagan political aide Stu Spencer.

Everybody knew that the black vote would go heavily for Carter, but the key was the turnout. Carter hoped to increase it by scaring blacks with the prospect of a Reagan presidency. The Republicans countered by securing the endorsement of some well-known black leaders, Ralph David Abernathy and Hosea Williams, former associates of Martin Luther King, Jr., and the mayor of Fayette, Mississippi, Charles Evers. These endorsements came less from conviction than from a calculation among these former black powers that they might regain some of their importance if Reagan should win; almost every other major black politician in the country backed Carter.

Among the very few groups in the country that viewed both men favorably were white southerners; they identified with Ronald Reagan on philosophy and with Jimmy Carter on regional heritage. If either candidate did well with working-class whites in the South, he almost surely would carry most of the region, both sides agreed.

Incumbency. The Carter White House was fully prepared to utilize all the advantages of the incumbency. The president devoted the opening part of a September 18 news conference to some patently political and partisan claims, prompting Adam Clymer of the *New York Times* to call the session "the most dramatic use of the power of incumbency yet in this presidential campaign."[12]

Federal largesse had a distinct political coloration, too. The *Wall Street Journal* noted that in October, a month early, the administration announced its quarterly grants to economically distressed areas; about $200 million in federal aid for local transit buses was similarly moved up before the election, as were drought-relief loans to farmers. Cabinet officers were used extensively to travel around the country praising Carter and assailing Reagan. Carter's half-dozen town meetings were almost always televised live by the local stations.[13]

Incumbency has liabilities, too. The influx of Cuban refugees hurt the president badly in Florida and Arkansas; the Soviet grain

---

[12] Adam Clymer, "Carter Speech: An Extra Edge," *New York Times,* September 19, 1980.

[13] Timothy D. Schellhardt, "Carter the Incumbent Excels at Using Office as a Campaign Asset," *Wall Street Journal,* October 1, 1980.

embargo was a political disadvantage in the farm belt; and rising Japanese auto imports were a negative in Michigan. In sum, the powers of incumbency are exaggerated as often as they are partially offset by drawbacks over which the president has little control.

The running mates. A common cliché of presidential politics is that vice-presidential candidates cannot help, but only hurt, a presidential contender. Like most clichés this is an oversimplification, and it was particularly so in 1980, for both Vice-President Mondale and George Bush were important symbols to key elements of the presidential candidate's constituency. Among Democrats, Mondale reassured liberals, labor, and Jewish voters who were lukewarm to Carter. On the GOP side, George Bush was very popular with the moderate, Jerry Ford–type Republicans and with independents, many of whom remained wary of Reagan.

Although neither running mate received much national attention, their tireless efforts paid off in local coverage. Invariably, they got top billing on local television stations and front-page coverage, and it was almost always favorable. Both Mondale and Bush were embarrassingly fulsome about their running mates, but both were also thoroughly professional performers who avoided mistakes and controversy—unlike some of their recent predecessors, such as Spiro Agnew and Thomas Eagleton.

The two presidential contenders, however, never fully utilized their number two men. The Reagan camp resisted doing separate Bush commercials until the very end of the campaign and gave Bush limited staff resources. The close governmental relationship between Mondale and Carter did not extend to the campaign. Real animosity existed between the vice-president and Carter's media director, Gerald Rafshoon, and Mondale was rarely used in any Carter commercials. And according to the vice-president's aides, tensions between Mondale and pollster Caddell were so great that sometimes the vice-president had to find out about the latest polling data surreptitiously; Caddell denies this.

Campaign organization. At the top, the Carter campaign enjoyed a clear edge. The four top decision makers—Jordan, Powell, Rafshoon, and Caddell—knew each other well, had complete control over their areas of expertise, and avoided most of the internal bickering that so often accompanies presidential campaigns. When a consensus developed among this group, decisions were reached and executed quickly.

By contrast, the Reagan high command was often splintered and indecisive. With Stu Spencer on the campaign plane, the traveling entourage had acquired considerable political skills. Back at the Arlington, Virginia, headquarters, it was another story. William Casey, the sixty-seven-year-old New York lawyer who took over the chairmanship of the campaign in February when Reagan fired his talented campaign chief John Sears, was in over his head; he lacked experience and political instincts, and other aides spent much time trying to bypass "the Casey problem."

The other top Reagan aides were all bright men (there were no women in the inner circle except the candidate's wife), but there were political problems with each of them. Pollster Richard Wirthlin is one of the best in the profession, but as both the campaign's chief pollster and its chief strategist, according to many insiders, he was overextended. Chief Reagan aide Ed Meese is knowledgeable about government and highly trusted by Reagan, but on political matters he was frequently indecisive. Former Ford and Bush campaign chief James Baker became an emerging force as the campaign progressed, artfully handling the television debate negotiations, for one thing. He was still new to the Reagan operation, however, and at times was reluctant to weigh in heavily. Similarly, political director Bill Timmons and Drew Lewis, working out of the Republican National Committee, were resourceful politicians but in the crunch often lacked sufficient clout. Accordingly, the campaign apparatus was cumbersome and factionalized. "If a crisis develops, we have no mechanism to make quick decisions," worried one top Reagan strategist.

Further down the hierarchy, however, the Reagan organization often looked a lot better than its Carter counterpart. The Reagan regional coordinators and campaign directors in the major states were uniformly talented; on the Carter side, the picture was more mixed. At the local level, the Reagan campaign was teeming with enthusiastic volunteers, whereas the Carter campaign offices were sparsely populated. Moreover, Democratic divisions in some areas hampered the Carter effort. In Chicago, for example, the presidential race took a back seat to the brutal battle between Democratic mayor Jane Byrne and Richard M. Daley, son of the late mayor and the Democratic candidate for Cook County state's attorney; when a Democratic machine like Chicago's is wracked by division, it undermines the entire ticket, and there was little Carter could do about it.[14]

The Republicans also enjoyed a decided financial edge. Both major-party candidates received $29.4 million in federal funds, and the national parties could spend another $4.6 million on their behalf.

---

[14] See Jules Witcover, "Chicago Party Feud Dims Carter's Hopes in Illinois," *Washington Star*, October 8, 1980.

Further, in 1979, Congress voted to allow state and local parties to spend unlimited amounts on prescribed presidential-campaign-related activities such as voter registration, campaign literature, buttons, bumper stickers, and telephone banks to get out the vote. The Republicans moved quickly to use this new vehicle, bringing in a top fund raiser, Tennessee businessman Ted Welch, to direct the effort. The Democrats assigned this a lower priority. The result: the GOP raised and spent almost $15 million on this effort, or about three times what the Democrats spent. This was a huge advantage in states like Texas—where Governor Clements directed a $2.5 million fund raiser in one night—as the Reagan campaign paid for almost all their field operations from this fund. In part, the Democrats' deficiency here was due to the drawn-out primary struggle, which made it difficult to raise money until after the August convention. Still, it is also true that the Republicans in recent years—particularly under the exceptionally able party chairman Bill Brock—outdistanced the Democrats with sophisticated direct mail fund-raising operations.

These expenditures turned out to be much more important than the more publicized ventures by so-called independent groups. The 1976 Supreme Court decision on the campaign financing law ruled that groups genuinely independent of a presidential candidate could spend unlimited sums on behalf of that candidate. Over the summer, numerous Republican and conservative groups were formed and boasted of plans to spend millions of dollars to help elect Ronald Reagan. Still, legal challenges by the Democrats and Common Cause, the self-styled citizens' lobbying organization, crippled the ability of these groups to raise funds. Although these challenges were eventually dismissed, the independent groups, except for a few efforts in some southern states, had only a minimal impact on the election.

The Final Three Weeks

At mid-October, the presidential picture remained muddled, although the trend and tide still seemed with Reagan. Once baseball's World Series ended, in another week, according to conventional political wisdom, voters would start really paying attention to the presidential choice. John Anderson was clearly out of the picture, but neither of the two other major candidates seemed able to pull away.

The Carter Strategy. The president was now on the road most of the time trying to gain the political offensive. As interest rates continued to climb, dampening White House claims of an increasingly bullish economy, Carter turned to a new culprit: the Federal Reserve Board, whose monetary policies, he charged, were "ill-advised." Carter neglected to mention that he had appointed five of the board's seven members, including the conservative chairman, Paul Volcker.

Indeed, Carter was on the attack constantly now. He charged that Reagan's 30 percent tax cut was "economic quicksilver" and would only fuel inflation; transferring federal welfare and educational programs to the states would result in skyrocketing personal property and state income taxes, he claimed. On the war/peace issue, the president worried aloud about Reagan's "macho" stands and warned that the Oval Office "is not a place for simplistic answers, is not a place for shooting from the hip, and is not a place for snap judgments." Almost the entire thrust of the Carter message was anti-Reagan; from both calculation and necessity, the president offered little vision of where he would like to lead the country or how a second Carter administration would differ from the first and perhaps avoid some of its problems.

Still, by October 15, Caddell was privately insisting that these assaults on Reagan were working: "All our data show Reagan's internals—feelings about his competency, leadership, and qualification—are collapsing." The Carter high command felt that the president had kept the race close enough that he could pull it out at the end, when voters seriously focus on the alternatives.

Caddell felt that New York was safe, and Illinois and Pennsylvania were moving Carter's way; Ohio and Michigan, he admitted, were tougher but still winnable. Most of the South, except for Texas and Florida, continued to look promising. Caddell continued to maintain that independent-minded Catholics were critical, and he sought to persuade Carter to go after Reagan's links with the Moral Majority; historically, with good reason, Catholics never have been comfortable with Protestant fundamentalists. "The Moral Majority issue is bubbling and it can be exploited," the president's pollster argued. The Carter operatives even saw a perfect forum: the traditional Al Smith nonpartisan dinner in New York on October 16, with both candidates in attendance.

Despite professed optimism, frustration permeated the White House at the same time. Ronald Reagan—an aging movie actor and political lightweight in the Carter staff's eyes—was not crumbling as they had envisioned. Carter aides soon located a handy rationale: the press. In particular, the Washington press corps, argued Gerald Rafshoon, "hates Carter so much that you're giving Reagan a free ride."

The Reagan Strategy. There was uncertainty in the Reagan camp, too. The polls looked good in most states, and the South especially was better then expected. "We've got him (the president) bleeding like a stuck pig in his own base and he's going to have to come back here to heal those wounds," said Lee Atwater, a South Carolinian and leading Reagan Dixie operative.

Yet there were problems, too. After five weeks of an error-free campaign, Reagan had stumbled badly one night in early October while talking to some businessmen in Steubenville, Ohio. Governor James Rhodes of Ohio is openly contemptuous of environmentalists and, as is his wont, brushed aside Reagan's protective staff that day. Also, Stu Spencer was elsewhere. In a rambling discourse, Reagan claimed that the volcano on Mt. St. Helens produced more sulfur dioxide than all automobiles had emitted over the previous ten years. He even suggested that the oil slicks off the coast of Santa Barbara, California, were once considered healthy in battling infectious diseases. In addition, he talked about some dangerous health hazards coming from trees. It was a silly performance, compounded a few days later when the candidate returned home to be greeted by one of the worst smogs in southern California history. (He also was welcomed by a sign on a tree reading: "Chop me down before I kill again.")

Further, despite Carter's complaints, the press was roughing up Reagan. He provided fodder with a series of issue flip-flops as he sought the middle ground. He moderated his stands on federal aid for New York City and the Chrysler Corporation, as well as on labor legislation. Similarly, he fudged on agriculture policies, defense spending, budget cuts, the social security program, and energy policy. On October 7, a long piece analyzing these reversals appeared on the CBS "Evening News." Correspondent Bill Plante contrasted the earlier, hard-line Reagan with the toned-down version this fall, and each time the television screen imposed a big X over Reagan's picture to reflect the discarding of the old position. It was a devastating analysis. The only good news, one Reagan insider joked, was that "it's a lot better to be called a sell-out than a nut."

Outside experts saw the Reagan drive stalling at this juncture. "For the first time, I feel the election may be starting to elude Ronald Reagan's grasp," ventured Democratic pollster Peter Hart about three weeks before the election. GOP poll taker Bob Teeter, who was helping Reagan's pollster Wirthlin, concurred: "In most big states, they both are sitting there in the high 30s and it's going to take 46 to 48 percent to win." And Wirthlin's October 14 national survey showed

Carter ahead—41 percent to 39 percent—the first time Reagan had trailed Carter in Wirthlin's national tests in months.

Neither man was striking any sparks. "We've had a war in the Middle East and people haven't rallied around the president," noted political analyst Michael Barone. "And there's an incumbent with very low job ratings and people haven't rallied around the challenger." This lack of enthusiasm was manifest in many newspaper editorials. Both Miami papers endorsed John Anderson, saying they could not stomach the two major-party aspirants. Lukewarm endorsements by the *New York Times* (Carter) and the *Chicago Tribune* (Reagan) essentially took the lesser-of-two-evils approach. The *Boston Globe* endorsed both Carter and Anderson, arguing only against Reagan, and the prestigious *Economist* headlined its October 18 endorsement: "Anybody but Carter."

Politically, it therefore seemed that whichever man got the most breaks would win, though throughout the campaign Reagan had more maneuverability. The astute *Washington Star* political editors Jack Germond and Jules Witcover ran a weekly count on the likely electoral scoreboard. On October 15, they showed Reagan leading in states with 240 electoral votes, Carter ahead in states with 139 votes, and 159 electoral votes in the toss-up category. In the big industrial states, Carter was put ahead in New York, and Reagan was up in Ohio, Illinois, and California. Still, Pennsylvania, New Jersey, Michigan, Wisconsin, and Missouri—with a combined 88 electoral votes—were all rated too close to call. In the South, Germond and Witcover had Reagan up in Florida, Virginia, and Mississippi and Carter ahead in North Carolina, Georgia, Arkansas, and Alabama. Still, Texas, Louisiana, South Carolina, Tennessee, and Kentucky—with 63 electoral votes—were in the toss-up category.[15] About this time, a Gallup survey indicated that 36 percent of the voters were not strongly committed to any candidate and could change their minds before election day.

The Second Debate. This tentativeness was causing both sides to reconsider the question of a head-to-head debate. The ball was really in Reagan's court. The Republicans had figured earlier that since they were ahead anyway, a debate would be too risky; Carter's refusal to include Anderson in any debate gave Reagan the excuse to avoid a direct confrontation.

---

[15] Jack Germond and Jules Witcover, "The Presidential Campaign Scoreboard," *Washington Star*, October 15, 1980.

Pollster Wirthlin, certain that the Reagan tide was inexorable despite his October 14 poll, and political director Timmons, argued against debating. They thought Reagan still was a little ahead, and the campaign had about $7 million—about twice as much as Carter had—to spend in the final two weeks. Campaign chairman Casey and staff chief Meese were ambivalent. Jim Baker and Drew Lewis and some of the second-tier political operatives were prodebate, but their influence was questionable.

The mood on the plane started to shift, however, and when quick decisions were essential, those physically closest to the candidate had an advantage. Later Lyn Nofziger recalled going into Stu Spencer's hotel room during a mid-October South Dakota stop and saying: "Looks like we're going to have to debate." Spencer said he was thinking the same thing. "I rode to the airport that day with Reagan," Nofziger said, "and even before I approached him he said, 'Looks like we're going to have a debate.'" Spencer later said the shift was easily explainable: "We leveled out in early October. That was bad news against an incumbent president; in the end, he's got the marbles."

Reagan and his wife, Nancy, were still personally apprehensive. But the final straw was the joint appearance with Carter at the October 16 Al Smith dinner hosted by Terence Cardinal Cooke. Carter, as privately planned, slashed away at Reagan's ties to the Moral Majority. The evening was supposed to be more fun-spirited, and the conservative Catholic audience reacted very negatively. Curiously, this seemingly unimportant event finally convinced Reagan that he could go head to head with the president. The timing was tailor-made. At that very moment the League of Women Voters was extending invitations to Reagan and Carter to join in one big debate; by now, the league figured its only hope of getting Carter meant excluding Anderson, which it did. On October 17, Reagan accepted the debate invitation while continuing to blame Carter for vetoing Anderson.

Reagan's acceptance caught Carter off guard. Indeed, at that very time the White House was preparing to rule out any debate if Reagan did not accept within the next few days. By now, some Carterites thought they were within striking distance of victory, and a debate would be too risky. "From early October on, I lived in terror that Reagan would change his mind and agree to debate," said Caddell. "Our feeling—based on our experience debating Ford in '76—was that a debate was likely to only help Reagan and hurt the incumbent. All Reagan had to do was not make a mistake and look like he was on par with the president. The biggest mistake we made in this campaign was not to cut off the possibility of a debate."

Despite such fears, once Reagan accepted, Carter was trapped. For one thing, the Democrats had assailed the GOP nominee for refusing a head-to-head encounter. Also, Caddell noted, "we still are hamstrung by our refusal to debate Kennedy in the primaries—it would have looked like we always duck debates." Thus caught by his own calculations, Carter was forced to agree to debate.

Neither side particularly wanted the League of Women Voters to sponsor the forum; people in both camps talked snidely about the "League of Women Vultures," feeling that they were opportunists. Yet the league was best situated to run the debate; so after considerable hassling, the two sides agreed to a ninety-minute debate in Cleveland on October 28, exactly one week before the election.

Much of the time now would be devoted to this possibly make-or-break event. Reagan did give a thirty-minute televised commercial on October 19 with a foreign policy speech. In it, he sought to portray himself as a man of peace, speaking as a "parent and grandparent" and noting, "I have known four wars in my lifetime and I don't want to see a fifth." Still, the two contenders devoted almost all of the four or five days before the Cleveland session preparing for the debate. Warm-ups included question-and-answer practice (both sides claimed afterward that they had anticipated all questions) and work on the sort of tone to be established on this key night.

Carter wanted to draw a sharp contrast with Reagan, but aides warned him against overkill in any attacks. "Reagan is the Muhammad Ali of American politics; he's like a butterfly the way he bounces off attacks," cautioned Caddell. Instead, the president's pollster stressed the need to "envelop Reagan, to build a bubble around him with as many specifics as possible. We want him pressed on specifics and we want the debate to center on our issues, particularly on war and peace and nuclear arms." (At one point during the debate preparations, Carter casually mentioned that he might talk about a recent conversation he had had with his thirteen-year-old daughter, Amy, about nuclear arms; aides, especially Rafshoon, ridiculed that suggestion and didn't think the president was serious.) The Carter advisers also wanted him to touch as many political bases—with appeals to blacks, women, labor, southerners—as possible.

Reagan, on the other hand, mainly wanted to avoid any costly mistake. He was briefed by experts for days, and they carefully rechecked the candidate's favorite facts and figures to guard against any embarrassing error. The former actor studiously rehearsed answers to many hypothetical questions and wrote and memorized much of his planned closing remarks.

Immediately before the debate two miniscandals broke. The

Wall Street Journal reported that Reagan's chief foreign policy adviser, Richard Allen, engaged in questionable conflict-of-interest practices during an earlier stint in government; Allen took a "leave of absence" from the campaign but immediately reappeared election night when the heat was off. On the other side, a leaked report from the Justice Department suggested that President Carter had been uncooperative in the investigation of his brother's links to the Libyans. Although both stories received prominent television coverage for one evening, they quickly faded; this was not an election to be won or lost on a last-minute scandal.

As both camps had figured, the format of the Cleveland debate was not conducive to serious give-and-take. The panelists asked both men the same questions, for instance, which most experts agreed was pointless. It was a shame that a more serious debate was not possible, for the issues dividing the two contenders were dramatic. Reagan favored huge increases in military outlays, massive tax cuts, and transfer of many federal social programs to state and local governments while opposing the strategic arms limitation treaty, all government controls on energy, and any national health insurance or other new social scheme. Although Carter was hardly a traditional liberal —the president's philosophy was usually defined by his opponent— he was clearly to the left of Reagan, favoring the SALT agreement and modest increases in both domestic and military outlays while opposing huge reductions in personal income taxes.

Both men came to the debate understandably nervous. The president went on the attack from the beginning. Reagan's proposed tax cut was "ridiculous," he charged. He talked of his native South and then, with an eye to organized labor, lambasted Reagan's earlier opposition to the minimum wage as a "heartless kind of approach, typical of many Republican leaders in the past." He saved his biggest shots for the war/peace and nuclear arms issues, however. Speaking of his "lonely" White House decisions, he railed against Reagan for "habitually" advocating the use of military force, charging that a Reagan administration would also "lead to a very dangerous arms race." Curiously, the president repeatedly stressed the matter of nuclear proliferation, although only a few weeks earlier he had successfully lobbied the Senate to approve a highly controversial uranium sale to India. He even said his thirteen-year-old daughter had told him controlling the spread of nuclear weapons was the most important issue in the campaign.

Reagan seemed on the defensive most of the time. During one Carter assault, the GOP nominee sighed, "There you go again," alluding to what he felt were false Carter charges. He did score some telling points on Carter's economic record and said the Iranian hostage issue was a national "humiliation." Yet much of the debate centered on foreign affairs, and Reagan frequently appeared hesitant and unsure. He recouped, though, with a brilliant closing statement. The basic questions, he said, were: "Are you better off than you were four years ago?" and "Is America as respected throughout the world?"

Predictably, both sides claimed victory. The Reagan camp insisted their man held his own with the president of the United States for ninety minutes. On the other side, Hamilton Jordan instantly proclaimed, "We won, we won," as the Carterites argued that the president was crisper and appealed to all the necessary constituencies. If there was any instant consensus among political experts, it was that Carter might have got the upper hand but did not score any knockout punch.

Within an hour, though, it appeared that the president did not even win the upper hand. For fifty cents, viewers could call ABC to indicate who they thought won the debate; this phone-in was unscientific, skewed to Reagan's advantage (more Republicans have phones), and journalistically irresponsible. Still, this survey, showing Reagan getting twice as much support, had an impact: "I saw lots of newspaper headlines the next day that read, 'Reagan wins 2-to-1,'" said James Brady of the Reagan staff. Other analysts argued that this survey might have persuaded some undecided voters that Reagan had really won the debate.

Although Carter may have been hurt unfairly by the ABC poll, the voter reaction to the debate, under any circumstances, was more favorable to Reagan. The *Wall Street Journal*, with pollster Peter Hart, went back to interview two dozen of the participants in earlier focus sessions, starting the day after the debate. The purpose was to determine how undecided voters were making up their minds as November 4 neared.

By a decisive margin, these people were more impressed with Reagan in the debate, including some who planned to vote for Carter. A major factor was the different expectations of the two candidates. Many of these voters wanted Reagan to assure them he was not a dangerous warmonger, and he did: "Reagan dispelled the theory of him being trigger happy," said Gail Colo, a thirty-seven-year-old Glassboro, New Jersey, secretary who only six weeks earlier had expressed concern about the GOP nominee on that score. They also wanted Reagan to demonstrate that he was sufficiently smart; merely going head to head with the president for an hour and a half and not crumbling enabled the GOP nominee to satisfy many here.

Carter's test was considerably tougher, according to these interviews. People wanted him to explain why things had not gone very well during the past four years and why he would govern better in a second term. This he plainly did not do.[16] "The one thing Carter wouldn't do was the one thing he had to do," noted John Sears, the respected Republican politician. "Namely, he had to show a little humility, confess some mistakes and assure people he had learned a lot."

What these interviews also suggested was that many of these voters, for all their apprehensions about Reagan, wanted an excuse to vote for him or, more probably, an excuse to vote against Carter. One of the very few analysts who all along had forecast a big Reagan win was *Washington Post* columnist Mark Shields, a former leading Democratic political strategist. Shortly before the election, Shields wrote a remarkably perceptive column suggesting that Reagan was what politicians call a "voting booth candidate," which he defined as one who "will consistently run stronger and better with actual voters on Election Day than he (or she) will in any preelection poll." Shields offered two other guidelines to reading the election: (1) How many people do you know who voted for Jerry Ford in 1976 and are voting for Jimmy Carter in 1980? (2) How many people do you know who voted for Jimmy Carter in 1976 and are not voting for him in 1980? Anyone spending any time with voters knew that the second group was much larger than the first.[17]

The Key States. Carter's problems also became more apparent from a look at the critical states during the last week of the campaign. In 1976, the Democratic nominee carried Texas, Ohio, and Pennsylvania, with a combined seventy-eight electoral votes. To win in 1980, it was widely agreed, Carter needed to win at the very least two of these three states. Yet in all three states Carter's political problems were enormous.

In 1976, Carter carried Texas by 129,000 votes out of 4.1 million cast. There had been significant slippage in this support in smaller rural areas, however, and about the only compensation, Democrats felt, lay in a bigger turnout among Mexican-Americans. Still, the Republicans were making a great effort in the Chicano community, too. Here, as elsewhere, the huge Republican financial and organizational edge was impressive. "If we're within three or four points of

[16] Albert R. Hunt, "Most Undecided on Journal Voter Panels Have Made Up Their Minds, Reluctantly," *Wall Street Journal*, October 31, 1980.

[17] Mark Shields, "Behind Closed Curtains," *Washington Post*, October 31, 1980.

Carter in the polls we'll carry Texas because of organization," predicted Reagan's southern coordinator, Paul Manafort, a view shared by many Texas Democrats.

In Ohio, Carter's 1976 margin was even less—11,000 out of 4.1 million votes. To win statewide, a Democrat usually has to carry heavily Democratic Cuyahoga County, consisting of Cleveland and its suburbs, by 125,000 votes; in 1976, Carter carried Cuyahoga County by only 94,000 votes. As a fresh face and born-again Baptist, however, Carter registered a 14,000-vote plurality in eleven small, conservative-leaning southern counties and did unusually well in other rural and Republican-leaning areas. Yet Carter supporters knew they could not repeat that showing in rural Ohio in 1980 and thus had to look elsewhere. The prospects were bleak. The unemployment rates in industrial Ohio were staggering: 13 percent in Youngstown and over 10.5 percent in Toledo, and Democrats in those areas said that not only would it not be possible to improve on Carter's 1976 margins but there was sure to be actual slippage.

Throughout industrial Ohio, labor leaders and Democratic politicians lamented that it was impossible to stir any passions for Carter. "Among our rank and file we can't find any enthusiasm for this election," worried Joseph Tomasi, the United Auto Workers regional director in Toledo. Tim Hagan, the bright young Cuyahoga Democratic leader, supported Kennedy in the primaries but as a party loyalist was trying to help Carter now. It was not easy, he acknowledged: "Most of our people don't think the guy [Carter] is a real Democrat. The only hope is to scare people about Reagan, but they're so turned off by Carter even that doesn't do much good."

Pennsylvania was supposed to be easier for the president. Carter had carried the state by 123,000 votes out of 4.6 million last time; over the last twenty years, Pennsylvania had voted Republican only in the 1972 presidential race. The president carried Philadelphia by 256,000 votes in 1976, but—evidence of his problems with traditional Democratic constituencies—he was clobbered there in the primaries by Ted Kennedy. In white ethnic South Philadelphia, ward leaders threw away Carter-Mondale literature, figuring Carter was a drag on their local candidates. The president would win the city's big black vote easily, but black leaders expected a disappointing turnout. Thus David Glancey, the aggressive new party chairman in the city, estimated that Carter's margin in Philadelphia would drop to around 175,000, and most other Democrats thought he needed to win by at least 200,000.

Some Carter operatives hoped that the falloff in Philadelphia might be offset by Reagan's problems in the suburbs; many moderate suburbanites along Philadelphia's affluent Main Line were apprehensive about the conservative Californian on social issues and foreign policy. Yet as election day neared, it seemed most of the voters were willing to swallow these reservations. Explained Faith Wittlesey, the leading GOP politician in big, suburban Delaware County: "Bush helps assuage some doubts, but more than anything else these people think Carter is such a disaster he has to go. Reagan isn't as popular as Jerry Ford in these areas, but he'll do better. The reason is Carter."

These states, along with Michigan, Illinois, and Florida, were the battlegrounds. Two days after the Cleveland debate, both sides did a national poll and agreed that Reagan was ahead, by seven points, according to Wirthlin, and by four to five points, according to Caddell. Gallup and Harris both showed Reagan with a small but clear lead, although the CBS News/*New York Times* poll showed a virtual dead heat.

In examining state and local polls, however, it is apparent that Reagan was on the move the entire last week of the campaign. On November 1, for example, Bob Teeter showed the GOP nominee six points ahead in Missouri and eight points up in Michigan; the same day the Carter-Mondale internal political report noted: "The latest Caddell poll (in Missouri) showed a drop of 15 points. Our supporters in the five largest counties think their support is holding firm and that the poll is wrong." To bolster morale, the campaign noted that Mahoning County, Ohio (in the Youngstown area), was moving to Carter, and experts anticipated a margin of about 1,200 votes; the problem here was that in 1976 Carter carried Mahoning County by more than 29,500 votes.

There was still, however, one last drama to play out—fittingly, the Iranian hostages, the issue that had so dominated American politics, especially Jimmy Carter's fortunes, for the preceding year. After off-again, on-again negotiations, the Iranian parliament finally, less than three days before the election, set four conditions for releasing the hostages. They included a U.S. pledge not to interfere in Iranian affairs, unfreezing of all Iranian assets, abandonment of all U.S. claims against Iran, and returning all the late shah's wealth to Iran.

Carter was in Illinois when this news hit. He had taken on an air of desperation. He was pulling out twenty-year-old Reagan statements to attack his opponent; he dropped by unannounced at an Italian sports banquet in Chicago and inexplicably called former baseball great Mickey Mantle one of the "greatest Italian athletes."

Campaign chief Jordan flew out to Chicago, and early Sunday morning—with the election only a little more than forty-eight hours away—Carter cut short his campaigning and returned to the White

House to deal with the hostage issue. Substantively and politically, however, the president had problems. Except for the pledge to stay out of Iranian affairs, the terms could not be met easily or quickly, as there were considerable legal complications. It soon became apparent that more negotiations were necessary, and the White House dream of securing physical release of the hostages before the election would not be realized.

Further, Carter had a credibility problem here. He had exploited the hostage issue for political advantage during the primaries; after he lost the New York and Connecticut contests, he faced a showdown with Kennedy in the April 1 Wisconsin primary. At 7:20 on the morning of that primary, Carter dramatically invited reporters and television cameras into the Oval Office, where he suggested that progress on the hostage issue was imminent. This was the only early morning news conference Carter held as president. He won the Wisconsin primary, but the promised progress never materialized. By now, both Carter and Reagan polls indicated growing public cynicism on the hostage question. "We dug our own trap on this issue and none of the options were good," lamented one White House aide.

After an entire day of consultations with his substantive and political aides, the president appeared on television, shortly after 6:20 Sunday evening, to say that the Iranian parliament's action was a "significant development," but he still could not say when the hostages might be freed. With days of buildup, this was a decided letdown. The hostages would not bail out Carter this time, and the president decided he had to go back on the campaign trail election eve: one final, exhausting, six-state, fifteen-hour trek across the country.

The Reagan campaign tried to prepare for a last-minute hostage break. Among the contingency plans were some hard-hitting commercials, Stu Spencer said, that "asked basic questions like: how did they get there and why are they getting out now?" Weeks earlier Reagan had already indicated agreement with most of the terms the Iranians eventually spelled out; so on that last weekend he took the high road. Under a prearranged plan, however, former president Gerald Ford and Henry Kissinger were much more critical in interviews on Sunday. Kissinger even suggested that acceptance of the demands would be "humiliating." Thus the Reagan campaign calculated it could play to public cynicism but keep its man above the fray at the same time.

The Reagan party was flying to Cincinnati from Dayton, Ohio, when the president came on television that Sunday evening. Although the plane was in the air, the networks' small portable television sets picked up the president as Reagan aides and dozens of reporters flooded the aisles and climbed over seats to watch. When the president finished, several top Reagan aides broke out in smiles; they knew the hostages were not getting out and they would not have to risk the television commercials or have their candidate take a position.

At the end, the mood among the candidates was markedly different. For weeks Anderson had known he could not win, but he was hoping to achieve a minimum 5 percent so he could get postelection funds. The independent candidate discarded his occasional stuffiness, however, and turned philosophical. He indicated to reporters that he just might run again.

In the last days Reagan was brimming with confidence. He started off the final day with Jerry Ford in Peoria, Illinois, and then flew back to his West Coast home base to wrap up the long campaign. That day Vince Breglio, Wirthlin's chief assistant, got the results of the final national poll in a makeshift office on the nineteenth floor of Los Angeles's Century Plaza Hotel. The poll showed Reagan eleven points ahead, and Breglio rushed to share the good news, but there were only two Spanish-speaking maids. He told them anyway, in English, and they grinned.

By contrast, Carter had the look of a loser, appealing to Anderson voters with the pitch that he shared much in common with the independent candidate he had treated with contempt for months. Monday night Caddell went to his Washington office and got the bad news: the campaign's final national poll put Reagan ten points ahead. Early in the morning on election day, Caddell called the president, who was flying back to his home town of Plains, Georgia, on Air Force One, and gave him the bad news: "It's gone . . . and it's going to be very big." The president, Caddell said, seemed to accept the news with little emotion, but a few hours later, talking to his townspeople, Carter broke down and cried a little.

Election night the Reagan entourage eagerly awaited the results in Los Angeles. The mood at the White House was gloomy, however, as news of the television networks' exit polls poured in during the day—all indications were of a Reagan sweep. Shortly before 7:00 P.M. press secretary Powell told reporters that the president would not concede before 11:00 P.M. eastern standard time (EST), when the polls on the West Coast would close.

Still, at 8:15 P.M. (EST) NBC declared Reagan the winner. Moreover, the Republican candidate was winning almost everywhere, taking all the major industrial states and sweeping the South except for Georgia. About then the president called Powell and said he wanted to concede soon; the concern that the polls were still open on the West Coast was apparently brushed aside. At 9:45 P.M., at the Sheraton Washington Hotel, scene of the Democrats' election night gathering, Jimmy Carter conceded defeat; voters in almost half the country were still going to the polls.

Carter had never established good relations with most other politicians, and many Democrats were horrified by his early concession. One with good cause was Jim Corman, a ten-term California Democratic congressman. Corman had been one of the president's stauchest supporters in Congress: he cast the decisive vote to secure passage of the president's first energy bill, he supported the White House consistently on the House Ways and Means Committee, and even though he had cosponsored national health insurance with Ted Kennedy, he endorsed Carter in the primary. Jim Corman was one of a handful in the entire Congress of what might be called Carter loyalists.

Corman was in the fight of his political life in 1980 against a well-known foe of school busing, an emotional issue in his San Fernando Valley district. After the president conceded, Democrats reported that thousands of West Coast voters left the voting lines; countless others never showed up. Corman aides, at the time, figured the president's action cost them a couple of thousand votes. That night Jim Corman lost reelection by 752 votes.

6

The Media in 1980:
Was the Message the Message?

Michael J. Robinson

Ask a European whether the media made much difference in the presidential campaign of 1980, and he or she will probably point out that Ronald Reagan is a movie star. Fair enough. When the president's credentials include *Bedtime for Bonzo* and *Death Valley Days*, it is hard to argue that the media do not count.

In fact, Reagan's background represents only one of several instances of media intrusion in the campaign. Walter Cronkite, for example, became even more important than usual in this, presumably the last, presidential campaign he will cover. In one of its spring issues, the *New Republic* quoted Cronkite as saying that John Anderson had asked him to be Anderson's vice-president—and that Cronkite had tentatively agreed. Cronkite also served as a channel for—and inadvertently helped to scuttle—the historic negotiations between Jerry Ford and Ronald Reagan at the Republican National Convention. In fact, the CBS staff came dangerously close to serving as national bagmen in that ill-fated "dream ticket" of Reagan-Ford. Starting with the notorious Mudd-Kennedy interview, media were *very* visible throughout the 1980 campaign.

Some famous Americans even talked as if the media actually *were* the election. In the midst of his own vice-presidential campaign, Walter Mondale called the evening news "the most indispensable power" in presidential politics.[1] And when asked about the meaning of the press in the campaign, John Connally put it more bluntly: "On a scale of ten the importance of media is at least eight and everything else is two."[2] For the last dozen years, the media have been to

[1] Kathy Sawyer, "The White House Has Become the Nation's Fire Hydrant," *Washington Post*, October 10, 1980.
[2] "John Connally Critiques His Press," *Washington Journalism Review*, July/August 1980, p. 20.

177

campaign "theory" what sex has been to clinical psychiatry—the first and foremost factor analyzed. Admittedly, no professional psychiatrist can completely ignore sex in considering the personal problems of clients, nor can a political analyst legitimately ignore the media in discussing any presidential campaign. Nevertheless, either factor— the media or sex—can be mistakenly applied when explaining a particular case.

Still, the more popular thinking holds that presidential campaigns grow more media determined as time goes by—that the 1976 campaign was *inevitably* more media based than the 1972 campaign, and so on. The growing power of media in elections has come to be regarded as almost inexorable. The assumption that media always get more important in presidential elections needs some rethinking, however, especially now that the 1980 campaign has become history. And despite Connally's rankings, despite Cronkite's dalliance in vice-presidential politics, despite Reagan's film relationship with Bonzo, I think that the 1980 campaign may prove, after all, to have been a "critical election," if not in terms of party alignments, then at least in our thoughts about the impact of media on politics.

If we look *beyond* strategy and at *outcomes*, the power of media in the 1980 campaign did not follow or build directly from the campaign that preceded it. I would argue, in fact, that the *results* in 1980 show that media do not inevitably become more important in determining outcomes, even if they do consistently dominate candidate schedules and campaign decisions.

Finally, it seems that 1980 saw less of a mass-media election than did 1976 for reasons that transcend the specifics of this campaign. And although much of the decline in the importance of media in the 1980 campaign was due to the uniqueness of the campaign, I believe that 1980 produced precedents that might make the media less important in the next few presidential campaigns than they have been in our recent past.

Paid Media

Before comparing the effect of media on the last two campaigns, we need to decide which media we are talking about. In this essay the greater focus is on "free media," news coverage and public affairs journalism. Paid media (advertising) are treated more incidentally. In fact the thesis offered here—that media played a somewhat less central role in 1980 than in 1976—pertains only to "free media." And although it would be relatively easy to build a discussion of paid media into that thesis, it probably would not be worth the effort.

The evidence from the past several elections, and from this election as well, indicates that paid media generally count for comparatively little in determining the turning points or the outcome of any given presidential campaign. The history of the limited effects of paid media in presidential politics is a comparatively long one—at least by the standards of history associated with television. In a statistical analysis of the presidential vote in 1956 and 1960, Gary Jacobson found no relationship between media expenditures and state-by-state voting patterns. In fact, in the 1956 campaign Jacobson found the precise correlation between dollars and votes to have been the almost never attained 0.00.[3]

In 1970 DeVries and Tarrance asked voters in Michigan about the things that influenced their perceptions of candidates for governor (the level of election most analogous to president). In a list of thirty-five factors that influenced voters, television spots ranked twenty-fourth in perceived importance. Television news, on the other hand, ranked first.[4] And again in the 1970s, paid media proved notably unimportant in presidential voting. Although in *The Unseeing Eye* Patterson and McClure heavily emphasized the fact that television spots in 1972 contained five times as much issue content as campaign coverage on the evening news, they eventually found that those spots were nearly impotent when it came to moving voters. According to Patterson and McClure, only 1 percent of the eligible electorate was actually "manipulated" by the television ads and, at the outside limit, only 2 percent of the sample was in any way influenced by them.[5]

In the Carter-Ford election, political science demonstrated how far we had come in establishing the superiority of free media to paid. The two major books coming out of the 1976 campaign dealing directly with the media virtually ignored advertising. An implicit, if inadvertent, conclusion drawn from both Tom Patterson's *Media Election*[6] and James David Barber's *Race for the Presidency*[7] is that paid media did not count at all in 1976. Paid media were not even discussed. In 1980 the established pattern holds up nicely—the

---

[3] Gary Jacobson, "The Impact of Broadcast Campaigning in Electoral Outcomes," *Journal of Politics*, vol. 37 (1975), p. 781.

[4] Walter DeVries and V. L. Tarrance, *The Ticket Splitters: A New Force in American Politics* (Grand Rapids, Mich.: William Erdmans, 1972), p. 77.

[5] Thomas Patterson and Robert McClure, *The Unseeing Eye: The Myth of Television Power in National Elections* (New York: Putnam, 1976), p. 134.

[6] Thomas Patterson, *The Mass Media Election: How Americans Choose Their President* (New York: Praeger, 1980).

[7] James D. Barber, *Race for the Presidency: The Media and the Nominating Process* (Englewood Cliffs, N.J.: Prentice-Hall, 1978).

campaign gives little, if any, support for the idea that paid media work in a presidential campaign. Even in the primary campaign, where paid ads have always proved more effective, 1980 produced precious little evidence for a paid-media effect.

The Primaries. Using data from the Federal Election Commission (FEC), I have identified the ten most hotly contested primaries, in terms of the highest campaign expenditures, for both the Republican and the Democratic parties.[8] Despite the fact that the figures from the FEC do not tell us how much was spent on radio and television, they do indicate the level of campaign effort in each state. Given that practically every candidate spends at least half of his total budget on media, these figures approximate rather closely how much was spent by each of the candidates on mass media in the 1980 campaign.

Figure 6–1 shows the dollars spent by each of the top four competitors—Carter, Kennedy, Reagan, and Bush—in each of the ten states in which the candidates spent the most money, calculated as a proportion of FEC spending limits. For the Democrats, not surprisingly, Jimmy Carter, the incumbent, outspent Edward Kennedy in nine of those ten states—but Carter lost in four. Kennedy, on the other hand, outspent Carter in just one of those ten states—New Hampshire. Kennedy, of course, lost there, and badly. In Iowa, where CBS kept track of money actually spent on television ads, Kennedy outspent Carter by over 10 percent—Carter clobbered Kennedy in Iowa.

Somewhat surprisingly, on the Republican side, George Bush outspent Ronald Reagan in seven of the ten most hotly contested Republican states. After Connally, Bush was, in fact, the big spending challenger. Yet Bush lost four of the seven primaries where he spent more, and Reagan lost big in one of the three states where he had outspent Bush. That was Iowa, Bush's greatest triumph. All told, for both parties in the top ten states in terms of campaign effort, the big spender won in only half the cases. In fact, big spenders did even worse than this statement suggests, given that Jerry Brown was far and away the spendthrift candidate in the Wisconsin primary, where he got only 12 percent of the Democratic vote.

Anyone familiar with the election understands that the Carter administration's vote against Israel in the United Nations in early March had a far greater impact than anybody's paid-media campaign

---

[8] Federal Election Commission, *FEC Reports on Financial Activity, 1979-1980,* interim report no. 7, *Presidential Pre-Nominations Campaigns* (Washington, D.C.: FEC, 1980).

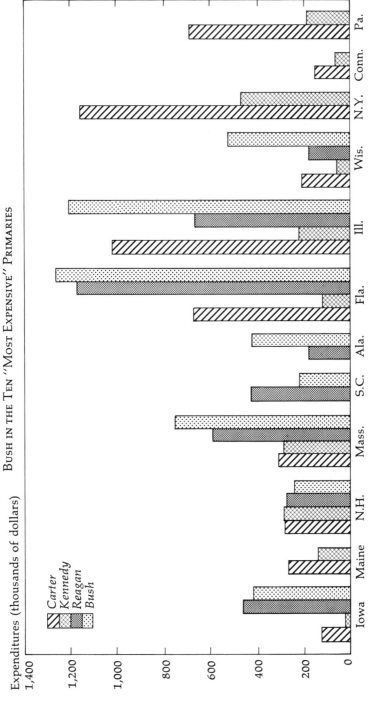

FIGURE 6–1

Campaign Expenditures for Carter, Kennedy, Reagan, and Bush in the Ten "Most Expensive" Primaries

—and that, of course, is the point. Paid media meant next to nothing in New York or Connecticut, given the critically important message in the free media being offered at the time.[9]

Kennedy's campaign proved to be a case study in this ironic aspect of paid media. Without much question Kennedy's greatest victory in vote percentage, and in political significance, came in New York. Although he was not expected to win, Kennedy carried New York with a plurality of 20 percent. Yet Carter had outspent Kennedy by more than two to one in that election. More important, perhaps, was the fact that the major ad in Kennedy's New York ad campaign—the one featuring Ethel Kennedy in tennis whites talking about Kennedy's family life—was considered to be among the year's worst in quality. The "Ethel ad" was labeled, in fact, "one of the worst in the history of political television."[10] Still, Kennedy did better in New York than in any other state save two—his native Massachusetts and heavily Catholic Rhode Island.

The Bush case is similar: Bush did best where he advertised least. Bush won in Iowa, where Reagan outspent him. Bush came in a distant third in Illinois, where he outspent both Reagan and Anderson—each by over half a million dollars. In Michigan, where Bush made his last real stand, he beat Reagan by nearly two to one in the popular vote, although Reagan outspent him in Michigan by more than three to one. Only in Pennsylvania could one make a credible case that Bush bought a primary victory.

The futility of the presidential paid-media campaigns is told best in the saga of John B. Connally. Connally, largely portrayed by the free media as the Fortune 500 candidate, refused public finance and matching funds. He was, therefore, able to spend whatever he could raise, wherever he chose to spend it. He spent as much (or more) and spent it as rapidly (or more rapidly) as any other candidate. And he spent most of it on paid media. His was the near-ultimate media campaign.

All told, Connally spent $12.5 million in three months and in the early months spent at an even faster rate than Reagan. Not only did Connally fail, but he failed more conspicuously than any other Republican. Despite his corporate-backed media extravaganza, he won no primaries, no caucuses. By the time he withdrew from the

[9] The one state where Carter people believe that they did buy a primary was Ohio. Carter outspent Kennedy there about two to one. Ohio was not, however, a major-effort state as defined here.

[10] Frank Greve, "How Media Advisors Bungled Job for Ted," *Miami Herald*, March 23, 1980. The quotation is attributed to Sidney Blumenthal.

race, he had won one convention vote—that of Ada Mills of Arkansas. The media dubbed Mills "the thirteen-million-dollar delegate" and enthusiastically reported on her eventual switch to Bush—testimony to Connally's ability to buy little more than disdain among the working press.

There is even some preliminary evidence from social science indicating that television ads in the 1980 primaries were "artistic successes but political duds." Edwin Diamond, at MIT, working with viewers of campaign ads from Iowa, New Hampshire, Massachusetts, New York and Connecticut, "found little evidence that they (the ads) influenced the votes of anyone." Primaries in 1980 prove again that candidates continue to increase their paid television budgets but that voters continue to exhibit little interest and even less vulnerability.[11]

The General Election. For quite some time we have know that advertising money buys fewer votes in November than in the spring primaries. In his seminal work concerning broadcasting expenditures and the vote, Gary Jacobson finds that paid media in the 1970s were three times as powerful in winning votes in primaries as they were in general campaigns.[12] Unfortunately, it is impossible to replicate Jacobson's research in the 1980 elections because the FCC no longer collects statistics on *broadcast* expenditures; the FEC collects figures only on total expenditures. Neither the Carter nor the Reagan campaign collected media budget figures, state by state, for the general election campaign. Network "media buys" make that kind of bookkeeping almost impossible. So there is practically no way to test how well Carter and Reagan did in the general campaign as a function of state-by-state radio and television advertising. What we do know suggests that the old Jacobson finding still holds—the electorate is much less malleable in the fall than in the spring.

Reagan, for example, chose not to spend any money in New York to buy ads—essentially writing off the state. Still, he did very well in New York, where Carter made his biggest media effort: despite forfeiting the ad campaign to Carter, Reagan beat him in New York by over 160,000 votes. Without television Reagan did about as well in New York as he did in the rest of the urbanized East.

Perhaps the most interesting evidence that advertising fails more completely in general elections than in primaries comes from a set of

[11] United Press International, day wire, April 9, 1980.
[12] Jacobson, "Impact of Broadcast Campaigning," p. 781.

miniexperiments conducted by Robert Kaiser, the 1980 political media analyst for the *Washington Post*. Kaiser conducted uncontrolled experiments with potential voters in Albany, New York, during the primaries and in Wilmington, Delaware, during the general campaign. Kaiser found that while Reagan and Carter did win the battle of the television ads in March when each was pitted against his primary opponents, by late October neither Carter nor Reagan was winning any real support with his general campaign ads. What makes this particular "October surprise" interesting is that Kaiser used *undecided* voters in his Wilmington experiment. While noting the limitations of his own "unscientific" study, Kaiser did conclude that "Jimmy Carter and Ronald Reagan just may be wasting most of the $15 million each is spending to advertise himself this fall."[13]

All this makes perfectly good sense. During the primaries voters look at a very large field without much information about many of the candidates, other than the information in the ads. And with primary voters inevitably choosing from a list of candidates within their party, party labels mean nothing in primaries; "image" means much more. During the general election, voters focus on a much more limited field—a field on which free media shower information day by day and candidate by candidate. And in general elections party labels become marginally meaningful again. The logical conclusion seems unavoidable—however overstated the impact of paid media may be on primary elections, the overstatement is much greater in general elections.

Perhaps the history of the last five presidential elections puts paid media into an appropriate perspective. In those elections where the media allegedly made the difference between victory and defeat— 1960, 1968, 1976—it was always the free media that made that difference. The first Kennedy-Nixon debate in 1960, television coverage of the riots in Chicago in 1968, Ford's "Polish freedom" gaffe in the second debate in 1976—all of these turning points involved news and public affairs, and none involved commercials.

It is also conceivable that paid media were less important in 1980 than in any other recent campaign—not because of any change

---

[13] Robert Kaiser, "$30 Million TV Spending May Do Little for Carter and Reagan," *Washington Post*, October 22, 1980.

The only evidence suggesting that paid media had any substantial impact is circumstantial and comes from Reagan's media blitz in the last ten days of the campaign. Reagan spent $600,000 a day for paid media in that period, and according to Richard Wirthlin, Reagan's pollster, that money produced much of the "November surprise." Still, Reagan's victory in the debate and the disappointment over the hostages also came during the last ten days.

in the electorate or technology but because of the law. The 1980 campaign was the first wholly uninterrupted, publicly financed campaign.[14] Public finance ensures that both candidates have equal funding in the general campaign. And even in the primaries, public finance means that the richest candidate cannot spend above the FEC limits for each state.

Public financing of presidential campaigns is *not* the most important factor in the comparative weakness of paid media. The most important factor is that presidential elections produce so much free media material about the candidates that voters need not rely on the ads for their impressions.[15] Still, public finance added one more limitation to the power of presidential paid media.

Paid Media in Nonpresidential Campaigns. Paid media did have their moments in 1980, but, as usual, those moments did not come at the presidential level. Some congressmen and some senators came very close to buying a seat in 1980—Robert Dornan, for example, spent $1.5 million on his race, the largest total ever, and was reelected in his Los Angeles district. In 1980, however, the impact of paid media was confined not merely to the traditional, individual campaigns for House or Senate.

1. *Republican congressional television ads.* In 1980 the Republican National Committee (RNC) did something with paid media that had never been done before—they staged a nationwide television campaign asking viewers to "Vote Republican, for a Change." Although the RNC had pioneered with national television in the 1978 midterm elections, spending about $1 million in that television campaign, their major effort began in 1979.

In November 1979, Republican pollster Robert Teeter released national survey data indicating that a majority of the electorate finally knew that the Democrats had controlled Congress for the last twenty years and that the Republican party had finally lost its image as the party of hard times. Buoyed by these findings, the RNC put up $5 million to test the impact of a well-designed ad campaign—a series of commercials both reiterating that Democratic control of Congress had lasted a long time and blaming the Democrats for inflation, energy shortages, and unemployment. These ads ran in three cities in the Midwest, where public response was measured both before and after the "buys." Teeter and his associates also conducted

[14] In January 1976, the Supreme Court ruling in Buckley v. Valeo eventually caused a holdup in matching funds—a delay that probably hurt Reagan the most.
[15] Jacobson, "Impact of Broadcast Campaigning," p. 774.

a second round of evaluations in those same test cities in April and June.

Although the RNC has not yet made its complete findings public, the results made available are stunning.[16] In one of the midwestern test cities, between January and June the percentage of respondents planning to vote Democratic in the congressional elections dropped from 49 percent to 29 percent. The RNC also found that in August, just after the $5 million national campaign had ended, the Gallup poll showed that 42 percent of its respondents planned to vote Republican in the November congressional elections, about five points higher than the usual Gallup figure for midsummer in an election year. It was also in early August that Harris shocked everybody by showing a one-point Republican lead among potential voters for Congress. Having concluded that its ads had made the difference, the RNC quickly decided to spend another $5 million on national advertising in the general election.

It would be foolish to attribute all or most of the Republican congressional gains to the ads alone. Still, the success revealed in Teeter's private research reinforces two important truths about paid media. First, once ad campaigns move below the rarefied atmosphere of presidential politics, they can work relative wonders. Second, when ad campaigns are not challenged by the other side—especially at the congressional level—they have considerably greater chance of success. If the sometimes poignant, sometimes funny RNC spots planned for 1982 go completely unchallenged—as was the case in 1980—they will help the Republicans in their bid to seize control of the House. A well-crafted, heavily financed, and *uncontested* ad campaign does influence congressional elections—1980 is substantial proof.

2. *Political action committee (PAC) television.* Republicans also benefited from a second innovation in paid media during 1980—the growth in PAC television. Under the law, political action committees can contribute to any political candidate, but the law also permits PACs to spend money *on behalf* of candidates. As long as this PAC money is expended "independently" of the candidate (that is, without the candidate's personal involvement or control), the normal spending limitations do not apply.

In the 1980 campaign the biggest PACs spent most of their money in "independent expenditures." In fact, according to Morton Mintz, 90 percent of the contributions from the three biggest PACs

[16] Statistics provided by Michael Baroody of the Republican National Committee.

were of the independent variety.[17] And because the law does require that PAC independent expenditures go into communication of one sort or another, PACs spend most of their independent funds on paid media. Thus the 1980 campaign was, as a matter of law and political reality, a watershed in the development of PAC television. Independent expenditures for media were not new in 1980—liberal philanthropist Stewart Mott pioneered with them in 1968 and 1972, first in favor of Nelson Rockefeller, then in opposition to Richard Nixon. And Environmental Action used independent contributions to defeat the congressional "Dirty Dozen" in 1972 and 1976. PAC television in 1980 was different, however.

First, in contrast to earlier years, almost all the large, independent PAC contributions went to conservative Republicans. Stewart Mott and Norman Lear spent over $200,000 on behalf of John Anderson, but their contributions were personal, not made through a PAC. The overwhelming bulk of the independent PAC money was spent by a relatively small handful of right-wing organizations. Biggest among all PACs were the National Conservative Political Action Committee (NCPAC), Jesse Helms's Congressional Club (CC), and the Fund for a Conservative Majority (FCM). These three PACs alone spent $17 million between January 1979 and November 1980 attacking Carter, defending Reagan, and targeting six incumbent liberal senators. NCPAC spent $1.2 million in its Senate campaigns against Birch Bayh, Frank Church, Alan Cranston, John Culver, George McGovern, and, eventually, Tom Eagleton.[18]

The second development in PAC campaigning involved the unprecedented reliance on television. In the past television had been considered too expensive, but this time conservative PACs used television as a preferred medium. As of September the five largest conservative PACs had planned to spend $12.5 million on anti-Carter media during the course of the general campaign.[19] Eventually they spent far less than that—under $2 million—mostly on broadcasting and mostly in the South. Yet nothing nearly as expensive, as visible, or as negative as this had ever happened before on television.

PAC television came of age in another way in the 1980 campaign: for the first time ever, somebody decided to evaluate the impact sys-

[17] Morton Mintz, "Conservative PACs Continue Late, Heavy Spending Flurry," *Washington Post*, November 2, 1980.

[18] Bill Keller, " 'New Right' Wants Credit for Democrats' Nov. 4 Losses, but GOP, Others, Don't Agree," *Congressional Quarterly Weekly Report*, November 15, 1980, p. 3372.

[19] James Dickenson, "Conservatives to Saturate Airwaves on GOP's Behalf," *Washington Star*, September 28, 1980.

187

tematically. NCPAC, the biggest and most professional of the conservative PACs, did *not* evaluate the effect of its independent media campaign on the presidential race. NCPAC did do considerable evaluation of its impact on the targeted Senate races, however. In fact, NCPAC undertook full-scale evaluation programs in four of the six states—Iowa, South Dakota, Idaho, and Missouri.

The most interesting evaluation took place in Missouri, where NCPAC had originally intended not to challenge Thomas Eagleton. But eventually NCPAC chose to use Missouri as a laboratory, to test the impact of its negative media campaign in a state where the incumbent was seen as unbeatable. Between May and June NCPAC set up a field experiment in the town of Springfield. Using a private pollster, NCPAC measured public attitudes just before and just after its radio and television blitz—one based on the NCPAC slogan "the closer you look at (Tom Eagleton's) record, the less you like what you see."

Focusing on Eagleton's record, the ads caused drastic changes in his public image. Figure 6–2 shows the percentage of those interviewed who held positive images of Eagleton's record in national defense, energy, taxes, and economics both before and after the two-week negative campaign. Before the test, according to these surveys, Eagleton's policy image was positive, on average, in just over one-third of the cases. After the ads had run, just two weeks later, less than one-sixth of the response was positive—his positive policy image had been cut by more than one-half.[20]

In the ultimate test—public voting intention—NCPAC ads proved just as effective. The percentage of those planning to vote for Eagleton no matter who opposed him fell from one-third to one-sixth. And in a trial heat with Gene McNary, Eagleton lost what had been an overwhelming lead. In May, Eagleton had 65 percent of the vote; in June, 31 percent!

We should remember that McNary eventually lost to Eagleton. And during the general election, the NCPAC ads themselves became a big issue, as targeted senators struck back at their opponents by attacking NCPAC for carpetbagging and hate-mongering. In fact, in the states where NCPAC had done year-long monitoring of the ad campaign, it found that a clear majority of those who said the ads had influenced them were influenced *in favor* of the targeted liberal. In South Dakota, for example, by November, among those having seen the ads, twice as many voters were *more* likely than were less likely to vote for McGovern because of the ads. Even so, NCPAC

[20] Terry Dolan, "To National Conservative Policy Advisory Council Members," memorandum, July 2, 1980, NCPAC files.

FIGURE 6–2

PERCENTAGE OF RESPONDENTS BELIEVING THAT SENATOR THOMAS
EAGLETON WAS DOING A GOOD JOB, MAY AND JUNE 1980

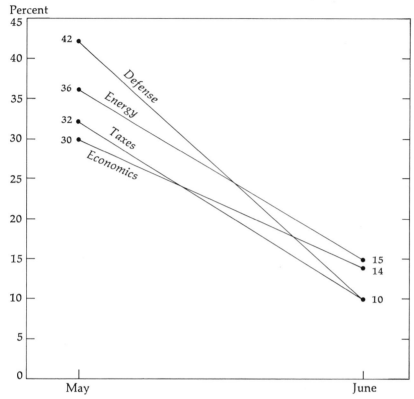

NOTE: Respondents evaluated Senator Eagleton's performance in the areas of defense, energy, taxes, and economics.

SOURCE: Terry Dolan, "To National Conservative Policy Advisory Council Members," memorandum, July 2, 1980, NCPAC files.

directors believe that the ads helped the conservative candidates more than they hurt, because the ads put liberal incumbents on the defensive and set the agenda of the campaign. NCPAC points out, for instance, that in South Dakota before the ads ran, voters did not think about McGovern in terms of his position on abortion, but after the ads McGovern's abortion stand was paramount in voters' minds.[21] Despite some backlash, NCPAC expects to continue its television campaign in 1982.

[21] NCPAC polls conducted by Arthur J. Finkelstein, provided to author through NCPAC. For a discussion of NCPAC's role, see Bill Keller, " 'New Right.' "

With two of the six targeted senators winning, the overall efficacy of the ad campaign remains unclear. What is clear, from both the Eagleton case and the McGovern case, is that paid media work well when public images of the candidate are vague, when the opponents let the paid media go unanswered, and when the incumbent is clearly on the "wrong" side of the issues. Because those conditions generally do not apply at the presidential level, however, paid media—NCPAC notwithstanding—fail to move presidential campaigns the way free media do.

Free Media

Reality and "Mediality" in 1980. Declaring that paid media are outside the scope of this chapter does not solve the more basic definitional problem in media research: distinguishing the effects of media from the effects of "reality." This is a theoretical, not merely a statistical, problem, because the medium alone is *not* the message. Unless we make some theoretical distinction between medium and message, we run the risk of confusing the effect of media with the effect of real events.

To handle this problem we can adopt a fourfold definition of campaign reality because, in any presidential election, four types of circumstances, beyond party loyalty, strongly affect the outcome. Together these four circumstances represent the "reality" of the campaign. First are *national conditions*—the state of the nation as the campaign begins. Is the nation at war or in a recession? Is it the Soviet army or the civil rights movement that has been on the march? As 1980 began, national conditions included an inflation rate of more than 10 percent and an international situation approximating the cold war. Second are the real *events*—events that force the public to reassess national conditions during the course of the campaign. The Iranian seizure of American hostages in early November 1979 constituted a classic instance of a real-world "event." Third are *political actions*—campaign events that are portrayed as discrete, meaningful news stories about the players in the contest. Gerald Ford's decision not to run in 1980 was a political action—a move with political significance under any plausible system of media imaginable. These three circumstances—national conditions, real events, and political actions—represent a best approximation of reality. Not so with the fourth circumstance—what I have chosen, for want of a better word, to call *mediality*.

Mediality is closely akin to both Daniel Boorstin's notion of

"pseudoevent"[22] and Jules Witcover's definition of a media event—
"the overblowing of an insignificant early phase of [the campaign]
for the purpose of satisfying the need for hard news."[23] Mediality
goes beyond both of those concepts, however, incorporating as well
the idea of news priorities and news themes. In other words, mediality
includes not only Bush's classic debating blunder in the New Hampshire primary but also the media agenda, especially when that agenda
lacks any clear objective base. Medialities are events, developments,
or situations to which the media have given importance by emphasizing, expanding, or featuring them in such a way that their real
significance has been modified, distorted, or obscured.

Argued most broadly, all conditions in national politics could be
considered medialities. It can, after all, be argued that even something as tangible as unemployment is more a mediality than a reality.
Without media coverage no substantial share of the electorate could
really know that unemployment had risen 1, 2, even 3 percent in the
space of a year, let alone every thirty days.

Without the Bureau of Labor Statistics and the national press
together offering monthly reports, unemployment would have meaning only under conditions that were literally boom or bust. Yet if
unemployment is considered a mediality, the term could define almost
any circumstance or political action. The problem is that some
analysts do just that—view reality and media as one and the same.
I prefer to see mediality as limited to those conditions and events that
fall well short of war, depression, inflation, and matters of state.
I prefer a definition of mediality that includes events, themes, and
blunders that clearly have meaning only as day-to-day campaign news
—that *become* news because they make the campaign seem important,
relevant, personally meaningful to potential audiences. Breaking
diplomatic relations with Iran is an event, a reality. Counting up,
day by day, the number of days our hostages have been held in Iran
is—just as plainly—a mediality.

Medialities, 1976 and 1980. Having defined medialities as media-based
situations that alter the shape or direction of a campaign, I should
note my major point, that there were fewer crucial medialities in
1980 than in 1976. This does *not* mean that candidates used free
media less—or tried to manipulate media less—in 1980. Since 1972
the media—especially television—have been the key concern of

[22] Daniel Boorstin, *The Image* (New York: Harper and Row, 1964), p. 34.
[23] Jules Witcover, *Marathon: The Pursuit of the Presidency, 1972–1976* (New
York: Viking, 1977), p. 202.

campaign strategy. Candidates build virtually everything around private polls and public presentation of self on the evening news. The obsession with getting on television and getting good television was at least as great in 1980 as in 1976.

In 1980 we witnessed a constant flow of embarrassing concessions by candidates to television. John Anderson, desperate for news coverage and justifiably worried that as an independent he would get no air time during the convention period, campaigned by touring both Europe and the Middle East. He even told the National Rifle Association that it should support gun registration—posing for film crews in the process.

Jimmy Carter, trailing badly in the polls, on two separate occasions left the White House and drove to northern Virginia to sign less than crucial bills into law: Carter's aides figured that the presidential motorcade and a mobile Rose Garden would get him the lead story on the evening news. (They were wrong.)

As front-runner, Ronald Reagan actually staged fewer "events" just for news time—he ran a low-key, accommodate-the-media campaign. Reagan's major concession to television involved having Lyn Nofziger hurl himself in front of cameras whenever Reagan departed from his text. Thus it seems that by 1976 we had already reached a ceiling in terms of television-based campaigning, and in 1980 there was no room to grow. Even if television did affect scheduling and strategy more in 1980, our principal concern here lies with outcomes, not with documenting the history of media campaigning. Although the 1980 campaign proved to be as television-strategic as the 1976 campaign, what was different was the extent to which any of it mattered—how much of the voting depended on mediality. The answer is: less in 1980.

Mediality and Outcome. The best evidence for my thesis comes from election results, especially the results of the primary campaigns. If one is willing to choose January as the starting date of the 1980 campaign, and if one is willing to define the nomination of front-runners or incumbents as indicators of media weakness, then the 1980 results suggest that the media in 1980 made less difference.

In 1976 the incumbent president came very close to losing his party's nomination; in 1980 the incumbent easily defeated his leading primary opponent. In 1976 the out-party nominated a man who began the year with the support of 3 percent of his party's identifiers; in 1980 the out-party nominated the man who had been front-runner for at least the preceding three years. As for the nominations, 1980 resembled 1948 more than 1976.

Nonshifting Sands in 1980. Obviously, just looking at the names and placements of the eventual nominees masks a great deal. Front-runners who win do not prove that media did not matter. In fact, if we use October 1979 as the start of the 1980 campaign, the front-runner for the Democratic nomination actually lost. Still, looking at the results from the entire election campaign also suggests that media were moving fewer grains of sand in 1980 than in 1976. It starts in the primaries. On the Republican side at least, stability in *real* opinion about candidates appeared throughout much of the spring. In a nine-wave panel survey conducted in New Jersey between October 1979 and July 1980, Zukin and Keeter found that the percentage of people having no opinion about George Bush fell only from 60 to 57 percent during those nine months.[24] Bush's case was not unique. New Jersey voters showed the same sort of nonopinion stability toward all the Republicans, even John Anderson. Zukin and Keeter attribute this form of stability to the noninformational quality of campaign news and to a lack of audience interest. Whatever the causes, media coverage of the Republicans in the 1980 primaries did not produce much solid opinion or meaningful opinion change about the contestants, at least not in New Jersey. But the conclusion that media moved less sand in 1980 is rooted in one simple observation: much less sand moved in this general election than in the one before it. Nothing much happened from September on.

In the absence of any major world event, in the absence of any real change in the national condition, shifts in political preferences might well be interpreted as media effects. But if the polls change little during the campaign, the implication is that campaign actions and campaign medialities are not influencing many voters—or, at the least, are influencing voters "both ways."

From January to June 1976 the Gallup poll's percentage of Democrats preferring Jimmy Carter for the party's nomination leaped forty-six points, with precious few real events—but many medialities —to explain the leap. The medialities began in 1975, when R. W. Apple of the *New York Times* reported that the then-unknown Carter was running a "surprisingly strong" campaign in Iowa, and ended on the day of the last primaries in June 1976, when Carter's loss of California and New Jersey was overshadowed by television's quicker reporting of his victory in Ohio. In the general election

---

[24] Cliff Zukin and Scot Keeter, "The Origin and Development of Voters' Images of Candidates during Presidential Primaries" (Paper delivered at the annual meeting of the American Political Science Association, Washington, D.C., August 1980), fig. 2.

campaign of 1976, again with no major event or change in condition, Gerald Ford gained thirty points in the Gallup poll in ten weeks' time—producing the greatest shift in political sand in the history of Gallup polls in general elections for president.

In 1980 public opinion was much less volatile. During the nine months before the election, Carter's approval score did ride a roller coaster, but much of Carter's image practically stood still. On the crucial issue of the economy—the issue most in evidence in the final vote—Carter's approval scores between November 1979 and August 1980 were 21, 27, 26, 23, 21, 18, 19—hardly evidence of shifting sand.[25]

Most important, the polls for the major contenders in the general campaign proved conspicuous in their stability. The Harris poll—which despite its reputation for inaccuracy proved to be the most accurate poll in 1980—presented an opinion graph looking considerably more like the Kansas plain than the Colorado Rockies. Harris, who came within 3 percent sampling error in his final predictions, found that from June on—after the nominations were settled and Anderson had declared his intentions—Reagan led Carter at every stage of the general campaign. Never once did Carter pull ahead of Reagan in the Harris poll, even allowing for sampling error. In terms of public opinion, the 1976 campaign was practically psychotic; the 1980 campaign was mental health. Even the last few weeks of the 1980 campaign were "uneventful." Reagan's own pollster, Richard Wirthlin, conducted 10,500 phone interviews during the last eighteen days before the election. Although most people imagine those days to have been highly volatile, they were not—at least according to Wirthlin's data—data that predicted an eleven-point Reagan victory, just one percentage point removed from the actual count (figure 6–3).

Reagan's popularity showed a shift of only three percentage points in those last two and a half weeks. Carter's popularity shifted a little more in the last week, but even the Cleveland debate added only one percentage point to Reagan's estimated total vote.

Two things must be said about these comparisons of the two campaigns. First, less movement in the polls is not direct proof that media were less effective in changing voters' minds. Clearly, with data like these we cannot know whether nobody was changing his mind or whether changes were cutting several ways at once. What is more, media could well have been a cause for stability. Still, these polls are

[25] Kathleen A. Frankovic, "Public Opinion Trends," in Gerald Pomper, *The Election of 1980: Reports and Interpretations* (Chatham, N.J.: Chatham House, 1981), p. 100.

FIGURE 6-3

VOTER PREFERENCE FOR REAGAN, CARTER, AND ANDERSON:
THE WIRTHLIN POLL, THE LAST EIGHTEEN DAYS

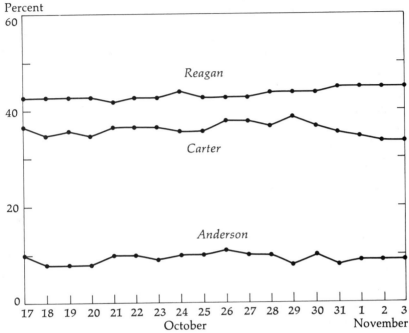

SOURCE: Surveys by Decision Making Information.

not comfortably consistent with either the notion that the Carter-Reagan debate was "unusually decisive" or the idea that the last-minute medialities—Amy's nuclear policy, the hostage anniversary, any of the late-autumn gaffes—caused an electoral earthquake. Second, these figures overlook Kennedy's fall of 1979—the last two months of the year, which did produce an opinional Mt. St. Helens within the Democratic party.

Before the seizure of the hostages on November 4, 1979, Kennedy was the preference for the nomination. In October, he led Carter among Democrats by two to one in all the major polls. In February, it was precisely the reverse: Kennedy dropped just over thirty points in the Gallup poll between October and March. Thus Kennedy's decline in 1979–1980 was almost as meteoric as Carter's rise in 1976.

The reason? It could have been the Roger Mudd interview; or the media's resurrection of Chappaquiddick; or the ill-conceived, ill-timed Kennedy remarks about the despotic shah; or simply the public's rallying to Carter after the seizure in Teheran and the occupa-

TABLE 6–1

A Listing of Major and Critical Medialities in the 1976 and 1980 Presidential Elections

1976

1. *Carter's media victory in Iowa*
2. *Reagan's $90 billion blunder*
3. *Reagan's "unexpected" loss in New Hampshire*
4. *Carter's victory coverage in New Hampshire*
5. Reagan's North Carolina victory and speech
6. Carter's "ethnic purity" comment
7. Carter's come-from-behind "miracle" in Wisconsin
8. Carter's Pennsylvania victory
9. "Super Tuesday's" press coverage
10. Carter's "lust in my heart" interview
11. Ford's "unexpected" success in the first debate
12. *Ford's Polish freedom fiasco*

1980

1. *Kennedy's Roger Mudd interview*
2. *Kennedy's blunder concerning the shah*
3. *Bush's "big" victory in Iowa*
4. *Bush's Nashua disaster*
5. The Anderson surprise in New England
6. Reagan little gaffes
7. Carter's meanness
8. The debate debate
9. The last debate
10. *The hostages*

NOTE: Critical medialities appear in italics.
SOURCE: Author.

tion of Kabul. Still, whichever reason one likes, "mediality" plainly marks Kennedy's fall from public grace.

An Inventory of Mediality. Can Kennedy's fall be reconciled with the thesis that media mattered less in 1980 than in 1976? I think so, if one remembers that the thesis is not that media failed to do anything in 1980 but that they did less. Medialities were *less* important in 1980, not unimportant. And although Kennedy's case probably represents the high-water mark in media consequences in the 1980 campaign, his was clearly not the only watermark on the campaign.

Table 6–1 lists my selection of the major and critical medialities of 1976 and 1980, with the critical cases listed in italics. It shows that 1980 had fewer entries and, more important, fewer "critical" entries—

critical medialities defined as those that really did turn someone's campaign around or upside down.

The table does not list some medialities that got considerable attention at the time: for example, the Clarence Kelly "valence" issue and the Mondale-Dole debate, in which Dole implicitly blamed the Democrats for 3 million war dead, are excluded from the 1976 list. Excluded from 1980 are Bush's successes in the 1979 straw polls and the Billy Carter issue of summer 1980. Aficionados of politics may remember these affairs, but they were important in terms neither of overall coverage nor of anyone's standing in the polls. To the extent that it is possible to reconstruct campaign history, I have listed only the "historic" medialities.

Medialities, 1976. The top dozen medialities of 1976 should be familiar to almost anyone who follows presidential politics. In the primaries we had (1) Carter's media victory in the Iowa caucuses, in which Carter got 28 percent of the vote and was enthusiastically declared the Democratic front-runner, despite the fact that 37 percent of the caucus participants voted "uncommitted"; (2) Reagan's "$90 billion plan," in which the press resurrected from a months-old speech a statement declaring that by turning back domestic policy to the states, the nation could save $90 billion—a remark that became a major issue in that year's New Hampshire race; (3) Reagan's unexpected loss in New Hampshire, in which Ford "surprised" the media in the year's most heavily covered primary, beating Reagan by a mere 1,100 votes; (4) Carter's victory coverage in New Hampshire, in which Carter drove two prominent liberals from the race and scored the major press victory of 1976 with a plurality of 7,000 votes, 29 percent of the total; (5) Reagan's North Carolina victory, in which he proved that he could win somewhere and made his coinciding national television appeal for funds a legitimate and successful one, enabling him to continue to campaign in the West; (6) Carter's "ethnic purity" gaffe, after which the press hounded Carter for days about his allegedly racist attitudes toward integrating neighborhoods; (7) Carter's pseudo come-from-behind Wisconsin "miracle," on a day in which Carter lost heavily to Jackson and Udall in the New York primary but the loss was obliterated by Carter's 7,000-vote victory in the Wisconsin primary (NBC and ABC had erroneously predicted a Udall victory, making Carter's "surprise" win the day's top story); (8) Carter's Pennsylvania media victory, in which Carter's 37 percent plurality convinced the media that Carter was unstoppable and caused the *Washington Post* to editorialize against Humphrey's entry in the race—an editorial Jules Witcover regards as the major factor in Humphrey's declination;[26] and finally (9), the extraordinary television coverage of the last day of the primaries, in which Carter's big victory in Ohio was reported first and fullest by the networks and thus overshadowed completely Jerry Brown's landslide victory in California and surprisingly large victory in New Jersey. Through that mediality, Carter got only 40 percent of the day's delegates but still won handily in the media, eventually shoving Mayor Daley and the nomination into his grasp.

The general election added three more medialities, at least one of them critical: (10) Carter's lust-in-my-heart interview with *Playboy*, in which Carter used the word "screw," admitted to desire, and then witnessed a six-point erosion in his standing in the Gallup poll; (11) the Ford victory in the first debate, in which Ford won in all the major polls, mostly because the press and public had expected him to lose; (12) the Polish freedom fiasco, in which Ford declared Poland free of Soviet control and the media decided that his comment was the major blunder of the year (Robert Teeter found a shift of fifty-five percentage points, from Ford to Carter, as to who had "won" within days after the debate), indicating just how crucial media "reviews" can be in deciding "who won."[27]

Even if we ignore some of the longer, more subtle medialities in the 1976 campaign, such as the media depiction of all-American football star Jerry Ford as physically inept, it may well be that that campaign produced the most media-determined election in modern history. Had the *New York Daily News* not run its infamous headline "Ford to City: Drop Dead" after Ford's decision not to bail out New York, it is entirely possible that Carter would have failed to carry the state and would have lost the election to Ford.

Medialities, 1980. Medialities in the 1980 campaign began before the calendar year, two of the most important coming in November and December of 1979. They were: (1) the Roger Mudd interview with Edward Kennedy on November 4, an hour-long special in which CBS helped lead the national press in resuscitating Chappaquiddick and Kennedy's marriage as campaign issues—so much so that in the Harris poll Kennedy fell seven points between November 10 and November 26 [28]—and (2) Kennedy's San Francisco blunder, in which

---

[26] Witcover, *Marathon*, pp. 314-15.

[27] Ibid., p. 601.

[28] The Mudd interview was not the first, or last, major piece of journalism to follow Kennedy's informal announcement of his candidacy—but it was the most famous bit of reportage in the campaign resurrecting the Chappaquiddick issue.

he seemed to be supporting the Iranians who seized the American hostages by claiming that the shah was one of history's greatest despots. That remark caused the *New York Post* to run its now-famous headline: "Teddy: The Toast of Teheran," and it was also accompanied by an even sharper drop in Kennedy's image than that following the Mudd interviews: after the shah blunder, Kennedy's popularity among Democrats dropped twelve points in twelve days.

The Kennedy medialities of late 1979 were not only among the most important, they were also among the most controversial. The shah coverage was perhaps less a mediality than a political event: Kennedy knew what he was saying, knew he was expressing a policy, knew he was on camera. Nevertheless, the mediality surrounding "Chappaquiddick revisited" was vintage—a classic case in which the media, not ongoing events, determined what the news would be.

In the two weeks surrounding Kennedy's formal declaration of candidacy, ABC, CBS, the *Washington Post*, the *Washington Star*, the *Wall Street Journal*, and the *New York Times* all ran specials, features, editorials, interviews, commentaries on Kennedy's personal life—none of which did much more than recapitulate the charges and countercharges and restate the questions that had gone unanswered since 1969. Still, that recapitulation, the mediality of "Chappaquiddick revisited," had a telling effect. Between November 1979 and April 1980 the percentage of people thinking that Kennedy had lied about Chappaquiddick virtually doubled.[29]

During the calendar year there would be eight more notable medialities: (3) George Bush's slim victory in Iowa, in which Bush beat Reagan by a meager 2 percent, in a caucus election that attracted almost as much media attention as New Hampshire. More important, perhaps, was the fact that the networks estimated Bush's plurality to be 6,000 votes, when in fact final figures showed a plurality of just 2,000 votes—but that mattered little, as Bush's media-based "big" victory helped build his following among national Republicans from 6 to 24 percent in less than a month.[30]

(4) The Nashua, New Hampshire, fiasco, in which Bush refused to allow four Republican candidates to join him and Reagan in debate. The media made that the top election story for the three days before

---

For a review of the mediality surrounding Kennedy's personal life after his formal announcement of candidacy, see Charles Seib, "Enough of Chappaquiddick," *Washington Post*, November 16, 1979.

29 CBS/*New York Times* poll, April 1980, part 1, p. 8.

30 CBS/*New York Times* poll, February 1980, p. 5.

the New Hampshire balloting, and Bush's popularity among the New Hampshire voters fell from 35 percent to 23 percent in the final week of the campaign;[31] and finally, in the primary period, (5) "Anderson's surprise," in which Anderson virtually tied Bush in Massachusetts and Reagan in Vermont—moral victories that reinforced, for a time, the media's fascination with the "Anderson difference" and quadrupled his support among independents and Republicans combined.[32]

In the general election, medialities were less pinpointed and more *thematic* in nature: (6) Reagan's late summer gaffes, planned and unplanned remarks through which Reagan called Vietnam "a noble cause," disputed Darwin, blamed trees for pollution, and accused Carter of being too cozy with the Ku Klux Klan. All these the media melded into a portrait of Reagan as buffoon, an image that helped produce Reagan's only real slide in the polls in the general campaign, in the dog days of late summer; (7) Carter's "meanness," in which the national media presented for several weeks the dark side of Carter's personality. Coming on the heels of Carter's accusations that Reagan was injecting racism and warmongering into the campaign, the meanness mediality got as much attention on the evening news in September as did the economy—it was, in fact, the fourth most covered "issue" of the month on television news;[33] (8) the debate debate, the continuing dialogue as to whether Carter would debate Anderson, or Reagan, or both, etc., an "issue" that led all the others on the evening news in September[34] and hurt Carter from the start— the CBS poll showing a five-point drop in support for Carter immediately after the Anderson-Reagan debate had taken place;[35] (9) the Carter-Reagan debate, in which Carter helped create an audience of 120 million Americans who could see for themselves that Reagan was not the kind of man Carter had been attacking and after which a very questionable ABC poll reported a national consensus that Reagan had won.

(10) Finally, there was the hostage mediality, especially during the "anniversary" coverage that began the last week of the campaign

[31] Hedrick Smith, "Reagan's Populist Coalition," *New York Times*, February 27, 1980.

[32] "Opinion Roundup," *Public Opinion*, April/May 1980, p. 39.

[33] Data from Media Analysis Project, George Washington University, Washington, D.C., September 1980 memorandum.

[34] Michael Robinson and Margaret Sheehan, "How the Networks Learned to Love the Issues: The Eleventh Hour Conversion of CBS," *Washington Journalism Review*, December 1980, p. 16.

[35] CBS/*New York Times* poll, September 1980, p. 1.

at precisely the same time that the "final" negotiations were falling to pieces. There is no question about the hostage coverage's being a mediality. The extent of the coverage alone was unparalleled in television history—and the same could perhaps be said of print. In 1980 there were 1,031 Iranian news sections on the network weekday evening news programs![36] (The *Washington Post* averaged three Iran stories a day.)[37] Yet it is still impossible to make any definitive statement about the electoral effect of the "America held hostage" mediality. The conventional wisdom argues, quite reasonably, that the hostage mediality helped Carter until April—when Carter blatantly tried to exploit the media on the morning of the Wisconsin primary by hinting that a settlement was near when none in fact was. After that, the hostage coverage probably hurt Carter, especially during the "first anniversary" coverage.

As it turned out, however, only a small percentage of Americans voted on the basis of the hostage issue—at least directly. Less than 1 percent of the exit poll respondents in the CBS survey listed Iran as the major factor in their vote—one-tenth of those voting the economy![38] Clearly the hostage issue meant more than that in terms of "image"; but with all the candidates saying little about Iran, and with all the candidates saying much the same things, the most obvious media issue of the campaign failed to materialize as a clear, clean "voting" issue.

The hostage issue was not the only mediality that failed to influence voters as one might expect. After what was certainly Carter's worst press of the year—media coverage of the Democratic convention—most analysts assumed that Carter would sink even further in the polls. On network television, in front of millions, Kennedy failed to clasp his hand to Carter's, Carter invoked the never-to-be-forgotten name of Hubert Horatio "Hornblower," and—as all the networks pointed out—even the victory balloons failed to fall from the ceiling.

Yet the critcial reporting of the convention had no more impact than the failure of the balloons—Carter went *up* thirteen points in the CBS poll, twelve points in the NBC poll, ten points in the Gallup poll, and nine points in the ABC poll.[39] The convention was a Carter

[36] William Adams and Phil Hyl, "Television and the Middle East: 1972–1980," in William Adams, ed., *Television Coverage of the Middle East* (Norwood, N.J.: Ablex, forthcoming, 1981).

[37] Don Oberdorfer, "Hostage Seizure: Enormous Consequences," *Washington Post*, January 23, 1981.

[38] CBS/*New York Times*, "Post Election Poll," November 1980, p. 8.

[39] "The Major Election Polls," *Public Opinion*, December/January 1981, p. 19.

disaster on television, but it evidently played well in Peoria. Obviously the convention was an exception—most medialities produced anticipated results. In 1980, however, those medialities often failed to produce results to the anticipated degree, and, overall, there were fewer of them.

Why Were the Media Less Important in 1980?

If it is true that free media played a less important role in 1980, the question becomes: Why? The answer does not seem to be that there were fewer blunders; there were not. Nor were there fewer candidates or fewer primaries or fewer debates or fewer of any of the things that usually increase the power of media.

Still, there were differences from the 1976 campaign that made mediality less important and made it appear less important as well. As for appearances, the major factor was the very real difference in the final vote in each election. In 1976 Jimmy Carter defeated the incumbent by just a million and a half votes—and by only 56 electoral votes. In 1980 Ronald Reagan buried the incumbent with a plurality of nearly 9 million popular votes and by a margin of 440 votes in the electoral college. Media and mediality are generally not used to explain landslides—especially when the landslide spills over into congressional elections. Media must inherently appear less important when the winner's margin over the loser is so large.

That explanation, however, begs the question. In fact there were real "environmental" differences that separated 1976 from 1980. I see three major differences in the media environment, differences that caused the press to determine less of the campaign in 1980 than it had in 1976. Only one of those differences was within the control of the media; the other two were outside. Still, all three worked to reduce the power of free media in the election returns.

1. In 1980 the Republicans Were the Out-Party. Republican voters and identifiers have traditionally proved themselves more issue oriented and more ideologically coherent than Democrats. Consequently Republicans as a class are less vulnerable than their Democratic brethren—less susceptible to any sort of "extraneous" influence such as media or personality or even events. In American politics, the Republican party is always the more cohesive, more sedentary party.

In this century, Republicans have never denied an incumbent renomination or forced an incumbent to decide against running again. Republicans, for that matter, rarely change their individual minds about who the party's nominee should be. In 1976 Jerry Ford started as the year's preferred Republican, and he reached the convention holding the same status. Even in the campaign of 1980, so famous for its volatility, the Republicans, when compared with Democrats, stood pat in their preferences for their nominee. In the critical months —November 1979 through March 1980—Reagan's popularity among Republicans shifted a mere five percentage points. Carter's position among Democrats in the same period moved twenty-nine percentage points.[40]

Yet Republicanism is not the only characteristic associated with greater stability; so is incumbency. Historically, the in-party tends to be almost as politically stable as Republicans in its choice for nomination. When the Democrats are "out," media have more fertile soil for generating change; when the Republicans are out, the ground is not so easy to till. Most of what we think about media and the nomination process in the new era comes from the 1972 and 1976 campaigns, when the Democrats were out. So the last few elections have proved only that the Democrats are vulnerable to medialities, that the Democrats turn away from early front-runners, that the Democrats nominate media-based candidates. In 1980 the Republicans picked from a long list of nonincumbent candidates. Medialities and media shaped the nomination process less in 1980 than in 1976 principally because Republicans take issues more seriously and media less seriously than the Democrats. In the argot of political science, we can conclude that our notions about nominations in the television age were "time-bound," much more relevant to the schizophrenic Democrats than to the unflappable GOP.

Bush's success after Iowa seems to run counter to the theory of the sedentary Republican. In fact, between January and February, Bush jumped eighteen points among Republicans in the CBS/*New York Times* poll. Coming out of Iowa with Bush, "Big Mo" was a textbook case of mediality. But, *among Republicans,* Bush never seriously challenged Reagan's lead, even after Iowa. Only once did Bush appear to be the front-runner in the polls, and that was an appearance based on data that combined Republicans and independents. After Iowa, independents, not Republicans, rushed toward Bush.

The best evidence for a theory of Republican sedentarism comes from the Anderson campaign. The media took Anderson's performance in the nationally televised Iowa debate as a sign that he had

---

[40] Gallup poll, cited in ibid., p. 39.

arrived. After the Iowa debate, CBS even used clips from a bit on "Saturday Night Live"—a phony missing person's report on candidate John Anderson—to conclude that Anderson "has been found."[41] In fact, Anderson's performance had pleased only the media and the politically independent. The Iowa poll, conducted before and just after the debate, indicated that Republican support for Anderson climbed a modest one point after that debate—jumping from zero to 1 percent.[42]

Following Anderson's surprising second-place finishes in Massachusetts and Vermont, both liberal states that permitted crossover voting, Anderson returned to Illinois hoping to win his home state's primary and use his momentum to bring Republican voters to his campaign. (In Massachusetts, despite his second-place finish, Anderson attracted only 23 percent of the Republican identifiers.)[43]

Illinois gave him another chance to debate. He brought with him his usual rhetorical skill and his "difference," but the debate proved to Republicans that Anderson was insufficiently Republican. In that primary, despite media momentum, Anderson got 26 percent of the vote among Republican identifiers, whereas Reagan got 59 percent.

In the CBS/New York Times poll, Anderson never got more than 10 percent of the Republican identifiers to support him for the nomination. And in June, although 17 percent of the Democrats supported his bid for the presidency, only 12 percent of the Republicans did so. Even after Anderson's fine showing in Massachusetts and Vermont, when his press coverage was more favorable than that of any other candidate at any time during the primaries (see below), his support among Republicans went up only six percentage points nationwide.

If Anderson was the preferred media candidate of 1980—and our content data show that from January through April he was just that[44]—his story points to three realities about media in 1980: (1) what the candidate says about policy counts (after his September debate with Reagan, Anderson *lost* support only among conservatives); (2) what one says counts more if one is a Republican (unlike Carter, Anderson never had any bandwagon momentum among the rank and file); (3) Republicans get less carried away than Democrats about winning or losing, medialities, or momentum—the "Big Mo."

[41] CBS Evening News, January 10, 1980.

[42] "Reagan Sags, Carter Soars in Iowa Polls," *Des Moines Register*, January 11, 1980.

[43] CBS/New York Times, "Massachusetts Primary Day Poll," March 4, 1980, p. 2.

[44] Michael Robinson, Nancy Conover, and Margaret Sheehan, "The Media at Mid-Year: A Bad Year for McLuhanites?" *Public Opinion*, June/July 1980, pp. 44–45.

The media threw a good deal of bad press against Reagan—the "age" issue, "Big Mo," the Anderson "difference," the Polish-Italian joke, the dumbness charge; Reagan received the most negative press of any Republican between January and June.[45] Yet it did not matter much to Republican identifiers. Each in his own way, both John Anderson *and* George Bush were running in the wrong party.

2. In 1980 the Nominees Offered Clearer Choices. It will be months before the final word on public perceptions of where the candidates stood comes down from Ann Arbor. Still, in the general election it seems inconceivable that Reagan and Carter failed to convey how much more they differed on public policy than Carter and Ford had. I can think of no big issue where Reagan was closer to Carter than Ford was. On Panama, ERA, abortion, Kemp-Roth, and détente, however, Reagan-Carter was obviously the clearer, cleaner choice.

Reagan was the difference, of course. In September 1980 an impressive 57 percent of the electorate felt that Reagan "has clear positions on the issues."[46] As early as March 1980 CBS found that 47 percent of the electorate already knew Reagan was the conservative candidate. CBS stopped asking the question at that point in part because it found almost complete awareness of Reagan's conservatism among those willing to respond. Reagan's conservatism was so clear that even Carter's history of appearing fuzzy came to an end as voters saw him in contrast with the avowedly conservative Reagan.

With the issue gap as wide as it was, medialities had less chance to move voters from one side of the gap to the other. As long as Reagan failed to give the media and the voters any real cause to see him as crazy, as a Goldwater, media influences could not dominate policy differences. And Reagan in the campaign gave no cause to believe that he was crazy.

The issue, however, transcends Reagan's "flawless" performance. For several elections now political scientists have been arguing that the size of the "issue vote" is as much a function of the differences between candidates on issues as anything else. But the same logic should apply to the size of the "media vote." When candidates differ only a little on the issues, medialities should provide more important cues for voters and have more weight in the final choice. When candidates differ more on the issues, medialities should mean less.

Evidence for this premise that media power is inversely proportional to issue differences is hard to come by. In fact the argument

---

[45] Ibid., p. 44.

[46] CBS/*New York Times* poll, September 1980, p. 19.

rests solely on the axiom that media, the ephemeral factor, matter least when other more tangible criteria are in sharp relief. Blunders matter less, style matters less, almost everything matters less when basic differences on policy between candidates come through clearly. Had Carter and Reagan waffled more on basic issues such as the economy, media issues and medialities of all types would have taken on greater importance; but neither candidate waffled much.

3. In 1980 the Media Corrected for Some of Their Most Important Consequences. Until now I have stressed the particulars of the 1980 campaign—specifically, the out-party status of the Republicans and the unusually wide issue gap between candidates—to explain the somewhat reduced impact of the media. There is a third factor, however, that is not so specific to this election, one that stresses change in the media themselves.

In the last analysis, the single most important mediality in the age of television has been the media-based bandwagon in the early campaign. Given that the national free media do not lie, do not invent, and do not practice anything close to blatant partisanism, bandwagoning has been the one singularly important consequence that their behavior has produced in the last several campaigns. We think of McCarthy, McGovern, and Carter—the big three media candidates —as media candidates primarily because their bandwagons began in mediality, not reality.

In 1968 and 1972 media-defined "moral victories" in New Hampshire spawned both the McCarthy movement and the McGovern juggernaut. Yet by 1976 the media, especially the networks, had already taken some steps to reduce the impact of moral victories in the early campaigns. In 1976 the media hit an all-time high in covering New Hampshire, but they refused to call anybody a moral victor, there or anywhere else.[47] Much to Ronald Reagan's dismay (he had come within 1,100 votes of beating an incumbent), the media used the actual vote totals in 1976 to determine who won and lost in New Hampshire, as well as Iowa, Florida, and most of the early states.

By 1980 the media had taken two other steps that made the message more important than the mediality. Having understood their increasingly important role in defining winners and losers, the national media began by planning to minimize their impact on the primary campaign. For the first time they actually poor-mouthed their own surprise candidates.

---

[47] Michael J. Robinson, "Media Coverage in the Primary Campaign of 1976: Implications for Voters, Candidates, and Parties," in William Crotty, ed., *The Party Symbol* (New York: Freeman, 1980), pp. 178–91.

CBS provides an interesting example of how the networks tried to cope with primary performances that went "better than expected." On the night after Anderson's surprise showings in Vermont and Massachusetts, Walter Cronkite led with Anderson's "strong" finish. Still, Cronkite also explicitly mentioned Anderson's having finished "second," and he noted that *in the sometimes convoluted logic of politics,*" Anderson was viewed as a big winner.[48] That news lead was not the sort that would have come in the preceding two campaigns, where the tone would have been more certain of Anderson's new importance.

And that lead typified the way the media treated all the primary surprises: as tentative. There were some exceptions: Tom Petit of NBC declared Reagan finished after the Iowa caucuses, but that conclusion was not offered on the evening news, and it was not representative of the "new tentativeness" that came with interpreting primary returns. The press relied on vote totals more and arbitrary expectations less in 1980 than in the recent past.

The major change in media coverage in 1980, however, was the increasing speed at which the national media moved to minimize their own bandwagon effects. After the Iowa caucuses in 1976, the media gave Carter almost three months of comparatively easy riding. It was not until Pennsylvania that the media went after Carter, using his "ethnic purity" remark as their justification.

The "ethnic purity" controversy was a media-sponsored crisis. Although nobody disputes that Jimmy Carter said what was alleged, it is also a matter of record that Martin Plissner, political editor at CBS News, dredged up the phrase—resurrecting it from an interview on page 134 of an old copy of the *New York Daily News.*[49] Plissner asked CBS correspondent Ed Rabel to question Carter about the remark at an open press conference, Carter repeated the phrase, and that repetition almost changed political history.

The "ethnic purity" episode indicates the extent to which the media had, by 1976, understood their new mission: removing the wheels from bandwagons that they had helped to create. (Who else could remove them?) In 1980, however, national media simply got better and quicker at dewheeling. The first case was George Bush in New Hampshire. The media did not force George Bush to do what he did in the Nashua debate—Bush acted on his own. Still, the media covered it with a passion merited only by a candidate with self-proclaimed "Big Mo"—*media-based* momentum. The night of and

[48] CBS Evening News, March 5, 1980, italics added.
[49] Witcover, *Marathon*, p. 302.

the night after the Nashua debate, Bush's blunder attracted seventeen minutes of news coverage on the weekend news shows—a huge share, considering all the other political activity *not* getting coverage that weekend, including the substance of the debate. When one considers what Bush actually did in Nashua—he simply stated that he and Reagan should stick with the debate plans they had earlied agreed upon—the media coverage looks like a case study in which the media turned on one of their own creations, either because they resented "Big Mo" or because they felt that a Big Mo candidate needed very close scrutiny.

The classic case of the media turning against media candidacies, however, is Anderson. From the moment he had established himself as the "different" Republican in the Iowa debate, Anderson was the darling of the press corps. In January and February, *before* Massachusetts, despite his 1 percent showing in the polls, John Anderson was given 400 news seconds—and two favorable features—more than any of the other second-tier candidates on the CBS "Evening News." He got more news time than Connally, three times as much as Crane, six times as much as Dole—all of whom led him in national popularity at the time (see figure 6–4).

What is more, Anderson's coverage was overwhelmingly favorable and exactly in keeping with his plan to be "different." In those first two months, before Massachusetts, CBS referred to Anderson as the "forthright" candidate, the "freshest face," the "candidate standing apart from the crowd," the one "many voters see . . . as the most articulate, honest, and best candidate" in the field. From the outset, even before he had become what one CBS reporter called the "candidate in vogue," all the networks treated Anderson comparatively well, and so did the national print press (except for Evans and Novak).

As soon as Anderson faltered—the day after the Illinois primary—the press changed its story. That night Walter Cronkite concluded his lead-in by announcing that "another big loser yesterday was John Anderson, Illinois congressman, whose expected strong challenge fell through." And moments later, Bruce Morton concluded that "John Anderson can go on, but he has to wonder. . . . Anderson was a considerable loser in his home state."[50]

After Illinois, the press turned on Anderson because he had failed with his best media shot. And there is something to be said in praise of that switch. As late as April, after Anderson looked dead in the

[50] CBS Evening News, March 19, 1980.

FIGURE 6–4

News Coverage Given Anderson, Connally, Crane, and Dole
on CBS Evening News, January–February 1980

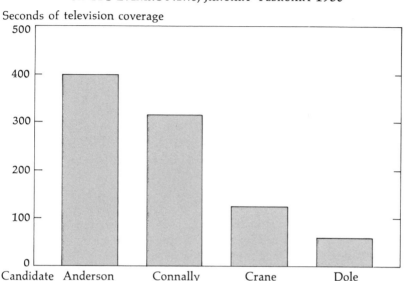

Seconds of television coverage

Candidate: Anderson (1%), Connally (5%), Crane (2%), Dole (2%)

Notes: Percentages are Republicans preferring candidate for Republican nomination, February 1980. Seconds of coverage are for CBS Evening News, January–February 1980, weeknights only.
Sources: CBS News; CBS News/ *New York Times* poll, February 1980.

media, in a National Press Club poll, Anderson was the clear favorite among newspaper people attending the spring association meetings in the District of Columbia. (He beat the next closest candidate, Kennedy, by two to one.)[51] Still, despite his personal popularity with the press, Anderson lost his media campaign as soon as the objective vote totals went unambiguously against him. The media, in the two weeks between Massachusetts and Illinois, realized that one of their own "creations" had failed his first real test, and they took away his media momentum. By summer Anderson was getting the *worst* press among the three remaining candidates, as the national media pilloried him for his image-building trip to Europe, his meeting with Kennedy, and his inconsistency about whether he might drop out of the race.[52]

[51] "Campaign Notes," *Washington Post*, April 2, 1980.
[52] See also Robert Kaiser, "On the Media Yo-Yo," *Washington Post*, September 11, 1980; and Robert Kaiser, "Anderson Debilitated by a Flurry of Negative Publicity," *Washington Post*, October 1, 1980.

The national media helped to make Anderson—in part because they liked him, but mostly because he was different and he seemed to be catching on. Yet when Anderson's campaign failed to achieve real viability, the media did what they generally do: they "told it like it was," and Anderson never overcame the loser image that he was given coming out of Illinois.

This is media power, but it is of a different form, more passive than that which preceded it. In 1980 the media used blunders or returns or some other reality to test more stringently and more quickly the candidates who were getting away with something (usually a media-based bandwagon), and those failing the tests were quickly in trouble. In the campaign of 1980 it is clear that the media moved fast against all the perceived front-runners—Kennedy in November, Bush in February, Anderson in March, and Reagan and Carter from then to the election.

Jimmy Carter lost five of eight contests on the last day of the primaries in 1980. And on the day he went over the top in delegates needed for nomination, Reagan lost Michigan to Bush by two to one. If 1980 serves as a media model for 1984, we should expect hard times for the original front-runners and even tougher times for the first surprise candidate who slips ahead of the pack. Winning in Iowa or New Hampshire is not exactly what it once was—in fact, winning early may no longer be absolutely essential. The media have learned to adjust to candidates whom they themselves help to create. As a consequence of treatment by the media, we should expect to see more and more candidates backing into a nomination.

Conclusion

Media have always mattered in presidential politics. In his newest study of the presidency and the press, James David Barber shows how Wilson, Willkie, and even Eisenhower were for the most part media creations of the press barons of their time.

Yet the capacity of media to influence the process is variable, not inexorable. We once agreed that the proliferation of primaries increased the power of the media to influence the nominating process. We should also be willing to agree that other changes in the political environment might render the media a little less important. The 1980 campaign merely provided conditions slightly less hospitable to media influence than the recent past.

Claiming that the media have power and consequences in presidential campaigns does not add much to our understanding. Even if we cannot know precisely how much power the media have, we should at least recognize which factors lead media to be more or less powerful. The experience of 1980 implies that media matter less when Republicans are the challengers, when issues more clearly divide candidates, when media try harder to keep any candidates from exploiting them or their audiences.

On the last day of 1980 Marshall McLuhan died in Canada. Until that day, McLuhan had, for fifteen years, stood as the living embodiment of the theory that, above all, the medium is the message. But the 1980 campaign failed to produce a McLuhan-style nominee—there was nothing like a Eugene McCarthy, a George McGovern, or a 1976 version of Jimmy Carter. Although we can all personally mourn the passing of Professor McLuhan, it does seem that there was precious little in the 1980 campaign to bring comfort to his universally famous —if overstated—theory of political communication. Sometimes, often when we least expect it, the media are the media, and the message is the message.

7

The November 4 Vote for President: What Did It Mean?

William Schneider

There is nothing wrong with the Republican Party that twelve percent inflation won't cure.

Richard M. Scammon, 1976, postelection analysis

The American people are not going to elect a seventy-year-old, right-wing, ex–movie actor to be president.

Hamilton Jordan, 1980, preelection analysis

The surprise of the November 4, 1980, presidential vote was that it was so decisive. Pundits and pollsters spent months of time and untold pages of print explaining how the election was going to be "too close to call," how independent candidate John Anderson might "steal" the election from Jimmy Carter—and possibly create a deadlock in the electoral college and throw the decision into the House of Representatives—how the vote would really be fifty-one separate state contests determined by local factors and conditions, how the popular vote might go one way and the electoral count another, and how a volatile, ticket-splitting electorate would undoubtedly swing different ways for different offices.

On November 4, however, the ax fell on the Democrats with breathtaking swiftness and severity. Ronald Reagan won the national popular vote by a definitive ten-point margin over his Democratic opponent. Indeed, Reagan won an absolute majority of the popular vote, so that even if one were to add all the Anderson votes to all the Carter votes, the Republican ticket still would have come out ahead. The swing was truly national. The Democrats' share of the presidential vote declined from 1976 to 1980 in every state. The Reagan-Bush ticket carried all the states that Ford and Dole had won in 1976 plus seventeen others that had gone to Carter and Mondale four years earlier. In 1976, the Republicans lost every southern state save Virginia; in 1980 they captured every southern state except Carter's native Georgia. The Republicans even took "the People's Republic of Massachusetts," whose fourteen electoral votes had gone, uniquely, to George McGovern in 1972.

The electoral vote tally said it all: Reagan-Bush 489, Carter-Mondale 49, a ten-to-one margin.

Perhaps not quite all. The Republicans buttressed their presidential victory by picking up thirty-three seats in the House of Representatives, the party's largest gain since 1966. No fewer than four House committee chairmen went down to defeat—the first time since 1966 that any House chairman had lost a general election. The GOP gained four governorships out of thirteen contested in 1980, plus a net gain of 189 state legislative seats. Five additional state legislative chambers came under Republican control, raising from twelve to fourteen the number of states with the Republicans in charge of both legislative houses and from five to seven the number of states with divided party control. These state-level changes are particularly important because the state governments elected in 1980 will be in charge of legislative redistricting to comply with the 1980 census. Thus, for example, Illinois, Ohio, and Pennsylvania are due to lose congressional seats in the redistricting process; the Republicans gained control of an additional legislative house in all three states, each of which already has a Republican governor.

Sweetest of all for the Republican party was the gain of twelve U.S. Senate seats. That gave the Republicans a Senate majority for the first time since 1954. Conservatives especially relished the defeat of such liberal senior Democrats as George McGovern (who had represented South Dakota in the Senate since 1962), Birch Bayh (Indiana, since 1962), Frank Church (Idaho, since 1956), Warren Magnuson (Washington, since 1944), and Gaylord Nelson (Wisconsin, since 1962).

In short, there was little ambiguity about the election results. There was considerable ambiguity about their interpretation, however. The *New York Times*'s headline after the election read, "Reagan Buoyed by National Swing to Right." Yet that same newspaper's nationwide poll of voters on election day revealed almost no change in the self-described ideology of voters between 1976 and 1980.[1] Conservatives have an interest in arguing that the 1980

[1] In the CBS News/*New York Times* nationwide exit poll of voters on November 4, 1980, 31 percent described themselves as conservatives and 18 percent as liberals. Four years earlier, in a similar poll of 1976 voters, 32 percent called themselves conservatives and 20 percent liberals. Reported in CBS News/*New York Times* poll, "Post-Election Poll, November 1980," released November 15-16, 1980, p. 4.

election was a mandate for more thoroughgoing conservative policies. Liberals, on the other hand, take refuge in the contention that
the voters were rejecting Jimmy Carter personally for his incom-
petence and his failure of leadership. Liberals, after all, had no special love for Carter and spent much of the campaign actively opposing him. Republicans like to think of the 1980 election as their
party's "1932," a watershed year when a new majority party comes
to power and consolidates its control for a generation to come.
Carter was, in fact, the first elected incumbent since Herbert Hoover
to be defeated after only one term in office. Democrats prefer the
1972 analogy—a purely personal victory that entails no lasting shift
in ideology or party loyalty. As evidence for this view, many Democrats point to the preponderance of negative sentiments about both
major candidates and parties, as well as the low level of voter turnout. Voters seemed to be settling for the best of a bad lot, and their
votes appeared to be motivated more by distaste for the opposition
than by real enthusiasm for their eventual choice.

An interesting analytical issue is presented by the 1980 election
as well, namely, the supposedly inherent "centrism" of American
politics. When a moderate or centrist candidate runs against a candidate perceived as more ideologically extreme, the moderate is
supposed to win—as happened in 1964 and 1972.[2] That is especially true if, as in those years, the moderate candidate is also the
incumbent. Both campaigns in 1980 seem to have been aware of this
"rule." The Democrats spent most of their time attacking Reagan
as an irresponsible extremist and reminding voters of the Republican
nominee's far-fetched statements and positions. During the October
28 debate between the two presidential candidates, Carter said,
"This is a contest between a Democrat in the mainstream of my
party . . . as contrasted with Governor Reagan, who in most cases
does typify his party, but in some cases there is a radical departure

---

[2] This "rule" is investigated in some detail by Norman H. Nie, Sidney Verba, and
John R. Petrocik, *The Changing American Voter* (Cambridge, Mass.: Harvard
University Press, 1976), pp. 334-44. "The conclusion seems obvious: if you want
to win, nominate a candidate close to the center. Or, if you must nominate a
candidate far from the center, hope that the other party will do so as well" (p.
339). In these authors' mock-election analysis (based on a survey administered in
1973), Ronald Reagan is considered a noncentrist Republican. Their tests showed
a correspondingly high level of issue voting and issue defection in contests involving Reagan as the Republican nominee (pp. 314-17). The authors caution,
however, that "continued movement in one direction or another [i.e., left or right]
by the public may convert extreme positions on the part of the candidates into
more centrist ones" (p. 341). This hypothesis as it applies to the 1980 election
is taken up later in this chapter.

by him from the heritage of Eisenhower and others." The Republicans tried to minimize the ideological distance between the candidates by conducting a self-consciously moderate campaign. Ever mindful of Barry Goldwater's catastrophic performance in 1964, Ronald Reagan gave a cautious and conciliatory acceptance speech at the Republican National Convention in Detroit. "It is essential," Reagan said, "that the integrity of all aspects of Social Security be preserved."

Did the perception of Ronald Reagan become substantially more moderate as the campaign progressed? Did the voters themselves move significantly to the right in 1980? We shall examine evidence on these points as well as on the impact of specific issues— the economy, foreign policy, social issues, and the candidates' personal characteristics—on the 1980 vote. An effort will also be made to interpret the nature of the "mandate" resulting from the 1980 election.

The Election Results

Approximately 160 million Americans were estimated by the Census Bureau to be resident and of voting age on November 4, 1980. Of that number, a total of 86,495,678 cast ballots for president, according to official state returns compiled by the Federal Election Commission. The resulting turnout, 54.0 percent of the age-eligible electorate, represents a slight decline from the 54.3 percent level recorded in the 1976 presidential election. The exact meaning of these turnout estimates is a matter of some dispute, since the voting-age population includes many people who are ineligible to vote.[3] Although the method may underestimate turnout in each election, it does show that since 1960, the percentage of the U.S. voting-age population participating in presidential elections has been gradually declining. Voter participation fell by about 1 percentage point from previous elections in 1964, 1968, and 1976. The decrease was an unusually high 5.4 percentage points in 1972, the first year eighteen-

[3] See, for instance, Ronald C. Moe, "Myth of the Non-Voting American," *Wall Street Journal*, November 4, 1980. Moe points out that the voting-age population, or "potential electorate," includes many aliens, prisoners, and service personnel for whom it is difficult or impossible to vote. Registration requirements also vary from place to place in the United States, placing a special burden on a highly mobile population. Moe attributes much of the decline in voter participation since 1960 to the growth in the under-thirty segment of the population (the postwar "baby boom" that first came of voting age in the 1960s and 1970s, augmented by the newly enfranchised eighteen- to twenty-year-olds in 1972); young voters show a persistently low rate of voter turnout.

to twenty-year-olds could vote nationwide. The drop-off from 1976 to 1980, at about one-third of 1 percentage point, actually represents a slower rate of decline than has been the case in recent presidential elections.

Between 1976 and 1980, the number of votes cast for president went up by about 5 million. (At the same time, the estimated population of voting age went up by about 10 million.) The Democratic ticket of Carter and Mondale lost about 5.3 million votes, from 40.8 million in 1976 to 35.5 million in 1980. The 1980 Republican total for Reagan and Bush, at 43.9 million, was 4.8 million votes higher than the 39.1 million cast for Republicans Ford and Dole in 1976. The South played a critical role in this increased Republican total. The eleven states of the Old Confederacy cast just under one-quarter of the total presidential vote in 1980. The Republicans, however, gained 2.4 million votes in those eleven states—amounting to *half* of the party's total nationwide gain.

The total votes cast for the two major parties fell only slightly from 1976 to 1980, from 80.0 million to 79.4 million. The big change was in the non-major-party vote. Independent and third-party votes went from about 1.6 million in 1976 to over 7 million in 1980, or from less than 2 to more than 8 percent of the total.

The bulk of the non-major-party vote in 1980 was cast for independents John Anderson and Patrick Lucey; they received 5.7 million votes nationwide, or 6.6 percent of the total. Following Anderson at some distance were Libertarian Ed Clark, with just under 1 million votes (1.1 percent), and Citizens party candidate Barry Commoner, with 230,000 votes (0.3 percent). If one assumes that the bulk of the Anderson votes were cast by people who would normally have voted for one of the two major parties—and the survey evidence suggests that this was the case—then the remaining minor-party vote was about the same in 1980 (1.6 percent) as it had been in 1976 (1.9 percent).

The percentage results reveal just how devastating the election was for the Democrats. The Democrats' share of the popular vote fell by over 9 percentage points, from 50.1 percent in 1976 to 41.0 percent in 1980. The Republicans' gain, however, accounted for less than one-third of this loss. The total Republican vote went up by only 2.8 percentage points, from 48.0 percent for Ford in 1976 to 50.8 percent for Reagan in 1980. The rest of the Democrats' loss was accounted for by the 6.3-percentage-point increase in non-major-party votes, mostly for Anderson. Thus a basic feature of the 1980 election outcome was that the Democrats lost more than the Republicans gained.

The shift appears more impressive if one expresses it in terms of the margin between the two major parties. In 1976 the Democrats had a modest margin of two percentage points over the Republicans. In 1980, the Republicans beat the Democrats by a margin of ten points. That is surely decisive, but it is not quite of the same magnitude as the historic presidential landslides of this century: Richard Nixon's margin of twenty-three points over George McGovern in 1972, Lyndon Johnson's twenty-three points over Barry Goldwater in 1964, Dwight Eisenhower's fifteen points over Adlai Stevenson in 1956, Franklin D. Roosevelt's successive landslides of eighteen points over Herbert Hoover in 1932 and twenty-four points over Alf Landon in 1936, and—almost unremembered—the greatest presidential landslide of them all, Warren G. Harding's defeat of James M. Cox by twenty-six percentage points in 1920. (Indeed, that last vote was followed by impressive Republican margins of twenty-five points in 1924 and seventeen points in 1928.) In retrospect, what created the impression of a Reagan landslide was the Republicans' enormous lead in electoral votes—10 to 1, compared with a popular vote margin of 5 to 4—plus the fact that the outcome was much more decisive than had been anticipated.

Even though Reagan's margin over Carter was, in historical terms, only middling in size, the Republican swing seemed to penetrate deeper in 1980 than in previous Republican victories. In 1952, the GOP returned to power with net gains of only twenty-two House seats and one Senate seat. Eisenhower was reelected in 1956 with a net gain for his party of only three House seats and no Senate seats. The Republicans picked up five House seats and seven Senate seats in 1968. Richard Nixon's massive presidential victory in 1972 was accompanied by a gain of only twelve Republican House seats and by *Democratic* gains of two seats in the Senate and one governorship. What was most impressive about 1980 was not the magnitude of Reagan's victory but the across-the-board rejection of the Democratic party.

• The Republicans gained an average of nine percentage points in the thirty-four Senate contests in 1980, picking up twelve additional Senate seats and majority control of that chamber.

• The Republican vote went up by an average of five percentage points over their 1976 totals in the thirteen states electing governors in 1980, for a gain of four additional state executives.

• The Republican vote rose three percentage points, on the average, in the nation's 435 congressional districts, producing a net gain of thirty-three seats in the House.

• Reagan appears to have had coattails, at least regionally. He ran ahead of the Republican congressional vote in thirty-four states and behind the party's congressional vote in fourteen states, the latter mostly in the Northeast and Great Lakes areas. In the South and West, Reagan led his party to victory.

The Republican sweep at all levels suggests that the 1980 election was more than a purely personal victory for the presidential ticket, like the Eisenhower elections of the 1950s or the Nixon vote in 1972. Unlike the landslide elections of 1936, 1956, 1964, and 1972, the 1980 vote was anti-incumbent. By throwing out incumbent Democrats across the board, the voters were sending out a clear message: it was time for a change.

Appendix A presents in detail the final presidential election results by state and region for 1976 and 1980. Figure 7–1 displays the 1980 Republican presidential vote compared with the 1976 Republican vote in each of the fifty states.

As one would expect, the 1980 Reagan vote and the 1976 Ford vote were strongly correlated: +0.73 for the fifty states. Reagan did well in the same states where Ford had done well, namely, the mountain states and the farm belt. Both candidates did relatively poorly in Carter's native South, Mondale's native Minnesota, and the urban and heavily Democratic states of the Northeast.

Figure 7–1 draws attention to changes in Republican support from 1976 to 1980. A state falling on the diagonal would have given exactly the same percentage to Ford in 1976 and to Reagan in 1980. (The state that came closest was Wisconsin. Ford lost Wisconsin in 1976 with 47.8 percent of the vote. Reagan won it in 1980 with 47.9 percent.) The parallel line above the diagonal defines a 2.8-percentage-point increase in the Republican vote, which was the size of the party's gain nationwide. The result is three groups of states: (1) twenty-eight states where the Republican share of the vote went up more than it did in the country as a whole, (2) eleven states where the Republicans gained, but at a lower rate than in the country as a whole, (3) eleven states below the diagonal, where the Republican share of the vote went down.

The Republicans made their greatest gains in 1980 in many states where Ford had done quite well and in many states where Ford had done relatively poorly. As a result, the correlation between the 1976 Ford vote and the *change* in the Republican vote from 1976 to 1980 was an insignificant −0.09. The ten states where the Republican vote increased the most included six mountain and farm belt states that had gone well for Ford (Nevada, North Dakota,

FIGURE 7–1

Republican Presidential Vote by State, 1976 and 1980

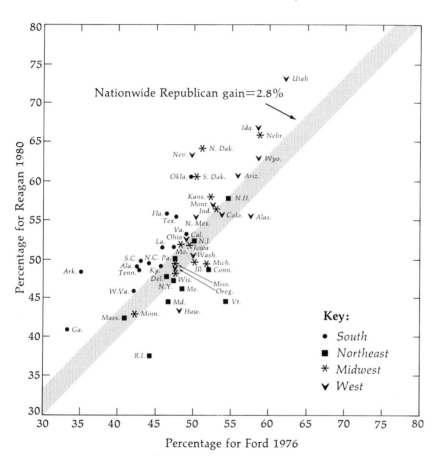

SOURCE: Official state returns, compiled and published by the U.S. Federal Election Commission, December 29, 1980.

Oklahoma, Utah, South Dakota, and Idaho) and four southern states where Carter had done well (Texas, Florida, Arkansas, and Carter's own Georgia, where the Republican vote went up eight percentage points).

Table 7–1 recapitulates the regional results from appendix A. In 1976 Carter's strongest support came in the South. He ran best in the deep South, followed by the outer South and the border states.

TABLE 7-1
Presidential Votes by Region, 1976 and 1980

Region	1976 (percent)			1980 (percent)				Change, 1976–1980 (percentage points)		
	Ford[a]	Carter[b]	Turnout	Reagan[a]	Carter[b]	Anderson[c]	Turnout	Rep.	Dem.	Turnout
New England	45.9	51.7	61.7	44.7	40.3	13.7	60.1	−1.2	−11.4	−1.6
Middle Atlantic	47.6	51.1	52.8	47.9	43.2	7.3	50.7	0.3	−7.9	−2.1
Deep South	40.8	57.9	46.7	47.6	49.1	1.8	49.5	6.8	−8.8	2.8
Outer South	46.7	52.1	48.2	53.4	42.1	3.6	49.5	6.7	−10.0	1.3
Border states	46.7	52.0	55.0	51.9	43.9	3.4	55.3	5.2	−8.1	0.3
Great Lakes	50.3	47.8	59.4	50.5	41.4	6.6	58.9	0.2	−6.4	−0.5
Farm belt	48.6	48.9	64.4	52.2	38.1	8.0	63.1	3.6	−10.8	−1.3
Mountain states	55.7	41.1	57.5	60.7	28.8	8.1	57.3	5.0	−12.3	−0.2
Pacific	49.4	47.3	53.3	51.6	36.5	9.0	53.0	2.2	−10.8	−0.3
United States	48.0	50.1	54.3	50.8	41.0	6.6	54.0	2.8	−9.1	−0.3

[a] Republican.
[b] Democrat.
[c] Independent.

Source: Official state returns (Washington, D.C.: U.S. Federal Election Commission, December 29, 1980), aggregated by author.

Many commentators were struck by the "East-West" pattern of the 1976 vote, the Northeast and South coalescing behind the Democratic ticket, more or less in the traditional New Deal pattern, whereas most of the Midwest and West went Republican. In 1980 Carter continued to run *relatively* well in the South and Northeast; Carter's continuing support in his native South, along with Reagan's western regional appeal, caused the East-West split to persist. Thus a high positive correlation resulted between the 1976 and 1980 votes.

The 1976 alignment was somewhat diluted, however, by the changes in the Republican vote noted above. These changes can be seen regionally in table 7–1: from 1976 to 1980, the Republican vote increased fastest in the deep South (6.8 percentage points), the outer South (6.7 percentage points), and the border states (5.2 percentage points), followed by the mountain states (5.0 percentage points) and the farm belt (3.6 percentage points). The so-called sunbelt coalition of South and West can be seen in the Republican *gains* from 1976 to 1980 more clearly than in the 1980 vote itself. Note, in figure 7–2, where the Republicans made higher than average gains. The rapidly growing southern and western states are the core of the conservative coalition that some have predicted would supplant the New Deal alignment of a Democratic East versus a Republican Midwest and West.[4]

As figure 7–2 shows, the Republican vote declined only in a few states, mostly in New England, plus Maryland (with a strongly government-oriented population) and Michigan (where Ford's 1976 support had been inflated by local pride). Interestingly, the Republicans also lost support in Hawaii (−5.2 percentage points) and Alaska (−3.3 percentage points). Non-major-party candidates did unusually well in those two states—John Anderson got 10.6 percent in Hawaii and libertarian Ed Clark won a phenomenal 11.7 percent in Alaska. (Clark came in third in Alaska, where his share of the vote was ten times greater than his national vote and four times greater than his next best state.) The high votes for minor candidates in Hawaii and Alaska may have been partly a time-zone effect. A large share of the electorate in both states voted after President Carter had conceded. With strategic considerations no longer relevant, many Hawaiian liberals and Alaskan conservatives probably felt free to vote for the candidates they really preferred.

According to table 7–1, the Democratic decline was fairly uni-

---

[4] Most prominently, Kevin P. Phillips, *The Emerging Republican Majority* (New Rochelle, N.Y.: Arlington House, 1969), especially pp. 25-42, 471-74. See also Kirkpatrick Sale, *Power Shift* (New York: Random House, 1975), for a broader cultural interpretation.

FIGURE 7–2
Change in Republican Vote by State, 1976 to 1980

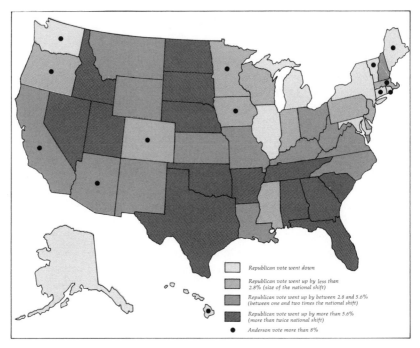

Republican vote went down

Republican vote went up by less than 2.8% (size of the national shift)

Republican vote went up by between 2.8 and 5.6% (between one and two times the national shift)

Republican vote went up by more than 5.6% (more than twice national shift)

● Anderson vote more than 8%

form throughout the country, including the Northeast where the Republicans picked up very little. The difference is accounted for by the Anderson vote. Thus in New England, where the Democratic presidential vote fell by over eleven percentage points, it was John Anderson, not Ronald Reagan, who benefited. All in all, the most prominent single characteristic of the 1980 election was the universal decline in support for the Democrats. In the South, almost all of the Democrats' loss went to Reagan. In the Northeast, almost all of the Democrats' loss went to Anderson. In the rest of the country, the Democrats' loss benefited both Reagan and Anderson in varying proportions, state by state. The entire country seemed to agree that the Democrats did not deserve reelection. There was somewhat less consensus behind the Republicans as an alternative.

If the Democrats' decline was universal and Reagan's gains were greatest in the South, the mountain states, and the farm belt, then Anderson must have done relatively well in the rest of the country (except Alaska). For instance, New England was the only region of the country where both the Democratic and the Republican shares of the vote declined from 1976 to 1980. It was also Anderson's best region by far; he got 13.7 percent in New England, more than twice his share of the vote in the country as a whole. Aside from New England, Anderson did relatively well in the liberal-inclined areas of the West Coast, the upper Midwest (Minnesota, Iowa), and fast-growing Colorado and Arizona—areas with either a liberal Republican "Yankee" heritage or a significant population of young "new class" professionals, or both (for example, Oregon). Anderson did not do particularly well in the major industrial states, including Pennsylvania, Ohio, Michigan, and his native Illinois.

It may be worth noting that there were fourteen states that Reagan carried where the Anderson vote was larger than Reagan's margin over Carter. These were the only states where it could be argued that Anderson played the role of a "spoiler," that is, where he might have taken electoral votes away from the Democrats. These included four New England states where Anderson did exceptionally well (Massachusetts, Vermont, Maine, and Connecticut), plus four northeastern and midwestern states where Reagan's margin was fairly close and Anderson did fairly well (New York, Delaware, Michigan, and Wisconsin). The other six "spoiler" states were, surprisingly, in the South—Tennessee, Arkansas, South Carolina, Mississippi, Kentucky, and North Carolina. As noted, Anderson did quite poorly in the South; he averaged only 2.2 percent of the vote in these six states. He could be said to have "stolen" these states from Carter only because Reagan's margin in them was so excruciatingly thin, averaging 1.2 percent. Suppose one makes the rather unrealistic assumption that every one of Anderson's votes in these fourteen states had gone to Jimmy Carter. That would have given Carter 158 additional electoral votes, for a total of 207—still considerably less than Ronald Reagan's remaining total of 331.

Table 7–1 also shows the change in turnout for each region of the country from 1976 to 1980. Turnout declined in most states outside the South, especially in the urban industrial states of the Northeast. Turnout rose conspicuously in the South, however, particularly in the deep South. This reversal of the national trend suggests that southerners were more enthusiastic about the Reagan-Carter choice than voters in other parts of the country, a conclusion also evidenced by Anderson's poor showing there.

Carter is, of course, a southern Democrat, while Reagan embodies the hard-line conservatism favored by most southern Republicans (and Bourbon Democrats). In the contest for the 1976 Republican nomination, Reagan won 47 percent of the convention votes, but he carried 73 percent of the votes cast by southern Republican delegates. In fact, Jimmy Carter and Ronald Reagan can be said to typify the *southern* party system, and that region of the country responded to the choice between them with some enthusiasm. For the rest of the country, the choice seems to have been a bit too conservative. That is one reason why John Anderson was in the race—to "broaden" the range of choice. Anderson's presence on the ballot does not appear to have stimulated turnout in liberal areas, however; the correlation between Anderson's vote and the change in turnout from 1976 to 1980 was —0.29 for the fifty states (—0.07 outside the South).

So far all the evidence presented on voter shifts has been aggregate in nature—that is, it shows *net* changes in the vote from 1976 to 1980, aggregated by state and region. It is certainly not true, however, that the only shifts were away from the Democrats and toward either Reagan or Anderson. Survey data can be used to uncover the changes at the individual level that resulted in the net outcome reported above.

Both ABC News and CBS News and the *New York Times* interviewed voters as they left their polling places throughout the country on election day (so-called exit polls). In addition, the *Los Angeles Times* conducted a nationwide telephone survey of voting-age Americans a few days after the election. All three surveys asked people how they voted in 1976 and 1980. The results show substantial agreement concerning voter shifts from 1976 to 1980.

The surveys indicate that between 60 and 63 percent of 1976 Carter voters who voted for president again in 1980 voted a second time for Carter. Among 1976 Ford voters, loyalty to the party ticket was substantially greater; between 79 and 83 percent voted for Reagan. Almost one-third of former Carter voters switched to Reagan in 1980 (29–31 percent), while only 10–13 percent of Ford voters switched to Carter. Moreover, defections to Anderson hurt Carter slightly more than they hurt Reagan. The polls show that 7–9 percent of Carter voters voted for John Anderson in 1980, compared with 5–6 percent of 1976 Ford voters. Finally, those 1980 voters who said they had not voted in 1976 also gave the edge to Reagan, by seven to eight percentage points in the three polls.

Thus Carter lost almost four out of every ten of his former supporters who showed up at the polls on November 4, and almost 80 percent of those he lost voted for Reagan. By contrast, the Republicans gave up only about two in ten of their former supporters, about two-thirds of them to Carter and one-third to Anderson. The former nonvoters (including those too young to vote in 1976) broke approximately five to four for Reagan over Carter, with about 10 percent for Anderson.

TABLE 7–2
VOTER SHIFTS, 1976 TO 1980
(percent)

1980	1976			
	Carter (Dem.)	Ford (Rep.)	Did not vote	Too young
Carter (Dem.)	37	11	10	12
Reagan (Rep.)	19	67	10	16
Anderson (Ind.)	5	4	1	3
Others	1	1	—	—
Registered, but did not vote	28	7	15	10
Unregistered	10	10	64	59
Total	100	100	100	100

NOTE: $N = 1,703$.
SOURCE: *Los Angeles Times* poll, November 7-12, 1980.

The postelection survey by the *Los Angeles Times* allows us to take the analysis one step further. Unlike the network exit polls, the postelection survey interviewed people who did not vote for president on November 4. Table 7–2 shows the reported behavior in 1980 of the entire electorate, including those who said they did not register or did not vote. The interesting comparison is in the "registered but did not vote" category. Former Carter supporters were four times as likely as former Ford supporters to report that they "sat out" the 1980 presidential election. Abstention siphoned off even more former Democratic voters than did defection to other candidates. The result was that Carter was able to hold on to only a little more than a third of those who had given him his scanty majority four years earlier, while Reagan retained two-thirds of the former Ford voters.

Clearly turnout was a major blow to the Democrats. A Gallup poll taken just before the election found that 48 percent of all registered voters called themselves Democrats and 23 percent said they were Republicans. According to the ABC News exit poll on election day, however, Democrats outnumbered Republicans by a significantly smaller margin, 42–29 percent, among actual voters. The CBS News/*New York Times* exit poll found virtually the same ratio, 43 percent Democrats to 28 percent Republicans.

In almost every election, Republicans are more likely to vote than Democrats because Republicans tend to be older, higher in socio-economic status, and more active politically. According to post-election surveys by the Center for Political Studies (CPS) of the University of Michigan, Republicans were about seven percentage points more likely to vote than Democrats in 1972 and about eight percentage points more likely to vote in 1976. The *Los Angeles Times* postelection poll indicates a 14 percent Republican turnout advantage in 1980.

Aside from its effect on the election outcome, the disproportionately large number of Democrats who decided to stay home on election day was probably one reason why the preelection forecasts underestimated the Reagan margin. Pollsters' corrections for "likelihood to vote" usually take into account background factors such as age, social status, and political activism, but not short-term political factors—like the unpredictable mood of the voters on election day.

The surprisingly large Republican margin on November 4 appears to have been the product of two factors, the bias in turnout and a late swing. Between November 7 and 12, CBS News and the *New York Times* reinterviewed 89 percent of the 2,264 registered voters whom they had originally interviewed a few days before the election. Among those reinterviewed after the election, 79 percent reported that they voted for the same candidate they had indicated preference for before the election. In this "stable" group of voters, Reagan led Carter 49–43 percent. Eight percent of those reinterviewed said they had decided to stay home on election day. These abstainers had originally indicated a strong preference for Carter over Reagan, 50–29 percent. Finally, 13 percent of those reinterviewed reported a change from their preelection preference. Before the election, this group divided 32 percent for Carter, 16 percent for Reagan, and 27 percent for Anderson, Clark, and others (the rest were undecided or said they would not vote). After the election, these "late swingers" reported that they had gone 52 percent for Reagan, 30 percent for Carter, and 18 percent for Anderson and others. In other words, this group switched from two-to-one for Carter to nearly two-to-one for Reagan in the last few days of the campaign.

Thus, according to CBS News, the original preelection sample was evenly split between Reagan and Carter, 43–43 percent on the weekend before the election. However, the vote among those in the original sample who actually voted on election day was, according to their report of it, 49 percent for Reagan to 41 percent for Carter— quite close to the final 51–41 margin. According to the *New York*

Times, "Economic arguments were cited most frequently by those who switched in a way that helped Mr. Reagan. About a third of them said either that the economy was the reason for their change or that it was the 'greatest failure' of Mr. Carter's term."[5]

The Issues

The economy was certainly the dominant issue of the campaign. In each of the major 1980 primaries, ABC News asked voters to identify the biggest problem facing the country; in every state, the answer most often given by both Democrats and Republicans was inflation. The CBS News/*New York Times* poll asked a similar question repeatedly during the fall campaign. Economic problems were named by about 60 percent of those interviewed in August, September, and October, and by 68 percent of those interviewed just after the election. Foreign policy, by comparison, was much less salient; the percentage mentioning war and peace, relations with the Soviet Union, the hostage crisis in Iran, and other foreign policy problems ranged between 14 and 19. Energy, other domestic issues (including taxes), and dissatisfaction with government were each designated by between 2 and 5 percent as the most important issue facing the country.

Gallup reports that economic issues generally, and inflation specifically, dominated voter concerns in 1980 to a much greater extent than in previous postwar elections. Foreign policy issues topped the list of most important problems in Gallup polls taken during every presidential campaign from 1948 through 1972: the cold war, relations with the Soviet Union, war and peace, and, later, Vietnam. Economic problems came into prominence in 1976, when 47 percent named inflation and 31 percent named unemployment as the country's most serious problem. In 1980, according to Gallup, 61 percent named inflation and 16 percent cited unemployment.[6] NBC News and the Associated Press (AP) posed the question directly by asking people whether, in deciding how to vote for president, they were "more concerned about the candidate's positions on the nation's economy and other domestic problems or about America's position abroad and foreign policy in general." Domestic problems consistently outweighed foreign affairs by margins of two or three to one. That was not good news for Carter and the Democrats. Figure 7–3 shows why.

[5] Adam Clymer, "Poll Shows Iran and Economy Hurt Carter among Late-shifting Voters," *New York Times,* November 16, 1980.
[6] *Gallup Opinion Index,* report no. 181 (September 1980), p. 11.

FIGURE 7–3

Job Ratings for Carter, September 1979–November 1980

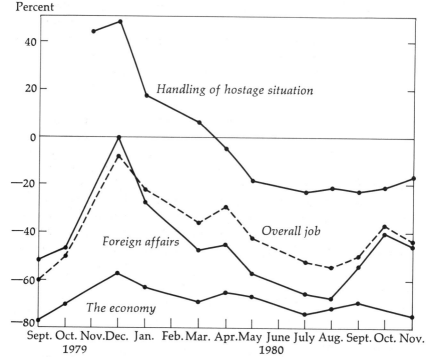

Percent

Sept. Oct. Nov.Dec. Jan. Feb.Mar. Apr.May June July Aug. Sept. Oct. Nov.
    1979   1980

NOTES: Hostage situation: The question was, "Have you heard or read anything about Americans being held hostage in Iran? (If yes) Do you approve or disapprove of the way President Carter is handling the situation?" Positive response = percentage who approve; negative response = percentage who disapprove.

Overall job: The question was, "What kind of job do you think Jimmy Carter is doing as president—do you think he is doing an excellent job, a good job, only a fair job, or do you think he is doing a poor job?" Positive response = percentage who said excellent or good; negative response = percentage who said only fair or poor.

Foreign affairs: The question was, "What kind of a job do you think Jimmy Carter is doing in handling our foreign affairs . . . ?" Positive response = percentage who said excellent or good; negative response = percentage who said only fair or poor.

The economy: The question was, "What kind of a job do you think Jimmy Carter is doing in handling the economy . . . ?" Positive response = percentage who said excellent or good; negative response = percentage who said only fair or poor.

SOURCES: Hostage situation: All NBC News, Associated Press polls.

Overall job: NBC News/Associated Press poll to September 1980; ABC News/Harris poll, October and November 1980.

Foreign affairs: NBC News/Associated Press poll to September 1980; ABC News/Harris poll, October and November 1980.

The economy: NBC News/Associated Press poll to September 1980; ABC News/Harris poll, November 1980.

Carter started out in September 1979—after a summer that included gas lines and the president's July 15 "malaise" speech in response—with extremely negative job ratings. The Iran and Afghanistan crises in November and December 1979 lifted the president's ratings considerably, although never to a net positive level. The period from January through August 1980 was marked by a steady erosion of presidential approval, interrupted temporarily and weakly by the Iran rescue attempt in April. By August, things looked about as bad for the White House as they had a year earlier. The campaign boosted the president's approval ratings slightly in September and October, particularly in the foreign policy area, but these gains were far from enough to pull the administration out of trouble.

Throughout this entire period, President Carter's marks on the economy remained abysmally low, always lower than his foreign policy and overall job ratings even when the latter were at their lowest. The lift the president got from the Iran crisis in the winter of 1979 and from the election campaign in the fall of 1980 hardly made a dent in the public's assessment of his economic performance. The public was strongly dissatisfied with the administration and overwhelmingly dissatisfied with its handling of the economy. After the election, CBS News and the *New York Times* asked people what they thought was the greatest failure of Jimmy Carter's four years as president; 31 percent named economic issues (12 percent named inflation, 3 percent cited unemployment, and 16 percent said, "the economy"), compared with 23 percent who mentioned the hostages in Iran.

The result, not surprisingly, was that Reagan consistently outpaced Carter as the better candidate on economic issues in the public's view. The ABC News/Harris poll asked repeatedly during the campaign which candidate "would do a better job of handling the economy." Reagan always came out ahead of Carter and Anderson. Indeed, Reagan's margin over Carter increased from 42–28 percent in August to 50-27 percent on November 2. The NBC News/AP poll also found Reagan consistently beating his opponents as the candidate "who would do the best job solving the nation's economic problems." In late October, the standings were Reagan, 39 percent; Carter, 21 percent; Anderson, 10 percent; and "no difference between the candidates," 25 percent. CBS News and the *New York Times* asked people whether they thought the economy "would get better, get worse, or stay about the same" (1) if Carter were elected and (2) if Reagan were elected. More people always said the economy would get worse rather than better if Jimmy Carter were elected (31 percent said worse and 19 percent said better in the final preelection poll). For Reagan, the reverse was true; 38 percent expected better under Reagan and 20 percent expected worse in the final poll.

Two additional considerations made the economic issue even more damaging for the Democrats. One is that inflation was felt to be a more serious problem than unemployment. CBS News and the *New York Times* found that to be the case in each of four polls taken during the 1980 campaign. An average of 58 percent said inflation and 26 percent said unemployment was the "more important problem facing the country." The CBS News/*New York Times* poll had shown a closer balance between the two concerns in 1976, when an average of 50 percent named inflation and 40 percent named unemployment as the more serious problem in three pre-election surveys.

Inflation is usually thought to be a better issue for conservatives, since government—and particularly government spending—can easily be blamed for the problem. Thus the public's initial response to rising inflation in 1978 took the form of the "tax revolt," which was, fundamentally, an attack on government waste and inefficiency.[7] Inflation was, accordingly, a very good issue for Ronald Reagan in 1980. Evidence to this effect can be seen in table 7–3. Next to strengthening the national defense, reducing inflation was the issue where Reagan was perceived to have the strongest advantage over Carter. A nationwide poll taken by the *Los Angeles Times* in October showed the same thing—47 percent chose Reagan, 2 percent chose Carter, and 12 percent chose Anderson as the best candidate for stopping inflation. In the CBS News/*New York Times* poll, Reagan was always in the lead among those who named inflation as a more important problem than unemployment.

The economic issue in 1980 created yet a second calamity for the Democrats: they lost the party's historically powerful advantage on the unemployment issue. In table 7–3, Reagan was preferred over Carter 41–32 percent as the best candidate for reducing unemployment, a margin only slightly smaller than his advantage on the inflation issue. The *Los Angeles Times*'s October poll confirms this finding; its sample preferred Reagan over Carter 43–30 percent as the candidate with the best policy for decreasing unemployment. The Democrats in 1980 were in the unusual position of presiding over a major recession; the recessions of the 1930s, the late 1950s, and the mid-1970s all occurred under Republican administrations and

[7] See Seymour Martin Lipset and William Schneider, "Is the Tax Revolt Over?" *Taxing and Spending*, vol. 3 (Summer 1980), pp. 73-78.

TABLE 7–3

CANDIDATE ISSUE RATINGS
(percent)

QUESTION: "This card lists various problems with which the man elected President this November will have to deal. Regardless of which man you happen to prefer—Carter, Reagan, or Anderson— please tell me which one you, yourself, feel would do a better job of handling each of the following problems."

	Reagan	Carter	Anderson	Don't Know
Reagan rated higher				
Strengthening national defense	55	28	7	10
Reducing inflation	44	29	13	14
Improving the economy	44	30	12	14
Spending taxpayers' money wisely	42	29	16	13
Increasing respect for the United States overseas	42	31	13	14
Reducing unemployment	41	32	14	13
Domestic affairs	42	36	14	8
Improving the energy situation	40	34	14	12
Handling the Iranian situation	39	33	11	17
Building trust in government	37	32	18	13
Carter rated higher				
Improving things for minorities including blacks and Hispanics	22	49	13	16
Keeping the United States out of war	25	50	12	13
Helping the poor and needy	24	49	14	13
Women's rights	23	48	17	12
Dealing with racial problems	26	47	15	12
Dealing with the Arab-Israeli situation	30	47	9	14
Foreign relations	37	43	11	9
Improving the environment and dealing with environmental issues	32	37	17	14
Dealing with Russia	37	40	11	12

NOTE: The poll was taken September 12-15, 1980 (nationwide sample of registered voters).
SOURCE: *Gallup Opinion Index*, report no. 181 (September 1980), p. 19.

therefore reinforced the Democrats' traditional advantage on the unemployment issue. In fact, the last major recession to occur under a Democratic administration was in the 1890s, when Grover Cleveland was president, and it was instrumental in creating a Republican majority that dominated American politics for more than thirty years.

The Carter recession got under way in the spring of 1980 and helped turn the Democratic primaries around for Edward Kennedy. In late June and early July, the *Los Angeles Times* poll asked, "Would you tend to vote more Democratic or Republican if inflation got worse?" Predictably, 52 percent answered "more Republican," and 32 percent, "more Democratic." The poll also asked, "Would you tend to vote more Democratic or Republican if unemployment got worse?" Here the Republican advantage was about the same—50 percent answered "Republican" and 34 percent, "Democratic." Indeed, 30 percent of Democrats in the poll said they would vote more Republican if unemployment got worse, and their preference at the time of the poll was just that—54 percent for Reagan to 18 percent for Carter. In the case of either higher inflation or higher unemployment, the voters indicated they would vote for a change, and in 1980 that meant voting Republican.

Since the 1930s, the Democrats, as the party of the New Deal, have normally held the advantage on economic issues. That advantage is evidenced by the Gallup polls, which have asked almost every year since 1951, "Which political party—the Republican or the Democratic—do you think will do the better job of keeping the country prosperous?" The Democrats have come out ahead on this issue in 37 out of 41 tests over the last thirty years. The Republicans were ahead only twice, by one percentage point at the end of 1955 and by three points in September 1972, just before the Nixon landslide. In the 1950s, the average Democratic margin on the prosperity issue was nine percentage points. In the 1960s, the Democrats' advantage rose to twenty-four percentage points. The party's advantage fell slightly, to seventeen points, in the 1970s. Most recently, the Democrats' margin on this issue has gone from eighteen points in March 1978, to six points in June 1980, to exactly one point in September 1980, when 36 percent said the Democrats were the best party for prosperity and 35 percent preferred the Republicans.[8] Thus a central theme of the Carter administration and of the 1980 election was the collapse of Democratic preeminence as the party of prosperity, whether thought of in terms of inflation or in terms of unemployment.

[8] *Gallup Opinion Index*, report no. 181 (September 1980), p. 8.

Gallup has also asked regularly since 1951, "Which political party do you think would be more likely to keep the United States out of World War III—the Republican party or the Democratic party?" The Republicans held the advantage on this issue from 1951 through 1960. Responses began to favor the Democrats in 1961, when John Kennedy took office, and continued to do so until early 1966. Then, with the intensification of the Vietnam war, the advantage shifted back to the Republicans and remained with them through the Nixon administration. Beginning in 1974, the Democrats were once again rated best for peace, by an average six-point margin through June 1980. In September 1980, the Democrats' advantage on the peace issue widened considerably, to seventeen points; 42 percent said the Democrats were most likely to keep the country out of World War III, and 25 percent said the Republicans were. That represents the largest Democratic advantage on the peace issue since 1964, when, with Barry Goldwater as the Republican nominee, the Democrats outdistanced the Republicans as the peace party by twenty-three points.[9]

Typically when the Republicans have won presidential elections, as in 1952, 1956, 1968, and 1972, they have done so by gaining supremacy in the foreign policy area in order to compensate for the party's usual disadvantage on economic issues. The 1980 election reversed that pattern. The Democrats lost their ascendancy as the party of prosperity, but they enjoyed an uncommonly strong lead on the peace issue.

Thus, in table 7–3, Reagan had a six-point advantage over Carter for handling domestic affairs, while Carter held a six-point advantage in foreign relations. Not all foreign policy issues worked to the Democrats' advantage, however. Peace certainly did; Carter led by twenty-five points, as shown in table 7–3, as the best candidate for keeping the United States out of war. Reagan had an equally strong lead, however, as the best candidate for strengthening the national defense. Reagan was also felt to be more capable of increasing respect for the United States overseas. But Carter was preferred for dealing with the Arab-Israeli situation. Generally, the distinction is between peace issues, which benefited Carter, and defense issues, where Reagan held the advantage. The issue of dealing with the Soviet Union involves both peace and defense, and so Carter was only narrowly preferred. In the *Los Angeles Times* poll, it was Reagan who was slightly ahead as the best candidate for dealing with the Soviet Union.

[9] Ibid., p. 9.

This ambiguity on foreign policy issues shows up in every survey. NBC News and the Associated Press asked which candidate would do the best job of keeping the United States out of war. Carter was ahead of Reagan each time the question was asked (the average for Carter was 41 percent and for Reagan, 16 percent). Reagan held the lead over Carter, however, when people were asked who would "do the best job in strengthening America's position in the world" (the average for Reagan was 38 percent and for Carter, 25 percent). In the ABC News/Harris poll, Reagan led Carter by thirty-five points as the candidate who "would keep U.S. military strength at least as strong as or stronger than the Russians'." People also felt, by a margin of twenty-three points, that Reagan "would stand up most firmly if the U.S. were threatened by the Soviet Union." By a margin of twenty-eight points, however, the public felt that Reagan "might be most likely to get the U.S. into another war." The result was that Carter ended up ahead as the candidate who "would best handle foreign policy"—but by only two points.

Both the CBS News/*New York Times* poll and the NBC News/AP poll asked people whether they felt that if Reagan were elected president he would get us into a war. Between 32 and 39 percent of the public answered yes in eight different polls. Significantly, women indicated greater concern on this point than men. That appears to be one reason why, throughout the campaign and on election day, Reagan did notably worse among women than among men. Men tend to give greater emphasis to defense, and women tend to give more to peace, in forming opinions on foreign policy. Reagan's toughness on foreign policy had a good deal to do with the differentiation of the candidates in this area. But so did Jimmy Carter's record. Preserving peace was Carter's one substantial accomplishment, and the voters seemed to be aware of it. After the election, CBS News and the *New York Times* asked, "No matter how you feel in general about the job he's done, what do you think Jimmy Carter has done best during his four years as President?" The answers most frequently given were keeping us out of war (15 percent), the Mideast peace agreement (11 percent), and foreign policy in general (7 percent)—as well as "nothing" (7 percent).

A third category of issues widely discussed during the 1980 campaign was the so-called social issues. These included, most prominently, two proposed constitutional amendments, the Equal Rights Amendment (ERA) for women and an amendment to prohibit abortions. Polls indicate that the public continues to take the "liberal" side on both issues—in favor of the ERA and against a ban on legalized abortions. Other social issues that received less attention during the campaign include handgun control, affirmative action for minority groups, and measures to censor pornography—all issues on which the public tends to favor the liberal side—as well as capital punishment, prayer in public schools, homosexual rights, and busing, where the conservative positions are usually more popular.[10]

What made these issues relevant to the 1980 campaign was that the candidates and parties took unusually strong and divergent positions on them. The Republicans, in their platform, went on record for the first time against the Equal Rights Amendment and in favor of a constitutional amendment to prohibit abortions, going so far as to require that any federal judge appointed by a Republican administration be explicitly opposed to abortion. The Democrats not only endorsed ERA and women's right to abortion; they went further and pledged to withhold party support from any candidate who opposed the ERA. On abortion, the Democrats supported the use of federal funds to subsidize abortions for poor women.

Did these issues have a significant impact on the vote? They were certainly less salient to the electorate than the economy and foreign policy. Few respondents in any poll spontaneously mentioned any social issue as a major problem facing the country. The ABC News exit poll of voters on election day presented a list of nine issues and asked respondents to check off the one or two of them "where you most like the stand of the presidential candidate you voted for." ERA came in sixth, with 18 percent, after government spending, foreign affairs, inflation, military strength, and tax cuts. Abortion came in last, with 6 percent, behind problems of the poor and elderly, and energy. Interestingly, those who checked ERA as a major issue voted for Carter over Reagan, 69 to 18 percent, while those who were concerned over abortion voted for Reagan, 52 to 35 percent.

It does not appear that social issues were a major factor influencing the vote on November 4. The ABC News exit poll, for example, asked respondents to take the same list of issues and check

[10] Several major polls published summary data on social issue trends just after the 1980 election. See the CBS News/*New York Times* poll, "Post-Election Poll, November 1980," released November 15–16, 1980; the Gallup poll, "Reagan, Public Not Eye-to-Eye on ERA, Abortion Ban" (November 16, 1980); and the ABC News/Harris survey, "Americans Oppose Conservative Stands on Key Social Issues," vol. 2, no. 152, press release, December 4, 1980. Both Gallup and Harris show that although the public continues to favor the Equal Rights Amendment, gun control, and affirmative action programs for blacks, opposition to all three has increased over the past few years. The Gallup data show, however, that attitudes toward abortion have remained stable or liberalized slightly since 1975.

off the one or two where they most *disliked* the stand of each presidential candidate. Only 9 percent named ERA and 6 percent named abortion as issues where they disliked Jimmy Carter's positions, far below the 37 percent who criticized Carter on inflation and the 31 percent who chose foreign affairs. ERA, however, was at the top of the list of issues on which voters disliked Ronald Reagan's position, with 29 percent, while 13 percent said they did not like Reagan's views on abortion. Can we conclude that these issues cost Reagan votes? Not necessarily. The fact is, the 29 percent who disliked Reagan's stand on ERA still voted for him over Carter, 47 to 39 percent. Those who disliked Reagan's stand on abortion voted for him by an even larger margin, 63 to 24 percent. By comparison, the 20 percent who said they disliked Reagan's stand on foreign affairs voted heavily for Carter, 58 to 27 percent.

After analyzing data from the June 1980 CBS News/*New York Times* poll, E. J. Dionne reported that 41 percent of the public disagreed with Reagan—that is, took liberal positions—on both ERA and abortion, while only 19 percent agreed with the Republican candidate and platform on both issues. As Dionne went on to point out, however:

> Critical for Mr. Reagan . . . is the fact that he seems not to be hurt among those who disagree with him on these issues, but is helped immensely among those who agree with him. . . . Among those who disagree with one or both of Mr. Reagan's positions on these matters, he still runs ahead of both Mr. Carter and John B. Anderson, the independent candidate. And those who want to ban abortions and stop the Equal Rights Amendment flock to Mr. Reagan and give him a 2-to-1 edge.[11]

The impact of economic, foreign policy, and social issues on the 1980 vote can be seen in table 7–4, which is based on the CBS News/*New York Times* exit poll of 12,782 voters interviewed across the country on election day. The table indicates how voters who took various issue positions cast their ballots for president on November 4. Table 7–4 also shows each group's *swing* to the Republicans from 1976 to 1980. Swing, a concept borrowed from British psephology, is simply the average of the Republican gain and the Democratic loss from one election to the next. In the country as a whole, according to the actual election results in table 7–1, the

[11] E. J. Dionne, "Even Carter's Successes May Be Helping Reagan," *New York Times*, June 29, 1980.

TABLE 7–4

Issues and the 1980 Vote

Question	1980 Electorate (percent)	1980 Vote (percent)			Swing to Republicans 1976–1980[a] (percentage points)
		Carter	Reagan	Anderson	
All voters	100	41	50	7	11.5
Which issues were most important in deciding how you voted today? (up to two answers)					
Inflation and economy	33	28	61	9	16.5
Jobs and unemployment	24	48	42	7	13
Balancing the federal budget	21	27	65	6	15
U.S. prestige around the world	16	31	61	7	16
Crisis in Iran	14	63	31	4	4
Reducing federal income taxes	10	29	64	4	14.5
ERA/abortion	7	50	38	10	14
Needs of big cities	2	77	13	7	1
Don't know/none	20	45	46	7	8
"We should be more forceful in our dealings with the Soviet Union even if it increases the risk of war."					
Agree	54	28	64	6	16
Disagree	31	56	32	10	8
"Cutting taxes is more important than balancing the federal budget."					
Agree	30	42	50	6	15
Disagree	53	37	53	9	11
"Unemployment is a more important problem today than inflation."					
Agree	39	51	40	7	11.5
Disagree	45	30	60	9	14

(Table continues)

237

TABLE 7-4 (continued)

Question	1980 Electorate (percent)	1980 Vote (percent)			Swing to Republicans 1976–1980[a] (percentage points)
		Carter	Reagan	Ander-son	
"I support the Equal Rights Amendment—ERA—the constitutional amendment concerning women."					
Agree	45	*49*	38	11	11.5
Disagree	35	26	*68*	4	14

NOTE: $N = 12,782$. Italics indicate the largest percentage in each row.

[a] Swing is defined as the average of the Republican gain and the Democratic loss, 1976 to 1980, in each group. The 1976 vote is measured by voter recall, which overstates Carter's support somewhat (57 percent Carter, 43 percent Ford for the sample as a whole).

SOURCE: CBS News/*New York Times* National Election Day Survey, at polling places nationwide on November 4, 1980.

Republicans gained 2.8 percentage points from 1976 to 1980 while the Democrats lost 9.1 percentage points. The average of these two figures gives a pro-Republican swing of six points. (Put in a slightly different way, the Republicans went from two points behind the Democrats in 1976 to ten points ahead of the Democrats in 1980; the increase in the Republicans' lead was therefore twelve points, which was brought about by a net change—"swing"—of six points.

The swing shown for all voters in table 7-4 is 11.5 percentage points, or almost twice the actual nationwide swing. The reason for this discrepancy is that respondents' voting behavior in 1976 was ascertained from a "recall" question in the 1980 poll ("In 1976, for whom did you vote?"). The voting behavior of the issue groups in table 7-4, unlike that of Republicans, women, college graduates, blacks, and so on, was not ascertained at the time of the 1976 election. Respondents in the CBS News/*New York Times* poll, like respondents in most polls, tended to overstate their level of support for the winning candidate in the previous election. Specifically, 57 percent reported voting for Jimmy Carter and 43 percent for Gerald Ford. Thus the swing among poll respondents was from a (reported) fourteen-point Republican deficit in 1976 to a nine-point Republican lead in 1980—an 11.5-percentage-point swing.

Even though the national swing figure in table 7–4 is error-based, it can be used to compare the relative magnitudes of voter shifts in different issue constituencies. By using swing figures, one can tell not just how a group voted, but whether the Republicans gained or lost support in that group from 1976 to 1980.

Take the case of those respondents—one-quarter of the sample—who said that "jobs and unemployment" was a major issue influencing their vote for president in 1980. According to table 7–4, this group voted for Carter over Reagan, 48 to 42 percent. The unemployment issue appears to have worked to Carter's advantage. This group, however, reported voting 66–34 percent for Carter over Ford in 1976. Therefore, among voters concerned about unemployment, a reported Democratic lead of thirty-two points in 1976 diminished to a Democratic lead of six points in 1980. The swing was thirteen percentage points toward the Republicans, or slightly more pro-Republican than in the sample as a whole. The swing calculation suggests that the unemployment issue helped the Republicans by cutting into the Democrats' previously commanding lead among voters concerned about it.

The Republicans made gains in 1980 in every issue constituency noted in table 7–4. The issue that helped Reagan the most was inflation and the economy; it was the issue most often chosen as important, and those concerned about it showed the strongest pro-Republican swing. Concern over U.S. prestige in the world also gained votes for the Republicans, although only half as many voters thought it was important as was the case with inflation. Finally, tax cuts, balancing the budget, and, as noted, unemployment, brought voters over to the Republican side. Two issues that held down the swing to the Republicans and therefore, relatively speaking, helped the Democrats were the Iran crisis and concern over the needs of big cities. Unfortunately for the Democrats, however, these issues were at or near the bottom of the list of the voters' interests. Otherwise, the Democrats did relatively well among voters who expressed no issue concerns at all—one-fifth of the sample.

The results for the social issues confirm the findings reported earlier. The CBS News/*New York Times* poll presented "ERA/abortion" as a single issue; although only 7 percent of the voters indicated that it was important to them, this group exhibited a relatively strong pro-Republican swing. In a separate question, voters were asked whether or not they supported the Equal Rights Amendment. Those who did *not* swung relatively strongly to the Republicans. Supporters of ERA, on the other hand, manifested the same swing as the overall sample. One reason is that John Anderson did comparatively well among ERA supporters and probably drained off more votes from Carter than from Reagan in this group, thus boosting the Republican swing. In sum, support for the ERA—the more popular position—did not seem to hurt the Republicans; if anything, it may have drawn otherwise Democratic votes to Anderson. On the other hand, the minority's opposition to the ERA appears to have helped Reagan directly.

The same pattern shows up in the case of two tough choices posed by the CBS News/*New York Times* poll. Respondents were asked to choose between unemployment and inflation as the more important problem and between cutting taxes and balancing the budget as the preferred policy. Those who gave priority to inflation and to cutting taxes evidenced a strong swing to the Republicans, but those who were more concerned with unemployment and balancing the budget behaved like other voters in the sample. They displayed no inclination to reward the Democrats.

The Reagan "Mandate"

The issues that were most important to the voters in 1980 were not deeply divisive ideological conflicts. They were "valence" issues, where everyone was on the same side: against inflation and unemployment, in favor of keeping peace, improving our military security, and increasing respect for the United States around the world. The argument was over how serious these problems had become, whether Jimmy Carter was responsible for them, and whether Ronald Reagan could handle them any better. In other words, the campaign centered on who would do better what everyone agreed needed to be done. Interestingly, one argument that worked in Carter's favor was that "today, regardless of who holds the office, no president can be very effective in solving our nation's problems." ABC News offered this statement to respondents in their exit poll. The more strongly people agreed with this view, the more likely they were to vote for Jimmy Carter.

The 1980 election was essentially a referendum on the Carter administration, precisely along the lines described by V. O. Key in his classic depiction of *The Responsible Electorate*:

> The major streams of shifting voters graphically reflect the electorate in its great, and perhaps principal, role as an appraiser of past events, past performance, and past actions. It judges retrospectively; it commands prospectively only

insofar as it expresses either approval or disapproval of that which has happened before.[12]

As figure 7–3 revealed, that could not have been good news for Jimmy Carter.

Indeed, given Carter's terrible job ratings, it is remarkable that the election was considered too close to call right up until the last minute. It may be worth noting that Carter entered the 1980 campaign with the lowest job approval ratings of any incumbent president since Gallup began taking these measurements in the 1940s. Gerald Ford had a 45 percent approval rating in the summer of 1976. Lyndon Johnson's approval rating in the summer of 1968 was 40 percent. Eisenhower was at 57 percent in June 1960. Truman's rating had been 32 percent in June 1952. In each of these years, the incumbent party was turned out of office. Jimmy Carter's approval rating in June 1980 was 31 percent, the lowest of them all. It dipped to a record low for any president, 21 percent, in July. Those ratings, which went widely unnoticed during the fall campaign, were ultimately to be the determining factor in the election outcome.

The campaign itself became largely a contest of personalities. The issue was not whether Jimmy Carter deserved to be reelected—most agreed that he did not—but whether Ronald Reagan could be entrusted with the presidency. That is where Reagan's image as an ideologue both helped him and hurt him.

Table 7–5 presents a comparison of the two major candidates by positive personality traits ascribed to them by the voters. Carter's strengths were mostly attributes of character—religiousness, morality, integrity, and personal sympathy. Carter was also clearly identified as the more moderate, middle-of-the-road candidate, normally a considerable advantage in a presidential election. Reagan's advantages were leadership, decisiveness, and conviction ("has a well-defined program," "you know where he stands," "imaginative, innovative solutions," "well thought out, carefully considered solutions," "clear understanding of the issues," and so on). Those can be counted as advantages accruing to an "ideological" candidate. People often admired Barry Goldwater, George Wallace, and George McGovern for being clear, forthright, and strong in their convictions ("speaks his mind," "you know where he stands"), especially in comparison with the "pragmatic" politicians who usually win our elections (Lyndon Johnson, Richard Nixon).

[12] V. O. Key, Jr., *The Responsible Electorate* (New York: Vintage Books, 1966), pp. 61-62.

TABLE 7–5

PERCENTAGE OF VOTERS ASCRIBING POSITIVE PERSONALITY TRAITS TO CARTER AND TO REAGAN

QUESTION: "Here is a list of terms—shown as pairs of opposites— that have been used to describe (Jimmy Carter/Ronald Reagan). From each pair of opposites, would you select the term which you feel best describes (Carter/Reagan)?"

	Carter	Reagan
Carter rated higher		
A religious person	87	40
Takes moderate, middle-of-the-road positions	82	48
Sympathetic to problems of the poor	68	41
A man of high moral principles	83	70
Sides with the average citizen	56	43
Says what he believes even if unpopular	57	54
Reagan rated higher		
Has strong leadership qualities	31	65
Decisive, sure of himself	37	69
Has a well-defined program for moving the country ahead	27	53
You know where he stands on issues	33	54
A colorful, interesting personality	50	70
The kind of person who can get the job done	39	56
Offers imaginative, innovative solutions to national problems	37	52
Has modern, up-to-date solutions to national problems	39	51
Has well thought out, carefully considered solutions for national problems	36	45
Has a clear understanding of the issues facing the country	50	55
No difference		
Bright, intelligent	73	73
Would display good judgment in a crisis	55	55

NOTE: Figures exclude respondents who did not express an opinion.

SOURCE: *Gallup Opinion Index*, report no. 181 (September 1980), p. 31. Poll was taken September 12-15, 1980.

The cost of being ideological is that one may appear divisive and extreme. When the *Los Angeles Times* asked which candidate best fit the description "He's too extreme," the results were Reagan, 41 percent; Anderson 24 percent; and Carter, 13 percent. Thus the strong beliefs that made many voters fearful of Reagan also attracted voters to him, since they suggested leadership and decisiveness—qualities widely felt to be lacking in the Carter presidency. (Carter's integrity and strength of character had been highly valued in 1976 for similar reasons.)

How extreme was the perception of Ronald Reagan? One argument holds that the voters moved sharply to the right during the 1980 campaign and so found themselves, in the end, relatively close to Reagan in ideology. Another argument is that Reagan's "moderate" campaign strategy was successful in that it shifted his image considerably closer to the center during the course of the campaign. Did either or both of these things happen? Tables 7–6, 7–7, and 7–8 present some surprising evidence on this point from several sources.

In January and February 1980, the Center for Political Studies of the University of Michigan asked respondents in a nationwide poll to locate their own position plus the perceived positions of several presidential candidates on a seven-point scale of political views, ranging from "extremely liberal" at one end to "extremely con-

TABLE 7–6

SHIFTS IN IDEOLOGICAL PERCEPTIONS DURING THE 1980 CAMPAIGN:
1. CENTER FOR POLITICAL STUDIES

| | Mean Scale Position[a] | |
Person Ranked	Jan.–Feb.	Sept.–Oct.
Yourself	+0.37	+0.31
Reagan	+1.08	+1.21
Carter	+0.35	−0.26
Anderson	N.A.	−0.43

NOTES: Minus = liberal. Plus = conservative. Jan.-Feb. $N = 1,008$./Sept.-Oct. $N = 1,004$. Seven-point ideology scale ran from −3 ("extremely liberal") to +3 ("extremely conservative"). N.A. indicates not asked.

SOURCE: University of Michigan Center for Political Studies (CPS), 1980 American National Election Study. Jan.-Feb.: P-1 Wave. Sept.-Oct.: C-3 Wave. *Gallup Opinion Index*, report no 181 (September 1980), pp. 33-36.

TABLE 7–7

SHIFTS IN IDEOLOGICAL PERCEPTION DURING THE 1980 CAMPAIGN:
2. CBS NEWS/NEW YORK TIMES POLL
(percent)

Person Ranked	March	September
Yourself		
Liberal	17	15
Moderate	43	46
Conservative	33	34
Margin[a]	+16	+19
Reagan		
Liberal	12	17
Moderate	18	15
Conservative	50	50
Margin[a]	+38	+33
Carter		
Liberal	17	24
Moderate	37	37
Conservative	28	21
Margin[a]	+11	−3
Anderson		
Liberal	16	29
Moderate	16	24
Conservative	11	15
Margin[a]	−5	−14

NOTES: March $N = 1{,}057$ registered voters; September $N = 810$ registered voters.
[a] Conservative percentage less liberal percentage, in percentage points.
SOURCE: Nationwide telephone surveys, March and September 1980, CBS News/ New York Times poll.

servative" at the other end, with "moderate, middle-of-the-road" at the center. Giving each scale position a numerical weight from −3 ("extremely liberal") to +3 ("extremely conservative"), one can calculate the mean scale position for the public as a whole and for the public's perceptions of the major candidates. The results for the public, Jimmy Carter, and Ronald Reagan are shown in table 7–6.

According to this calculation, the public saw itself as slightly to the right of center at the beginning of 1980—and Jimmy Carter was perceived at almost exactly the same position. Reagan, however, was seen as significantly farther to the right. Thus the conventional

TABLE 7–8

SHIFTS IN IDEOLOGICAL PERCEPTION DURING THE 1980 CAMPAIGN:
3. GALLUP POLL
(percent)

Person Rated	May	September
Yourself		
Liberal	20	17
Moderate	40	44
Conservative	28	28
Margin[a]	+8	+11
Reagan		
Liberal	16	16
Moderate	21	24
Conservative	42	46
Margin[a]	+26	+30
Carter		
Liberal	21	29
Moderate	39	35
Conservative	26	21
Margin[a]	+5	−8
Anderson		
Liberal	23	25
Moderate	38	26
Conservative	15	15
Margin[a]	−8	−10

[a] Conservative percentage less liberal percentage, in percentage points.
SOURCE: *Gallup Opinion Index*, report no. 181 (September 1980), p. 32.

wisdom about the campaign seemed to be true at its outset: the public and Carter were close to the center, whereas Ronald Reagan was relatively "extreme."

The ideology scale question was repeated in the September-October cross-section wave of the CPS 1980 election study. The mean scale positions for the respondents themselves and for candidates Carter, Reagan, and Anderson are also shown in table 7–6. Neither the public's own views nor its perception of Ronald Reagan had changed very much. Jimmy Carter, however, who had been placed slightly to the right of center at the beginning of the year, was now seen as slightly to the left of center. John Anderson came out somewhat further to the left than Carter.

Tables 7–7 and 7–8 present evidence from other sources of perceived ideological shifts during the campaign. In March and September, the CBS News/*New York Times* poll asked respondents to identify themselves and the candidates as "liberal," "moderate," or "conservative." The Gallup poll administered similar tests in May and September 1980.

Tables 7–7 and 7–8 confirm the shifts observed in table 7–6. The public's own political views hardly changed at all between the spring and the fall of 1980 (at most, people were a few points less likely to describe themselves as liberal), nor did the perception of Reagan change significantly. He was seen as a conservative in the spring, and he remained a conservative in the fall. Both comparisons, however, show Carter shifting from just right of center in the spring (more people calling him a conservative than a liberal) to just left of center in the fall (more people calling him a liberal than a conservative).

The consistency among these comparisons is striking. They suggest that neither of the initial hypotheses is correct. The public did not move sharply to the right during the campaign, nor was Reagan seen as moving significantly closer to the center. In fact, the public's perception of itself and of Ronald Reagan had not changed very much since the fall of 1976, when the Center for Political Studies asked the same scale questions. In 1976, the mean scale score for the public was a slightly conservative +0.34, almost exactly the same as in 1980. Gallup and the CBS News/*New York Times* poll have also published data showing little change in the public's ideological self-perception from 1976 to 1980.[13] The mean scale position for Reagan in 1976 was +1.31, or about the same as it was four years later.

It was Jimmy Carter whose ideological image shifted during the 1980 campaign. It moved to the left, most likely because Carter was a "conservative" running against Kennedy for the Democratic nomination in the spring and a "liberal" running against Reagan as the Democratic nominee in the fall. (In the fall of 1976, according to the

---

[13] See note 1, above. According to the Gallup poll, when asked to place themselves on a left-right scale, the public in 1976 turned out to be 31 percent conservative, 45 percent moderate, and 24 percent liberal. The 1980 results showed a slight decrease in the proportion on the left and a corresponding increase in the center: 32 percent conservative, 49 percent moderate, and 19 percent liberal. Thus, in an interesting parallel to the 1980 election results, the evidence suggests some decline in identification with liberalism but no corresponding surge in support for conservatism. Gallup Poll, "Little Evidence of Shift to Right Seen in Reagan Victory" (November 13, 1980).

CPS poll, Carter was perceived as much more liberal, with a mean scale score of −0.88). Carter's shift to the left, which may have been necessary for him to get the Democratic nomination and hold the party together, certainly did not improve his situation strategically. In the early polls, as shown in tables 7–6, 7–7, and 7–8, the public's position was very close to Carter's and relatively distant from Reagan's. As perceptions of Carter moved to the left, however, the public ended up in between Carter on the left and Reagan on the right. In other words, by the time of the fall campaign, Carter's ideological advantage had been lost; the public was not much further from Reagan than from Carter. (In an absolute sense, of course, Reagan was always more "extreme" than Carter, since Reagan was always further to the right than Carter was to the left.)

Finally, it should be noted that John Anderson was perceived as further to the left than Jimmy Carter among those respondents who had any idea where to place him (many did not). That was not where Anderson had intended to be. He advertised himself as in between the two major-party candidates ideologically, to the left of Reagan on social issues and to the right of Carter on economic issues. Nevertheless, he ended up being perceived as the most liberal candidate in the race, and both the nature and the extent of his support reflected that fact.

Why did people vote for Reagan in the end? Two reasons stood out in a list presented to respondents in the CBS News/*New York Times* exit poll—"It is time for a change" (cited by 38 percent of Reagan supporters) and "He is a strong leader" (cited by 21 percent). The election results raised many questions about the nature of the Republicans' "mandate," whether the voters had chosen Reagan because of his strongly conservative issue positions or in spite of them. The notion presented here of the election as a referendum on Carter seems to suggest the latter. In fact, this question was put directly to the public in a survey done for *Time* magazine by Yankelovich, Skelly, and White in January 1981: "Do you agree with people who feel that the Reagan victory was a mandate for more conservative policies in our country, or do you feel it was mostly a rejection of President Carter and his Administration?"[14] The results were one-sided: 63 percent said the Reagan victory was mostly a rejection of the Carter administration, whereas 24 percent felt it was a mandate for conservatism. Even Republicans (54 to 34 percent) and self-described conservatives (57 to 30 percent) felt that the elec-

---

14 John F. Stacks, "New Beginnings, Old Anxieties," *Time*, February 2, 1981, p. 22. Additional data were provided by *Time*, the sponsor of the poll.

tion was more a rejection of Carter than a conservative mandate.

This dichotomy, however, is in many ways a false one that misrepresents the nature of American elections. The voters were voting for a *change*, and they were certainly aware that the type of change Reagan was offering was going to take the country in a more conservative direction. They were willing to go along with that, not because they were convinced of the essential merits of the conservative program, but because they were willing to give conservatism a chance. It is as if, having got nowhere for the past four years with Jimmy Carter at the wheel, the voters turned to Ronald Reagan and said, "O.K.—you drive."

As many political scientists have argued, our electoral and party systems are not well designed to give voters a clearly defined, programmatic choice on election day.[15] Thus Key concluded that voters in our system do not "command prospectively"; they judge retrospectively and, in doing so, produce a "mandate" for the new administration to solve the problems that caused the old administration to be defeated.

Franklin Roosevelt was elected in 1932 to end the depression. It certainly did not matter to the voters that he did not do so by fulfilling his campaign promise to balance the budget. Richard Nixon was elected in 1968 with a mandate to end the war in Vietnam. The voters did not "command" that he do so by being either a "dove" or a "hawk." Indeed, they were quite unable to decide which Nixon was in 1968, according to the survey evidence.[16] (Nixon executed this ambiguous mandate rather faithfully after he took office by being a dove and a hawk at the same time, withdrawing troops while increasing the bombing.) Four years later, the voters had reason to believe that the Nixon administration had not fulfilled its mandate to end the war, and they had to be reassured by proclamations that "peace is at hand." Reagan's mandate is to restore the economy, curb inflation, and increase the nation's military security. If he chooses to do so by "getting the government off our backs," or by some mysterious combination of tax cuts, budget balancing, and higher defense spending, that is the prerogative of the president and his party. The voters simply reserve the right to let him know in four years whether they believe those policies have worked.

[15] Most prominent among them was E. E. Schattschneider, *The Semi-Sovereign People* (New York: Holt, Rinehart and Winston, 1960); see especially pp. 108-15.
[16] See Benjamin I. Page and Richard A. Brody, "Policy Voting and the Electoral Process: The Vietnam War Issue," *American Political Science Review*, vol. 66 (September 1972), pp. 979-95.

Realignment

Every election offers voters both a plebiscitary choice—How do I feel about the way the government is being run?—and an ideological choice—Which party or candidate is closer to my beliefs? Jimmy Carter tried to keep the 1980 campaign focused on the ideological decision, as when he described the election in his acceptance speech at the Democratic National Convention as "a stark choice between two men, two parties, two sharply different pictures of America and the world. . . . It is a choice between two futures." Ronald Reagan emphasized the plebiscitary context of the voters' decision—the election as a referendum on the past and present rather than the future. In his closing statement in the October 28 debate, Reagan advised voters to ask themselves,

> Are you better off than you were four years ago? Is it easier for you to go and buy things in the stores than it was four years ago? Is there more or less unemployment in the country than there was four years ago? Is America as respected throughout the world as it was? . . . If you answer all of those questions "yes," why, then I think your choice is very obvious as to who you'll vote for. If you don't agree, . . . then I could suggest another choice that you have.

The argument presented here has been that the ideological context of the 1980 election was largely displaced by the plebiscitary context. That is why Reagan won.

Explaining the ultimate significance of the 1980 election, however, involves more than explaining why Reagan won. The election must also be interpreted in relation to long-term changes in American voting behavior. When the broader meaning of the election is considered, ideology becomes more important.

There is evidence that American politics began to undergo an ideological shift in the mid-1960s. In their analysis of survey data from the mid-1950s through the early 1970s, Nie, Verba, and Petrocik found a sharp rise in liberal-conservative "attitude consistency" in the American electorate at the time of the 1964 election. A comparison of the distribution of political beliefs in 1956 and 1973 revealed a decline in the proportion of the electorate with centrist or inconsistent political beliefs and "a large growth in the proportion of citizens taking consistently left or right views across . . . issue spheres."[17]

[17] Nie, Verba, and Petrocik, *The Changing American Voter*, p. 144. The five issue spheres in their analysis were the size and power of the federal government,

A shift in the geographical pattern of presidential voting could also be detected beginning with the 1964 election. In an earlier essay, two distinct regional alignments were identified in the data on state presidential and congressional voting from 1896 to 1976:[18]

1. The first was the New Deal party system, which allied the Democratic South and Northeast against the Republican midwestern and mountain states. This "East-West" or New Deal configuration dominated American voting behavior in the 1940s and 1950s. The issues sustaining it were primarily economic, including class differences (as in conflicts between business and labor) and disagreement over the role and power of the federal government. Voters in rural midwestern and western states have historically been mistrustful of federal power, whereas the New Deal received its strongest support from urban workers and from the rural poor in the South.

2. The second alignment, labeled "ideology," basically involved social and cultural issues—primary among them, race. The ideological alignment differentiated the conservative South from the core areas of historic "Yankee liberalism"—New England, the upper Midwest, and the Pacific Northwest. This sociocultural pattern prevailed before the New Deal in the "system of 1896," when the Republicans were the majority party in the North and the Democrats had their base in the "solid South" and among Irish Catholics elsewhere. Social polarization reemerged with the civil rights conflicts of the 1950s and the 1960s. The 1964 election was a turning point because it marked the first sharp differentiation between the two major parties in terms of social ideology. The Democrats, who had endorsed the civil rights cause and sponsored the Civil Rights Act, were now clearly identified as the liberal party, whereas the Goldwaterites gave the Republican party an aggressively conservative orientation that proved especially appealing in the South.

Table 7-9 shows how state voting patterns in presidential elections from 1960 to 1980 related to these two alignments.

The pattern of the 1960 vote was basically that of the New Deal partisan alignment. The presidential elections of 1964, 1968, and 1972 encompassed a period of intense ideological polarization over

---

government action to improve conditions for blacks, school integration, social welfare policy, and attitudes toward the cold war. See pp. 142-44 and pp. 281-84 for a discussion of these changes.

[18] William Schneider, "Democrats and Republicans, Liberals and Conservatives," in S. M. Lipset, ed., *Emerging Coalitions in American Politics* (San Francisco: Institute for Contemporary Studies, 1978), pp. 183-267.

TABLE 7–9

FACTOR ANALYSIS OF
PRESIDENTIAL VOTES BY STATE, 1960–1980

	Varimax Rotated Factor Matrix[a]				
Presidential Votes, by State	Factor I: ideology (+ liberal, − conservative)		Factor II: partisanship (+ Democratic, − Republican)		
1960					
Kennedy (50%) D	.19		.84		
Nixon (50%) R		−.01		−.87	
1964					
Johnson (61%) D	.68		.55		
Goldwater (38%) R		−.68		−.55	
1968					
Humphrey (43%) D	.69		.62		
Nixon (43%) R		.01		−.91	
Wallace (13%) I			−.80		.19
1972					
McGovern (38%) D	.69		.50		
Nixon (61%) R		−.68		−.43	
1976					
Carter (50%) D	.11		.78		
Ford (48%) R		−.15		−.76	
1980					
Carter (41%) D	.18		.74		
Reagan (51%) R		−.40		−.71	
Anderson (7%) I			.57		.06

NOTES: For an explanation of the factor analysis and the 1900–1976 matrix, see Schneider, "Democrats and Republicans," table A-2, pp. 255-67. D = Democrat. R = Republican. I = Independent. Weighted N = 37 nonsouthern states (excluding Alaska and Hawaii), plus 11 southern states weighted equal to 1. Percentages of total vote are given in parentheses.

[a] Partial results.

race, the Vietnam war, social protest, and cultural radicalism. The distinctive features of these three presidential elections can be seen in table 7–9:

• The ideological alignment showed up quite clearly in presidential voting behavior. In all three elections, the conservative

South defected from its historic loyalty to the Democratic ticket while the liberal Northeast trended toward the Democrats.[19]

• The New Deal alignment did not vanish during this period. It simply became less salient than it had been in the previous twenty years, as New Deal party loyalties were disrupted by social conflict.

Thus, in the 1960s, the Democrats became associated with social and cultural as well as economic liberalism; hence the increased left-right "issue consistency" discovered by Nie, Verba, and Petrocik. In the course of moving to the left, the party wrote off a large part of its conservative southern support. The Republicans picked up most of these conservative Democratic defectors in 1964 and 1972, although in 1968, the racist vote in the South and the law-and-order backlash vote in the North tended to go to George Wallace. (Table 7–9 indicates that Nixon's 1968 vote was traditionally Republican and ideologically "centrist.") The distinctive feature of presidential voting behavior between 1964 and 1972 was the salience of *both* dimensions of conflict. It was during this period that commentators began to notice a new North-South sectionalism in American politics, with the southern and southwestern sunbelt states moving toward a new conservative-Republican alliance.

The 1976 presidential election brought much of this realignment theorizing to a halt. Conflict over race, Vietnam, and cultural radicalism diminished, while economic issues regained prominence. Moreover, the Democrats nominated a culturally conservative southern white governor as their standard-bearer. The result was to bring large numbers of traditional Democrats—and the South—back into the party fold and to reverse the trend toward ideological polarization. Commentators began to write about a revival of the traditional New Deal Democratic coalition. According to table 7–9, the East-West configuration of the 1976 vote looked very much like the pattern of the 1960 vote, with no sharp ideological differentiation of the candidates. Was the 1964–1972 system, then, an aberration, a temporary disruption of the New Deal party alignment occasioned by the intense but transitory ideological conflicts of the 1960s?

[19] In 1964, the Democrats enjoyed a margin of twenty-three points over the Republicans in the national presidential vote. The Democratic margin was only eight points in the South, whereas it was thirty-seven points in the Northeast. In 1968, the Republicans had a three-point margin over the Democrats in the South, but the Democrats held a seven-point advantage in the Northeast. In 1972, Nixon led McGovern by sixteen percentage points in the Northeast—less than the nationwide Republican margin of twenty-three points—but Nixon led by thirty-eight points in the South. U.S. Bureau of the Census, *Statistical Abstract of the United States: 1979* (Washington, D.C.: U.S. Department of Commerce, 1979), p. 501.

Table 7–9 suggests that the 1980 vote was more or less an intermediate situation between the predominantly partisan alignment of the 1976 election and the three previous "ideological" elections. The partisan factor remained about as strong in 1980 as it had been four years earlier; the reasons for this outcome have already been discussed—the continuing importance of economic issues in 1980 and the renomination of Jimmy Carter, who retained considerable appeal to his fellow southerners. The *change* in the vote from 1976 to 1980, however, was in the direction of increasing ideological alignment. Reagan's vote displayed a more conservative contour than Ford's had four years earlier; as noted, Republican gains between 1976 and 1980 were greatest in the South. It was not Jimmy Carter, however, but John Anderson who did relatively well in the strongholds of social and cultural liberalism.

Table 7–9 confirms the fact that the partisan confrontation between Carter and Reagan on economic issues was the principal focus of the 1980 election. But it also suggests that a secondary "social issue" conflict emerged between Reagan and Anderson. Anderson represented the "new politics" liberal tradition of the 1960s, a commitment that many liberals found weak or lacking altogether in Jimmy Carter. Had the party's liberals got their way and nominated Edward Kennedy, it is quite likely that the ideological confrontation between the two major party nominees would have been considerably more intense.

Some realigning tendencies can also be detected in table 7–10, which shows the presidential vote in 1976 and 1980 for major demographic groups.

Jimmy Carter lost support in every social group except non-whites, a category that includes mostly blacks. The Republicans gained four points among white voters but lost five points among nonwhites. Thus the difference between the races widened between 1976 and 1980.

The difference between men and women reversed, from slightly more support for Ford among female voters in 1976 to slightly more support for Carter among female voters in 1980. Historically, women have been reluctant to support hawkish candidates like Goldwater in 1964 and Wallace in 1968. They have been more likely than men to support "peace candidates" like Eisenhower in 1952 and McGovern in 1972. The Republicans were apprehensive about Reagan's problem with female voters throughout the campaign, with the candidate going so far as to promise to appoint a woman to the U.S. Supreme Court if elected. In the end, the difference between

TABLE 7-10

1976 AND 1980 PRESIDENTIAL VOTES, BY GROUPS

Group	1976 Vote (percent)		1980 Vote (percent)			Change (percentage points)	
	Carter	Ford	Carter	Reagan	Anderson	Dem.	Rep.
All	50	48	41	51	7	−9	3
Men	53	45	38	53	7	−15	8
Women	48	51	44	49	6	−4	−2
Whites	46	52	36	56	7	−10	4
Nonwhites	85	15	86	10	2	1	−5
College	42	55	35	53	10	−7	−2
High school	54	46	43	51	5	−11	5
Grade school	58	41	54	42	3	−4	1
Professional/ business	42	56	33	55	10	−9	−1
White collar	50	48	40	51	9	−10	3
Manual workers	58	41	48	46	5	−10	5
18–29 years old	53	45	47	41	11	−6	−4
30–49 years old	48	49	38	52	8	−10	3
50 and older	52	48	41	54	4	−11	6
Protestants	46	53	39	54	6	−7	1
Catholics	57	42	46	47	6	−11	5
Jews	64	34	45	39	14	−19	5
Labor union families	63	36	50	43	5	−13	7
Democrats	82	18	69	26	4	−13	8
Independents	38	57	29	55	14	−9	−2
Republicans	9	91	8	86	5	−1	−5
East	51	47	43	47	8	−8	—
South	54	45	44	51	3	−10	6
Midwest	48	50	41	51	6	−7	1
West	46	51	35	52	10	−11	1

NOTE: Postelection poll, November 1980, $N = 2,393$.

SOURCES: Gallup poll, "Dramatic Changes Seen in Vote Given Carter in '76 and '80," press release, December 21, 1980. Data for regions are from CBS News/ New York Times poll, November 4, 1980, $N = 12,782$; and CBS News poll, November 2, 1976, $N = 14,836$.

the sexes was in the expected direction, although Reagan actually carried the vote among women as well as men.

While Carter lost support in all groups except nonwhites, Reagan was not always the direct beneficiary. Reagan's gains over Ford were greatest among Democrats, labor union families, manual workers, southerners, Jews, Catholics, older voters, and the non-college-educated—*all groups that had been core supporters of the New Deal Democratic coalition.* The support that Carter lost among women, the college-educated, young voters, Protestants, higher-status groups, Republicans, independents, and nonsoutherners tended to go disproportionately to Anderson. Notably, Carter suffered his sharpest decline among Jewish voters, as shown in table 7–10. Jews are probably the group with the strongest historical loyalty to the New Deal Democratic party. Between 1976 and 1980, Jewish support for the Democratic ticket dropped by almost one-third. The flow of Jewish votes away from the Democrats did not go in one direction, however; it went about two-thirds to Anderson and one-third to Reagan.

Thus what happened in 1980 might be described as an unraveling of the strained fabric of New Deal Democratic loyalties. It was Jimmy Carter's weakness—not in itself an ideological issue—that allowed the threads to unravel. But once the fibers started to come apart, they were pulled in different directions, some to the right by Reagan and some to the left by Anderson. In other words, ideology had more to do with the direction of change than with the momentum behind it.

This unraveling process can be seen in greater detail in table 7–11, which takes advantage of the large sample sizes in the CBS News exit polls to break down the 1976 and 1980 votes simultaneously by partisanship and ideology. The results show that Carter's losses among liberal Democrats went overwhelmingly to Anderson. His losses among moderate Democrats went in about equal proportions to Anderson and Reagan, and his losses among conservative Democrats went mainly to Reagan.

Both table 7–10 and table 7–11 indicate that Reagan's gains came entirely from Democrats. It was Anderson who picked up the support Carter lost among independents, while Carter's minimal Republican backing in 1976—less than 10 percent—remained about the same in 1980. Interestingly, support for the Republican ticket went down among self-described Republicans between 1976 and 1980 (by five percentage points according to Gallup). As table 7–11 shows, the loss occurred mostly among liberal and moderate Republicans and it went mainly to Anderson. In the end, however, Reagan's

TABLE 7–11

1976 AND 1980 PRESIDENTIAL VOTES
BY PARTISANSHIP AND IDEOLOGY

	1980 Elec- torate (percent)	1976 Vote (percent)		1980 Vote (percent)			Change (percentage points)	
		Carter	Ford	Carter	Reagan	Ander- son	Dem.	Rep.
Democrats								
Liberals	9	86	12	70	14	13	−16	2
Moderates	22	77	22	66	28	6	−11	6
Conservatives	8	64	35	53	41	4	−11	6
Independents								
Liberals	4	64	29	50	29	15	−14	—
Moderates	12	45	53	31	53	13	−14	—
Conservatives	7	26	72	22	69	6	−4	−3
Republicans								
Liberals	2	17	82	25	66	9	8	−16
Moderates	11	11	88	13	81	5	2	−7
Conservatives	12	6	93	6	91	2	—	−2

NOTES: November 4 $N = 12,782$. November 2 $N = 14,836$. Data for the 1980 electorate do not total 100 because respondents who did not identify either their party or their ideology were excluded.
SOURCE: CBS News/*New York Times* poll, November 4, 1980. CBS News poll, November 2, 1976.

losses on the Republican left were more than compensated for by his gains on the Democratic right. Conservative and moderate Democrats outnumbered liberal and moderate Republicans by more than two to one among 1980 voters.

A bit more might be said about John Anderson's role in the 1980 election. Anderson's campaign was predicated on the assumption that there would be widespread dissatisfaction with, if not active protest against, the choice between Reagan and Carter. His expressed intention was to draw votes from a broad cross section of the electorate who felt that Carter should not be reelected but that Reagan was an unsuitable alternative. He presented himself as a candidate of "National Unity"—the label he gave his campaign— and appealed to voters to reject the false divisiveness of the two major parties. Anderson tried to portray himself as a candidate of the center, to the right of Carter on economic issues and to the left of Reagan on social issues. Thus he would be ideally situated to lead a broad-based coalition of discontent rather than a narrow, ideologically delimited protest movement.

Two problems arose with this strategy.

The first is that discontent with the Carter-Reagan choice was not nearly widespread or intense enough to provide the basis for a viable Anderson coalition. Survey data taken during the campaign did not reveal an extraordinarily high level of displeasure with Reagan and Carter, both of whom were nominated in the most open and participatory selection process in American history. In a *Los Angeles Times* poll taken in October 1980, 59 percent of likely voters said they had a favorable impression of Carter and 67 percent felt favorable toward Reagan. Anderson's support was precisely a function of people's feelings about Reagan and Carter, just as he intended it to be. Among those who liked either Carter or Reagan—or both of them—Anderson's support never rose above 16 percent. Yet his support was an overwhelming 75 percent among those who disliked both major party nominees. The problem was, the latter category included a mere 5 percent of the prospective electorate.

Anderson expected that, given President Carter's disastrously low approval ratings and the apparently irreparable split in the Democratic party between Kennedy and Carter, Carter would simply collapse in the polls and become the third-placed candidate, with Anderson then emerging as the principal alternative to Reagan. The Anderson forces dreamed of the day when they could say, "A vote for Carter is a vote for Reagan." That day never came. Instead, Carter got a lift in popularity after the Democratic National Convention, and our electoral system performed its customary task of ruthlessly suppressing third-party candidates. People accepted the argument that Anderson could not win and that, by voting for him, they might be helping to elect the candidate they like least.

The second problem with Anderson's strategy was that he failed to keep himself positioned in the center, as the evidence in tables 7–6, 7–7, and 7–8 showed. More than most candidates, Anderson could not afford to ignore his base, and his base, including most of the passion and the financial support for his campaign, was on the left. Anderson's issue positions, his National Unity platform, and his effort to make a deal with Kennedy all signaled a leftward tilt in his campaign. He became, in fact, the archetypal candidate of the upper-middle-class, suburban-oriented New Politics constituency—moderate on fiscal issues but resoundingly liberal on social and cultural issues and on foreign policy (despite the conspicuous conservatism of his record, which he renounced).

Throughout the campaign and in the final election results, Anderson's strongest support came from liberals, college-educated voters, and the young.[20] He had hoped to appeal to the broad spectrum of voters who felt that Carter and Reagan were too incompetent to be president. Instead, he got the vote of the much smaller group who felt that Carter and Reagan were too conservative to be president. It was among liberals that dissatisfaction with the Carter-Reagan choice ran deepest in 1980, and so it was not surprising that John Anderson gravitated in their direction.

How then should the 1980 election be characterized in realignment terms?

The 1980 election appears to have been a continuation of the long-term realignment that began in 1964 and was temporarily interrupted in the mid-1970s. Since 1964, the parties have been moving apart ideologically, the Democrats to the left on social and cultural issues and the Republicans to the right.

The realignment was initiated in the 1960s, during the period of intense national polarization over race and foreign policy. The civil rights movement, the antiwar movement, and the law-and-order backlash were its earliest manifestations. These issues all died down in the 1970s and were replaced by narrower conflicts, such as abortion, feminism, gay rights, nuclear power, environmentalism, and busing.

An interesting characteristic of these ideological issues is that they did not reenforce the cleavages associated with the New Deal party system. Instead, they *cut across* class, religious, and party lines. In the 1960s, middle-class voters divided into liberal (McCarthy, McGovern) and conservative (Goldwater, Reagan) segments. Working-class voters were also split left (Humphrey) and right (Wallace). White Protestants now include some of the most conservative (Moral Majority) and some of the most liberal (National Council of Churches) elements in the electorate. There are now right-wing as well as left-wing Catholic factions. Jews too are split, although in their case it is between "new left" and "old left" tendencies (New Politics liberalism versus neoconservatism).

The political parties have had to make major readjustments in order to accommodate these conflicts. Liberal Republicans and conservative Democrats have been pushed out of their respective parties; they represent anomalies associated with the "old" party

[20] See Everett C. Ladd, Jr., and G. Donald Ferree, "John Anderson: Candidate of the New Class?" *Public Opinion*, June/July 1980, pp. 11-15.

system. John Anderson, the last voice of liberal Republicanism, could not win a single Republican primary in 1980 and was forced to run as an independent. Most of his supporters were Democrats and independents. The Republican new right has tended to attract many former conservative Democrats, particularly in the South and West. Strom Thurmond, Jesse Helms, John Connally, S. I. Hayakawa, and Ronald Reagan were all once Democrats who, as conservatives, found themselves out of place in their party.

Democrats have gained a base among affluent, upper-middle-class suburban voters outside the South. These New Politics voters cannot abide the reactionary social conservatism of the new Republican party. On the other hand, the Democratic party has tended to lose much of its traditional support among white southerners, conservative Catholics, and blue-collar voters who feel threatened by social and cultural change. The realignment trend has been clearest in the South, where the Republican party has become dominant in presidential voting, competitive in statewide contests, and increasingly a factor in local elections. The Democratic presidential ticket failed to carry the South in 1964, 1968, 1972, and 1980. Even in 1976, according to the exit polls, most white southerners voted for Ford.

The mid-1970s temporarily reversed this realignment trend. There were three reasons: (1) Watergate, (2) the most severe recession since the 1930s, presided over in 1974–1975 by a Republican administration, and (3) the nomination in 1976 of a Democratic candidate who was culturally conservative—and, as it turns out, out of step with his party.

Between 1964 and 1972, most white blue-collar voters were cross-pressured between economic insecurity and racial fear. Racial fear predominated during this early period, and many of them defected from their traditional party loyalty to vote for law-and-order Republicans and backlash candidates. In 1974 and 1976, economic insecurity brought most blue-collar whites back to the Democratic fold, a move made easier in the presidential election because Jimmy Carter did not seem threatening to them on social and cultural issues. The return of many renegade southerners and "white ethnics" seemed to give the old New Deal party a fresh breath of life.

The larger realignment trend has been confirmed by the 1980 election, however. It now appears that 1976 was the aberration. Voting differences by class and religion—the traditional bases of the New Deal alignment—were lower in 1980 than in any year since

FIGURE 7–4

THE REPUBLICAN VOTE FOR PRESIDENT BY RELIGION AND BY OCCUPATION
(percent)

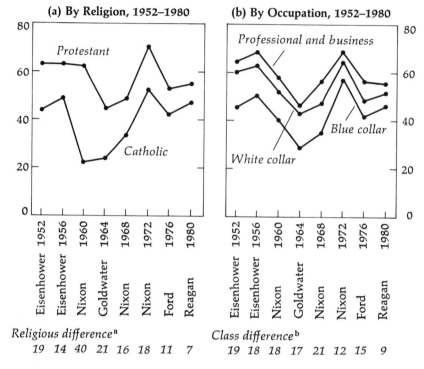

(a) By Religion, 1952–1980

Protestant

Catholic

Eisenhower 1952
Eisenhower 1956
Nixon 1960
Goldwater 1964
Nixon 1968
Nixon 1972
Ford 1976
Reagan 1980

(b) By Occupation, 1952–1980

Professional and business

Blue collar

White collar

Eisenhower 1952
Eisenhower 1956
Nixon 1960
Goldwater 1964
Nixon 1968
Nixon 1972
Ford 1976
Reagan 1980

Religious difference[a]

19 14 40 21 16 18 11 7

Class difference[b]

19 18 18 17 21 12 15 9

[a] Religious difference: Protestant % minus Catholic %.
[b] Class difference: Professional and business % minus blue collar %.
SOURCES: 1952-1976: *Gallup Opinion Index* (December 1976), pp. 15-16; 1980:
Gallup Poll, "Dramatic Changes Seen in Vote," press release, December 21, 1980.

1952[21] (see figure 7–4). And despite the renomination of Jimmy
Carter, the South went Republican once again.

It is not clear from the polls that Ronald Reagan's appeal to blue-
collar voters was primarily social or cultural, although such issues
obviously helped him make inroads among white southerners and
conservative Catholics. For the most part, blue-collar voters defected
to Reagan in 1980 because of economic discontent. That is also
part of the realignment process: by being the first Democratic presi-

[21] See Ladd's discussion of the "inversion of the New Deal class order" in Everett
C. Ladd, Jr., with Charles D. Hadley, *Transformations of the American Party
System* (New York: W. W. Norton, 1975), pp. 233-46.

dent to preside over a recession since the 1890s, Carter weakened the economic ties of blue-collar Democrats to their party. The Democratic party can no longer claim to protect their economic interests as it did in the 1930s. Thus economic self-interest is no longer a compelling reason to stick with the Democrats, and a majority of blue-collar voters and Catholics did not in 1980.

Reagan's victory confirmed the Republican party's shift to the right. It gave party control to the conservatives who first emerged as a protest faction against the party establishment in 1964. Kennedy's failure to win the Democratic nomination suggests that the liberal protest faction that challenged the Democratic party establishment in 1968 and 1972 does not enjoy comparable control over the other major party. Yet it was clear in the late primaries, at the Democratic National Convention, and in the election results that Kennedy more than Carter defines the essential values and philosophy of the Democratic party today. Like Reagan in 1976, Kennedy lost the nomination but carried the platform and essentially won the party. What Kennedy came to represent in 1980 was a new party consensus, a kind of "deal" between the party regulars and the New Politics liberals who had spent so many years fighting over Vietnam: the liberals would accept the "big government" economic programs and the commitment to organized labor that Democratic party regulars had long stood for, while the regulars would accede to a less interventionist foreign policy and a more progressive stance on social issues.

It is impossible to say at this point whether this new consensus, or even Kennedy himself, will have a prevailing influence over the Democratic party in opposition. Much depends on the success or failure of the Republican administration's program. It should be noted, however, that a good deal of the pressure on the Democratic party to "move toward the center" has a distinctly liberal tinge to it. New Politics liberals like Senator Paul Tsongas (Democrat, Massachusetts) have argued that, in light of the election results, the party ought to relieve itself of the burden of defending big government but retain the liberal faith on social and foreign policy issues— in other words, the party should move toward a purer New Politics ideology than even Kennedy was espousing.[22]

Whatever happens, there is little doubt that the ideological conflicts of the past fifteen years have had a polarizing influence on our

[22] Tsongas was making this argument even before the election was over. See Paul E. Tsongas, "Update Liberalism or It's a 60's Relic," *New York Times*, June 30, 1980.

party politics. At the same time, the economic crises of the 1970s have shifted the voters' attention away from ideology and toward management and performance. What the voters want are solutions to the enormous problems facing the country—inflation, unemployment, low productivity, the energy crisis, crime, and the deterioration of American power in the world. They may be forced to choose between sharply defined ideological alternatives, however, in part because moderates in both parties have been given a chance and are seen as having failed. The country now has the opportunity to see whether the right, and perhaps later the left, can come up with any better answers.

8
The Republican Surge in Congress

Thomas E. Mann and Norman J. Ornstein

Ronald Reagan's stunning sweep of electoral votes was the obvious highlight of the election of 1980. For the Republican party, however, the more enduring and important story may well have been the Republican surge on Capitol Hill. With its second straight good election—a phenomenon the party had not experienced since 1950–1952—the GOP took control of the Senate for the first time in twenty-six years and made sizable gains in the House, finally erasing the Watergate disadvantage it had suffered since 1974.

The Republicans did not erase at one stroke the fifty-year hegemony Democrats had enjoyed in Congress and in the country, but they exceeded their fondest expectations. Having relied upon a party-based, national campaign, the GOP strategists were confident that they had not merely experienced a one-shot, temporary gain. This would not be a 1972, when a landslide win of the presidency had crumbled into party disaster in two short years. Rather, this time, the Republicans had built a base for control of Congress and the White House throughout the coming decade.

Undeniably, the Republicans had made their impressive gains from a position of total weakness after Watergate. The devastating election of 1974 had left the GOP in its worst position since the depression. Thus, their 1980 victory was doubly sweet. How that victory was structured and what it might portend for 1981, 1982, and beyond are the subjects of this chapter.

Party Strategies after 1976

On November 2, 1976, the fortunes of the Republican party were as low as they had been in many years. After a protracted struggle with Ronald Reagan for the presidential nomination, Gerald Ford rallied from eighteen points down in the general election campaign but fell short of overtaking Democrat Jimmy Carter. The Repub-

263

licans were out of the White House only eight years after what some party strategists thought was the beginning of a GOP era in American politics. The Watergate disaster of 1974 had dealt a severe blow to the party's hopes, but its problems went well beyond Watergate. After all, Richard Nixon's 1972 landslide reelection victory over George McGovern was conspicuously top-heavy—the Republicans gained only twelve seats in the House, leaving them well short of a majority, and they actually dropped two seats further behind in the Senate. In 1976, a year in which they expected to recover from the "abnormal" losses of two years earlier, the GOP came away from the November elections empty-handed: no seats gained in the Senate, House, or state legislatures and a further loss of governorships, leaving them with the short end of a more than two-to-one Democratic majority in the House, only 38 of the 100 Senate seats, twelve of the fifty statehouses, and about a third of the 7,500 seats in state legislatures.[1]

The efforts to rebuild the Republican party after 1976 were spearheaded by Bill Brock, who took over as chairman of the Republican National Committee (RNC) in January 1977. Although Brock may have been justified in saying that the Republicans in 1976 were at their "lowest point in 40 years in terms of elective officers, membership and public perception,"[2] all was not gloomy with the GOP. In 1976 the RNC raised a record $19 million ($12.7 million excluding fund-raising costs), and Brock inherited a file of 250,000 Republican donors, more than twice the number currently on the Democratic National Committee (DNC) roster.[3] In addition, the Republican congressional campaign committees were already light-years ahead of their Democratic counterparts in direct-mail fund raising. Brock therefore began with a substantial financial base, which permitted him to launch new party-building programs at the same time he reinvested funds to expand the pool of direct-mail donors. Over at the Democratic National Committee, Chairman Kenneth Curtis and his successor John White were still paying off 1968 campaign debts.

The Republicans devised a strategy consistent with a number of recent findings about voters and elections in contemporary American

---

[1] The rebuilding efforts of the Republican party are described in Morton Kondracke, "The G.O.P. Gets Its Act Together," *New York Times Magazine*, July 13, 1980; Michael J. Malbin, "The Republican Revival," *Fortune*, August 25, 1980; and Timothy B. Clark, "The RNC Prospers, the DNC Struggles As They Face the 1980 Elections," *National Journal*, September 27, 1980.

[2] Quoted in Clark, "The RNC Prospers," p. 1617.

[3] Ibid., p. 1618.

politics. With fewer voters identifying with one of the major parties and with much less loyalty among those who do, the GOP recognized that voting has become increasingly candidate centered. Winning elections, therefore, requires good candidates and vigorous campaigns. Recruiting good candidates for congressional races is made easier by (1) having a pool of elected officials at lower levels of government, (2) having a national climate favorable to one's party, and (3) making available enough campaign resources to increase the probability of success. Waging vigorous campaigns requires, in addition to able candidates, (1) money, (2) technical expertise, and (3) a set of issues that resonate with the voters.

Good campaigns depend on understanding the advantages—and limitations—of incumbency. House incumbents have an enormous electoral edge based upon their ability to generate favorable publicity back home; that advantage is manifest at an early stage in the congressional career, especially in the "sophomore surge." Incumbency is not an automatic advantage, however; rather it is a *resource* that members are more or less successful in exploiting. Some incumbents are vulnerable; identifying them requires a member-by-member, district-by-district analysis. Incumbency is much less of an advantage in the Senate, partly because senators are less able to control their own press coverage, partly because statewide resources permit a more vigorous challenge.

Finally, party images can be important even when party loyalties are not; candidates can be helped or hurt at the margin by the generalized feelings that voters have about their party.

Whether Republican officials explicitly articulated these findings is beside the point. What matters is that the GOP strategy after 1976 did not respond to narrower interests within the party but focused instead on programs compatible with broader, objective observations about voters and elections. The Republican program included the following elements:

- a local elections division at the RNC, which helped recruit and train candidates for state legislatures and other local offices and which contributed directly to their campaigns
- a Campaign Management College, where congressional candidates were given sophisticated training in campaign techniques
- a program of targeting House and Senate seats most favorable to Republican takeover and recruiting the ablest candidates to run for those seats
- developing and articulating party positions on issues, through advisory councils of elected officials and party figures and spe-

cialized publications designed for a sophisticated audience
- direct financial assistance to congressional candidates (most of which was to be done by the congressional campaign committees).

On the last element, the Republicans realized that federal campaign law allowed the national party committees to spend up to $34,720 in direct contributions and coordinated expenditures on behalf of House candidates and, depending upon the voting-age population of the state, between $76,380 and $987,548 on behalf of Senate candidates.[4] They were determined to raise enough money to give the maximum amounts to their strongest candidates.

The GOP strategy was to restock the primary recruitment pools for congressional candidates; to win control of enough state legislative chambers to prevent Democratic gerrymandering when districts were redrawn after the 1980 census; to offer sufficient incentives to attract more able Republican candidates in targeted states and districts; to develop party positions on issues that would be viewed as attractive alternatives to those of the Democratic administration; and to amass enough money for an ambitious program of direct contributions and coordinated expenditures for House and especially Senate candidates.

An early test of the Republican efforts in 1978 produced mixed results at the national level—the pickup of fifteen seats in the House (four in by-elections) and three in the Senate was modest by historical standards—but the state and local results were much more promising. The GOP gained seven governorships and more than 300 state legislative seats, recouping almost half the seats it lost in 1974.

After the 1978 elections, the Republican party redoubled its efforts along the lines described above, but it also added an important dimension. A small band of junior Republicans in the House pushed the party to adopt a more confrontational, election-oriented stance within Congress, drawing the sharpest possible contrast between its party's position on a number of important issues and that of the Democrats. At the same time, the GOP launched a $5 million television advertising campaign designed to blame the country's ills on the twenty-five-year Democratic control of Congress. (The television budget was later increased to $9 million.) The hard-hitting commercials—variously featuring a Tip O'Neill lookalike, an unemployed factory worker, and a truck driver—all lambasted the Democratic Congress and urged viewers to "Vote Republican—For a Change."

As the 1980 political season opened, then, the Republican party appeared to be playing it both ways: locally, waging vigorous cam-

[4] Larry Light, "Republican Groups Dominate in Party Campaign Spending," *Congressional Quarterly Weekly Report*, November 1, 1980, p. 3236.

paigns with able candidates and, nationally, presenting an aggressive new look to the party.

As we might well expect of a majority party that now controlled the presidency on top of its long-time domination of both houses of Congress, the Democrats had no offensive strategy during the period after the 1976 elections. In fact, all of their efforts were geared toward damage limitation. The Democratic National Committee, already constrained by its debt and its modest budget, acted largely as a political arm of the Carter administration, seeking a set of party rules that favored Carter's renomination and enough money to spend the maximum amount allowed by federal law on behalf of the presidential campaign.

Congressional Democrats were generally content to run for re-election as individuals, and, as always, they did not expect much help from their party. Two developments in Congress after the 1978 elections, however, revealed their apprehension about 1980. First, Democrats (and a handful of Republicans) sought to limit the role of political action committees (PACs) in House campaigns. The Obey-Railsback amendment, which passed the House on October 17, 1979, by a vote of 217 to 198 but was blocked in the Senate by threat of fili-buster, would have reduced the amount one PAC could give a House candidate in a primary and general election campaign from $10,000 to $6,000; it also would have put a $70,000 ceiling on funds a House candidate could receive from all PACs during a two-year election cycle. Although Democrats had done quite well by PACs in past campaigns (labor giving almost exclusively to Democrats and corpo-rate and trade association PACs contributing heavily to incumbents of both parties), there were signs late in the 1978 campaign that the rapid growth in PACs might ultimately make Republican challengers the major beneficiaries. The motivations of its supporters no doubt varied, but the Obey-Railsback measure would have limited one source of potential damage to Democratic incumbents in 1980 and beyond—Republican challengers heavily financed by PACs.

The second development was the on-again, off-again flirtation of some Senate and House Democrats with Edward Kennedy and his quest for the presidential nomination. The dump-Carter movement on Capitol Hill was strongest when Carter was weakest in the public opinion polls, during the summer and fall of 1979, up to the taking of the American hostages in Iran. Having no special personal affec-tion for Carter or any real partisan commitment to his adminis-tration, Democrats in Congress simply sought to limit the damage to their candidacies from the top of the ticket. For a while, it appeared that Kennedy could give the Democratic ticket a boost. Later, when

Carter's stock rose after the events in Iran and Afghanistan and Kennedy's fell after a rash of unfavorable publicity, most of the life went out of this movement. It resurfaced, however, during the weeks before the Democratic convention, as Carter's approval ratings sank once again. The open-convention forces, based primarily in the House, sought to preserve a rule that theoretically gave the convention the power to nominate someone other than Jimmy Carter. Ultimately, sixty-seven Democratic members of the House were willing to permit their names to be associated with the open-convention movement. As recounted in chapter 2, it failed, and Democratic candidates, for better or for worse, were forced to run with President Carter at the top of their ticket.

From the perspective of the resources and the strategies of the two national parties, then, the 1980 campaign opened with the Republicans much better prepared than the Democrats and in a position to make substantial gains across the board.

The Senate Campaign

Republican hopes in 1980 for the U.S. Senate were bright and shining long before the November election. Indeed, early in 1979 soon after the 1978 contest, as he surveyed the list of seats up for challenge in 1980—twenty-four Democratic seats to only ten Republican—Senate GOP campaign chairman John Heinz was suggesting to observers the possibility of a Republican majority in the Senate in 1981.

Few political professionals took such predictions at face value, but nearly all incumbent Democratic senators up for election in 1980 viewed their own potential races as dangerous from the start. Many were alarmed by the unexpected defeats in 1978 of moderate Thomas McIntyre in New Hampshire and liberal Dick Clark in Iowa and the decisive losses at the same time of Democratic liberals Floyd Haskell (Colorado), William Hathaway (Maine), and Wendell Anderson (Minnesota). Others saw 1980 as a year of danger for incumbents generally. By July 1979—a full sixteen months before the election—*Congressional Quarterly* was reporting that "Senate incumbents facing reelection next year, including an unusually large class of liberal Democrats, have collected record amounts of campaign money at an early stage in the 1980 political season."[5] Senators who had raised the most money in the first six months of 1979 included Alan Cranston (Democrat, California), Bob Packwood (Republican, Oregon), Donald Stewart (Democrat, Alabama), Thomas Eagleton

---

[5] *Congressional Quarterly Weekly Report*, July 28, 1979, p. 1539.

(Democrat, Missouri), Paul Laxalt (Republican, Nevada), Ernest Hollings (Democrat, South Carolina), Frank Church (Democrat, Idaho), and Warren Magnuson (Democrat, Washington). Senator Richard Stone (Democrat, Florida) had the largest party campaign war chest, nearly one-half million dollars. Incumbents with the slowest start in financing for 1980 included Jacob Javits (Republican, New York), Robert Morgan (Democrat, North Carolina), Barry Goldwater (Republican, Arizona), and John Durkin (Democrat, New Hampshire). Both Javits and Goldwater contemplated retirement at the end of their terms and did not form early campaign committees or seek funds.

Congressional Quarterly suggested that the general political climate had caused nervousness in several Democratic incumbents who had no visible opposition and who were in little apparent danger of losing; Thomas Eagleton and Gaylord Nelson (Wisconsin) were given as examples. Five other vulnerable Democrats—George McGovern (South Dakota), John Culver (Iowa), Birch Bayh (Indiana), Cranston, and Church—faced the dual threat of strong potential Republican challengers and the targeted, well-financed opposition of an independent ideological organization, the National Conservative Political Action Committee (NCPAC), which began negative television commercials against Church and McGovern early in 1979. Yet other Democrats—Russell Long (Louisiana), Richard Stone, Mike Gravel (Alaska), Herman Talmadge (Georgia), and Donald Stewart—feared substantial primary opposition.

Although Democratic incumbents were nervous—exceedingly nervous—the prospects for dramatic Democratic losses in the Senate were not great from the perspective of July 1979. To begin with, history suggested that party change in the Senate would not be substantial. Of seventeen elections in the post–World War II period, only two had resulted in a double-digit loss of seats for a party (1946 and 1958). Even in years of political upheaval at other levels, such as 1952, 1964, and 1972, the Senate had changed little, if at all. The average party shift in seats in the Senate in this thirty-two-year period was only 4.5.

Second, many potentially vulnerable Democratic incumbents, such as Church, Magnuson, Bayh, McGovern, Cranston, and Eagleton, were veteran, savvy campaigners who had overcome stiff challenges before. Other, more junior senators, such as Culver, Hart (Colorado), Leahy (Vermont), and Durkin, were aware early of their vulnerability and were prepared for their uphill struggles. None would get caught by surprise as Thomas McIntyre had in November 1978.

Third, not all Republican senators up for reelection in 1980 felt confident this early in 1979. The Republican National Committee political operations director, Norm Turnette, commented, "As a group, the Senate is vulnerable."[6] Bob Packwood, Robert Dole of Kansas (running a presidential effort as well as his Senate campaign), Jake Garn of Utah, and Paul Laxalt were busy early, raising money and discouraging strong challenges. Packwood and Dole had some potential problems; Democrats also eyed greedily the open seats of retiring GOP senators Richard Schweiker (Pennsylvania) and Henry Bellmon (Oklahoma) and the potentially open seats of Javits and Goldwater. If they were able to win even two or three of these seats—a reasonable expectation—the odds were overwhelmingly against the Republicans winning enough seats to capture the first GOP control of the Senate in twenty-six years.

As 1979 moved into 1980, Democratic apprehensiveness and Republican optimism remained. On February 25, 1980, Senator Javits ended months of speculation about his possible retirement and announced his reelection bid, calling himself "an orthodox Republican." Even as he announced, Javits faced opposition from within his own party, led by Hempstead Township supervisor Alfonse D'Amato, a conservative who had announced his own candidacy on January 7 and was endorsed by New York's Conservative party on March 22. Democrats, who also viewed Javits as vulnerable, looked toward their own hotly contested primary, the three main candidates being consumer adviser Bess Myerson, Congresswoman Elizabeth Holtzman, and former New York City mayor John Lindsay, with Myerson the early favorite.

In the Senate campaign overall, the early months of 1980 were dominated by coming primaries and by the aggressive independent campaign of NCPAC. The first primary, on March 18, was in Illinois, and it provided bad news for the Republicans. The GOP's high hopes of capturing the open Senate seat vacated by popular retiring Democrat Adlai E. Stevenson III were dimmed by a tough Republican primary contest colored by charges of income tax evasion against the favorite, moderate GOP state attorney general William Scott, who had been viewed as having an excellent chance of capturing the seat. Scott was tried on the eve of the primary; though no verdict emerged until afterward,[7] he lost by five percentage points to conservative lieutenant governor David O'Neal. O'Neal, more colorless and less

---

[6] Ibid., p. 1541.

[7] Scott was found guilty of one count of tax fraud the day after the primary.

popular than Scott, was immediately labeled an underdog to Democratic candidate Alan Dixon, the Illinois secretary of state.

The NCPAC campaign grew more aggressive in the early part of 1980—and more controversial. George McGovern of South Dakota, trailing Republican Congressman James Abdnor in the polls and faced with a hard-hitting multimedia campaign targeted by NCPAC against him, hit back in April and May. On May 2, the South Dakota Democratic party formally complained to the Federal Elections Commission that the National Conservative Political Action Committee was not acting independently—that in fact it was providing aid and advice to Republican candidate Abdnor and was therefore exceeding campaign spending limits. The Democratic party complaint was seized upon by McGovern and by Abdnor's primary opponent, Dale Bell, throwing both Abdnor and NCPAC on the defensive.[8] Abdnor easily survived the primary on June 3 (McGovern had a tough primary himself, the first in his long career), but McGovern's attacks on NCPAC and its direct ties to Abdnor continued unabated, amid speculation that the anti-McGovern campaign could backfire. Indeed, by early July, NCPAC suspended its anti-McGovern advertising and channeled the resources into a campaign against Senator Thomas Eagleton of Missouri. Nevertheless, McGovern continued to do poorly in South Dakota polls.[9]

In Indiana, Birch Bayh faced the same problem; the NCPAC attacks, combined with those of antiabortion groups and of Bayh's opponent, Republican Congressman Dan Quayle, shrank Bayh's lead in polls from a 58 to 34 percent margin in fall 1979 to a mere ten percentage points by June 1980.[10] Bayh, too, began to fight back, attacking the "outside" interests and their ties to Quayle.

Similar themes were reiterated by Frank Church in Idaho. As early as January 1980 Church was both attacking NCPAC and tying it directly to his likely opponent, conservative Republican Congressman Steve Symms. An early NCPAC television commercial showed a Republican state legislator standing in front of an empty missile silo to underscore the complaint that "Senator Church has almost always opposed a strong national defense." Church struck back at the advertisement as misleading and fabricated, noting that the silo was empty because it was designed for a now-mothballed

---

[8] See *Political Report*, vol. 3, no. 19 (May 9, 1980), pp. 6–8.

[9] See "McGovern, Trailing, Campaigns Harder Than Ever," *Washington Post*, July 8, 1980.

[10] Jack Germond and Jules Witcover, "Bayh Facing a Cliffhanger Again This Year," *Washington Star*, June 27, 1980.

Minuteman, which Church had supported. Church's press secretary, Cleve Corlett, added to the attack by noting the presumably independent NCPAC's connection with Symms: "Symms is on the board of a lot of these committees operated by Richard Viguerie, of which NCPAC is just one."[11]

John Culver, targeted in Iowa, took a rather different campaign tack, going against the conventional wisdom in a way that captured national attention. Mindful of his state colleague Dick Clark's defeat two years earlier, Culver decided to take the unequivocal offensive in his campaign, proudly defending his liberalism, honesty, and consistency. Like the others, Culver vigorously criticized NCPAC. He attacked the new right as "a dangerous, alien force that is exploiting the fears and anxieties of a lot of decent and sincere people."[12] He urged Iowa to reject "the hate factories of the East."[13]

Unlike his fellow targets, however, Culver spent more time proclaiming his philosophy and record than attacking his opponent. Said Culver, "I'm proud of my record, I don't have any trouble calling myself a liberal."[14] Culver proudly defended his vote to scrap the B-1 bomber, defended SALT II, criticized the nuclear aircraft carrier, and supported the Equal Rights Amendment (ERA).

In contrast, even George McGovern hedged at least a bit on his staunch liberalism under the relentless barrage of NCPAC. Thus, Culver's campaign attracted more than the usual amount of attention; the up and down poll results reported in the *Des Moines Register* were watched with interest by other endangered liberals, by Democrats in general, and by the *Washington Post, Wall Street Journal,* and CBS.

One other NCPAC "target," Senator Alan Cranston of California, was not so vigorous either in denouncing the committee or in trying to tie its negative campaign to his opponent—largely because Cranston was not facing, as his colleagues were, a unified, aggressive campaign from an accomplished challenger. Although a number of California Republicans jumped into the race against Cranston or made early soundings, the GOP nomination contest came down to a struggle between a political novice, sixty-seven-year-old Paul Gann, the lesser

---

[11] James M. Perry, "Liberal Incumbents Are Main Targets of TV Ads," *Wall Street Journal,* January 25, 1980.

[12] James R. Dickenson, "Culver Goes Toe to Toe with Right Wing in Iowa," *Washington Star,* October 5, 1980.

[13] Helen Dewar, "Iowa Liberal Culver Rejects Bending to Conservative Winds," *Washington Post,* July 9, 1980.

[14] Dennis Farney, "The Feisty Culver Campaign," *Wall Street Journal,* September 26, 1980.

known co-leader of California's tax revolt (Proposition 13 was the "Jarvis-Gann" proposal), and a sixty-five-year-old perennial candidate, former Los Angeles mayor Sam Yorty. Gann won the June 3 primary, after a gaffe-filled, unfocused campaign, but his performance did not improve in the general election campaign and Cranston was never seriously challenged.

The controversy over NCPAC dominated the national attention paid in the first half of 1980 to the Senate elections. As the campaign year entered its second half, a number of primaries in both parties presaged later general election face-offs and ultimate results. Several incumbents fought early for their political lives in tough primary battles, including Democrats Herman Talmadge, Donald Stewart, Mike Gravel, and Richard Stone and Republican Jacob Javits. Other Democratic incumbents, such as Warren Magnuson, Patrick Leahy, John Durkin, Gaylord Nelson, and Gary Hart, breezed through to their party's nomination but watched their state GOP engage in vigorous and often bitter struggles to choose their opponents.

Herman Talmadge, veteran Agriculture Committee chairman, faced an unpleasant (and unprecedented) uphill primary because of a highly publicized scandal involving a broken marriage, alcoholism, and, most significant, an alleged impropriety involving misuse of office funds that resulted in his being denounced by the U.S. Senate. A host of challengers jumped into the Georgia Democratic primary on August 5 against Talmadge, led by moderate Lieutenant Governor Zell Miller, former judge Norman Underwood, and Congressman Dawson Mathis. In spite of his troubles, Talmadge led in most polls and sought mainly to go over the 50 percent mark to avoid a runoff on August 26; historically in Georgia, incumbents who are forced into runoffs lose them.

Talmadge did not achieve his goal, indeed falling far short (40.9 percent). Joining him in the runoff was Miller, who garnered 24.6 percent.[15] Largely unnoticed in this overwhelmingly Democratic state, Republican state chairman Mack Mattingly won the GOP nomination without a runoff. Although Talmadge's poor showing in the initial primary indicated the degree of statewide disapproval of his actions, he was made the runoff favorite, against historical odds, because of the weakness of his opponent. "Anybody but Zell Miller could have beaten Talmadge in the runoff," one close observer of Georgia politics speculated in a personal interview, "but Miller is

---

[15] See *Congressional Quarterly Weekly Report*, August 9, 1980, pp. 2321-22.

simply too flamboyant and too liberal. The small town businessmen and bankers won't go for him." They didn't. Talmadge won the runoff convincingly (58 to 42 percent) and moved confidently into the general campaign in Jimmy Carter's home state against an unknown Republican opponent.

Alabama's Stewart felt especially vulnerable. He had been in the Senate only two years, having won the right to the remainder of the term of the late Senator James Allen by beating Allen's widow, Maryon, in a divisive interim election. Stewart's juniority, his moderate stance on issues, a charge of campaign finance scandal raised by columnist Jack Anderson, and the bitterness remaining from that election combined to offset his popularity, vigor, and skill as a campaigner and made his primary against Jim Folsom, Jr., son of the ex-governor, and several other opponents a horserace. Here too, though, the major question was whether front-runner Stewart would be forced into a runoff. On the GOP side in an increasingly two-party state, there was also a hard-fought primary, between longtime Republican politician Armistead Selden and a political novice and former Vietnam prisoner of war, Jeremiah Denton. Selden, a mainstream conservative, was backed by the Alabama Republican establishment; Denton, by the Moral Majority.

The September 2 open primary resulted in a Democratic party runoff and a comfortable GOP victory for Denton. Stewart outdistanced the field but fell barely short of the 50 percent necessary to capture the nomination outright.[16] Folsom finished second, with 36 percent to Stewart's 49 percent. In the September 26 runoff, following the pattern typical of southern primary runoffs involving an incumbent, Stewart was unable to improve his standing. He was edged out, 50.8 percent to 49.2 percent, by the young public service commissioner, Jim Folsom, Jr.

Alaska's Mike Gravel was a flamboyant and controversial senator who had gained notoriety by releasing the original Pentagon papers from his privileged post as a Senate subcommittee chairman. He achieved even more notoriety in Alaska through his feud with the state's other senator, Republican whip Ted Stevens, over the proper legislative strategy to follow in the Senate on the Alaska lands bill.

Gravel's erratic behavior had made him an early 1979 target of the GOP and led to a strong primary challenge by Clark Gruening, the grandson of the man Gravel had beaten to win his seat in 1968,

---

[16] See *Congressional Quarterly Weekly Report*, September 6, 1980, p. 2658, and *Political Report*, vol. 3, nos. 37 (September 20, 1980), pp. 1-2, and 38 (September 26, 1980), pp. 1-2.

but his hard-line, no-compromise position on Alaska lands increased his popularity in polls to a point where most observers, by June 1980, gave him an even chance to hold his seat.[17] A successful high-pressured campaign by Gravel to raise funds pushed him into a comfortable lead over Gruening in early August, three weeks before the August 26 primary.[18]

Gravel's strategy of focusing his campaign on the Alaska lands bill backfired, however, when he failed to kill the bill in the Senate. He achieved only 30.3 percent of the vote to Gruening's 37.9 percent. A multicandidate Republican primary nominated a Fairbanks banker, Frank Murkowski, to oppose Gruening. Gravel's unexpected defeat threw the Alaska race into uncertainty for both parties. Democrats were unsure whether the bitter race would cause Gravel and his supporters to fail to endorse or work for Gruening. At the same time, a Republican strategist noted, "We had planned to make Gravel the issue, but now we will have to change our strategy."[19]

Florida, represented by Richard Stone, a one-term incumbent Democrat, also faced vigorous, multicandidate primaries in both parties. Stone was attacked from the left and the right by three other major candidates and was forced into a runoff with the state insurance commissioner, William Gunter, whom he had bested six years earlier in a primary for the seat. Stone barely led the September 9 primary, with 31.9 percent to Gunter's 30.9 percent. On the GOP side, public service commissioner Paula Hawkins was forced into a runoff with former congressman Louis Frey, 48.6 percent to 26.6 percent.

In a bitter Democratic runoff, the two candidates traded charges and countercharges, Stone accusing Gunter of misusing his office to obtain contributions from insurance interests, Gunter lambasting the generally conservative incumbent for, among other things, supporting the Panama Canal Treaty. Gunter won, 51.7 to 48.3 percent. The popular Hawkins coasted to a GOP primary victory with 62 percent of the vote, and a month before the election she moved into a position of narrow favorite for the seat.

Thus, three incumbent Democratic senators—Stewart, Gravel, and Stone—lost their seats in primaries, two of them in runoffs. One veteran Democrat, Talmadge of Georgia, was forced into a runoff but managed to escape with his party's nomination. On the other side, only one Republican incumbent had a difficult road to nomination.

[17] *Political Report*, vol. 3, no. 29 (July 25, 1980), pp. 1-4.

[18] See David Ignatius, "For Campaign Gold, Alaska Puts the Rush on Donors," *Wall Street Journal*, August 8, 1980.

[19] *Political Report*, vol. 3, no. 34 (August 29, 1980), p. 6.

In that case, in a bitter and divisive New York primary, the twenty-four-year veteran Jacob Javits was beaten by his conservative challenger, Alfonse D'Amato.

Javits, as noted earlier, had not announced his intention to run until relatively late in the campaign, but once he formally entered the race, he campaigned hard, focusing on the June 19 Republican state convention. On June 14, Javits, as usual, received the designation of the Liberal party, ensuring a place for him on the November ballot. On June 19, he easily won the official designation of the Republicans, receiving 64.3 percent of the votes cast at the convention. D'Amato, however, after the withdrawal of a third candidate, Bruce Caputo, won 35.7 percent of the vote and therefore the right to oppose Javits in the September GOP primary.[20] D'Amato, too, was assured a spot in November, having been designated as the nominee of the Conservative party.

Javits began the primary effort with a wide lead over D'Amato; June polls showed him with a 68 to 20 percent margin.[21] D'Amato, however, ran a "hardhitting and brutal" campaign,[22] portraying Javits both as an old-line liberal out of step with his party and, capitalizing on Javits's disclosure of his debilitating motor neuron disease, as an old man on the verge of death—whose seat, if vacated soon after the election, would be filled by a Democratic governor. Javits countered with filmed endorsements by former president Gerald Ford and other Republican notables. In spite of indignant protests by a deeply offended Javits, D'Amato's negative campaign worked. He moved forward steadily in the polls, and beat Javits handily on September 9 by 56 to 44 percent. Javits, however, vowed to stay in the race on the Liberal ticket. On the Democratic side, a tough primary saw liberal Congresswoman Elizabeth Holtzman come from behind to beat moderate Bess Myerson.

The dean of the Senate, Democrat Warren Magnuson, had disappointed many ambitious young politicians in the state of Washington with his decision early in 1980 to seek a seventh term. His race also made national Democrats nervous; in spite of "Maggie's" longevity and undisputed power, he faced a vigorous challenge from Attorney General Slade Gorton, a popular moderate Republican who began to campaign actively for Magnuson's seat as early as summer 1979.

[20] New York Republican party rules enable any candidate with 25 percent or more of convention votes to appear on the party primary ballot.
[21] See *Political Report*, August 29, 1980, p. 2.
[22] Ibid.

Gorton's campaign momentum was brought to a halt in June 1980, however, when conservative broadcast executive Lloyd Cooney announced his candidacy as an alternative to Gorton. As the president and general manager of KIRO in Seattle, Cooney broadcast nightly station editorials on his CBS-TV affiliate and was one of the best-known figures in the state. Through June and July, Magnuson held a wide lead in polls as Cooney and Gorton pointed toward the September GOP primary. Gorton's early Republican lead evaporated (by August the two challengers were virtually tied in statewide samples),[23] and he moved from concentrating his campaign on Magnuson to attacking Cooney.

Gorton's tactics, plus a large number of Democratic crossovers, gave him a primary victory over Cooney, 55 to 41 percent, and the right to challenge Magnuson in November. The seventy-five-year-old Magnuson planned a scaled-down campaign with few live appearances. He refused to debate Gorton (which the Republican made a major campaign issue) and emphasized his power in Washington, D.C., and his ability to bring federal dollars to the state, the Mt. St. Helens disaster being the most recent example. Gorton ran a low-key campaign emphasizing his health and vigor—and by implication, Magnuson's elderly status. Sensitive to the age and health issue—especially after Javits's primary defeat—Magnuson retorted, "I may be old and slow, but the meetings don't start until I get there, and they don't end until *I* bang the gavel." The age factor and Magnuson's visibility as part of the Capitol's "establishment," however, clearly made a difference to Washington voters. The incumbent's early lead vanished. A Maritz poll in early October showed Magnuson with 46 percent of the vote, Gorton with 45 percent, and the remainder undecided.[24]

In Vermont, Senator Patrick Leahy, who had served only one term, waited anxiously for months in late 1979 and early 1980, anticipating a very tough contest with popular at-large Republican Congressman James Jeffords. Jeffords declined to make the race, however, and six lesser-known Republicans jumped into a primary battle for the right to face Leahy. Only one of the six candidates—former lieutenant governor T. Garry Buckley—had ever held elective office. Only two of the six—Buckley and former Republican state chairman Jim Mullin—had substantial name recognition. Besides these two, the appointed state commissioner on banking and insurance, Steward Ledbetter, a moderate, was also seen as a strong contender. The conservative Mullin, who campaigned for the nomination for over a

[23] See *Political Report*, vol. 3, no. 36 (September 12, 1980), p. 8.
[24] *Political Report*, vol. 3, no. 40 (October 10, 1980), p. 6.

277

year and had spent, by July, nearly half a million dollars (most raised out of state), started with an early lead, but the moderate Ledbetter used a walking campaign to counter and underscore Mullin's free-spending out-of-state connections. Ledbetter won on September 9, with 36.5 percent of the vote to Mullin's 26.4 percent, and turned his attention to Leahy for the remaining eight weeks of the campaign.

New Hampshire's John Durkin also found himself in a precarious situation as he approached the end of his first term. Durkin's first election effort, in 1974, had resulted in a disputed deadlock with Republican Louis Wyman, with the Senate, after months of wrangling, calling a special election. Durkin won but recognized that his hold on New Hampshire voters was anything but secure. His Democratic state colleague Thomas McIntyre's shocking loss to a political novice in 1978 made Durkin's situation appear even more precarious. As the 1980 campaign approached, the feisty and controversial incumbent followed a combative strategy of loudly criticizing President Carter, detaching himself from the goals and policies of the administration, and supporting the Kennedy candidacy.

Durkin's obvious vulnerability acted like a honey pot to a pack of hungry Republican bears. A full eleven aspirants entered the race on the GOP side and fought out a long, bitter, and confusing primary. The early favorite was conservative former governor Wesley Powell, endorsed by the *Manchester Union Leader*. Powell refused to accept any campaign contributions, however, and did not actively campaign for the nomination. Running second in most polls was Warren Rudman, a moderate and a former state attorney general. The rest of the pack included conservatives Tony Campaigne, chairman of the New Hampshire Conservative Caucus; John Sununu, an engineering professor at Tufts University; Edward Hager, a physician, who was supported by "new right" Senator Gordon Humphrey; and such lesser-known moderates as State Senator David Bradley and State Representative George Roberts.

Because of Powell's noncampaign, no clear favorite emerged through months of confusing Republican electioneering. As a result, Durkin's chances were seen by most observers as improving through July and August. When the dust cleared after the September 9 primary, the moderate Rudman had edged out the numerous conservative challengers, winning the nomination with a bare 20.3 percent of the vote. Running on a ticket in an uneasy alliance with ultraconservative gubernatorial candidate Meldrim Thomson, Rudman was not regarded as a clear favorite for the Senate seat as the general election campaign began.

Senator Gaylord Nelson, a former governor of Wisconsin and popular three-term veteran of the Senate, was nervous about his own campaign for months before he had any declared opposition. As possible opponents surfaced, Nelson's concern began to be shared by other Democrats. In April 1980 syndicated columnists Evans and Novak reported that private polls showed Nelson with only a narrow lead over former congressman Robert Kasten, the favored candidate, which represented a serious decline for Nelson over a three-month period. They noted, "One worried liberal political action group has changed its evaluation from 'leaning Nelson' to 'tossup.' "[25] The private polls confirmed survey results published in late March by the *Milwaukee Journal*.

By June, however, Nelson's prospects were improving. Kasten was locked in a four-way primary battle with businessman Terry Kohler, radio executive Doug Cofrin, and Lieutenant Governor Russell Olson. The wealthy Kohler and Cofrin spent $700,000 and $1.3 million, respectively, on their primary efforts, putting front-runner Kasten on the defensive throughout the summer. Many political professionals, remembering that Kasten had previously blown an early lead and lost a gubernatorial primary to Lee Dreyfus, discounted his chances. He prevailed in the September 9 primary, however, with 36.7 percent (to Kohler's 29.1 percent) and immediately focused his campaign on Nelson's liberalism.

Gary Hart, in Colorado, was one of several Democratic senators whose state colleague had been beaten convincingly by a conservative Republican challenger in 1978. Hart, a moderate, was made a midsummer favorite in his state, because of the topsy-turvy politics surrounding the Republican efforts to pick his opponent. At the June 7 GOP state convention, where 20 percent of the votes were necessary for a candidate's name to appear on the September 9 primary ballot, three candidates made the cutoff.[26] But another candidate, the well-known and highly popular moderate liberal secretary of state, Mary Estill Buchanan, finished a surprisingly poor fifth, eliminating her from contention.

Buchanan, however, angry at the result and convinced that conservatives had blocked her candidacy on ideological grounds, considered pursuing a petition drive to put her name on the primary ballot. Early in July, Buchanan began the effort to collect before the

---

[25] As reported in *American Political Report*, vol. 9, no. 16 (April 25, 1980), p. 8.

[26] They were, in order of votes received, moderate John Cogswell (26 percent), conservative Sam Zakhem (24 percent), and conservative Howard "Bo" Callaway (20 percent).

July 25 deadline the 10,000 or so signatures necessary to get her on the ballot. Buchanan's efforts irritated party conservatives, but the flap over her convention failure got substantial press coverage across Colorado. Buchanan appeared to collect the requisite number of signatures by the deadline, but a state hearing officer disqualified numerous signatures, and various Republican officials tried to block her efforts to amend her petitions.

The dispute went to state courts, and on September 3—less than a week before the primary—the Colorado Supreme Court put her on the GOP Senate primary ballot. To many Colorado voters Buchanan was seen as the underdog who had battled—and beaten—the party establishment, and the momentum from her legal victory carried her through to a narrow primary win, 30.8 to 30.1 percent over Bo Callaway.

Buchanan's favorable image as an underdog persisted, to her advantage, into the general election campaign. A September 24 GOP poll showed her leading Hart 53 to 37 percent, with 10 percent undecided, while a Denver television station poll showed Buchanan ahead 46.5 to 41.6 percent.[27] The numbers were disputed by the Hart campaign and many disinterested observers; Hart generally remained a favorite to hold his seat in November. Yet the contrary poll results made the outcome far from certain.

September 9 was the major primary day for Senate elections, with seven states choosing candidates that Tuesday. For all intents and purposes, the final leg of the 1980 Senate elections, the general campaign, began the next day. Through the first eight and one-half months of the 1980 Senate campaign, assessments of the likely November outcome had fluctuated considerably. The initial GOP euphoria had cooled slightly by midyear. In early May, the *Washington Post*, noting the extraordinary opportunity for Republican gains on Capitol Hill, cautioned:

> Even in the view of Republican strategists, the chances of the party's regaining control of Congress next year for the first time in a quarter century are remote—slight in the Senate and non-existent in the House.[28]

The *Post* article said Republicans predicted a gain of three to six seats in the Senate—although the piece also noted that Democratic leader Robert C. Byrd of West Virginia admitted that "it is conceivable" that

---

[27] *Political Report*, vol. 3, no. 39 (October 3, 1980), p. 3.

[28] Helen Dewar, "Republicans, by Adding Seats This Year, Hope to Gain Control of Congress in '82," *Washington Post*, May 4, 1980.

his party could lose its majority in the Senate. The same article suggested that, to Republicans, the Democrats' endangered list included Gravel, Culver, Church, McGovern, Bayh, Durkin, Hart, and Magnuson; vulnerable Republicans in the view of Democrats included Dole, Goldwater, and Javits. Democrats also expected to gain one or two among the open seats, holding Illiniois and Connecticut and perhaps picking up Pennsylvania and Oklahoma.

Overall assessments did not change much in the ensuing few months. In late July, Republican-oriented analyst Kevin Phillips predicted a net GOP gain of three to six seats in the Senate, giving them forty-four to forty-seven seats in the Ninety-seventh Congress, and with at best a slim chance of winning a majority.[29]

The consensus estimates of April and July were offered with little confidence. As many as a dozen Democrats were seen to be in some significant trouble, and a handful more faced at least a slim prospect of danger. Republicans faced trouble holding the two open seats of Pennsylvania and Oklahoma, as well as the seats of Javits in New York and, less likely, Goldwater in Arizona. The three-to-six range of Republican gains was based on Democrats' losing about half of their endangered Senate candidates and Republicans' dropping two or three of their own seats. Late fall trends, however, in the presidential contest or in voter attitudes generally, not to mention unpredictable gaffes or events in individual state races, could potentially mean a very large Democratic loss—or no net change whatsoever in party margins.

In the aftermath of the primaries, as the campaign moved toward its final few weeks, Republican optimism had waned a bit more. Several Democratic incumbents who had been trailing in state polls made noticeable comebacks. Some, like Culver and Nelson, moved into narrow leads; others, like McGovern and Church, remained behind but reduced the margin substantially. The trend, to political observers, was a familiar one: the embattled incumbent gets momentum to pull ahead of an inexperienced challenger. McGovern, Bayh, and Church had all faced numerous tough campaigns in the past where that particular pattern prevailed.

One month before the election, in the *Washington Post's* comprehensive survey, David Broder concluded,

> There is no evidence of a dramatic upsurge in Republican strength or a massive turnover in Congress. . . .
> Overall, the consensus estimate is that Republicans may

---

[29] *American Political Report*, vol. 9, no. 22 (July 18, 1980), p. 4.

gain two to four seats in a chamber where Democrats now outnumber them 58–41. Other than Holtzman, the best Democratic prospects for gains are in vacant seats in Oklahoma and Pennsylvania. The top Republican targets are in Alaska, Florida, Idaho, Indiana, Iowa, New Hampshire, South Dakota and Washington.[30]

The *Washington Post* survey also pointed to tough races in Vermont, for incumbent Democrat Leahy; North Carolina, for incumbent Democrat Robert Morgan; Wisconsin, for incumbent Democrat Nelson; and Colorado, for incumbent Democrat Hart, but viewed them as less likely GOP prospects. Incumbent Herman Talmadge of Georgia was seen as comfortably ahead, as was Democrat Jim Folsom in Alabama.

A week later, the *Congressional Quarterly*'s election outlook offered a similar projection:

> Earlier in the year, Republicans were predicting heavy Senate gains, and some were optimistic about capturing the 10 seats necessary to insure control. . . .
>
> . . . The picture became less bright as the year progressed. For one thing, more of their own seats have become shaky. . . .
>
> At the same time, Democrats started to surge back from their summer lows. Culver of Iowa, who last June was 17 points behind his GOP challenger Rep. Charles E. Grassley, had pulled even by the beginning of September. . . .
>
> As a result, Republicans probably will pick up Senate seats this November, but they will probably be less dramatic gains than at first anticipated. . . .
>
> . . . with four of their own seats now in jeopardy, their chances of winning a Senate majority are almost nil.[31]

In the last ten days of the 1980 campaign, the outlook changed—but not dramatically. As the hostage release failure and the debate seemed to swing public sentiment away from Carter and toward Reagan, the estimates by Democratic and Republican professionals about the Senate tilted accordingly. Instead of assuming that "tossup" seats would break evenly for the parties, observers assumed a few more would go to the GOP. Republicans gave optimistic figures; Democrats, pessimistic ones. As late as the day before the election, however, none would privately or publicly predict a net Republican gain of more than seven.

[30] David S. Broder, "The Post Survey," *Washington Post*, October 5, 1980.
[31] "Elections 1980: A Test of Incumbency," *Congressional Quarterly Weekly Report*, October 11, 1980, pp. 2984, 2985.

The House Campaign

The challenge to House incumbents in most districts was so inconsequential that no visible, credible alternative was presented to the voters. Nonetheless, *changes* in each party's record of recruiting able candidates did make a big difference in the November outcome.

Whether or not a vigorous challenge materializes in a particular district depends on many factors: the strength of the opposition party, the popularity of the incumbent, the availability of money and other campaign resources, and so on. How well a party does *overall* in fielding a slate of attractive candidates depends much more upon the national political climate.[32] President Carter's poor standing during the summer and fall of 1979 created a mood in which potential Republican candidates were encouraged to compete for seats held by Democrats, and Democratic candidates were discouraged from contesting Republican seats. The efforts of the national Republican party —the television advertising campaign, training seminars, and direct contributions—reinforced this political climate and, as *Congressional Quarterly* put it in its February 1980 outlook on the elections, also helped

> motivate a better crop of GOP candidates to run than the party fielded in 1976 and 1978. Once recruited, those Republican candidates may feel less isolated in waging a difficult challenge to a Democratic incumbent if they know that there is a larger effort behind them. And it will give those contenders themes on which to run individual campaigns.[33]

This does not mean that strong Republican candidates emerged in all Democratic-held seats or even in a majority of them. Recent history showed the tremendous power of incumbents (three-fourths of those seeking reelection have won big, with 60 percent or more of the vote) and the weakness of challengers (the mean expenditure in 1978 by challengers in these districts was $32,564, an insignificant sum compared with the $200,000-plus budgets of winning challengers and candidates in open seats).[34] Even optimistic Republicans had no reason to expect all Democratic districts to become more competitive in 1980,

[32] Gary C. Jacobson and Samuel Kernell, *Strategy and Choice in Congressional Elections* (New Haven: Yale University Press, forthcoming).

[33] *Congressional Quarterly Weekly Report*, February 23, 1980, p. 437.

[34] Thomas E. Mann and Raymond E. Wolfinger, "Candidates and Parties in Congressional Elections," *American Political Science Review*, vol. 74 (September 1980), p. 627.

but they had every reason to expect Republican fortunes to improve in the smaller number of already competitive districts as well as in some significant portion of the open seats. If things went their way, the Republicans might also pick off some complacent and comfortable "safe" incumbent Democrats.

In 1976 the Republican strategy centered on taking aim at the members of the Democratic class of 1974. Congressman Guy Vander Jagt, chairman of the National Republican Congressional Committee, predicted a gain of "76 in '76." The GOP ended up in the embarrassing position of losing two *more* seats rather than gaining seventy-six.[35] In 1978 the Republicans changed, concentrating much of their fire on the open seats; yet their net pickup was only two in seats without incumbents running. In 1980 their approach seemed to have shifted once again. In August, Vander Jagt spelled out the GOP strategy as follows: "We made a conscious decision to recruit outstanding candidates to confront Democratic 'leaders' and 'committee chairmen.' Even if they are not all defeated, the survivors will be frightened enough so that they will become more conservative once they return."[36]

The Republicans in 1980 actually targeted a much more diverse set of seats than implied by the Vander Jagt statement and by much of the press commentary that followed. Because the number of retirements declined from the unusually high levels in the four previous elections, the Republicans were perforce obliged to concentrate much of their attention on Democratic incumbents. Throughout the two-year cycle preceding the election, the Republicans maintained a list of seventy to eighty Democratic seats that they thought could be won. The list included incumbents of every level of seniority—freshmen, members of the class of 1974, and senior Democrats such as Morris Udall (Arizona), John Brademas (Indiana), Thomas "Lud" Ashley (Ohio), and Thomas Foley (Washington). Decisions about which seats should be targeted were based on many factors: the partisan coloration of the district, its recent electoral history, the availability of potentially strong and well-financed challengers, how good a job the incumbent had done of staying close to his constituents, whether the incumbent appeared to be out of step ideologically with mass sentiment in the district or vulnerable on any specific issues or aspects of his or her personal reputation. Districts moved on and off the list

---

[35] Alan Ehenhalt, "GOP House Candidates Face Task of Beating Entrenched Incumbents," *Washington Star*, January 6, 1980.

[36] Quoted in Richard E. Cohen, "A Chairmanship No Longer Guarantees a Lengthy Career in Congress," *National Journal*, October 25, 1980, p. 1795.

as local conditions changed. As often as not, the first step in mounting a serious challenge was taken in the district; the Republican hit list registered this development rather than initiated it.

A good case in point was the race in Oregon between Democrat Al Ullman, chairman of the Ways and Means Committee, and Republican Denny Smith, the son of a former Oregon governor. In early 1979 most observers (including national Republican party officials) agreed with the assessment that Ullman should not be expected to face any significant political difficulty in his home district. A September 1979 poll registered a 61.6 percent favorable job rating for Ullman and a 59 to 12 percent lead over Smith, who was then unrecognized by 82.8 percent of the district voters.[37] Ullman appeared to bring on some political problems for himself when he announced his support for a national value-added tax (VAT). The proposal was vigorously attacked in Oregon, and in April 1980 Ullman withdrew the proposal, admitting it had little support.[38] The national Republican party still showed little interest in the district. Then Ullman, facing a politically unknown candidate who did not campaign, barely won his May primary election 55 to 45 percent. A June poll in the district revealed that Ullman's favorable job rating had dropped to 41.6 percent, that the percentage of voters who did not recognize Smith had been cut in half, and that Ullman's lead over Smith had dropped to 46/40 percent.[39] After Smith had been campaigning for some ten months and had spent $175,000 in the primary, the district was finally targeted by the national Republican party.

This case illustrates an important point about the Republican strategy in 1980. Although the Republican party was unusually active and aggressive in targeting Democrats during 1980, the system remained highly decentralized. Potential candidates and donors in congressional districts made their own rational calculations about whether to run or whether to contribute; these decisions were only partly influenced by the national party. The much-heralded Republican strategy of targeting Democratic leaders in the House did not exist until after it became clear that many of them were already in trouble, mostly for reasons peculiar to their individual districts: in addition to Ullman, James Corman (California), a senior member of the Ways and Means Committee, was threatened because of his position on busing; Harold "Bizz" Johnson (California), chairman of the Public Works Committee, because of age and several controversial public

[37] *Political Report*, vol. 3, no. 27 (July 3, 1980), pp. 4-5.
[38] Cohen, "A Chairmanship," p. 1798.
[39] *Political Report*, July 3, 1980, pp. 4-5.

works projects; majority whip John Brademas, because of an attractive, well-financed challenger in a district he had never been able to make safe; Interior Committee chairman Morris Udall, because of an influx of Republican residents and too much exposure as a national liberal; Agriculture chairman Thomas Foley, because of a reluctance to "work his district" in the manner of new-style congressmen; and John Murphy (New York) and Frank Thompson (New Jersey), chairmen respectively of the Merchant Marine and House Administration committees, because they were Abscam defendants. Not only did the Republicans articulate this strategy well after local challengers had made their move; they did so largely as a publicity tactic to get more national press attention on House races, which in turn led to more local press much needed by Republican challengers and stimulated more direct-mail contributions. These resources were then channeled to wherever Republicans thought they could win.

The Democrats, being generally on the defensive in 1980 and having a much less active national party apparatus, were geared more to holding their own seats than to replacing Republicans. The first priority was assisting threatened incumbents, although the party had too few resources to be of any significant help. The second priority was to try to hold the block of Democratic seats being vacated by retiring incumbents or by those seeking higher office. In some of these districts, the Democrats realized early that the Republicans were heavy favorites to take control; so their challenge was only halfhearted. For example, when conservative Democratic Congressman David Satterfield of Richmond, Virginia, announced his retirement after sixteen years in the House, the *Washington Post* reported that the local notables, in a manner reminiscent of old-style nomination politics, "selected former Richmond mayor Thomas J. Bliley, Jr., assured him enough money to crush two opponents for the Republican nomination and thereby frightened off a half dozen prospective Democratic challengers. The result: Bliley faces only token opposition this fall on his way to becoming Richmond's first GOP Congressman since Reconstruction."[40] Republicans also made a strong, early claim to the Thirty-second Congressional District of New York, where Democrat James Hanley had managed to stay afloat in Republican territory. In others, like the Fourth District of Massachusetts, where Father Robert Drinan retired in response to the Vatican's decision to tighten its rules forbidding priests to hold elective office, the Democrats fought hard to save the seat.

[40] Glenn Frankel, "The Making of a Congressman by Richmond's GOP Kingpins," *Washington Post*, June 14, 1980.

Overall, in the twenty-seven open Democratic seats, no real election contest developed in ten (two Republicans were home free, eight Democrats); Democratic candidates built a solid lead against Republican opponents in five; and a tight race with two active candidates developed in the remaining twelve. Democrats had designs on many of the sixteen open Republican seats; they managed to run serious campaigns in eleven of these districts and had a reasonable chance going into the last phase of the campaign of winning in eight of them. The level of competition in the open seats was in general much higher than in seats with incumbents running, but there was no sign from the way in which the contests shaped up that the Republicans would make a large net gain.

Democrats also had a target list of vulnerable incumbents, but it was much shorter than the Republican list, and there was little in the way of national party resources to back it up. Late in the campaign, *Congressional Quarterly* identified nineteen Republican incumbents who were sufficiently pressed by their challengers to leave the outcome in doubt, including two congressmen publicly involved in homosexual incidents, Robert Bauman (Maryland) and Jon Hinson (Mississippi); Texas Congressman Ron Paul, a pure conservative who appeared to enjoy voting against projects that clearly benefited his Houston-area district; Robert Dornan of California, rematched in a multimillion-dollar campaign with the son of actor Gregory Peck; Illinois Congressman Paul Findley, who incurred the ire of many for championing the cause of the Palestine Liberation Organization; and a sizable number of freshmen Republicans.[41] These individual challenges all proceeded largely on their own, however, with no relationship to a national Democratic strategy and little assistance from outside the district, at least not from the national party.

As the Ullman-Smith example revealed, the shape of many races is not determined until after the primary election. In the extreme case, the incumbent is defeated. Typically, only a handful of congressmen are denied renomination each election; 1980 was no exception. Six representatives were defeated in primaries, two Republicans and four Democrats. Republican Richard Kelly, who became an underdog for renomination after receiving Abscam notoriety, placed a distant third in a three-man primary. Veteran John Buchanan of Alabama, the other Republican loser, fell victim to a more conservative opponent who claimed to have had the support of 2,500 volunteers from the Moral Majority; Albert Lee Smith's upset victory turned

---

[41] Christopher Buchanan, "Modest GOP Congressional Gains Expected," *Congressional Quarterly Weekly Report*, November 1, 1980, pp. 3242-47.

a safe Republican seat into a tossup in November.[42] California Democrat Charles H. Wilson faced not only two strong opponents, including a former House member; he also faced the prospect of being censured by the House for alleged financial misconduct. Democrat Edward Stack of Florida, at age seventy the oldest freshman to be seated in more than a decade, was surprised by a late-charging opponent who stressed that he would be a more energetic legislator than Stack. Democratic Congressman Bennett Stewart suffered from a wave of antiorganization sentiment in the Chicago primary. Finally, an Appropriations subcommittee chairman, Democrat Robert Duncan of Oregon, who did not realize he was in trouble until two weeks before the election, fell victim to a challenger who spent $100,000 and mobilized hundreds of volunteers from the Oregon Gray Panthers.

Of course, primaries can shape House contests in other ways as well. Ullman's narrow primary victory signaled Republican party officials and opened up the campaign coffers for his opponent. In North Dakota, a divisive Republican primary gave an advantage to the Democratic nominee in the race to replace Senate-bound Republican Mark Andrews. Similarly, a split in the Democratic ranks following the retirement of thirty-two-year incumbent Tom Steed gave the GOP a chance to win the seat in Oklahoma's Fourth District for only the second time since statehood. Close primaries can also have important delayed effects. Liberal Texas Democrat Bob Eckhardt's unexpectedly narrow primary victory in 1978 set the stage for tough primary and general election challenges in 1980.

After the dust had settled on the scramble for candidates and the parties had trained their sights on the most accessible targets, most observers could agree that the election would turn on the outcome in roughly one hundred congressional districts and that the Republicans were almost certain to increase their numbers in the House because more Democratic than Republican seats were being seriously contested. There was, however, great uncertainty about the likely size of the GOP pickup.

The Republicans were buoyed by a Market Opinion Research poll, released by the National Republican Congressional Committee on July 7, which showed that public confidence in the Republican party's ability to handle major problems increased dramatically during 1980; it also registered a modest shift toward the Republicans in terms of party identification.[43] A month later Louis Harris released

[42] Joe McFadden, "Moral Majority Forces Help Fell Rep. Buchanan," *Washington Post*, September 4, 1980.
[43] Cited in Malbin, "The Republican Revival," p. 86.

a poll showing that, for the first time in decades, a majority (50 percent to 49 percent) of the electorate intended to vote for the Republican candidate for Congress. At the same time, just before the Democratic convention, Ronald Reagan held a lead of twenty-eight percentage points over Jimmy Carter. For a moment it appeared that 1980 might in fact be a watershed year for the Republicans, that GOP control of the House was possible. The mood quickly shifted again, this time against the Republicans. First, Gallup released the results of his poll, taken at the exact time as Harris's, which showed the Democrats ahead in the race for the House, 57 to 42 percent. Then, another Harris poll conducted two weeks later gave the Democrats a 55 to 45 percent lead over the Republicans. Finally, Reagan's margin over Carter dropped to six percentage points as the Democrats enjoyed a boost in public sentiment immediately after their convention. The tightness of the presidential contest during the ensuing months dampened most predictions of a Republican landslide in the House.

All predictions of the net shift in seats obscured the fact that many highly contested races took on their own dynamic, which often ran counter to national trends. Democratic Congressman Morris Udall, of Arizona's Second District, knew he faced a difficult election in 1980: His district was becoming increasingly Republican, his victory margin in 1978 plummeted to only 52.5 percent, and he expected a very well financed opponent this time around. Republican challenger Richard Huff ran his first television commercials in November and December 1979, both to increase his name recognition and to stimulate early contributions; a second series of television ads with the same purpose in mind was run the following spring. Huff's major television onslaught, however, budgeted at about $200,000, appeared between September 2 and November 4, 1980. Huff's commercials stressed that Udall was out of touch with the district, that he was closely tied to eastern liberals, that he was a decent man who voted wrong. Polls always had Udall in the lead, but by October the margin closed to 55 to 39 percent, with much of Udall's support very soft. The Udall campaign shifted gears and went on the offensive, stressing that Huff was a "packaged candidate" whose commercials were imported from other districts, that he was afraid to debate, and that Arizonans deserved better representation in Congress. It was the first time in his congressional career that Udall had attacked an opponent. As election day approached, the race became increasingly heated, and both candidates were expected to spend well over

$500,000. Udall was favored slightly because of his superior organization and the perceived effectiveness of his counterattack.[44]

The aggressive, well-financed challenge to House majority leader Jim Wright of Texas's Twelfth Congressional District shocked many political observers. Wright had never won less than 60 percent of the vote; in 1978 he had 68.5 percent. Nevertheless, Jim Bradshaw, Fort Worth mayor pro tem, encouraged by the surprise victory of Republican Governor Bill Clements two years earlier and by the president's unpopularity, ran ads emphasizing "why voters need to know that Jim Wright has become Jimmy Carter's lackey." Wright countered by raising an impressive campaign kitty and by attempting to discourage others from contributing to his opponent. At one point he wrote to a number of corporate PACs, urging them to stay neutral rather than support Bradshaw, on the grounds that he (Wright) would be reelected and they would have to continue doing business with him. Wright pictured himself as a moderate who had done a great deal for the district; he also attacked some of Bradshaw's actions as mayor of Fort Worth. Near the end of the campaign, a Fort Worth journalist concluded: "I would be surprised if Bradshaw won, but I wouldn't be stunned. . . . If people are mad enough at Carter, Bradshaw could just pull this off."[45] Wright's goals went well beyond just winning, however. As an almost certain candidate for Speaker when Tip O'Neill retires, he wanted to demonstrate to his colleagues in the House that he had his district well under control.

The number-three man in the Democratic leadership—whip John Brademas of Indiana—acted more like a challenger than an eleven-term veteran. His district had been marginal for many years, the sentiment was strongly in favor of Republican presidential candidate Ronald Reagan in a state whose ballot form encouraged party-line voting, and the Republicans fielded a young and articulate candidate, the strongest in many years. Moreover, a July Market Opinion Research poll showed twenty-seven-year-old GOP challenger John Hiler with a lead of three to four points. Brademas, who in past campaigns had simply tried to ignore his opponent, attacked Hiler's positions as "simplistic" and tried to tie him to "big oil." Hiler emphasized his philosophical differences with Brademas on economic policy, but also tried to identify the incumbent as part of the congressional leadership, which must accept responsibility for the country's ills. Brademas

[44] *Political Report*, vol. 3, no. 41 (October 17, 1980), pp. 5-6; and personal interview with Udall's campaign staff.
[45] Quoted in *Political Report*, October 17, 1980, p. 8.

chose to respond to the latter charge by arguing that he had clout and could get things done for the district, pointing to the revitalization of downtown South Bend as a prime example. Although Brademas was expected to outspend Hiler two to one, he entered the last phase of the campaign as the underdog.[46]

The Ullman-Smith contest in Oregon had begun quite differently from the Brademas-Hiler race—Ullman had appeared safe until the unfavorable reaction to his VAT proposal and his poor showing in the primary—but by the final weeks of the campaign, the two elections looked very much alike. Ullman's lead in the polls had dropped to only a few percentage points, and Smith had by mid-October raised over half a million dollars. The GOP challenger attacked Ullman's support for a value-added tax and tried to hold him, as a member of the House leadership, responsible for many of the economic problems facing the country. Ullman counterattacked, branding Smith a "right-winger" who wanted to cut spending for cancer research and "devastate" the social security system. Ullman also stressed his ability to get things done in Washington for the Second Congressional District. Perhaps the most notable feature of the race was Smith's way of dramatizing his charge that Ullman had lost touch with the district. The television ad began with a shot of a post office box. A voice said, "This is Al Ullman's residence." The voice then said that Ullman had "recently moved." The camera panned to a different post office box. The scene then changed to show a picture of Ullman's house in suburban Washington, D.C. Finally, a picture of Republican challenger Smith's family and home in Oregon appeared on the screen. As the November 4 election neared, many observers believed that Ullman was on the defensive and Smith had a good chance of winning.[47]

Senior Democrats were not the only incumbents hard pressed for reelection. Many members of the Democratic class of 1974 who came from districts previously represented by Republicans faced vigorous challenges in 1980. Most, however, were savvy campaigners who had faced and beaten tough opponents before. Congressman Andrew Maguire (New Jersey), for one, anticipated a very difficult campaign; he faced a rematch with his last opponent, Margaret "Marge" Roukema (who had won 47 percent of the vote in 1978), in a year when the national tide would most likely be working against him in Republican Bergen County. As described by Larry Light, Maguire's "outreach" program was one of the best:

46 Ibid., pp. 1-2.
47 Ibid., pp. 2-3.

Every weekend, Maguire returned to his New Jersey district for a round of appearances. Every week, his Xerox 1700 computer terminal answered letters from constituents about his issue stances. Every few months, his office sent a newsletter to voters detailing his accomplishments. And every day, his staffers straightened out problems that district residents had with the federal government.[48]

The articulate Maguire combined a sophistication on the issues with a flair for publicity and a reputation for constituent service; these assets, he felt, combined with a well-organized campaign, gave him a reasonable chance of succeeding once again. Roukema, in a well-financed challenge that included ads on New York television stations during the last two weeks of the campaign, argued that Maguire was too liberal for the district on both economic and defense policy. She stressed that during his six years in the House he had not once voted for a defense appropriations bill. A Maguire poll in June 1980 showed him with a 55 to 32 percent lead; by September his margin had slipped only slightly to 51 to 38 percent. Just a few days before the election, a Republican poll showed that Maguire was ahead by seven percentage points. On election eve, the Roukema campaign staff feared they had fallen short once again.

As election day approached, the uncertainty about the size of the certain GOP pickup remained. Some observers, noting the attractive crop of Republican candidates and the more than five-to-one GOP advantage over the Democrats in party spending, felt their gain would be twenty-five to thirty seats or more.[49] On the other hand, *Congressional Quarterly*, based upon its final survey of House races on the eve of the election, predicted only moderate GOP gains, most likely ten to fifteen seats.[50]

The Senate Results

Long before midnight on election Tuesday, Democrats were sitting stunned at the results and projections reported by the television networks. The loss of the White House had been forecast well in advance, but the sweep of the Republican victory in the Senate far exceeded everyone's expectations. By the next morning, when the

---

[48] Larry Light, "Crack 'Outreach' Programs No Longer Ensure Re-election," *Congressional Quarterly Weekly Report*, February 14, 1981, p. 316.

[49] Thomas E. Mann and Norman J. Ornstein, "1980: A Republican Revival in Congress?" *Public Opinion*, October/November 1980, pp. 16-20, 56.

[50] Buchanan, "Modest GOP Congressional Gains Expected," p. 3242.

final close races were decided and the net Republican gain registered at twelve, it was clear that 1980 represented the biggest year for the GOP in the Senate since 1946, when the Republicans had gained thirteen seats and control of the chamber. It also represented the first GOP control of *either* house of Congress since 1954.

In fact, the closest analogy may be neither 1946 nor 1954 but 1958, an election in which the *Democrats* gained 15 seats and in the process solidified their unbroken control of the Senate for more than two decades. In the ten elections from the 1958 Democratic sweep through 1978, no party had gained more than 6 seats net in the Senate, the average party shift being 2.7 seats. So 1980, with a net shift of 12 to the Republican column, was a real departure from the recent past.

The Republicans in 1980 picked up twelve of the twenty-four Democratic seats up for contest and, remarkably, did not lose a single one of their ten contested seats. Nine Democratic incumbents went down to defeat on November 4, joining the three Democrats and one Republican (Javits) defeated earlier in primaries.

Nationally, the shifts in seats in a Republican direction were striking. In twenty-five of the thirty-four Senate seats, there was a percentage shift (compared with 1974, when these same seats were last contested) in a Republican direction. Even among those Democrats who held their party's seat in the face of the Republican sweep, a majority lost ground compared with the last election.

The shift in seats cut across all regions, with the Democrats particularly losing ground in the South, the Midwest, the Great Plains, and the Pacific Coast regions. Democrats losses in the deep South left them holding a bare majority of the twenty-two Senate seats there—a dramatic change from the consistent 100 percent of those seats the party held from the 1920s right into the 1960s. Democrats fell to a mere 25 percent of the Senate seats in the Great Plains region.

A look beneath the surface of this tremendous GOP sweep of the Senate in 1980 suggests that the election trend, while broad, was shallow. Many individual races were extremely close, shifting party columns by the narrowest margins and affected clearly by the last-minute movement and idiosyncrasies of the national campaign. Indeed, if one could shift barely 50,000 votes—less than one-hundredth of 1 percent of all votes cast—one could move *seven* Senate seats from the GOP to the Democrats [51] and change the election

---

[51] The seven seats are Alabama, Alaska, Arizona, Georgia, Idaho, New Hampshire, and North Carolina.

into a typical one. With a Democratic loss of only five seats, the party would have retained firm control of the Senate, fifty-four to forty-six, and the analysis of 1980 would have focused almost exclusively on the personal defeat of Jimmy Carter.

Of course, one cannot shift votes after an election. The incredible closeness of so many of these races tells us something about the firmness of the electoral foundation on which the massive Republican victory was built. Nevertheless, with twenty-one Democratic seats up in 1982 and only twelve GOP seats on the line, and with few of the Republican seats initially seen as vulnerable, the Republicans have an excellent chance of retaining their control of the Senate—possibly even of gaining more seats.

A closer analysis of the returns can also shed some light on ideological trends in the 1980 Senate races. There can be no question that the electorate in 1980 opted for a much more conservative Senate (as it had in 1978). With the exception of John Culver, most liberal Democratic incumbent senators were on the defensive throughout the 1980 campaign, tempering their viewpoints and downplaying their voting records. Conservative challengers were clearly on the offensive, proclaiming proudly their ideological points of view. The nature of the campaign, combined with the highly visible defeats of Church, McGovern, Bayh, Culver, Magnuson, Nelson, and Durkin and the victories of a dozen staunchly conservative GOP freshmen, leads to the inescapable conclusion that 1980 was partly a referendum on liberalism versus conservatism—and liberalism lost.

The returns suggest, however, that there was more to the 1980 elections in the Senate. Although a number of liberal Democratic incumbents lost, an equal number won—some by very comfortable margins. Inouye in Hawaii (78 percent), Glenn in Ohio (71 percent), and Cranston in California (59 percent) combined with the victories of Eagleton, Leahy, and Hart to offset the liberal losses enumerated above. Moreover, in two *open* contests where a clearly liberal Democrat was opposed by a clearly conservative Republican—Illinois (Dixon versus O'Neal) and Connecticut (Dodd versus Buckley)—the liberal won convincingly. In another open contest, in Pennsylvania, the Republican (Spector) who won was more liberal than the Democrat (Flaherty) he beat.

Additional evidence casts doubt on a simple ideological explanation for 1980. It was not only liberals who had trouble or lost. Two conservative Democrats, Morgan and Talmadge, were defeated in their bids for reelection. The Republican who came closest to relinquishing his seat to the Democrats in this great conservative tide

TABLE 8–1

VOTE CHANGE FROM 1974 TO 1980 FOR INCUMBENT SENATORS
(percentage points)

	Democrats		Republicans	
	Junior	Senior	Junior	Senior
Liberal	−3.8 (5)	−10.5 (8)	—	+3.0 (2)
Nonliberal	−10.0 (3)	−10.5 (2)	+17.5 (2)	+2.5 (2)
Overall	−6.1 (8)	−10.5 (10)	+17.5 (2)	+2.8 (4)

NOTE: Liberals include senators whose conservative coalition support scores for 1980 were thirty or under. Nonliberals include all senators with scores over thirty. Junior senators are those who had served one term or less; senior senators had served two terms or more. The figure in each cell is the average vote change in percentage points for the party group represented for their Senate seats between 1974 and 1980; the numbers in parentheses indicate the actual number of senators.

was none other than the dean of conservatism, Barry Goldwater of Arizona.

Some of this evidence suggests another partial explanation for the 1980 results. A public fed up with Washington took its frustration out on those most closely identified with Washington. Thus, *seniority* and *visibility* hurt as much, in many instances, as ideology. The poor showings of veterans Magnuson, Talmadge, Javits, and Goldwater fit here, at least in part. So too do the figures displayed in table 8–1. This table compares the 1980 results with the 1974 figures for incumbent senators, dividing them by party, seniority, and ideology. For the thirty-three Senate seats contested, the Republican vote, on average, went up 9.5 percentage points.

As the table shows, for Democrats, the group that performed best (that is, suffered the smallest percentage losses to the Republicans) was the *junior liberals*, who dropped an average of only 3.8 percentage points from 1974 to 1980. This group included Hart, Culver, Glenn, Durkin, and Leahy. Other Democrats—junior nonliberals (Bumpers [Arkansas], Ford [Kentucky], and Morgan); senior liberals (Church, Bayh, McGovern, Magnuson, Nelson, Inouye, Cranston, Eagleton); and senior nonliberals (Talmadge, Hollings)—did equally poorly, and much worse than the junior liberals.

All Republicans did well. Comparisons among Republicans show that the two junior incumbents, Laxalt and Garn, both nonliberals, did extremely well, while senior incumbents, liberal *and* conservative, did rather poorly given the overall GOP trend. The senior liberals,

Mathias (Maryland) and Packwood, did a little better, though, than the senior conservatives, Goldwater and Dole.

Although the role of party, issues, and philosophy in the election should not be downplayed, these figures suggest that seniority too was a factor in the 1980 contests. In an anti-Washington, anti-establishment year, it paid to be less visibly attached to the past and the status quo—even if you were a liberal.

The House Results

In a fashion less dramatic than displayed in the Senate, the Republicans registered a net gain of thirty-three seats in the House, still their best showing since 1966 and their second largest pickup since 1946. When added to the fifteen seats the Republicans gained in 1978, the 1980 harvest returned them to the level of strength they enjoyed in the House (44 percent of the seats) before their devastating losses in the 1974 election, indeed to the exact number of seats (192) they had held after both the 1966 and the 1970 contests. Initial reports on the election indicated that the Republicans actually won a majority of votes cast nationwide for the House.[52] The Republicans apparently increased their percentage of the total vote between 1978 and 1980 by three to four percentage points.

The Republicans won most of their new seats by defeating incumbents: twenty-seven Democratic incumbents lost to Republican challengers while only three Republican representatives were defeated, producing a net GOP pickup here of twenty-four seats. (These figures do not include Democratic Congressman Claude "Buddy" Leach, who lost to another Democrat in Louisiana's unique electoral system, or former congressman Michael "Ozzie" Myers of Pennsylvania, who was expelled from the House just before the election and was subsequently defeated for reelection by an independent who joined the Democratic caucus in the Ninety-seventh Congress.) Eleven open seats shifted party control, only one to the Democratic column, for a net GOP gain of nine seats. Overall, just under 8 percent (30 of 392) of seats with incumbents running and 26 percent (11 of 43) of the open seats changed party control. With primary elections included, 91 percent of all incumbents seeking reelection were successful, close to the average for the past several elections. Among the successes were Morris Udall in Arizona and Jim Wright in Texas,

---

[52] The official statistics, which, unlike the preliminary figures, include all votes cast for uncontested incumbents, are expected to show a slight Democratic majority or plurality.

both of whom won comfortably after stiff challenges. John Brademas in Indiana and Al Ullman in Oregon were not so fortunate.

Half of the twenty-eight defeated Democratic incumbents had served in the House for at least ten years; eight had been in the House for eighteen years or more. Almost two-thirds of the Democratic losers (four committee and fourteen subcommittee chairmen, as well as the whip) were part of the majority leadership. Many of the senior Democrats who lost—Brademas, Ullman, Johnson, Corman, and Ashley—were well-publicized Republican targets. Others were taken completely by surprise. Lionel Van Deerlin of California, who had won each of his previous five races with at least 69 percent of the vote, was upset by a thirty-two-year-old political novice after leading him in a September poll 66 to 21 percent. Lester Wolff of New York, after leading his twenty-seven-year-old opponent in September by an even wider margin, fell prey to a late media blitz criticizing Wolff's frequent trips around the world. One Republican incumbent—Samuel Devine of Ohio—was also defeated somewhat unexpectedly, although he had won by small margins in 1974 and 1976.

Six of the thirty-one defeated incumbents were tainted with scandal: Democrats John Jenrette (South Carolina), John Murphy, and Frank Thompson were implicated in the FBI's Abscam operation; Republican Robert Bauman was charged with soliciting sex from a sixteen-year-old boy; "Buddy" Leach allegedly violated federal election law in his 1978 victory; and Bill Burlison (Democrat, Missouri) was accused of using his influence to get special treatment for a fired postal worker in his district.

Another nine Democratic defeats were suffered by members of the class of 1974, who, before this election, had been remarkably resilient. (Included among them was Andrew Maguire of New Jersey.) Of the seventy-five Democrats first elected in 1974, two were defeated in the 1976 general election, seven in the 1978 election; a full forty-eight remain in the Ninety-seventh Congress.

Just what role the Reagan landslide played in the defeat of the Democratic incumbents is difficult to say. Eight representatives lost by extremely small margins—less than 5,000 votes—and virtually all ran ahead of President Carter even while losing. Yet the Democrats who lost suffered an average decline of fourteen percentage points from their 1978 vote—well in excess of the national swing. Only a third of the losers had won with less than 55 percent of the vote in 1978; almost half had margins of 60 percent or more. Therefore, although the Reagan vote probably made the difference in some of the Democratic losses, the congressional candidates and their local campaigns were dominant.[53] One striking illustration of the importance of these local effects is the record of the Democratic class of 1978. Even though many were first elected by extremely narrow margins, not one was defeated by the Republicans in 1980. By utilizing the extensive resources of incumbency at their disposal for the first time, they enjoyed the now classic "sophomore surge."[54] A Republican presidential landslide could not deny them reelection. Another piece of evidence on the same point is the pattern of swing between 1978 and 1980 across all congressional districts. The increasing localization of political forces in the House elections, measured by a tripling of the variance in swing between 1958 and 1978, continued unabated in 1980.[55]

The Republican "victory" in the House was much less shallow than that in the Senate. Although a shift of just over 25,000 votes would have saved the Democratic incumbent in eight districts (Alvin Baldus [Wisconsin], Bob Carr [Michigan], James Corman, Bob Eckhardt, Herbert Harris [Virginia], Peter Kostmayer [Pennsylvania], Richardson Preyer [North Carolina], and Al Ullman), another seven Democrats and only one Republican survived with margins of fewer than 2,500 votes each. The Republicans fell well short of the votes needed to take control of the House, but their thirty-three-seat pickup was by no means a fluke.

In fact, if one examines those districts in which the incumbent survived but with a greatly reduced margin from 1978, it becomes clear that more Democrats than Republicans appear vulnerable in 1982. Democrats who sustained a drop of ten percentage points or more include John Burton (California), Fortney "Pete" Stark (California), George Brown (California), Paul Simon (Illinois), Neal Smith (Iowa), Harold Volkmer (Missouri), Leo Zeferetti (New York), Raymond Lederer (Pennsylvania), J. J. Pickle (Texas), and Jack Hightower (Texas). Republicans in the same category include Paul Findley (Illinois), Carl Pursell (Michigan), Manuel Lujan (New Mexico), James Martin (North Carolina), and Marc Marks (Pennsylvania).

Finally, considering both those who were defeated and those

[53] Jimmy Carter's early concession may have had a more telling effect on several outcomes than Ronald Reagan's coattails. See Albert R. Hunt's discussion of this point in chapter 5.

[54] See the discussion in Albert Cover and David Mayhew, "Congressional Dynamics and the Decline of Competitive Congressional Elections," in Lawrence C. Dodd and Bruce I. Oppenheimer, eds., *Congress Reconsidered* (New York: Praeger, 1977), pp. 59-72.

[55] Thomas E. Mann, *Unsafe at Any Margin* (Washington, D.C.: American Enterprise Institute, 1978), chap. 5.

who survived with greatly reduced margins, one can find no sign of an ideological mandate in the House returns apart from the obvious Republican party victory.

Conclusion: The Ninety-seventh Congress

Whatever the causes of the Democratic losses in November 1980, the central effect most certainly was a more conservative Congress. Of the 16 freshmen Republican senators sworn in for the Ninety-seventh Congress, at least 12 can be classified as staunch conservatives; the net swing in the 100-member Senate was perhaps 8 votes in a right-ward direction. Similarly, the fifty-two Republican freshmen in the House were, as a group, strongly conservative, and they shifted the House several degrees to the right.

The addition of conservative Republicans to the House and the Senate, however, was not the only—or the most—interesting or significant effect of the 1980 congressional election. The change within the Democratic party was noteworthy. Democrats, to begin, were thrown into confusion and disarray by the election. Democrats in the Senate found themselves in the minority, a new experience for forty-four of the forty-seven.[56] The fits and starts of the first few months of the new Congress demonstrated their difficulty in adjusting to the new and different role.

Democrats in the House retained their majority status, with the attendant staff, chairmanships, leadership posts, and control over the agenda. Still, the loss of the Senate clearly shook them up. The loss of 33 seats still left House Democrats with a seemingly comfortable majority (243/192), but the Senate election created a universal nervousness. "For the first time," commented one House veteran, "we can *really* see the possibility of losing *our* majority in '82."[57] One result of this reaction is a greater concern among individual House Democrats with their party and party policy—and a concomitant rise in partisanship on the part of the Democrats. One observer noted:

> For a long time, Democrats have run for Congress as individuals, confident that they were insulated from national trends. But in 1980, they saw an ominous trend. Many Democrats, especially in the Senate, who had served their

[56] Senators Stennis (Mississippi), Long, and Jackson (Washington) had served previously in the minority, Stennis in both the Eightieth and the Eighty-third congresses.

[57] Personal interview with authors.

constituents faithfully and done their homework well, were swept up in a broader tide and thrown out of office. They know it could happen to them next time.[58]

These Democrats saw a party-based national Republican campaign pay dividends. As a result, they are more party-conscious and more resentful of Republican partisan tactics. Their partisanship is enhanced as well by their reduction in numbers after the 1980 election, making Democratic party unity more important on any given vote.

All of these things combine to encourage Democratic schizophrenia in the House. On the one hand, having read the election returns and observed the repudiation of their party and philosophy, Democrats are not anxious to step forward proudly as warriors carrying the spear of New Deal liberalism. The party in the House did not organize a campaign against the Reagan budget cuts or work out a coherent party strategy to fight the Reagan approach. On the other hand, many House Democrats are determined to prevent the worst excesses, as they see it, of rigid conservatism and have acted to provide a counterweight to the Jesse Helmses and James McClures of the Republican right. Thus, in February 1981 in the House Foreign Affairs Committee, Democrats ousted one subcommittee chairman and twice bypassed a senior member to install two aggressive junior liberals in key chairmanships; at the same time, they deliberately changed the name of another subcommittee from the innocuous International Organizations to the politically charged Human Rights and International Organizations. By mid-March of 1981 it was not clear which strain of Democratic strategy—the timid or the aggressive—would be dominant.

The typical relationship between an election and public policy outcomes is tenuous, at best.[59] The 1980 election provided as clear and distinct a message of general policy direction as any election since 1964. It is hazardous to project policy outcomes so soon after an election, but our early observations suggest that, in Congress, the results of the 1980 election produced a clear and distinct change in the *political dialogue* and *the political agenda*, with both Democrats and Republicans talking about and focusing on the need to reduce public spending, balance the budget, and shore up our national defense. The change in direction and substance has been evolutionary,

[58] Personal communication with authors.

[59] See Anthony King, "What Do Elections Decide?" in David Butler, Howard R. Penniman, and Austin Ranney, eds., *Democracy at the Polls: A Comparative Study of Competitive National Elections* (Washington, D.C.: American Enterprise Institute, 1981), pp. 293-324.

not abrupt, but if one can recall the items discussed on the political agenda in 1968, or 1972, or 1976, the change is nonetheless remarkable.

The effect of the election on concrete policy—public laws—remains to be seen. There are many indicators that suggest that the sharp right turn evident in the Senate outcomes and, to a slightly lesser extent, the House returns will not mean more sharply conservative policy outcomes in the Ninety-seventh Congress.

True, the 1980 election removed a large number of liberal Democrats from the Senate and brought into the chamber an even larger number of very conservative Republicans—and in the process made Republicans the chairmen of all Senate committees and subcommittees. One must also consider, however, the following points:

• Senior Republicans, who chair all the key committees, are considerably more moderate or liberal in orientation than their junior counterparts. Chairmen such as Hatfield (Appropriations), Packwood (Commerce), Stafford (Environment), Mathias (Rules), and Percy (Foreign Relations) are at least as liberal as their Democratic predecessors. Even conservatives like Dole (Finance), Tower (Armed Services), Garn (Banking), and Domenici (Budget) are very little different in their views on matters confronting their committees from the previous Democratic chairmen. Only in a handful of panels— Judiciary (Thurmond), Energy (McClure), and Labor and Human Resources (Hatch)—are the chairmanship changes dramatic.

• Even with the "new right" surge, a majority of Republicans in Congress are centrists, or moderate conservatives. The junior group in the Senate includes Gorton, Rudman (New Hampshire), Spector, and Andrews from the class of 1980, along with Durenberger (Minnesota), Boschwitz (Minnesota), Kassebaum (Kansas), Cochran (Mississippi), Cohen (Maine), Pressler (South Dakota), Heinz (Pennsylvania), Danforth (Missouri), and Chafee (Rhode Island). In the House, where a band of thirty or so conservative Democrats can join with the Republicans to make a majority on the floor, that majority would be, basically, slightly to the right of center, and not at an extreme.

• An ambitious conservative agenda, ranging from a subminimum wage for youth, repeal of the Davis-Bacon Act, and dismantling the Federal Trade Commission to constitutional amendments on a balanced budget, abortion, school prayer, and busing, requires in each instance a new piece of legislation enacted into law. Any Congress, Republican or Democratic, conservative or liberal, has difficulty passing a lot of new and sweeping laws.

• The ability and desire of the still-Democratic House of Representatives to check the enthusiasm of a conservative Republican Senate was enhanced by the movement up in seniority of a number of tough, aggressive moderates and liberals from the class of 1974. Many now occupy key subcommittee chairmanships in energy, economic, and foreign policy areas. They will dominate the House side on conference committees, often forcing compromises with the Senate on legislation.

Thus, policy in the Ninety-seventh Congress will probably consist of an occasional conservative initiative intermixed with deadlock and eventual compromise on most other matters.

Under typical circumstances, this set of expectations should leave Democrats optimistic about 1982 and Republicans apprehensive. History suggests a Democratic rebound; in every off-year election since 1934, the party in control of the White House lost seats in the House. Still, early in 1981, at least, the opposite sentiments prevailed. Democrats, as we have suggested, continued to reel from the effects of November 1980 and to hesitate over an appropriate response to the Reagan and Republican program.

Republicans looked ahead more eagerly to 1982, planning an impressively financed campaign to strengthen their hold on the Senate and take control of the House. National Republicans hoped to top their 1980 contributions to candidates; overall, the House Republican Campaign Committee announced plans to spend $20 million in 1981 alone, and its Senate counterpart hoped to raise $25 million for the 1982 campaign.[60] In spite of some internal friction over Reagan appointments and policies, the Republicans started the year ebullient over their victory, convinced that the country was behind them, and hopeful that 1982 would continue a basic realignment—making the Republicans the majority party in America. Yet Republican success in 1982 was by no means a sure thing, given the intractable nature of many economic problems and the recent penchant of the American public to transform their dissatisfaction into votes to throw the rascals out. Republicans had good reason to be optimistic about the Senate, given the large number of Democratic seats up once again. A Democratic party comeback in 1982, at least in the House, would signal that 1980 was an aberration, but a continuing Republican surge would indicate a more significant long-term change. In the wake of the elections of 1980, for many in both parties, the 1982 elections were taking on considerably more significance than the typical off-year election.

[60] "GOP Mapping Multimillion-Dollar Fund Drives for Senate and House," *Washington Post*, March 5, 1981.

9

How Not to Select
Presidential Candidates:
A View from Europe

Anthony King

All over Europe in the autumn of 1980, wherever people met to talk politics, there was only one topic of conversation: How on earth had a great country like the United States, filled with talented men and women, managed to land itself with two such second- (or was it third-?) rate presidential candidates as Jimmy Carter and Ronald Reagan?

Europe's political leaders had, of course, to be circumspect in what they said publicly; but the press had no such inhibitions. Newspapers like *Le Monde* of Paris and the *Neue Zürcher Zeitung* were tepid in their response to the two candidates. Leading British newspapers were more outspoken:

> In Europe, there is great bewilderment that the Americans should be landing themselves with a choice between two such mediocre figures. (*Financial Times*)

> It is no wonder that Americans feel that there has been some malfunction of their political system. The President talks perfectly good sense, but his reasonable words and good intentions are somehow converted into unsuccessful policies. Governor Reagan does not sound sensible at all. (*The Times*)

> In short, neither of the two main candidates gives much impression of knowing how they want to lead America in the complicated and difficult years ahead. . . . One sighs for a man of stature. (*Daily Telegraph*)[1]

[1] For typical articles in *Le Monde* and the *Neue Zürcher Zeitung*, see "Un lourd processus," *Le Monde*, November 5, 1980, and "Jimmy Carter trotz allem," *Neue Zürcher Zeitung*, August 18, 1980. The three quotations from British newspapers are from, respectively, "A Hard Choice for the U.S.," *Financial Times*, July 31, 1980; "A Great and Noble Campaign," *The Times* (London), September 3, 1980; and "Presidential Antics," *Daily Telegraph*, September 12, 1980.

Asked to develop their views of the two men in more detail, the great majority of European politicians and public officials would probably have responded roughly like this:

> Carter? A nice enough chap in his way. Certainly well-meaning, undoubtedly intelligent—but, as we all know, hopelessly inept. Raises issues, claims to attach great importance to them, then unexpectedly drops them, often with the result that friends and allies are left out on a limb. No consistent goals or policies; no follow-through. Treats everything on a case-by-case basis: cannot seem to see that in politics everything is interconnected. A curious tendency to moralize everything: whoever heard of a *moral* energy policy!? Came to Washington knowing little about American national politics, or about NATO, or about Europe; after nearly four years, has seemingly learned almost nothing. Surrounds himself with people who are as ignorant of the world as he is. In short, a decent man but hopelessly out of his depth.

> Reagan? Probably no better than Carter, possibly a good deal worse. Like Carter, a man with no real experience of national-level politics; like Carter, too, a man with no previous experience of foreign affairs. An accomplished platform performer, but apparently without any real grasp of the complexity of economic and foreign-affairs issues. Evidently not very bright: seems actually to believe his simple-minded slogans! Said to be lazy. To be sure, a tolerable governor of California, but then that was hardly a difficult post to fill with the state's economy growing as fast as it then was. Most that can be hoped for: that Reagan would choose able people, then delegate a good deal of authority to them. In short, possibly a disaster, at best a sort of down-market Eisenhower.[2]

Such views may have been unfair; they may have been ill informed. But they were certainly widely—indeed almost universally—held in Europe in 1980. This chapter seeks to explain how two men who probably could not have been selected in any European country could become their parties' presidential nominees in the United States, and at the same time to point up certain contrasts between European methods of selecting party leaders and the methods currently being employed in America. Before we proceed, however, it is worth making

---

[2] These are not real quotations but a sort of montage of the views of European politicians, journalists, and businessmen. It is doubtful whether any large number of informed Europeans would have dissented from them.

the point that the views just expressed of Carter and Reagan were not confined to skeptical, world-weary Europeans; they were widely held in the United States itself.

American Views of Carter and Reagan

The available evidence suggests that the two main presidential candidates in 1980 were less well thought of by the American people than any other pair of candidates since at least the 1930s. To a remarkable degree, the year's political jokes were aimed not at Carter or Reagan separately but at the two together. A bumper sticker to be seen in the streets of New York read: "Your candidate is even worse than my candidate." The *Cincinnati Enquirer* published a cartoon showing a campaign committee room with two entrances. The sign outside one read, "Anybody but Carter Hdqtrs," the sign outside the other, "Anybody but Reagan Hdqtrs." The committee room was manned by John Anderson. The cover of *Public Opinion* magazine in June/July 1980 depicted a man wearing four campaign buttons on his lapel. The first three were for Carter, Reagan, and Anderson; the fourth said, "No thanks."[3]

Likewise, the views of newspapers and magazines in America were very similar to those of the European press. "The present prospects are dismaying," the *New York Times* commented in July. The *Washington Post* remarked somewhat later in the campaign:

> There is no way, given the nature of the two prime contenders for the office, that this country is going to elect a president in November who is especially gifted in or suited to the conduct of the office. And that is that.

On the eve of election day itself, *Time* magazine began its concluding story on the campaign:

> For more than a year, two flawed candidates have been floundering toward the final showdown, each unable to give any but his most unquestioning supporters much reason to vote for him except dislike of his opponent.

A survey of more than 1,600 American daily newspapers found that, whereas in 1976 only 168 had refused to endorse any candidate, in 1980 fully 439 insisted on remaining neutral.[4]

[3] The New York bumper sticker was seen by the present writer. The *Cincinnati Enquirer* cartoon was reprinted in *Public Opinion*, June/July 1980, p. 25. The man with the lapel buttons appeared on the cover of the same issue of *Public Opinion*.
[4] The survey was reported in *Newsweek*, November 10, 1980, p. 39. The other quotations are taken from "It's Still 'None of the Above,' " *New York Times*,

TABLE 9–1

VOTERS GIVING "HIGHLY FAVORABLE" RATING TO MAJOR-PARTY PRESIDENTIAL CANDIDATES, 1952–1980

	Percentage of Voters Giving Rating		
	Republican candidate	Democratic candidate	Total
1952	47	37	84
1956	59	33	92
1960	40	42	82
1964	16	49	65
1968	38	25	63
1972	41	21	62
1976	28	41	69
1980	23	30	53

SOURCE: Gallup Poll, *New York Times*, October 31, 1980.

The most important views, however, were the views of the American people themselves. Beginning in 1952, the Gallup poll has asked a sample of voters every four years to rate each of the presidential candidates on a ten-point scale ranging from very favorable to very unfavorable. If the two highest points on each candidate's scale ($+5$ and $+4$) are merged to form a single "highly favorable" rating, then the results for the last eight presidential elections are as shown in table 9–1. Carter individually, it appears, was not as unpopular as Hubert Humphrey in 1968 or George McGovern in 1972; similarly, Reagan individually was not as unpopular as Barry Goldwater in 1964. Taken together, however, the two 1980 candidates were given a "highly favorable" rating by fewer voters than in any of the previous seven Gallup surveys. To take the extreme cases, in 1956, 92 percent of the electorate thought highly of either Dwight Eisenhower or Adlai Stevenson, whereas in 1980 the proportion of voters holding Carter and Reagan in equally high esteem was a mere 53 percent. America's citizens manifested their lack of enthusiasm by

reprinted in *International Herald Tribune*, August 1, 1980; "Using Presidential Power," *Washington Post*, October 20, 1980; and "Battling Down the Stretch," *Time*, November 3, 1980 p. 18.

turning out to vote on November 4 in smaller numbers than at any presidential election since 1948.[5]

In the rest of this chapter, we shall assume for the sake of argument that the instincts of the American people were right—that, compared with the other talent available, Carter and Reagan were (and are) pretty unimpressive political leaders. Such an assumption will clearly not please the minority of ardent Carter and Reagan enthusiasts; but even they may accept that there is some validity in the analysis that follows.

A European Contrast

No system of selecting political leaders can guarantee success. The ancient Athenians chose Pericles but also Alcibiades; the system that resulted in the nomination of Abraham Lincoln was essentially the same system that produced James Buchanan. All that a procedure for choosing leaders can do is make it more or less probable that men and women with certain characteristics, abilities, and aptitudes will emerge. America's presidential candidates in recent years have not, most people now believe, been altogether satisfactory. There may be a connection between this fact and the way in which presidential candidates are currently nominated.

One way of appreciating the peculiar features of America's way of selecting candidates for the country's highest office is to compare it with what happens in other countries. Britain provides an especially useful comparison, partly because it is better documented than most of the others but chiefly because it would be hard to imagine a system more unlike that of the United States; in most respects, as will become clear, the American and British systems are polar opposites. The British system is, moreover, not unusual. Party leaders in Australia, New Zealand, and Japan are selected in much the same way as in Britain, and the leadership-selection systems in most Western European countries certainly resemble the British system more closely than the American.[6]

---

[5] The lowest previous turnout since 1932 was 51.5 percent in 1948. From 1920 to 1932 turnouts in presidential elections ranged from 44.2 percent (1920) to 52.9 (1932). In 1936 turnout rose to 57.5 percent and, except for 1948, has stayed above 54.0 percent until the 1980 election. For a brief discussion, see Richard A. Watson, *The Presidential Contest* (New York: John Wiley, 1980), chap. 4.

[6] Unfortunately, no general comparative study of this subject exists; but see L. F. Crisp, *Australian National Government* (Melbourne: Longmans, 1974); Stephen Levine, *Politics in New Zealand* (Sydney: George Allen and Unwin, 1978); Robert E. Ward, *Japan's Political System*, 2d ed. (Englewood Cliffs, N.J.: Prentice-Hall, 1978); and Anthony King, "Executives," in Fred I. Greenstein and Nelson W. Polsby, eds., *Governmental Institutions and Processes*, vol. 5, *Handbook of Political Science* (Reading, Mass.: Addison-Wesley, 1975), pp. 183-94.

At the time in 1980 when the Democratic and Republican presidential nominees were being chosen in the United States, the leaders of Britain's two largest parties, the Conservatives and Labour, were Margaret Thatcher and James Callaghan. The reader is asked to consider the process by which these two people rose to the leadership of their respective parties. (Both also became prime minister either immediately or later; but it is the process of *selecting* party leaders rather than of *electing* prime ministers that we are concerned with here.)[7]

Margaret Thatcher, a tax lawyer, fought her first parliamentary election in 1950 at the age of twenty-four. She finally entered the House of Commons nine years later at the age of thirty-four. After serving on the Conservative back benches for two years, she was promoted to junior ministerial office in 1961 at the age of thirty-six. She held the office of parliamentary secretary to the Ministry of Pensions and National Insurance until the Conservative party was defeated at the general election of 1964. For the next six years, while the Conservatives were in opposition, she spoke for her party in the House of Commons on housing, pensions, transport, energy, economic affairs, and, latterly, education. Edward Heath, then the Conservative leader, appointed her to his "shadow cabinet" in 1967. When the Conservatives were returned to power in 1970, she entered the real cabinet as secretary of state for education and science, a post she held until the Conservatives were again defeated in February 1974. In the new Parliament, she was first chief Conservative spokesman on housing and local government matters, then her party's shadow chancellor of the exchequer (that is, chief spokesman on economic and financial affairs).

By this time, Edward Heath's political star was sinking fast. The Conservatives had lost three of the four general elections that it had fought under his leadership, and the 1970–1974 Heath government was generally considered a failure. In October 1974 Margaret Thatcher decided to stand against him for the leadership. The election took place some four months later, in the first half of February 1975. All of the candidates were Conservative members of the House of Commons; so were all of the electors. No one outside the House of Commons participated in the election, except as observers. The various candidates' "campaigns," if that is the right

---

[7] The ensuing account of how Thatcher and Callaghan were selected is largely drawn from Anthony King, "Politics, Economics, and the Trade Unions, 1974-1979," in Howard R. Penniman, ed., *Britain at the Polls, 1979: A Study of the General Election* (Washington, D.C.: American Enterprise Institute, 1981), and also from the sources listed there.

word, consisted solely of canvassing and lobbying their fellow members of Parliament (MPs). Thatcher led on the first ballot, but not by quite enough to secure her election outright; on the second ballot, a week later, she won easily. The views of the mass public appear to have played little, if any, part in determining the outcome; opinion polls in 1975 indicated that at least two other prominent Conservatives were more highly regarded than Thatcher. Nevertheless, in becoming Conservative leader, she became automatically her party's candidate for prime minister.

James Callaghan, a minor trade union official, was elected to Parliament at his first attempt in 1945. He was then thirty-three, having served in the navy during the war. In the postwar Labour government, he served in two junior offices, first as parliamentary secretary to the Ministry of Transport, later as parliamentary and financial secretary to the Admiralty (a less important office than it sounds). Labour was defeated in 1951 and spent the next thirteen years in opposition. During this time, Callaghan became a member of the shadow cabinet and gradually a more and more prominent figure in his party; he served both as shadow colonial secretary and as shadow chancellor. When Labour finally returned to power in 1964, he became chancellor of the exchequer, remaining at the Treasury for three years before becoming home secretary in a sideways move in 1967. He was again a member of the shadow cabinet between 1970 and 1974, speaking mainly on foreign affairs; and when Labour was again elected in February 1974, Callaghan became foreign secretary and chief British negotiator with the European Community.

By 1976 Callaghan had probably abandoned his previous ambition of becoming his party's leader and prime minister; but in March 1976 the incumbent prime minister, Harold Wilson, suddenly resigned. Under Labour's rules, a new leader of the party had to be elected immediately. Callaghan stood, together with five other candidates. As in the case of the Conservative party, all of the candidates were MPs; so were all of the electors. Wilson resigned on March 16. The first ballot was held on March 22, the second on March 29, the third on April 5. Callaghan was runner-up on the first ballot but established a commanding lead on the second and finally won on the third. Unlike Thatcher, Callaghan was the most popular of the various contenders so far as the mass electorate was concerned. On becoming Labour leader, since his party was in power at the time, he immediately took over as prime minister.

Eight points need to be made about the British leadership-selection process, if it is to be compared with the American. Several of them have been hinted at already.

1. *The winners had entered politics at an early age and had served for a considerable number of years in Parliament before becoming their party's leader.* Not only had Thatcher been an MP for sixteen years and Callaghan for thirty-one, but also most of their rivals had been around for just as long, in some cases even longer. William Whitelaw, Thatcher's main rival, was first elected to Parliament in 1955; Michael Foot, who finished second to Callaghan, was first elected to the House at the same time as Callaghan, in 1945.

2. *The winners had served in a number of different national-level offices.* Thatcher was somewhat unusual in having been a minister in only two departments (Pensions and National Insurance, and Education), but she had spoken for her party on a wide variety of other subjects. Callaghan was also unusual but in the opposite direction: he is the only prime minister in British history to have previously held all of the other principal offices of state: chancellor of the exchequer, home secretary, and foreign secretary. Most of the other contenders in 1975 and 1976 were at least as experienced as Thatcher, several of them more so.

3. *The candidates were assessed and voted upon exclusively by their fellow politicians.* All of the voters in the two leadership elections had had an opportunity to observe the various contenders at first hand—on the floor of the House of Commons, in committee, in party meetings, in some cases around the cabinet table. Most of them were on first-name terms with the people they were voting for; they were in an excellent position to know their strengths and weaknesses. More than that, they had a powerful incentive to arrive at the right decision since they personally would have to live with the consequences. They would have to work in the House of Commons with the new leader; if they made the wrong decision, they would suffer electorally and possibly also in career terms.[8]

4. *The leadership campaigns were very short.* In one sense, cam-

---

[8] It should perhaps be explained for the benefit of American readers that voting in Britain since well before World War II has largely been party voting. That is, voters have been far more concerned with which party nationally would make the better government than with the personalities and voting records of their individual local candidates. It follows that members of Parliament deciding how to vote in 1975 and 1976 had to consider what effect any given leadership candidate would have on the party's chances nationally and therefore on their own chances locally. Furthermore, whether the party won nationally would determine whether or not they had any chance of becoming government ministers. In short, their personal stakes were high—far higher than, say, the stakes of voters in primary elections in the United States.

paigns for the leadership of Britain's major parties are never-ending, since ambitious politicians, from the moment they first set foot in the House of Commons, are trying to establish their reputations, to have themselves noticed by their parliamentary colleagues; but the time taken for an actual leadership election is highly telescoped. Thatcher declared her candidacy in October 1974; the result was known by mid-February 1975, only twelve weeks later. The Labour contest lasted less than three weeks.

5. *The leadership campaigns involved very little wear and tear on the part of the candidates and their families.* Indeed the very term "campaign," as has already been suggested, is something of a misnomer. Public rallies and national tours have played no part in the election of British party leaders; even television appearances have mattered only insofar as they have influenced the occasional wavering MP. The arena in which the election has historically been fought has been almost entirely the House of Commons. In the weeks between October 1974 and February 1975, Thatcher probably accepted rather more speaking engagements in the country than she would have done otherwise; she undoubtedly appeared more often on television— though always being interviewed or addressing public meetings, never speaking straight-to-camera or trying to sell herself in "Thatcher commercials" (of which there were, and could be, none).[9] The only significant difference that the election probably made to Thatcher's life—apart from the emotional strains inherent in the occasion—was a much increased media interest in her comings and goings. Photographers congregated outside her house; she and other members of her family were pestered for interviews. The interest of the press and television was increased by the fact that she was the first woman to be a serious contender for the leadership of either major party. Nevertheless, her life was not radically disrupted by the contest, except possibly during the last few days, and the House of Commons remained her main base of operations. In the case of Labour, the leadership contest made even less difference to the contenders. With Labour in power, all six candidates were already senior cabinet ministers. They all had big jobs to do; they were already in the public eye; they actually had to meet together several times a week to discuss government business. To be sure, they were photographed

[9] There could be none because in Britain candidates for office are not permitted to buy time on television or radio to advertise themselves. At general elections, political parties are allotted a certain amount of free time; but this was not a general election. Even if the candidates had been able to buy time, it is doubtful whether they would have done so: a television spot seen by millions of people is not the most efficient way to reach some 250-300 people, whom one is anyway in a position to see almost every day.

rather more often than usual; they were the subject of minibiographies on television; their wives were endlessly rung up by women's magazines. But that was about it.

6. *The leadership campaigns cost next to nothing*—largely for the reasons just given. Thatcher and her supporters undoubtedly had to do a certain amount of entertaining of their fellow MPs, and they must have run up considerable telephone and taxi bills. In the Labour party, entertaining has less part to play, but the telephone and taxi bills were probably about the same. At a guess, the Conservative leadership contest cost all of those involved a total of about £2,500—say, $6,000. It is doubtful whether the total cost of the Labour contest, to both the party and all of the participants, was more than £1,000—call it $2,500. Certainly there was no need to raise funds, and there were therefore neither fund raisers nor campaign contributors.

7. *The process of electing the leader in each case was entirely a party process.* The rules governing the internal affairs of political parties in Britain are, in effect, like the rules of a private club. Legislatures and courts neither determine what they should contain nor (except in very rare cases) decide how they should be applied. Thatcher was chosen by members of the Conservative party, Callaghan by members of the Labour party. The mass public played no part in the two contests; neither, except very marginally and indirectly, did television and the press. The parties made the decisions; outsiders merely watched.

8. *Electoral considerations did not loom large in the minds of most MPs as they decided how to cast their ballots.* Somewhat surprisingly, since the personality of the party leader is likely to have at least some bearing on how well the party does at the next general election, the evidence suggests that most MPs, in deciding whom to vote for, are not overly influenced by electoral considerations—or at least by opinion-poll findings. Thatcher was not the most popular Conservative in the country in 1975, but she won. Callaghan was the most popular Labour figure in the eyes of the electorate a year later, but it took him three ballots to defeat the much less popular Michael Foot. MPs appear to be chiefly influenced by considerations of policy and ideology and, probably to a lesser extent, by which of the contenders they think will make the better prime minister. This is a subtle, little-researched point, and there is no need to go into greater detail here.[10]

[10] British MPs, wisely or unwisely, behave as though they believe either that ideological and policy considerations are more important than electoral ones or

So much for how the people who led Britain's two major political parties in the summer of 1980 were originally selected. Now contrast the processes just described with the processes that resulted in Jimmy Carter's and Ronald Reagan's becoming the presidential nominees of the Democratic and Republican parties in the United States. To do so is to enter a different world.[11]

Carter, a small-town businessman and former naval officer, first ran for the governorship of Georgia in 1966. He was then forty-two and had already served two terms in the Georgia state senate. His first attempt at the governorship failed, but he then spent the whole of the next four years campaigning around the state, and in 1970 his efforts were rewarded; he won a runoff election by a handsome margin, defeating a previously popular incumbent. Although he lacked any experience of national politics and government, Carter's eyes were already on the presidency, and in 1972, halfway through the one term that Georgia's state constitution allowed him as governor, he and his advisers decided that he should make a bid for the Democratic presidential nomination in 1976. George McGovern had proved an appallingly bad candidate in 1972, and the race for the 1976 nomination looked as though it were going to be wide open. In order to make himself better known nationally, Carter volunteered to serve as the Democrats' campaign coordinator for the 1974 midterm congressional elections. He announced his presidential candidacy in December of that year.

For the next eighteen months, the ex-governor of Georgia campaigned full time for his party's nomination. He began by dispatching 500,000 letters to potential campaign contributors. In the course of 1975, he traveled from coast to coast, spending time in forty-six states and the District of Columbia. To win the nomination, he needed, in some states, the support of state and local party leaders; but his main appeal had to be to the millions of ordinary citizens

---

that whomever they elect can be counted on, as the result of increased television exposure and such like, to become an acceptable national figure. Alternatively, they may be misinformed about opinion-poll findings or may simply not believe them. The point is discussed briefly at various points in King, "Politics, Economics, and the Trade Unions."

11 The ensuing account of the nominations of Carter and Reagan is based largely on Martin Schram, *Running for President: A Journal of the Carter Campaign* (New York: Pocket Books, 1977); James Wooten, *Dasher: The Roots and Rising of Jimmy Carter* (New York: Warner Books, 1979); Jules Witcover, *Marathon: The Pursuit of the Presidency, 1972-1976* (New York: Viking, 1977); Hedrick Smith et al., *Reagan: The Man, the President* (New York: Macmillan, 1980); and Richard Harwood, ed., *The Pursuit of the Presidency 1980* (New York: Berkley Books, 1980).

eligible to vote in the twenty-nine primary elections due to be held in 1976. The primaries would choose or bind nearly 75 percent of the 3,008 delegates to the Democratic National Convention in July. In the end, Carter's name appeared on the ballot in twenty-six states, and he campaigned actively in most of them. Altogether some 15.6 million people turned out to vote in the Democratic primaries; 6.3 million of them voted for Carter. He won the first primary in New Hampshire in February and had the nomination effectively sewn up by the beginning of June. His victory in the primaries and the state caucuses was ratified on the first ballot at the party's nominating convention in New York City. Democratic senators, congressmen, and governors played little part in the selection process—beyond, in most cases, casting their own primary ballots. In 1980, although he was president, Carter was forced to campaign again for the Democratic nomination.

Ronald Reagan, a retired film actor and professional after-dinner speaker, fought his first election in 1966 when he was already fifty-five years old. He was elected governor of California at this first attempt and was reelected to a second four-year term in 1970. He had had a certain amount of previous political experience, raising money and speaking for Barry Goldwater during the latter's ill-fated presidential campaign in 1964. Although, like Jimmy Carter, Ronald Reagan lacked firsthand experience of national government, Reagan's thoughts, like Carter's, soon turned toward the White House. He sought the Republican presidential nomination in 1968, though in that year he did little campaigning on his own behalf. Matters were quite different when it came to the 1976 nomination. By this time Reagan, no longer governor of California, was free to devote his whole time to his drive for the presidency—a circumstance that gave him a considerable advantage over the incumbent president, Gerald Ford. Reagan announced his candidacy in the summer of 1975 and, with the aid of crossover votes from conservative Democrats and independents, fared well in the Republican primaries in the following year, winning 50.7 percent of the vote to Ford's 49.3 percent. Ford, however, had a slight edge among delegates to the Kansas City convention and was able to win the nomination on the first ballot.

By the summer of 1976, Ronald Reagan had been working toward the presidency for nearly eight years—only part time between 1968 and 1975 but virtually full time in the months since then. For the next four years, throughout the lifetime of Jimmy Carter's presidency, he went on working. He visited nearly every state in the union, taping radio commentaries, giving thousands of speeches, shaking thousands of hands, traversing hundreds of thousands of miles. When in November 1979 he formally announced that he intended to run, he already had the support of most Republican leaders in states where such support counted; but his main objective, like Carter's four years before, was the amassing of votes in primary elections. As it turned out, Reagan's path was even smoother than Carter's in 1976 (and far smoother than Carter's in 1980). He drubbed his chief rival, George Bush, in New Hampshire in February and by the time of the Michigan primary in May had won enough delegates to secure the nomination. Of the 12.8 million votes cast in the Republican primaries, Reagan won 7.6 million (60 percent). In the Republican party, as in the Democratic, public officeholders played no formal role—and very little actual role—in the contest. When Reagan was finally acclaimed at his party's convention in Detroit in July 1980, he was sixty-nine years old. He had been campaigning for the presidency for the better part of a dozen years.

These events in the United States can easily be compared, point by point, with the events surrounding the selection of Margaret Thatcher and James Callaghan as party leaders on the other side of the Atlantic.

1. *The two winners in the United States had entered politics in middle age, and neither had very much experience of government.* Carter first ran for statewide office at the age of forty-two, Reagan at the age of fifty-five. By contrast, Thatcher first stood for Parliament when she was only twenty-four, Callaghan when he was thirty-three. At the time he won the Democratic nomination, Carter had spent four years in the Georgia state legislature and another four years as the state's governor; Reagan had spent eight years as California's governor in Sacramento. These two stints of eight years compare with Margaret Thatcher's sixteen years in the British House of Commons and James Callaghan's thirty-one.

2. *Neither winner in the United States had ever served in any capacity in the national government, whether in Washington or overseas. Moreover, at the time of their nomination neither held any public office whatsoever.* Indeed it is scarcely too strong to say that America's presidential nominees were drawn from the ranks of the unemployed. This was not true of all of the contenders for the two major parties' nominations in 1976 and 1980. Apart from the incumbent presidents in both years, in 1976 Democrats Henry Jackson (Washington) and Frank Church (Idaho) were both long-serving U.S. senators, and Democrat Morris Udall (Arizona) was a prominent member of the House of Representatives. Carter's chief rival in 1980, Edward Kennedy (Massachusetts), was also a U.S. senator.

Among the Republicans in 1980, Howard Baker (Tennessee) was the Senate minority leader, and John Connally had served in the federal executive branch as secretary of the navy under John Kennedy and secretary of the treasury under Richard Nixon. George Bush had had the most varied experience, having served two terms in the House of Representatives and subsequently as ambassador to the United Nations, chief of the U.S. liaison office in Peking, and director of the Central Intelligence Agency. Bush, however, lost—and so did all of the others. Thatcher was relatively inexperienced by British standards when she became Conservative leader, but she had been a member of the Macmillan, Home, and Heath administrations for six and a half years and a member of the Heath cabinet for three and a half. Callaghan, as mentioned earlier, had held all three of the top posts in the British system. Moreover, at the time of their selection as party leaders both Thatcher and Callaghan were members of Parliament. Callaghan was also foreign secretary.[12]

3. *The candidates in the United States were assessed and voted upon by party activists in some states but mainly by voters in primary elections. No special weight was attached to the views of public officeholders or to the views of those who had worked with the candidates or had had a chance to observe them at first hand.* Senators, congressmen, governors, and others were in a position to endorse whichever candidates they preferred, and the candidates' own extensive travels enabled thousands of voters at least to catch a glimpse of them; but most activists and primary electors probably paid little attention to the endorsements, and of course the great majority had never been in the physical presence of any of the candidates, let alone done business with them. Instead they were forced to form their impressions from what they could read in the printed media or see on television. The candidates' performances were all there was, and except for the incumbent presidents, Ford in 1976 and Carter in 1980, the performances that mattered were not in high office but on the small screen. Hence the large role played by the mass media in the selection of American presidential candidates; hence also the uneasiness of many people in the American media about the role that they play.[13] The contrast with the British

---

[12] Much the best, indeed almost the only, comparative study of the selection of British prime ministers and American presidents is Hugh Heclo, "Presidential and Prime Ministerial Selection," in Donald R. Matthews, ed., *Perspectives on Presidential Selection* (Washington, D.C.: The Brookings Institution, 1973). Heclo, writing in 1973, emphasized the experience of American presidents and presidential candidates; in 1981 the picture looks somewhat different.

[13] See, for example, David Broder's remarks about the "unhealthy and unnatural

system in this connection is complete. Thatcher and Callaghan were chosen by their fellow MPs—that is, by political insiders—and by no one else.

4. *The campaigns of would-be presidential nominees in the United States last for a very long time.* There is hardly any need to labor this point. Thatcher's campaign for the leadership of the Conservative party took twelve weeks; Reagan's campaign for the leadership of the Republican party took the best part of twelve years. The Labour party in March/April 1976 took three weeks to elect its new leader; Carter was on the campaign trail more or less continuously from the summer of 1974 until the summer of 1976. In the United States, staying power is at a premium.

5. *Campaigns for presidential nominations in the United States involve an enormous amount of wear and tear on the part of the candidates and their families.* "Wear and tear" is not easy to measure, and that which exhausts one person can be counted on to exhilarate another. Nevertheless, anyone reading accounts of would-be presidential nominees stumping the country must be impressed by the heavy toll that the whole process exacts: loss of sleep, loss of privacy, disrupted schedules, news conferences at which no one shows up, the endless room-service meals, the long, dreary hours in airport lounges. The same words keep cropping up: "grueling," "exhausting," "tiredness," "fatigue." Vignettes stick in the mind: Edmund Muskie weeping in the snows of New Hampshire, Jimmy Carter sprawled full-length on a sofa at LaGuardia Airport waiting for a long-delayed plane and seizing "an opportunity to at least make up for nights of lost sleep."[14] The essential point is that someone who wishes to compete for a major-party presidential nomination in the United States has to cast his life in an entirely new mold. Campaigning in primaries and caucuses is not something that one does part time, in the midst of other activities. It becomes, in itself, a way of life—"a severe test," in the words of Morris Udall, "of your stamina, your digestion, your marriage and your sense of humor."[15] Among recent candidates, only Ronald Reagan seems to have been able to avoid

---

significance [of] the role of the mass media," in *Choosing Presidential Candidates: How Good Is the New Way?* (Washington, D.C.: American Enterprise Institute, 1979), p. 11, and also a large number of the comments in John Foley, Dennis A. Britton, and Eugene B. Everett, Jr., eds., *Nominating a President: The Process and the Press* (New York: Praeger, 1980).

14 Schram, *Running for President*, p. 118.

15 Quoted by Saul Pett, "Ex-Candidates, on Presidential Race: Mad, Mad Marathon," *New York Times*, August 30, 1980. The Pett article is full of good stories about the awfulness of campaigning for the presidency.

some of the strain. Even when he first ran for the governorship of California at the age of fifty-five, he often managed a nap in the afternoon.[16] Again, the contrast between the all-consuming nature of American presidential nominating politics and the more low-key, contained way in which Thatcher and Callaghan were elected in Britain is striking.

6. *The campaigns in the United States cost enormous sums of money, and the candidates and their staffs have to devote a great deal of time and effort to raising money.* Jimmy Carter launched his campaign for the Democratic nomination by writing to potential campaign contributors, and raising money is one of the key tasks of American campaign organizations, even at the prenomination stage. Television and radio time have to be paid for; so do newspaper advertisements, direct mailings, travel facilities, staffers, consultants, opinion polls, and telephone calls. While the Federal Election Campaign Act has relieved some of the pressure on fund raisers by providing for federal underwriting of both primary and general election contests, at the same time the new legislation forces candidates to raise much larger numbers of small contributions. Quite apart from changes in the law, the costs of campaigning in the United States are high—much higher than in most other countries—and continue to rise. In 1976, the Democratic and Republican preconvention campaigns cost the participants and the federal government roughly $67 million; in 1980, the total was nearer $100 million.[17] If the rough estimates given above of the costs of Britain's two party-leadership elections in 1975 and 1976 are accepted as broadly accurate, then the costs of selecting American presidential candidates are some eight to ten thousand times greater than the costs of selecting party leaders in Britain.

7. *The process of selecting presidential candidates in the United States is by no means an exclusively party process.* On the contrary, as has often been pointed out, American political parties in the 1980s are not stable organizations, like parties in most other countries; they are rather prizes to be competed for. Most recent presidential aspirants have had long associations with the Democratic or the Republican party; but they need not have had. More to the point, those deciding who will be the party's standard-bearer in a presidential election include people who regard themselves as party regulars; but

[16] Adam Clymer, "A Star Is Born," in Smith et al., *Reagan*, p. 11.

[17] For the 1976 figures, see Stephen J. Wayne, *The Road to the White House: The Politics of Presidential Elections* (New York: St. Martin's Press, 1980), p. 28. The 1980 figures are taken from Herbert E. Alexander, "Financing the Campaigns and Parties of 1980" (Paper delivered at Sangamon State University, Springfield, Illinois, December 3, 1980).

they also include, in far greater numbers, people with no continuing commitment to the party, people with no commitment to any party, and even people strongly committed to the opposition party. Such are the consequences of opening the candidate selection process to ordinary voters in primary elections. Yet again, the contrast with Britain is marked—indeed total.

8. *Electoral considerations may have loomed large in the minds of many of the party regulars who attended caucuses in 1976 and 1980, but they probably figured scarcely at all in the minds of most voters in the primaries.* American presidential nominating contests used to be concerned, in large part, with "picking a winner." The delegates to the quadrennial conventions wanted a man to head the ticket who would pull in the party's other candidates on his coattails. Those days are gone. Not only are presidential candidates' coattails badly frayed in an age of split-ticket voting, but those who select candidates for the presidency—chiefly voters in primaries—are hardly concerned with complicated tactical considerations. They seldom ask, Which of these candidates do I think other people would be most likely to vote for if he were the candidate of my party? Rather, they ask simply, Who would I like to be president? Even more important is the fact that those who vote in primary elections are in no sense a microcosm of the electorate as a whole. Not only are they vastly fewer in number (32.3 million people voted in the primaries in 1980, 86.5 million in the November election), but all of the available studies indicate that they are a highly biased sample of the total population; they are more highly educated, more interested in politics, and considerably more likely than the electorate as a whole to hold extreme views.[18] In addition to all this, the system, as it now functions, makes it possible for a contender to "win" the primaries and to go on to become his party's presidential candidate even though he has won substantially less than half of the votes cast in the primaries; for example, in 1976 Carter "won" the Democratic primaries with only 39.9 percent of the total vote.[19] In other words, under the present system a party's candidate can be the choice of a minority of a

[18] Voters in primary elections are still just about the most understudied major participants in American political life; but see Austin Ranney and Leon D. Epstein, "The Two Electorates: Voters and Non-Voters in a Wisconsin Primary," *Journal of Politics*, vol. 28 (1966), pp. 598-616; Austin Ranney, "The Representativeness of Primary Electorates," *Midwest Journal of Political Science*, vol. 12 (1968), pp. 224-38; and Austin Ranney, "Turnout and Representation in Presidential Primary Elections," *American Political Science Review*, vol. 66 (1972), pp. 21-37.

[19] Gerald M. Pomper et al., *The Election of 1976: Reports and Interpretations* (New York: Longmans, 1977), pp. 14-15.

minority—and a biased minority at that. The bizarre outcome in 1980 was that the most open, most "democratic" leadership-selection system ever devised resulted in the nomination of the two least-respected and least-admired presidential candidates in modern American history. There should, however, have been no surprise about this, given the nature of the primary electorate. Even if there were a national primary, or a system in which would-be candidates had to secure 50 percent plus one of the primary vote in order to be nominated, it would still be perfectly possible for the minority of primary voters to plump for candidates whom the majority of the whole electorate did not want. More surprising, perhaps, is the fact that in Britain members of Parliament, who might be thought to have a personal stake in picking a winner, nevertheless frequently, like voters in primaries in the United States, choose a leader who is not the person that the voters at large prefer.[20]

Despite this last, rather unexpected similarity between the British and American systems for choosing party leaders and presidential candidates, the two systems are otherwise different in almost every particular: in who the potential candidates are, in who does the choosing, in how the choices are made. The contrast, in fact, is virtually complete.

Assessing the American System

The facts having been established, we now need to offer some assessment of them. Needless to say, it is not the purpose of this chapter to argue that "British is best." The British case was chosen, as we said earlier, partly because it is well documented, partly because it offers such a striking contrast to the American, but chiefly because the leadership selection systems in most liberal democracies resemble the British more closely than the American; the American system could equally well have been compared with, say, the Australian or the Swedish. In any case, the British system is neither perfect nor immutable. The Conservatives adopted their present arrangements as recently as 1965; the Labour party in 1980–1981 was taking active steps to adopt an entirely new system, one that would give a large say in the election of Labour leaders—and hence of potential Labour prime ministers—to the massed battalions of Britain's trade unions and to the party's activists in the constituencies.[21]

---

[20] See section "A European Contrast" and n. 10.

[21] At its regular annual conference in Blackpool in October 1980, the Labour party voted to extend the franchise in its leadership elections beyond the parlia-

The contrast between the British system and the American does, however, serve to point up certain weaknesses inherent in the present American system, weaknesses of which many people in the United States are well aware.

To begin with, the length of the American nominating process and its grueling character undoubtedly have the effect of causing many able men and women to eliminate themselves from the race before it has even begun. Candidates in any system are, of course, compared with other candidates, but they should also be compared with non-candidates—people who might have run but chose not to. We ought to ask: Are there able and qualified persons who might make good presidents but are deterred from seeking their party's presidential nomination by the present arrangements? Suppose for the sake of argument that the pool of potential presidential candidates is taken to consist of serving U.S. senators and congressmen and state governors. Are there people in this pool who, contemplating the race as it now is, a combination of high hurdles and marathon, say to themselves, "I want no part of it"? It would be amazing if such people did not exist; rumor suggests that they do.[22] The most famous case of someone who did enter the race but abandoned it after completing the first lap is Walter Mondale, later vice-president under Carter. Mondale stumped the country between 1972 and 1974 with his eye on the 1976 Democratic nomination, but he did not like what incessant campaigning was doing to himself and his family, and he quit in November 1974, more than a year before the first primary. He announced in a public statement:

> I found I did not have the overwhelming desire to be President which is essential for the kind of campaign that is required. . . . I don't think anyone should be President who is not willing to go through the fire. . . . I admire those with

---

mentary party. At a special conference in Wembley in January 1981, it decided that trade unions should have 40 percent of the vote in Labour leadership elections, constituency activists 30 percent, and Labour members of Parliament, who had hitherto had 100 percent, only the remaining 30 percent. Hardly had the Wembley decision been taken, however, than there were moves afoot to try, at the next regular conference in Brighton in October 1981, to improve the parliamentary party's position. Whatever the outcome of that conference, it seemed all but certain in the summer of 1981 that Labour's leadership-election system described earlier in this chapter had gone forever. The conservatives' system, however, was likely to remain the same.

[22] The present writer is personally aware of at least one member of the House of Representatives, who, although he might well make an electable presidential candidate and a first-class president, decided long ago that the race was simply not worth running: the costs are too great, the chances of success too slight.

the determination to do what is required to seek the presidency, but I have found I am not among them.[23]

How many other able men and women have, to the nation's cost, made the same discovery?

Mondale made his abortive bid for the presidency while a senator and a leading member of his party in the upper house. He knew perfectly well that, in his bid, he was handicapped as a candidate by being a senator and handicapped as a senator by being a candidate. So time- and energy-consuming has the pursuit of the presidency become that those who currently hold high public office are at a distinct disadvantage compared with those who do not. Not only can those who have left office behind them, or indeed never held it, devote more time and energy to campaigning, but they do not constantly have to choose between fulfilling their primary office-holding responsibilities and following the dictates of their personal ambition. "That was very clearly illustrated by Senator Jackson who in 1976 was continually torn between the needs of a presidential campaign and the needs of being in the Senate, especially for discussion of those issues on which he [had] the greatest expertise." [24] Howard Baker was probably putting it a little strongly in 1980 when he suggested that the current American system "requires you to be unemployed to be a successful candidate"; but the fact remains that, vice-presidents and incumbent presidents apart, three of the last four presidential nominees—Nixon, Carter, and Reagan—held no public office, major or minor, at the time of their nomination.[25] If those who hold no public office are indeed at an advantage over their office-holding rivals, it follows that future presidents of the United States, like the last two on the day of their inauguration, are likely to be

---

[23] Quoted in Arthur T. Hadley, *The Invisible Primary* (Englewood Cliffs, N.J.: Prentice-Hall, 1976), p. 38. Portions of the Hadley volume concerning Mondale are reprinted in James I. Lengle and Byron E. Shafer, eds., *Presidential Politics: Readings on Nominations and Elections* (New York: St. Martin's Press, 1980), pp. 69-77. Michael J. Robinson has similarly observed: "The primary system has made it so that the nice guys, including the competent ones, stay out of the whole ordeal. Right from the start, the primary system means that only those who possess near psychopathic ambition and temperament will get involved and stay involved." These and other similar remarks are quoted in Herbert B. Asher, *Presidential Elections and American Politics: Voters, Candidates, and Campaigns since 1952*, 2d ed. (Homewood, Ill.: Dorsey Press, 1980), p. 307.

[24] Jeane J. Kirkpatrick in Jeane J. Kirkpatrick et al., *The Presidential Nominating Process: Can It Be Improved?* (Washington, D.C.: American Enterprise Institute, 1980), pp. 9-10.

[25] Baker is quoted in Pett, "Ex-Candidates, on Presidential Race."

individuals without, as Howard Baker put it, "current information about the problems that confront the country."[26]

Presidential candidates under the American system may well not be immersed currently in national and international problems; it is also true that they may never have been so immersed. Carter in 1976 had never been nearer Washington (let alone London, Paris, Bonn, Moscow, or Peking) than Atlanta; Reagan in 1980 had never been nearer than Sacramento.[27] In the British and most other leadership-selection systems, the formal rules, or alternatively the informal norms, require that would-be national leaders should have had substantial national-level political experience, typically in both the executive and the legislative branches of government. Even if the rules and norms in these countries did not so require, it is still likely that, in any system in which those who choose national party leaders include a significant proportion of people who are themselves national-level politicians, the results will tend to favor people from similar backgrounds; whatever the rules, national politicians will tend to choose other national politicians. In the United States, by contrast, neither the rules and norms nor the men and women who select presidential candidates—whether voters in primaries or delegates to state caucuses and conventions—appear to attach any great significance to high-level experience of government in Washington. On the contrary, both Carter and Reagan were able to make a virtue out of being their party's non-Washington, even anti-Washington, presidential candidate. They arrived in Washington the first two presidents since Woodrow Wilson wholly innocent of national-level governmental experience.[28] Most observers thought that the results were all too apparent in Carter's four-year term of office; it remains to be seen whether Reagan will learn more and faster.

More generally, a disjunction seems to have developed in the United States between the qualities required to win the presidential nomination of one's party and the qualities required to be a good president. To win the nomination, a person needs to be able to attract media attention, to be able to communicate easily with ordinary

---

26 Ibid.

27 The literal-minded may protest that both men had traveled widely and that Carter had played a prominent part in the so-called Trilateral Commission. But of course that is not the point: to visit Washington, even on business, is not the same as working there. Carter as president showed no real understanding either of politics in Washington or of how the world looked from the vantage point of foreign capitals.

28 See the table in Heclo, "Presidential and Prime Ministerial Selection," pp. 31-32.

citizens, above all to be able to project an attractive image of himself on the small screen. He needs, in other words, to be someone who can convey a lot in a few words to a very large number of people. Some of these skills are required by an incumbent president, but some of them are not (presidents of the United States have no need to attract media attention: they have far too much already). More to the point, to win a presidential nomination in the age of caucuses and primaries, a person no longer has to do business with others, to build coalitions, or to bargain with people who possess things that he should acquire if he is to achieve his goals. It is enough that he be a supersalesman of himself. Before 1968 in the United States, a man who wanted to be president had to build a coalition out of the very same elements— members of Congress, big-state governors, big-city mayors, the leaders of major interest groups—upon which he would have to rely if and when he reached the White House. Not so in the 1980s:

> In the present nominating system, he comes as a fellow whose only coalition is whatever he got out of the living rooms in Iowa. If there is one thing that Jimmy Carter's frustration in office ought to teach us, it is that the affiliation and the commitment that is made on Iowa caucus night and New Hampshire primary day is not by itself sufficient to sustain a man for four years in the White House.[29]

Such problems are, of course, short-circuited in a leadership-selection system like the British: The people with whom a party leader will have to work are the very people who elected him.

Underlying both the lack of experience exhibited by recent presidential candidates, and also doubts about whether they have the requisite political skills, is the fact, all but unique to the modern American political system, that the elected officeholders of a party play almost no part in selecting the party's presidential nominee. This fact has been mentioned before, but it needs to be emphasized again. In almost every political system but the American, the man or woman who wants to make it to the top needs to acquire the support of people who have been in the best position, usually over a considerable period of many years, to observe him or her at close range: namely, the individual's fellow national politicians. Such politicians are better placed than anyone else could possibly be to assess their colleague's strengths and weaknesses, many of which are likely to manifest themselves, not in front of the television cameras, but in the cut and thrust of legislative debate or behind the closed doors of committee rooms.

---

[29] David Broder in *Choosing Presidential Candidates*, pp. 7-8.

In most political systems, these national-level politicians act as a sort of screening device or filter between the political parties and the mass electorate; they provide, in the American jargon, an element of "peer review." This element is entirely missing in the United States today.[30]

The primary-centered method of choosing presidential candidates is also part cause and part consequence of the general decline of America's political parties. Parties in the United States, as has often been pointed out, no longer provide cues to the electorate on the scale that they once did; they no longer even control their own nominations. The results are hard to disentangle from other important changes taking place within the American polity; but it seems reasonable to associate the decline of parties with the further blurring of lines of responsibility and accountability in the American system, the increasing alienation and frustration of the American electorate, the continuing assertiveness of interest groups, especially single-interest groups, the personalization of American politics, the seeming inability of Congress and the presidency to work together, and, more generally, a tendency in American government, reminiscent of the French Fourth Republic, toward immobilism and stalemate. If America's parties were to disappear completely—

> the candidate organizations, the women's caucuses, the black caucuses, the right-to-life leagues, and the like would become the only real players in the game. The mass communications media would become the sole agencies for sorting out the finalists from the original entrants [in presidential nominating politics] and for defining the voters' choices. And the societal functions of interest-aggregation, consensus-building and civil war–prevention would presumably be left to the schools, the churches, and perhaps Common Cause and Nader's Raiders.[31]

If such an outcome is to be avoided, changes will almost certainly need to be made in the way in which presidential candidates are selected. A larger strictly "party" element in the selection of presidential nominees will have to be reintroduced, if not on the British model, then on some other.[32]

---

30 On the question of peer review, see David Broder in *Choosing Presidential Candidates*, p. 3; and Austin Ranney in Kirkpatrick et al., *The Presidential Nominating Process*, p. 6.

31 Austin Ranney, "The Political Parties: Reform and Decline" in Anthony King, ed., *The New American Political System* (Washington, D.C.: American Enterprise Institute, 1978), p. 247.

32 For a variety of suggestions on how the presidential nominating process might be reformed—or, rather, improved—see Kirkpatrick et al., *The Presidential*

Another consequence of the primary-centered method of choosing presidential candidates is to increase greatly the political vulnerability of first-term presidential incumbents. Once upon a time, a president of the United States, however disastrous, could count on being renominated by his party (always assuming that he wanted to be). To so great an extent did incumbency matter. It now matters a great deal less, and in an era of intractable international and economic problems may even be a handicap. Ford in 1976 and Carter in 1980 only just managed to fight off the challenges of rival candidates within their own parties; Reagan will be very lucky not to face a similar challenge in 1984. Opinions differ about the desirability of first-term presidents' being vulnerable in this way. On the one hand, it can be argued that the fear of formidable challenges in the primaries makes American presidents more sensitive to the wishes of the American people than they used to be; on the other, it can be alleged that, precisely because they are fearful of such challenges, they may conduct themselves from the moment of their inauguration with one eye on the electorate. Whatever the merits of this particular debate, it is clear that for the foreseeable future first-term presidents will spend enormous amounts of time and energy in their third and fourth years in office trying to make sure that they are renominated as well as reelected. Whether presidents can afford to spend quite such large quantities of time and energy in this way is open to question.

Finally, it is worth commenting on one rather strange consequence of the virtually total elimination of the element of peer review from American presidential politics. Peer groups, to be sure, have a way of becoming completely obsessed with their own internal dynamics, of becoming oblivious of the needs and desires of the outside world; but at the same time such groups often have the ability to make very accurate judgments about their own members—to overlook their superficial characteristics and to evaluate them at their true worth. In Britain in recent years, the Conservatives have been adventurous enough to choose a woman as their leader; similarly, the Labour party, in electing Michael Foot as James Callaghan's successor toward the end of 1980, showed itself prepared to elect a somewhat improbable-looking old man with untidy hair, thick spectacles, and a walk like Charlie Chaplin's. It is clear that in both cases their chances of selec-

---

Nominating Process, pp. 15-27; Everett Carll Ladd, "A Better Way to Pick Presidents," *Fortune*, May 5, 1980, pp. 132-37; and Tom Wicker, "The Elections: Why the System Has Failed," *New York Review of Books*, August 14, 1980, pp. 11-15. Almost all the suggestions for improvement involve giving a larger say in the nominating process to a party's public officeholders and more generally to people with a continuing commitment to the party.

tion were considerably greater among their fellow MPs, their peers, than if the choice had been made by millions of ordinary voters with no more to go on than what they could see on their television screens. One does not have to be an especial admirer of either Thatcher or Foot to acknowledge the possibility that a small-group, face-to-face system, containing a large element of peer review, may considerably widen the range of potential national leaders. "Presidents today," as Jeane Kirkpatrick has written concerning the post-1968 presidential nominating process, "must be fit and not fat, amusing not dull, with cool not hot personalities."[33] She might have added that they must also be white and male. It is, however, not proven that great American presidents are to be found only in the ranks of the thin, the amusing, the cool, the white, the male, the glib, the invariably smiling, and the televisually presentable—even though the present arrangements for choosing American presidential nominees clearly assume that they are. By a strange but not uncommon irony, a system designed to maximize "openness" has probably had the unintended effect of barring the way to the top in American politics of a very large proportion of America's population.[34]

No system of selecting political leaders, as we said right at the beginning, can guarantee success; none is foolproof. Other countries, including Britain, have produced their duds; the old ways of nominating presidential candidates in the United States yielded such second-raters, all within the same decade, as Warren G. Harding, James M. Cox, Calvin Coolidge, and John W. Davis. It may be that in 1984 the American people will be offered a more impressive choice than they were in 1980. It may be, too, that Ronald Reagan will turn out to be a better president than many people expect; it certainly behooves the rest of the world to suspend judgment. All the same, it must be said that America's friends abroad view with considerable apprehension the prospect of a long line of Carters and Reagans as presidential candidates. It does seem that recent developments in the American presidential nominating system have greatly increased the probability

[33] Jeane Kirkpatrick, *Dismantling the Parties: Reflections on Party Reform and Party Decomposition* (Washington, D.C.: American Enterprise Institute, 1978), p. 7.

[34] This argument must not be pressed too far. A peer group may be extraordinarily conventional in its judgments if its members are guided not by what they think but by what they think others think. To take the obvious case, it took a primary election, in West Virginia in 1960, to persuade the leaders of the Democratic party that a Catholic could be elected president. Most European systems differ from the American in that voters are being asked to vote for a party as a whole, not for a single individual. Under these circumstances the personality of the leader is likely to be less important electorally.

that men will be nominated who lack relevant experience and have no evident aptitude for one of the most demanding and powerful jobs on earth. Changes in the system that had the effect of reducing the role of primary elections and of providing for an increased element of peer review would be enormously welcomed by most of America's friends and allies in Europe and—dare one say it?—probably in the end by most Americans too.

10

The Party of Government, the Party of Opposition, and the Party of Balance: An American View of the Consequences of the 1980 Election

Aaron Wildavsky

The election of 1980 is pregnant with many possibilities. It could be the beginning of a Republican renaissance, but it could just as well be the beginning of the end of the Republican party. It could be the herald of smaller government, we hear, but perhaps it is the siren song of big government, dashing on the rocks of desire for power the naive hopes that less could be more. The point is that the importance of an event is not only inherent in it but also in what it becomes. When we ask whether 1980 was a critical election, we are asking about more than whatever is in the Reagan administration and its supporters. We are asking what the world will do to them as well as what they will try to do to it.

With a Republican administration in the White House, a slim Republican majority in the Senate, and gains in the House of Representatives, it is easy to imagine the Republican party in the ascendant. Still, as the song says, "It ain't necessarily so." From the early 1930s until 1980, at least, the United States could reasonably be characterized as having a party-and-a-half system. Something like two-thirds of the potential electorate (including so-called independents who lean toward one party or the other) identify themselves as Democrats. Governorships and state legislative majorities are preponderantly of the Democratic party persuasion. The Senate in the past twenty years (again until the 1980 election) has been largely

I am grateful to Austin Ranney and Byron Shafer for their helpful comments.

Democratic, the House overwhelmingly so. One can gauge the weakness of Republican representation in Congress by observing that until after the election of 1980 it was difficult to imagine any election that would give that party control of the House. Is it a whole party when it is not even a potential majority party?

Just as one swallow does not a summer make, a single election does not restore a party to the position of a constant contender. Only winning the enduring loyalty of a near majority of voters can do that. To begin to do that, the Republican administration must be seen to be successful in maintaining peace and securing prosperity. In view of the turbulence of the international economy and the less than perfect understanding of the domestic economy, however, no government is able to ensure success in simultaneously reducing inflation and decreasing unemployment. Nor can any government, hawkish or dovish, ensure peace.

I mention this only to suggest that even the short-term, let alone the long-term, future of the Republican party is not assured. It would not take all that much—a decline in the standard of living, a nasty little war, a scandal or two—to diminish Republican representation below its pre-1980 levels. Then there would be talk about the disappearance rather than the resurgence of the Republican party.

As soon as the clamor over the "imperial presidency" of Vietnam and Watergate subsided, the presidency appeared less conquering than conquered, more impotent than potent. The decline of multi-issue coalitions, the rise of single-issue interest groups, the fragmentation of power in Congress and within the executive branch, the concentration upon government as a solver of national problems, all these and more have been cited as reasons for the unsatisfactory performance of presidents in recent times. Can it be coincidental, Americans wonder, that presidents fear to run for a second term or are defeated when they do? Is it mere happenstance that the loser of the last three presidential debates—Kennedy versus Nixon (Nixon had been vice-president in the Eisenhower administration), Ford versus Carter, Carter versus Reagan—has been the incumbent? Hard luck? Systemic defect? Unforgiving environment? Whatever the explanation, the proficiency and popularity of presidents does appear problematic.

Now that we know the future is still ahead of us, instead of taking refuge in a wistful desire to escape the past, we are in a position to ask how we might discern the shape of things to come. History remains contingency. Retrodiction (or predicting the past, which we call history) is still superior to prediction. Speaking in the voice of this skeptical spirit, I shall set out certain forms of accounting for measuring the institutional and policy legacy of the 1980 election. If we can never be entirely sure of where we are going, we can at least learn a little about where we have been.

The outcomes of an election, as I have suggested, are a joint product of what happened then and what the future will do to that potential. Two vectors may be put into operation if one analyzes the internal aspirations of the victorious forces (the purposes and cohesion of the Reagan administration) and the external forces working on them (the constraints facing any president). Then we can ask whether and to what degree there is a fortunate coincidence or an ill-fated opposition between what the new administration would like and what it can get, between how it begins and what it actually becomes.

Political parties usually are discussed primarily in terms of formal organization. In this chapter, by contrast, I am going to refer to parties as doctrinal tendencies competing for the allegiance of the American people. Sometimes these doctrines are espoused by formal party organizations, sometimes not; whether they are or not can be discovered only by observation.

My argument is that there are three significantly different ways of looking at how a government ought to be run, three doctrinal parties; each "party" will follow a somewhat different line of policies. The Reagan administration comes in as a "party of opposition," but only its policies will tell us whether it is truly that or another right-leaning "party of fiscal balance." A particular group of leaders may start out thinking it is one kind of party when in fact it is another. The policies it tries—as well as the success or failure of those policies—depend not only upon the group itself but also on conditions external to it. What makes the Reagan administration so interesting is that it is the best bet for a party of opposition we have had in a long time.

Commentators usually criticize Republicans for being *only* the party of opposition. The usual critique is that all the party does is slow things down a bit. Thus these critics would say, "Don't be just the party of opposition; strike out with something new." In today's terms the argument would be, "Don't be just the party of balance, be something new—a party of opposition to big government."

The Party of Opposition versus the Party of Responsibility

There are three doctrinal parties competing for control in the United States—the parties of government, of opposition, and of balance. The "party of government," as its name implies, is literally for expanding the role of government—more is better. The citizens it seeks to create are employees of, producers for, or beneficiaries of government. Name the problem—energy, inflation, employment, poverty, pollution—and the party of government has a governmental solution—rationing, price control, entitlements, welfare, regulation. The "party of opposition" is opposed to growing government; it is for increasing the absolute and relative size of the private sector—less is more. The citizens it creates seek limited government. Placed in this crude conceptual vise, parties race for the allegiance of citizens, one party (in our time, Democratic) trying to tie them to government, the other (now, Republican) trying to tear them away.

What and where is the third party? It is the "party of fiscal balance," or just the "party of balance," composed of the deviant wings of the major parties. Though Democrats generally prefer to meet difficulties with increased spending, their wing of balance will, when inflation strikes, decrease spending and increase taxation. Though Republicans prefer to decrease spending, their wing of balance will, when faced with unemployment, increase spending and, with deficits, increase taxation.

The party of balance is not a conservative but a conserving force. It is reactive. It tends to preserve whatever is there. If government is small, it will remain so; but if government is large to begin with, it will end up the same way it started. The difference is that the party of balance will curb what it sees as excess. If government has been growing too speedily, the party of responsibility will slow it down. If it has been growing too slowly, the party of balance will speed it up. Stability is the name of the game for the party of balance.

To understand the central tendency of the party of balance, one must set it in the context of its main rival in modern times, the party of government, against which it reacts. The politics of the party of government may be expressed in the same word Samuel Gompers used to characterize the demands of trade unions—"more." The party of government promises more subsidies and more loan guarantees and more tax expenditures to business; and it promises more entitlements and more indexing and more welfare to individuals. Ultimately, it promises success, for its various policies are held together by the desire to guard against failure. This is how the social insurance state, whose purpose was to place a floor beneath the worst individual adversity, became the state of success in which no one—business or person—is allowed to fail.

The political appeal of promising more needs no explication by me. Benefits appear in the present and costs only in the future. By this time, a majority of Americans receive some sort of stipend (a tax expenditure like housing deductions and loan guarantees for middle-class students counts as well as welfare for poorer people). What we need to explore briefly is how the party of balance relates to these perennial promises.

Two things turn out to be destabilizing—making future promises and failing to honor past ones. More promises are destabilizing because the debt created leads to inflation and the future resources required lead to higher taxes that lead to less investment. Slow down while there is still time is the advice. Social stability, however, according to the party of balance, requires that past promises be perpetuated. To do otherwise would cause social unrest, upset expectations, depress morale. The end result is not the same size of government but the larger size inherent in past promises.

Look at the likely financial consequences of a policy of fiscal balance: the rate of spending increase is slowed down and the rate of tax increase is speeded up. The spending slowdown, it must be understood, is not a spending decrease but a pause to enable revenue to catch up, thus bringing the economy into some sort of balance. Spending decreases result in direct deprivation of groups accustomed to receiving largess; by contrast, tax increases appear relatively painless—indirect taxes, like those paid by employers on payrolls, and direct taxes, like the "bracket creep" that pushes people into higher categories in an inflationary period, are favorite devices. When a party of balance leaves office (Jimmy Carter's and Gerald Ford's administrations may serve as prototypes), the effective tax take is much higher than when it took office, and so is spending, except that it has not risen as fast as in prior years.

What happens, we may ask, when elections are fought between parties of balance? The question is relevant because most elections in the United States are fought on this basis: the moderate left offers somewhat more and the moderate right somewhat less spending. If the responsible right appears disadvantaged, at least for all offices except the presidency, that may be because promising more has an advantage over promising less, or the people may trust politicians who want government to do marginally more to do just that. The answer to our question, however, lies less in what the parties promise than in what they do: What happens when parties of balance succeed parties of government?

Let us take Lyndon Johnson's time in office as the party of government. In 1968 Johnson was replaced by Nixon, who resigned under threat of impeachment and was succeeded by Ford, who lost to Carter. The time from 1968 to 1980, according to my criteria, was one of the party of balance, first conservative, then liberal. During that period, Republicans were in power in eight out of twelve years. Looking at trends in spending and taxing, one can easily see that both have gone way up. Taxes take a considerably larger proportion of income and spending a substantially larger proportion of the gross national product (GNP), and this during a period when inflation-adjusted spending on defense, despite the Vietnam war, remained constant. What spending would have been had the party of government been in power one can only imagine; it has certainly risen substantially in real dollars and in proportion to the private sector. Evidently the momentum in the programs inherited from the party of government was sufficient to go far, even when the brake was gradually applied. The effective tax increases during this period (those on social security, on windfall profits on oil, and as a result of inflation were among the largest in peacetime in American history) no doubt helped to sustain the upward spiral of spending.

It is the political legacy of balance that is of interest to us. To the degree that a party of balance is successful, taxes are higher than they were, and expenditures are lower than they would have been. Such a situation constitutes the ultimate opportunity for the party of government, which can promise spending increases without immediate increases in taxes. Since the rate of spending has slowed down but is still going up, the base for building future increases has been enhanced, and since the tax base has been enlarged, the flow of resources has been speeded up. This is how promising more spending without increasing taxes becomes politically palatable.

The party of opposition is in a less advantageous position to succeed a party of balance. Driving down spending calls for large and visible decreases; talk of "waste" has to give way to elimination of, or multibillion-dollar reductions in, existing programs; neither course of action is easy, and both take time. Tax cuts are politically promising but economically dangerous. Since spending is still high and deficits grow, it is tempting to bring spending down before reducing taxes. Before its adherents know what is happening, the party of opposition has become the party of balance.

An illustration of the difference that being in (or about to be in) government makes comes from David Stockman, whom Reagan selected as director of the budget. An advocate of immediate tax cuts, a member of the putative party of opposition, Stockman believes that tax cuts are necessary. Asked about the "windfall profit" tax on oil company revenue, however, Stockman, admitting it was not a desirable tax, nevertheless went on to say that the tax is a "pretty prodigious source of revenue" so that, in view of the growing deficit, he would not abolish the tax, at least not right away.[1] In this case, "not now" means "never."

As things stand, the party of government and the party of responsibility rule. Some countries (Israel is an example) have only parties of government. Others, like Britain, have largely been ruled by parties of responsibility, whatever name they give themselves. The similarities shown by parties in office are due to the fact that there are only modest differences between a party of balance on the left that allows spending to keep up and one on the right that holds spending increases down. Though Prime Minister Thatcher's government is widely believed to be a party of opposition, for instance, it came into office by increasing the value-added tax (comparable to a sales tax) by 15 percent. What would a government of opposition have done? It would have cut the value-added tax, for that alone, like a reduction in the taxes employers pay on wages in the United States, would have lowered prices instead of increased them. How would the government have made up the loss in revenue? By deeper cuts in public spending and by fewer contributions to state industry. The deficit would have been used to compel cuts in spending, not increases in taxes. How would the government cope with the resulting increase in unemployment? By lower taxes to spur industry. Suppose there is social unrest? Suppose the policy does not work as well or as quickly as desired? Nothing guarantees success. A genuine party of opposition, if it has to lose, wants to lose on the issues that matter to it—the relative sizes of the public and private sectors.

The discussion on domestic policy within the Reagan camp reveals doubt over whether government is to be limited or merely slowed down so as to be better prepared for the great leap forward. For instance, in a recent book, *The Future under President Reagan*, Congressman Jack Kemp (Republican, New York) writes:

> To be credible in its effort to control the growth of spending, the Administration must also lower budget authority now for future years. This is what affects expectations of future inflation, and therefore, long-term interest rates. Above all, controlling the growth of spending depends on success in reducing the rates of inflation and unemployment. A huge share of federal spending is tied to the "misery index"—the indicators of inflation and unemployment. Of

[1] Christopher Conte, "Tax Cut Ought Not to Be Delayed Despite a Record Budget Gap, Reagan Aide Says," *Wall Street Journal*, January 9, 1981.

the $36 billion cost overrun between June and November, 1980, for example, $26 billion—almost three quarters— could be traced to such automatic factors as indexed federal benefits, unemployment and welfare payments, interest costs, and other spending which is triggered by a worsening economy.[2]

He advocates tax reduction to increase investment in order to improve productivity, which would enable the government to afford a larger defense effort. Therefore he is caught up in arguments over whether lower taxes will increase economic activity sufficiently to raise revenues enough to offset the decrease in rates. If lower taxes were part of the social program of the party of opposition (as well as useful in attracting political support), he would not have to ask whether they are responsible economically, for there are always other ways—cutting tobacco and milk subsidies or entitlements, for example—to reduce the deficit.

Parties of government and of balance, to be sure, are not oblivious to the signs of the times. What these might be and how they might react we will discuss later. The point here is that these are parties with a social vision to which economic doctrines are subordinate. No doubt they have their priorities among objects of expenditure and types of taxation. No doubt the party of government is more enamored of central control and the party of opposition of market mechanisms. After all, the "owners" of the party of government are the employees and beneficiaries of government, and the party of opposition is made up of the "owners" of the private sector. Whether markets or regulations work in specific instances (policy analysts know that no instrument of policy is good for all purposes) is less important to them than realizing their separate social visions— life under larger and smaller public and private sectors.

Adherents of the parties of opposition and of government, insofar as they believe in their view of the good life, abide by certain precepts and follow certain rules derived from them. When in doubt, what they do depends on these precepts: (1) The size of spending is more important than its purpose; *how much* government does is more important than *what* it does. (2) The size of revenue is more important than its composition. For the party of opposition, the rule is that lower taxes and less spending are always desirable, even if the wrong expenditure or tax is cut. The party of opposition takes it where it can get it. For the party of government, the rule is that any

2 Wayne Valis, ed., *The Future under President Reagan* (Westport, Conn.: Arlington House, 1981), p. 68.

tax is a good tax, even if it would prefer another one. Every spending increase is a good one, even if the object is less desirable than another. Once spending and taxing are at higher levels, strengthening this party and weakening its opponents, the party of government may make adjustments to push one program ahead faster than others, thereby coming closer to its spending priorities as well. Similarly, the party of opposition will lower certain tax rates more than others when it can, meanwhile regarding any tax cut as doubly desirable for the revenues it reduces and the spending cuts it induces.

Whereas a party of opposition considers driving down taxes and spending good in and of itself, a party dedicated to social stability insists that spending and taxing be balanced. This is easier to do by keeping taxes high. Since a party, once in office, always needs money to satisfy demands, the result is that taxes stay up. Thus the next party of government can use the proceeds of restraint—temporarily lower spending increases and permanently higher effective tax rates—to build a bigger government.

Which way will President Reagan's government go? Will there be more citizens independent of government after his time, as befits a party of opposition, or will there be as many or more dependent on it, as would emerge from a party of fiscal balance? To put the matter in policy terms, is there to be a balanced budget at higher or lower levels of spending and taxation? Speaking in terms of social philosophy, one may ask, Is the domestic government to be made smaller because that is desirable or is it to remain larger because to do otherwise would be "simplistic"?

Will we hear less about "waste," and will we hear more about the desirability of providing fewer services? If the answers are yes, then we know the president belongs to the party of opposition. After he leaves government, will President Reagan say, as the former governor of California did, that he reduced the rate of increase in spending? If the answer is yes, then we will know that he stood with the party of balance. By painting a portrait of the kinds of policies a party of opposition would find desirable, we will better be able to offer an accounting of whether and to what extent the Reagan administration fits the picture of a slimmer Uncle Sam or a decaying Dorian Gray.

Adjusting to External Turbulence and Internal Fragmentation

Ours has not been a great time, as President Carter discovered, for the party of responsibility. The party's old constituency has been lost, and a new one has not been created because no one knows enough to manipulate the government and the economy successfully. That is what is meant when officials lament that "fine-tuning" does not work any more.[3] There are so many programs bumping into one another that government spends most of its time dealing with the distortions its own policies have introduced into the society, economy, and polity.[4] So much energy is used by government in cleaning up after itself that it has little left to adapt to emerging circumstances. Knowledge of what to do is deficient, partly because a multitude of programs interacting with great frequency overwhelms our understanding. Marginal moves do not work well because the base from which the move is made is itself not understood or is out of control. A multitude of comprehensive changes overloads the political system (Carter's first two years), and a plethora of minor adjustments increases complexity without improving control. Acting precipitously leads to unanticipated consequences, and delay allows presidents to be overwhelmed by the sheer momentum of events. The stability the party of responsibility seeks to achieve turns out to be the indispensable assumption of making its methods work.

In a time when unpredictable international pressures on the dollar can cause the imposition of deflationary measures, the party of government might be compelled to act against its desires. Cutting budgets instead of increasing them is not likely to please either the party or its constituents. Nevertheless, the party of government need not be entirely hostage to events. If it resists the demand for fiscal balance—selling out its adherents, one may say—it can try to make the government big enough so that government becomes the only possible solution to its own problems. What such a solution might look like can best be ascertained by looking at a genuine party of government—the British Labour party—that has just jettisoned its responsible wing.

---

[3] A party of balance believes in "fine-tuning." Small adjustments are its trademark. Thus a party that seeks to fine-tune the supply of money is not that much different from the party that seeks to adjust the level of spending. In a memorable phrase, John Biven, who was then financial secretary to the Treasury in Mrs. Thatcher's government, explained to his MPs that "m-3," a measure of money supply, was a "wayward mistress." Biven should have been asked why a party of opposition was pinning its hopes on a funny number (all statistics are made up, not natural to the world) instead of its social philosophy. Had the Thatcher government said it was reducing the size of government because that was a good thing to do, it would not have been in the anomalous position of succeeding in lowering inflation while the instrument supposed to do that was climbing out of sight.

[4] See Aaron Wildavsky, *Speaking Truth to Power* (Boston: Little, Brown, 1979), "Policy as Its Own Cause," chap. 3, pp. 62-85.

Some people say that this purist Labour party will destroy itself; the voters will refuse to elect it, or the trade unions will abandon it when asked to make sacrifices, or its policies will lead to financial ruin. Maybe, but not certainly. The outlines of a coherent (I do not say correct) party program are beginning to emerge. Where would a Labour government, the question is, get the resources to make government grow without first increasing national product? By withdrawing from the European Economic Community (EEC), as it is pledged to do, Labour will save a substantial sum. Naturally, the prospects of failure it fears from economic competition (the Labour dog does not want to be eaten by the big bully across the channel) will also be diminished. By using the same logic through which it has come out for nuclear disarmament—nuclear arms are immoral, and besides Britain does not make a difference—a Labour government could run down conventional defense, thus releasing billions for domestic purposes. A party that thinks the only real foreign peril could come from American miscalculation and that sees domestic inequities meanwhile crying out for concern needs no defense. After the savings gained from the EEC and defense budgets have been absorbed, however, how will Britain maintain, let alone increase, its standard of living? By erecting high tariff barriers (economist Wynn Godley at Cambridge University has provided a reasonable rationale), it will protect domestic industry. The strong will subsidize the weak, thus increasing equality. And if there is less to go around, the Labour party may well argue that it is better to enjoy the equality of a more leisurely life than an economically richer but socially poorer existence.

Just as every party has an internal problem, Labour has to be concerned about retaining the support of the unions, whose members want to maintain pay differentials in a class-conscious society. Early on, the new money this party of government raises from EEC withdrawal, savings on defense, higher tariffs, and perhaps selected tax increases may maintain these differences so that some workers remain more equal than others. Later on, when government has grown gigantic, so that appeals against it lack resonance, because there is no one to hear, the hierarchical principle inherent in a command economy and in the British tradition of governments that exercise full sovereignty may combine to confront union power. Indeed, the major difficulty the Conservative party has in acting as the party of opposition may well be that it also believes in its bones that government, as the repository of sovereign power, should solve problems by direct action.

In some ways an American party of government would find it easier, because its country is so much richer, to enter and stay in office. In other ways, because fragmented government is the norm, its life would be more difficult. The internal problem of the American party of government is its division between the "small is beautiful" and the central-command crowds. This division may be papered over by a phenomenon that could be called "bureaucracy without hierarchy." There are many rules, regulations, and bureaucracies, but there are no priorities among them. Programs may be split among different levels of government, passed on to the private sector in the form of regulations or tax incentives mandating or encouraging the desired action, even divided among the branches of the same government as with independent agencies and legislative vetoes. The important thing, at first, is that government grow, no matter where. Suspicion of interest groups and unlimited power is countered by the offsetting public power and decentralized administration of programs. When government gets big enough so that government's doing less is equivalent to citizens' doing without and there is no alternative, the confusion caused by bureaucracy without hierarchy may be remedied by imposing the latter on the former.

Is this, then, the time of the party of opposition? It is easier to diminish government when outside forces are squeezing down in the same direction. Real tax reductions (those that go beyond the "bracket creep" caused when inflation pushes people into paying more) may prove as popular as spending increases. Yet the swan song of responsibility—balance this, fine-tune that, don't rock the republic—may prove irresistible to a party that is the government while only imagining it is in opposition.

The consequences of the election of 1980 that brought a would-be party of opposition to the White House under President Ronald Reagan depend on whether the party is able to remain true to itself while maintaining sufficient social support to govern. No one who knows anything about American politics can believe this will be easy. Whether the party of opposition can succeed depends on its ability to create more citizens who wish to be independent of government faster than citizens are created who are dependent on it.[5] That in turn

[5] As Richard Rose has written in a recent paper, "In everyday bureaucratic politics, big government involves an exponential increase in interorganizational contacts. An increase of from 10 to 12 operating units increases the potential number of paired relationships between any two organizations by 16 percent, whereas an increase from 20 to 22 increases paired interactions by 41. The growth of government has even bigger implications for interaction between governmental and nongovernmental organizations. In a society in which 10 percent of organized activities were the responsibility of the government, and 90 percent the responsibility of the private sector, then if organizational interacting were random, four-fifths of society's organized affairs would involve interaction

requires (1) the willingness to formulate policies appropriate for a party of opposition, (2) the ability to get support from Congress, and (3) the capacity to implement the resulting programs. All three requisites are, to say the least, problematic. By envisaging the policies a party of opposition might pursue, we shall better be able to appraise its chances.

Policies for a Party of Opposition

How would a party of opposition deal with inflation? By cutting taxes and spending. Which would it do first? Both together; but if there has to be a choice, taxes first. Cutting spending is more difficult because individual programs are popular, because legislation may have to be changed, because there are so many programs with which to cope, and because some potential cuts—such as student loan guarantees and support for the elderly—affect the party's own constituents. Some cuts may be successful, but others may be blocked by a Congress not committed to opposition. The famed "iron triangle" of interest groups, agencies, and congressional committees will reassert itself on individual items. If tax cuts come first (say, a Kemp–Roth bill of 10 percent a year extended to four years, to go them one better, which would thereby cut real rates, not just keep up with inflation and taxes for social security), deficits will undoubtedly grow. Indeed, given a political propensity to cut taxes faster than spending, the initial deficit under President Reagan may be larger than the one he inherited from President Carter. What does this matter? It matters in that the size of the deficit may be used as a propellant to drive spending down further. Using the failure to cut spending as a rationale for raising effective tax rates belongs to the party of balance, not of opposition.

The usual political wisdom, taken apart from the kind of party for which it is intended, is that spending must be reduced before taxes can be cut. Otherwise, congressmen may claim credit for cutting taxes without being willing to take the blame for reducing spending. For the party of balance following a party of government (for which the size of the deficit is the least important consideration), this advice is essential. It is the strategy par excellence, since balance in the

---

between private organizations, and only one-fifth would involve government as one or both partners. But if the proportion of society's organized activities that were the responsibility of government rose to 30 percent, then more than half of all organized interactions would involve government as a partner." ("What, If Anything, Is Wrong with Big Government?" *Journal of Public Policy*, in press.)

economy, like stability in society, is of the essence. For the party of opposition, however, the advice may be misplaced. Of course, the cutting of both taxes and spending simultaneously is the best in the best of all possible worlds. Life, however, is not often so neat. Waiting for both may mean waiting forever. Internal bargaining on both may lead to each one's being cut far less than it might be alone. The party of opposition, therefore, takes whichever can come first, using lower taxes to lower spending and vice versa.

Which taxes are lowered and in what order? The party of responsibility wants to lower taxes on capital by rapid depreciation so as to increase productivity. The party of opposition, although it will take any tax cut it can get, places priority on cuts in personal tax rates because increasing take-home pay is both the symbol and the reality of its program—increasing the size of the private sector and trusting the people to spend their own money.

There is more, however. Suppose inflation is still too high? A more direct attack on price increases (other than wage and price controls, as advocated by the party of government) would be to reduce the taxes employers pay on wages. A combination of lower real prices and higher take-home pay does wonders for political popularity.

I have left monetary policy for last because I think it is politically (though not economically) least important. Restraint in money supply may be essential—certainly everyone gives lip service to it, but not everyone does what is desired. Every administration asks the Federal Reserve Board to do its bit. But it is not wise, as Mrs. Thatcher's experience suggests, to tie one's fortune to any particular measure of the money supply.

A different approach to money supply, giving it a subordinate but important political place, might be more helpful. A party of opposition is committed to strengthening the private sector. This means economic growth. By setting a reasonable rate for growth—say 4 percent a year—the president could give the federal reserve a relia- ble signal: calibrate money supply to this target rate of growth. If growth is less than desired, sell assets to increase supply; if growth is more, buy assets to decrease the supply. Instead of focusing atten- tion on an exotic number for money supply, it should be seen as an adjunct to the vision of the party of opposition—a vibrant private sector.

The emphasis on economic growth is useful also in providing a perspective on unemployment. Whereas the party of government wants to put people to work in or for the public sector, the party of opposition wants them to work in the private sector. Without at least modest growth, there will be substantial and sustained unemployment, driving out of office the party of opposition. Its choice, by no means guaranteed to succeed, is to create employment through growth of the private sector. If that fails, the party of opposition has failed in the right way by testing its vision of the good life against reality.

Apart from resisting the temptation to act as the party of balance, which industrial interests may prefer because they do not like uncertainty and do depend on subsidy, the party of opposition must be careful about how it deals with social issues. It is divided between libertarians, for whom almost any restraint on expression is anathema, and moralists, who want their traditional norms of family life and social deference respected.[6] As symbolic leader, the president can lend the moralists what they say they want—moral support. He can unite libertarians and moralists by removing governmentally sponsored interventions to which they object, such as subsidies for abortions. Going beyond this negative phase to a positive position of attempting to legislate morality, however, will seriously split the party of opposition.

If moralists want to improve morality, they will have to do it in the same way as everybody else in the private sector—on their own. By getting industry to put away the tin cup (if government intervenes to prevent big steel from losing money, why should its executives receive more than anyone else on welfare?), moralists will find it easier to convince others that morality begins at home and not in Washington.

Consistency is the key, especially where the party of opposition is tempted to act otherwise, that is, in defense. At this time there appears to be a general consensus that defense spending should increase, but people do not necessarily agree about how much or in which areas. Although a party of opposition might support increased spending on defense or in some other area, it must not abandon its view that government cannot solve problems merely by, as the phrase goes, "throwing dollars at them." It is essential, therefore, to show that a major effort is being made to improve, for example, the capability of the officer corps, perhaps by reducing its ranks and by adapting the strategy of warfare to contemporary conditions.

Polls of public opinion show that most people think government spending is too high, but most also favor many programs. Suspicion of inefficiency is strong. The Reagan administration can build support

[6] For an excellent article on these two tendencies, see James Q. Wilson, "Reagan and the Republican Revival," in *Commentary*, vol. 70 (October 1980), pp. 25-32.

by demonstrating increased effectiveness in the area where it proposes to increase spending—namely defense.

As time goes on, the party of opposition can expect to be swamped with efforts to reinstate spending programs and to modify tax provisions. Efforts to get around spending cuts through loans, entitlements, and tax expenditures will also accelerate. The administration can deal with them either retail, item by item, year by year, or wholesale, setting up schemes to deflect and direct these demands. At the moment of the inaugural, sure of its own strength, thinking, in the words of its director of the budget, that all that is necessary is "political will,"[7] retailing is the order of the day. Before too long, however, as it gets worn down by fighting simultaneously on so many fronts, the administration will reconsider its position. When it comes to the more profound understanding that, as the party in government, it is part of the problem—tax money is useful to balance budgets, to relieve strains among departments and their clientele, to respond to this or that exigency—the party of opposition may go wholesale so as to project its position.

On the tax side, once rates are down, it may seek a system of uniform rates for income taxes—say, 10, 15, 25 percent top—with no exemptions and deductions. The well-nigh universal belief that everyone else is cheating at taxes, legally or otherwise, would diminish, thus increasing the legitimacy of government in the eyes of citizens. The work of accountants and lawyers would decline, thus freeing these professionals for productive work.

On the spending side, a constitutional amendment to limit spending to the present level plus the increase in national product would take the pressure off the president. Agencies would fight each other—more for one agency means less for another—rather than the president.[8]

Obviously, low uniform income tax rates and spending limits are, if not utopian, at least visionary. I mention them only to show what a party of opposition might do to institutionalize its doctrines.

Though it is not desirable to run through the gamut of domestic programs, it is possible to capture the essence of the problems they pose in two words—subsidy and equality. Business and citizen are subsidized in so many ways, from soup—the expense-account lunch—to nuts—payments to peanut farmers—it is hard to count them. A structure of privilege so laboriously constructed will be difficult to

[7] *Wall Street Journal*, January 9, 1981.

[8] See Aaron Wildavsky, *How to Limit Government Spending* (Berkeley: University of California Press, 1980).

tear down. It will take time. All I wish to say here is that an even-handed approach will make it easier. If farmers are asked to give up or to accept lower price supports in times of abundance, for example, they must also be able to cash in on times of plenty. Forbidding food exports because they raise prices and then cutting subsidies when farmers are about to make money is not equitable.

The rationale for most social programs is equality. No red-blooded American, certainly no president, is going to deny that. What the party of opposition needs is its own version of equality. It is not against the "social insurance state," ensuring poor people against adversity, provided the sums do not keep growing so that the public overwhelms the private sector. Equality of opportunity is a must. But equality of result is not. What, then, is to take the place of equality of result?

Equality as variety is one answer. Each individual should be allowed to develop his or her potential in different ways. Variety as equality is like friendship; one does not treat friends equally, that is, like everyone else, but in their own unique way.

The political form most appropriate for generating variety is federalism. Whereas Americans once used to glory in the diversity of our federal system, however, today there is a tendency to condemn it as incoherent. No doubt the virulent pluralism that characterizes the American polity today does appear incoherent. Congeries of governments, interest groups, and professionals are mixed together in ways difficult to fathom. The one uniformity is that total public spending goes up. Adding functions to the government at a prodigious rate is bound to cause confusion among programs and consternation among the public.

Were states encouraged to differentiate themselves, by contrast, citizens could choose among different levels of services and of taxation. By stressing variety at the state level, the nation would be able to make better use of interest groups. By turning off the pump of federal funds, the government could divert energies into local channels. By reducing federal revenues, the federal government would leave room for states to step in—if they wished. There is evidence that people are moving from high-tax, high-service states to the opposite. If that trend continues, such states seeking to retain their population will have to change their policies, or if they choose to keep their amenities, they will have to support them by other means. Thus what would appear as chaos, were it sponsored from the top, appears as interesting experimentation below. In this way the party of opposition might make use of, rather than regret, political fragmentation.

So far this discussion has been abstract and internal. What would the parties of government, balance, and opposition like to do, has been the question, apart from dealing with whatever is imposed on them by specific circumstances of the time? The current question, of course, is whether the Republican party under Ronald Reagan will become a party of opposition or of balance. Let us look at what we can see in the entrails of our time and apply these readings to the parties of government, balance, and opposition. Then I will attempt an appraisal of the political feasibility of implementing the program of a party of opposition.

The Future

Just as the importance of the 1932 election was determined by 1936 and the elections that followed, the significance of the 1980 election depends on what happens afterward. The most likely result of any election, however, is that things will be much the same afterward as they were before. There are reasons things are the way they are, and these are usually powerful reasons based on more than inertia. Following the path of least resistance, then, the Reagan presidency should look, if not like Carter's, then at least like Ford's. Like most of his predecessors, President Reagan will get some of what he wants (none, needless to say, got all). Spending and taxation will be lower than they would have been but probably not—in real terms—lower than they are now. Government will grow but not as fast and not quite in the same direction as before. The party of opposition, in other words, will give way to the party of balance, and the 1980 election will signify continuity rather than change.

A less likely but not negligible possibility is that the Reagan administration will be unable to get any of its programs passed. Perhaps circumstances it does not anticipate will lead it into a series of ad hoc responses similar to those that characterized the Carter administration. The election of 1980 would then be notable for giving rise to an even more acute concern over the viability of the American political system.

The least likely eventuality is that a party of opposition will emerge full-blown out of the brow of the Reagan administration. For one thing, it may not have sufficient support in the Congress or the country. The American people may not want a much more limited government than they have now. They may want a better run government of about the same size or a bit larger. Should that be so, converting opposition to balance would be in line with popular sentiment, no small matter in a democracy.

For another, a party of opposition is not the same as a single-shot administration. A governing party implies both a coherent doctrine and an ability to compromise among factions. A narrow sect cannot win and maintain office. A party without a program cannot govern. In between the two is a broad-based party combining regions, races, and interests. A party that lasts implies attention to organization and to actions that give it a role to play, such as sending significant numbers of party officials to national conventions and funneling campaign funds through them. Since a party of opposition is at best a long-term affair, invigorating and maintaining party machinery is indispensable. To get to the long run, however, the party must survive in the short term.

Its very emphasis on doctrine may split the party of opposition. The intensity of individual concern that leads its adherents to join such a party may make collective action difficult if not impossible. Advocates of social regulation may clash with opponents of economic regulation. Proponents of increased defense spending may find themselves at odds with those who wish less total spending. As the world of experience begins to intrude on the realm of ideology, any progress that is attainable may be judged too little and too late. The leader of the party of opposition when in office, namely, the president, must be cognizant of pleasing the public as well as his own partisans. Being a party of opposition while in office may turn out to be a contradiction in terms. We will see.

Nevertheless, in my opinion, the attempt to establish and maintain a party of opposition would be neither futile nor hopeless. Futility does not reside in giving the citizenry an opportunity to select or reject a different vision of the role of government, one in which government might be both smaller and more effective. Even rejection of a party of opposition would clarify the course the country will take in the next several decades. A party of opposition is not a hopeless proposition either. Some signs of the times, as we have seen, are favorable. I do not think anyone can say more than that the political feasibility of reducing tax rates is high and of reducing spending overall is moderately good, without necessarily specifying how much they will decline or which taxes or expenditures will decline most.

Keeping its eye on the strategic direction of a party of opposition—any way that taxes and spending decline is desirable compared with the opposite—is essential if the Reagan administration is to make it through the first term and especially the first two years. If it insists that cuts be made in some precise order and magnitude, the administration will be unable to make necessary compromises. If it can keep its cool, giving here, taking there, so long as the direction of the size of government is down, it may be able to retain sufficient coherence and viability to take its case to the people over a series of elections. And, in a democracy, that is all any party can ask.

Like everyone else, the Reagan administration must start from where it (and the country) is. Unlike its opponents, however, the Reagan administration is committed to changing the course of national policy. This task is more difficult because governments in the Western world have been growing larger (absolutely and relative to the private sector) for a good hundred years. The first facts to be faced are that the Republican party has only a small majority in the Senate and is in a substantial minority position in the House of Representatives. Without give-and-take, it cannot get even part of its program through. On what bases should it stand firm or compromise?

A prototypical illustration of the choices that will face the administration is contained in this effort to teach a lesson in politics to the new and naive party of opposition:

> The incoming Office of Management and Budget director, David Stockman, and other administration officials have indicated the food-stamp program would be one of the first places where budget savings will be sought.
>
> Food stamp supporters in Congress already are gearing up for battle over the probable blitz on the program, which is to be reauthorized this year as part of a general farm bill.
>
> The new chairman of the Senate Agriculture Committee, Jesse Helms, R-N.C., long a critic of growing costs of the program, has talked about major reductions in food-stamp spending, ranging as high as 40 percent.
>
> But Rep. Frederick Richmond, D-N.Y., chairman of the House Agriculture subcommittee that oversees food stamps, warned recently that Reagan, Stockman and Helms are playing with fire.
>
> He said any efforts to "emasculate" the program would seriously jeopardize urban-suburban legislators' backing of other farm commodity support programs Reagan and Helms are likely to advocate.
>
> "This Stockman is not very realistic," Richmond said. "He is talking through his hat, overreacting because he is totally inexperienced in the politics of farm legislation.
>
> "Without a food-stamp program as part of the package, there is no way a general farm bill can pass. I have conveyed that idea to Sen. Helms and he realizes the tobacco supports

so important to his state will not go through without food stamps.[9]

The desire of senators from farm states for crop subsidies is held hostage to preservation of the food-stamp program at present levels of funding. Economically, abolition of the entire farm program would be a boon; politically, loss of support from farm-state senators and representatives might be disastrous.

Obviously, accommodation is in order. But what kind? Sufficient reduction in spending to move it below that of the prior year and to encourage fiscal conservatives to support tax cuts is acceptable. If the cuts mainly affect urban legislators and they insist on trimming farm supports in return, that is also acceptable; apportioning cuts among the elements of the farm package is a good way to go. Alternatively, as Governor Reagan did in California, cuts may be made while still allowing a smaller number of recipients (those most in need) to do as well as or better than before. The only kind of compromise that is not acceptable is one that adds up to more money than before. If that is the prospect and other areas do not make up the difference, the Reagan administration, if it wishes to be a party of opposition, must be prepared to see the farm bill stalled in Congress. No bill at all would be better than one that increased spending, because increased spending would be deemed worse than retaining some support while losing all substance.

I see no evidence in polls or in private conversation that the people of America are demanding an ever-increasing standard of living. Moderating inflation—say, 1 percent a year for four years—without worsening unemployment might be more than acceptable.

Given the good fortune, or the foresight and the acumen, not only to propose but to pass bills that raise economic growth, the clash of interests may be moderated. With the private sector growing faster than the public sector, there can be increases in real personal income and in government spending. This happy set of circumstances is by no means inevitable, less likely, perhaps, than not. But it is by no means impossible or highly unlikely. There is, and this is all I wish to say, a sufficient prospect for success—defined as giving the electorate an opportunity to vote in or out a potential majority party of opposition—to make it worth pursuing.

Immediate implementation of tax and spending cuts, once Congress has acted, poses no particular problems. Compared with service

[9] Ward Sinclair, "Budget Chief Proposes Food-Stamp Program Cut," *Oakland* (Calif.) *Tribune*, January 29, 1981, p. A-3.

349

programs, taxes and spending are easy to administer. The follow-up, however, involving the way in which program reductions are administered—causing the least versus the most disruption—will require painstaking care. If this "cutback management" is ignored, the same spending will surface in different forms as the only alternative to chaos.

In sum, the 1980 election is more likely to be an election to confirm past trends than it is to realign parties or programs. If the election does turn out in retrospect to have been critical—and it is the analytic purpose of this chapter to provide a mechanism of accounting for that purpose—it will be because it began the first stirrings of a fledgling party of opposition. Whether that party can be kept together to fight future elections is being decided now. Should such a party prosper, winning its share of future elections, the doctrine of American exceptionalism would live again in our time.

Appendixes

Appendix A

	Change, 1976–1980 (percentage points)			1976 (percent)			
Region and State	Rep.	Dem.	Turn-out	Ford	Carter	Other	Turnout
Nation	2.8	−9.1	−0.3	48.0	50.1	1.9	54.3
Total vote	—	—	—	39,147,793	40,830,763	1,577,333	81,555,889
New England							
Conn.	−3.9	−8.4	−1.9	52.1	46.9	1.0	62.4
Maine	−3.3	−5.8	1.1	48.9	48.1	3.0	65.0
Mass.	1.4	−14.4	−2.8	40.4	56.1	3.4	61.6
N.H.	3.0	−15.1	0.1	54.7	43.5	1.8	58.8
R.I.	−6.9	−7.7	−1.0	44.1	55.4	0.6	61.5
Vt.	−10.0	−4.7	2.9	54.4	43.1	2.5	56.9
Total vote	—	—	—	2,455,126	2,765,874	129,853	5,350,853
Percent	−1.2	−11.4	−1.6	45.9	51.7	2.4	61.7
Middle Atlantic							
Del.	0.6	−7.1	−2.4	46.6	52.0	1.4	58.4
D.C.	−3.1	−6.7	2.1	16.5	81.6	1.9	33.3
Md.	−2.5	−5.6	0.8	46.7	52.8	0.5	49.9
N.J.	1.9	−9.4	−2.8	50.1	47.9	2.0	58.1
N.Y.	−0.8	−7.9	−2.8	47.5	51.9	0.7	50.8
Pa.	1.9	−7.9	−2.1	47.7	50.4	1.9	54.7
Total vote	—	—	—	7,626,448	8,182,914	204,628	16,013,990
Percent	0.3	−7.9	−2.1	47.6	51.1	1.3	52.8

PRESIDENTIAL ELECTION POPULAR VOTES BY STATE AND REGION, 1976 AND 1980

Reagan	Carter	Anderson	Clark	Other	Turnout
50.8	41.0	6.6	1.1	0.5	54.0
43,899,248	35,481,435	5,719,437	920,859	474,699	86,495,678
48.2	38.5	12.2	0.6	0.5	60.6
45.6	42.3	10.2	1.0	1.0	66.1
41.8	41.7	15.2	0.9	0.4	58.8
57.7	28.4	12.9	0.5	0.4	58.8
37.2	47.7	14.4	0.6	0.1	60.5
44.4	38.4	14.9	0.9	1.4	59.8
2,443,081	2,205,666	748,946	42,152	27,346	5,467,191
44.7	40.3	13.7	0.8	0.5	60.1
47.2	44.9	6.9	0.8	0.2	55.9
13.4	74.9	9.3	0.6	1.8	35.4
44.2	47.1	7.8	0.9	0.0	50.7
52.0	38.6	7.9	0.7	0.9	55.3
46.7	44.0	7.5	0.8	1.0	48.0
49.6	42.5	6.4	0.7	0.8	52.6
7,517,431	6,775,422	1,147,310	123,833	125,256	15,689,252
47.9	43.2	7.3	0.8	0.8	50.7

(Table continues)

| Region and State | Change, 1976–1980 (percentage points) | | | 1976 (percent) | | | |
	Rep.	Dem.	Turn-out	Ford	Carter	Other	Turnout
Deep South							
Ala.	6.1	−8.3	2.7	42.6	55.7	1.7	47.2
Ark.	13.2	−17.4	1.3	34.9	65.0	0.1	52.2
Ga.	8.0	−11.0	0.9	33.0	66.7	0.3	43.3
La.	5.2	−6.0	6.0	46.0	51.7	2.3	49.8
Miss.	1.7	−1.5	4.7	47.7	49.6	2.8	49.5
S.C.	6.3	−8.0	1.4	43.1	56.2	0.7	41.7
Total vote	—	—	—	2,556,157	3,630,664	81,405	6,268,226
Percent	6.8	−8.8	2.8	40.8	57.9	1.3	46.7
Outer South							
Fla.	8.9	−13.4	2.7	46.6	51.9	1.4	51.5
N.C.	5.1	−8.1	1.7	44.2	55.2	0.6	44.1
Tenn.	5.8	−7.5	1.1	42.9	55.9	1.1	49.6
Tex.	7.3	−9.7	0.4	48.0	51.1	0.9	47.3
Va.	3.7	−7.6	1.1	49.3	48.0	2.7	47.7
Total vote	—	—	—	5,635,314	6,285,459	154,095	12,074,868
Percent	6.7	−10.0	1.3	46.7	52.1	1.3	48.2
Border							
Ky.	3.5	−5.1	2.3	45.6	52.8	1.7	49.1
Mo.	3.7	−6.8	1.1	47.5	51.1	1.4	57.7
Okla.	10.5	−13.8	−1.2	50.0	48.7	1.3	55.6
W.Va.	3.4	−8.2	−3.6	41.9	58.0	0.0	58.1
Total vote	—	—	—	2,319,763	2,582,460	61,734	4,963,957
Percent	5.2	−8.1	0.3	46.7	52.0	1.2	55.0
Great Lakes							
Ill.	−0.5	−6.4	−1.7	50.1	48.1	1.8	60.6
Ind.	2.7	−8.0	−2.7	53.3	45.7	1.0	60.8
Mich.	−2.8	−3.9	1.0	51.8	46.4	1.7	58.7
Ohio	2.9	−8.0	0.1	48.7	48.9	2.4	55.4
Wis.	0.1	−6.3	0.3	47.8	49.4	2.8	65.9
Total vote	—	—	—	8,447,461	8,034,576	327,036	16,809,073
Percent	0.2	−6.4	−0.5	50.3	47.8	1.9	59.4
Farm belt							
Iowa	1.8	−9.9	−1.1	49.5	48.5	2.1	63.7
Kans.	5.4	−11.6	−2.5	52.5	44.9	2.6	58.4

Reagan	Carter	Anderson	Clark	Other	Turnout
48.8	47.4	1.2	1.0	1.6	49.9
48.1	47.5	2.7	1.1	0.6	53.5
41.0	55.8	2.3	1.0	0.0	44.1
51.2	45.7	1.7	0.5	0.8	55.8
49.4	48.1	1.3	0.6	0.5	54.2
49.5	48.2	1.6	0.5	0.2	43.1
3,384,743	3,491,458	127,253	56,427	45,682	7,105,563
47.6	49.1	1.8	0.8	0.6	49.5
55.5	38.5	5.1	0.8	0.0	54.2
49.3	47.2	2.8	0.5	0.1	45.8
48.7	48.4	2.2	0.4	0.2	50.8
55.3	41.4	2.5	0.8	0.0	47.7
53.0	40.3	5.1	0.7	0.9	48.8
7,250,044	5,711,482	485,514	97,781	23,223	13,568,044
53.4	42.1	3.6	0.7	0.2	49.5
49.0	47.7	2.4	0.4	0.5	51.4
51.2	44.3	3.7	0.7	0.1	58.8
60.5	35.0	3.3	1.2	0.0	54.4
45.3	49.8	4.3	0.6	0.0	54.5
2,739,231	2,318,087	179,022	38,137	8,397	5,282,874
51.9	43.9	3.4	0.7	0.2	55.3
49.6	41.7	7.3	0.8	0.5	58.9
56.0	37.7	5.0	0.9	0.5	58.1
49.0	42.5	7.0	1.1	0.4	59.7
51.5	40.9	5.9	1.1	0.5	55.5
47.9	43.2	7.1	1.3	0.6	66.2
8,824,365	7,221,140	1,148,745	178,331	85,767	17,458,348
50.5	41.4	6.6	1.0	0.5	58.9
51.3	38.6	8.8	1.0	0.3	62.6
57.9	33.3	7.0	1.5	0.4	55.9

(Table continues)

Region and State	Change, 1976–1980 (percentage points)			1976 (percent)			
	Rep.	Dem.	Turn-out	Ford	Carter	Other	Turnout
Minn.	0.7	−8.3	−2.0	42.0	54.9	3.1	71.4
Nebr.	6.4	−12.4	0.1	59.2	38.5	2.3	56.1
N.Dak.	12.6	−19.5	−2.9	51.6	45.8	2.6	67.2
S.Dak.	10.1	−17.2	3.3	50.4	48.9	0.7	63.8
Total vote	—	—	—	2,619,690	2,637,630	135,296	5,392,616
Percent	3.6	−10.8	−1.3	48.6	48.9	2.5	64.4
Mountain							
Ariz.	4.2	−11.6	1.2	56.4	39.8	3.8	48.6
Colo.	1.0	−11.5	−2.1	54.0	42.6	3.4	60.4
Idaho	7.1	−11.6	7.9	59.3	36.8	3.9	61.6
Mont.	4.0	−13.0	1.0	52.8	45.4	1.8	63.7
Nev.	13.4	−18.5	−0.5	50.2	45.8	4.0	47.5
N.Mex.	4.4	−11.3	−1.4	50.5	48.1	1.4	54.6
Utah	10.3	−13.1	−1.5	62.4	33.6	3.9	69.4
Wyo.	3.3	−11.8	−4.0	59.3	39.8	0.9	58.1
Total vote	—	—	—	2,124,180	1,569,739	120,985	3,814,904
Percent	5.0	−12.3	−0.2	55.7	41.1	3.2	57.5
Pacific							
Alas.	−3.3	−9.1	11.7	57.9	35.7	6.4	48.3
Calif.	3.3	−11.7	−0.4	49.3	47.6	3.1	51.3
Hawaii	−5.2	−5.8	−1.6	48.1	50.6	1.3	48.1
Oreg.	0.5	−8.9	0.6	47.8	47.6	4.6	62.1
Wash.	−0.3	−8.8	−1.5	50.0	46.1	3.9	61.1
Total vote	—	—	—	5,363,654	5,141,447	362,301	10,867,402
Percent	2.2	−10.8	−0.3	49.4	47.3	3.3	53.3

SOURCE: Official state returns (Washington, D.C.: U.S. Federal Election Commisson, December 29, 1980), aggregates and percentages calculated by William Schneider. Note that these are preliminary figures and are subject to minor revisions when the final state canvasses are completed in 1981.

		1980 (percent)			
Reagan	Carter	Anderson	Clark	Other	Turnout
42.7	46.6	8.6	1.5	0.6	69.4
65.6	26.0	7.0	1.4	0.0	56.2
64.2	26.3	7.8	1.2	0.4	64.3
60.5	31.7	6.5	1.2	0.1	67.1
2,927,358	2,138,463	448,786	75,794	21,616	5,612,017
52.2	38.1	8.0	1.4	0.4	63.1
60.6	28.2	8.8	2.1	0.2	49.8
55.1	31.1	11.0	2.2	0.7	58.3
66.5	25.2	6.2	1.9	0.2	69.5
56.8	32.4	8.0	2.7	0.0	64.7
63.6	27.4	7.2	1.8	0.0	47.0
55.0	36.8	6.5	1.0	0.8	53.1
72.8	20.6	5.0	1.2	0.5	67.9
62.6	28.0	6.8	2.6	0.0	54.2
2,635,648	1,251,261	353,390	83,171	17,102	4,340,572
60.7	28.8	8.1	1.9	0.4	57.3
54.6	26.6	7.1	11.7	0.0	60.0
52.7	35.9	8.6	1.7	1.1	50.9
42.9	44.8	10.6	1.1	0.7	46.5
48.3	38.7	9.5	2.2	1.3	62.7
49.7	37.3	10.6	1.7	0.7	59.6
6,177,347	4,368,456	1,080,471	225,233	120,310	11,971,817
51.6	36.5	9.0	1.9	1.0	53.0

Appendix B

ELECTORAL VOTES FOR PRESIDENT BY STATE AND REGION, 1976 AND 1980

Region and State	1976 Rep.	1976 Dem.	1980 Rep.	1980 Dem.	Change, 1976–1980 Dem. to Rep.	Stayed Rep.	Stayed Dem.
Nation	240[a]	297	489	49	248	241	49
New England							
Conn.	8		8			8	
Maine	4		4			4	
Mass.		14	14		14		
N.H.	4		4			4	
R.I.		4		4			4
Vt.	3		3			3	
Total	19	18	33	4	14	19	4
Middle Atlantic							
Del.		3	3		3		
D.C.		3		3			3
Md.		10		10			10
N.J.	17		17			17	
N.Y.		41	41		41		
Pa.		27	27		27		
Total	17	84	88	13	71	17	13
Deep South							
Ala.		9	9		9		
Ark.		6	6		6		
Ga.		12		12			12
La.		10	10		10		
Miss.		7	7		7		
S.C.		8	8		8		
Total	0	52	40	12	40	0	12

Region and State	1976		1980		Change, 1976–1980		
	Rep.	Dem.	Rep.	Dem.	Dem. to Rep.	Stayed Rep.	Stayed Dem.
Outer South							
Fla.		17	17		17		
N.C.		13	13		13		
Tenn.		10	10		10		
Tex.		26	26		26		
Va.	12		12			12	
Total	12	66	78	0	66	12	0
Border							
Ky.		9	9		9		
Mo.		12	12		12		
Okla.	8		8			8	
W.Va.		6		6			6
Total	8	27	29	6	21	8	6
Great Lakes							
Ill.	26		26			26	
Ind.	13		13			13	
Mich.	21		21			21	
Ohio		25	25		25		
Wis.		11	11		11		
Total	60	36	96	0	36	60	0
Farm Belt							
Iowa	8		8			8	
Kans.	7		7			7	
Minn.		10		10			10
Nebr.	5		5			5	
N.Dak.	3		3			3	
S.Dak.	4		4			4	
Total	27	10	27	10	0	27	10
Mountain							
Ariz.	6		6			6	
Colo.	7		7			7	
Idaho	4		4			4	

(Table continues)

359

Region and State	1976		1980		Change, 1976–1980		
	Rep.	Dem.	Rep.	Dem.	Dem. to Rep.	Stayed Rep.	Stayed Dem.
Mont.	4		4			4	
Nev.	3		3			3	
N.Mex.	4		4			4	
Utah	4		4			4	
Wyo.	3		3			3	
Total	35	0	35	0	0	35	0
Pacific							
Alas.	3		3			3	
Calif.	45		45			45	
Hawaii		4		4			4
Oreg.	6		6			6	
Wash.	8 [a]		9			9	
Total	62	4	63	4	0	63	4

[a] One Washington Republican elector voted for Ronald Reagan for president and Robert Dole for vice-president.

SOURCE: Official state returns (Washington, D.C.: U.S. Federal Election Commission, December 29, 1980), aggregates and percentages calculated by William Schneider.

Appendix C

Presidential Primary Election Results and Turnout, 1980

TABLE C-1

PRIMARY RESULTS AND TURNOUT BY STATE

	Democrats				Republicans								Total Turnout,
Primary	Turnout	Brown[a]	Carter	Ken-nedy	No pref-erence	Turnout	Ander-son[b]	Baker[c]	Bush[d]	Con-nally[e]	Crane[f]	Reagan	No pref-erence	Both Parties[g]
Puerto Rico (D-3/16; R-2/17)	870,235	0.2%	51.7%	48.0%		186,371		37.0%	60.1%	1.1%				—[h]
New Hampshire (2/26)	111,930	9.6	47.1	37.3		147,157	9.8%	12.9	22.7	1.5	1.8%	49.6%		39.4%
Massachusetts (3/4)	907,332	3.5	28.7	65.1	2.2%	400,826	30.7	4.8	31.0	1.2	1.2	28.8	0.6%	30.4
Vermont (3/4)	39,703	0.9	73.1	25.5		65,611	29.0	12.3	21.7	1.3	1.9	30.1		29.3
South Carolina (3/8)						145,501	0.5	14.8	29.6		54.7			—[h]

(Table continues)

TABLE C-1 (continued)

Primary	Democrats					Republicans								Total Turnout, Both Parties[g]
	Turnout	Brown[a]	Carter	Kennedy	No preference	Turnout	Anderson[b]	Baker[c]	Bush[d]	Connally[e]	Crane[f]	Reagan	No preference	
Alabama (3/11)	237,464	4.0	81.6	13.2	0.7	211,353		0.9	25.9	0.5	2.4	69.7		16.6
Florida (3/11)	1,098,003	4.9	60.7	23.2	9.5	614,995	9.2	1.0	30.2	0.8	2.0	56.2		24.9
Georgia (3/11)	384,780	1.9	88.0	8.4	1.0	200,171	8.4	0.8	12.6	1.2	3.2	73.2		16.1
Illinois (3/18)	1,201,067	3.3	65.0	30.0		1,130,081	36.7	0.6	11.0	0.4	2.2	48.4		29.0
Connecticut (3/25)	210,275	2.6	41.5	46.9	6.4	182,284	22.1	1.3	38.6	0.3	1.0	33.9	2.3	16.9
New York (3/25)	989,062		41.1	58.9										—[h]
Kansas (4/1)	193,918	4.9	56.6	31.6	5.8	285,398	18.2	1.3	12.6	0.7	0.5	63.0	2.4	27.3
Wisconsin (4/1)	629,619	11.8	56.2	30.1	0.4	907,853	27.4	0.4	30.4	0.3	0.3	40.2	0.3	44.6
Louisiana (4/5)	358,741	4.7	55.7	22.5	11.6	41,683			18.8			74.9	5.3	14.4
Pennsylvania (4/22)	1,613,223	2.3	45.4	45.7	5.8	1,241,002	2.1	2.5	50.5	0.9		42.5		33.0

State														
Texas (5/3)	1,377,354	2.6	55.9	22.8	18.7	526,769	26.9		47.4			51.0	1.5	19.7
District of Columbia (5/6)	64,150		36.9	61.7		7,529			66.1		3.6			15.1
Indiana (5/6)	589,441		67.7	32.3		568,315	9.9		16.4			73.7		30.1
North Carolina (5/6)	737,262	2.9	70.1	17.7	9.3	168,391	5.1	1.5	21.8	0.7	0.3	67.6	2.7	22.3
Tennessee (5/6)	294,680	1.9	75.2	18.1	3.9	195,210	4.5		18.1		0.8	74.1	2.5	15.3
Maryland (5/13)	477,090	3.0	47.5	38.0	9.6	167,303	9.7		40.9		1.3	48.2		21.2
Nebraska (5/13)	153,881	3.6	46.9	37.6	10.4	205,203	5.8		15.3		0.5	76.0		31.5
Michigan (5/13)	78,424	29.4			46.4	595,176	8.2		57.5			31.8	1.7	10.3
Oregon (5/20)	343,050	9.7	58.2	32.1		304,647	10.1		34.7		0.7	54.5		33.9
Arkansas (5/20)	448,290		60.1	17.5	18.0									—[h]
Idaho (5/27)	50,482	4.1	62.2	22.0	11.8	134,879	9.7		4.0		0.8	82.9	2.6	29.2
Kentucky (5/27)	240,331		66.9	23.0	8.0	94,795	5.1		7.2			82.4	3.3	13.2
Nevada (5/27)	66,948		37.6	28.8	33.6	47,395			6.5			83.0	10.5	21.4
California (6/3)	3,323,812	4.0	37.7	44.8	11.4	2,512,994	13.6		4.9		0.9	80.2	10.5	34.4

(Table continues)

363

TABLE C-1 (continued)

Primary	Democrats					Republicans								Total Turnout, Both Parties[g]
	Turnout	Brown[a]	Carter	Kennedy	No preference	Turnout	Anderson[b]	Baker[c]	Bush[d]	Connally[e]	Crane[f]	Reagan	No preference	
Montana (6/3)	125,002		51.6	37.2	11.2	76,716			9.7			87.3	3.0	36.0
New Jersey (6/3)	560,908		37.9	56.2	3.5	277,977			17.1			81.3		15.5
New Mexico (6/3)	157,499		41.9	46.1	6.1	59,101	12.1		9.9		7.5	63.7	2.2	24.9
Ohio (6/3)	1,183,499		51.0	44.1		854,967			19.2			80.8		26.5
Rhode Island (6/3)	38,327	0.8	25.8	68.3	2.0	5,335			18.6			72.0	6.5	6.3
South Dakota (6/3)	67,671		45.9	48.2	5.9	88,325	6.3		4.2		0.5	82.1	5.8	32.2
West Virginia (6/3)	314,985		61.9	38.1		133,871			14.4			85.6		33.1
Total	19,538,438	2.9	51.2	37.6	6.6	12,785,184	12.3	1.4	24.0	0.6	0.8	59.7	0.5	25.3

a Brown withdrew April 1.
b Anderson withdrew April 24.
c Baker withdrew March 5.
d Bush withdrew May 26.
e Connally withdrew March 9.
f Crane withdrew April 17.
g Calculated by dividing the total number of votes cast in both parties' primaries by the estimated voting-age population in each state.
h Not calculated because of missing data.

Source: Rhodes Cook, "Carter, Reagan Exhibit Similar Assets in Preference Primaries," Congressional Quarterly Weekly Report,

TABLE C–2: PRIMARY RESULTS AND TURNOUT BY REGION, SYSTEM, AND PHASE

	Democrats						Republicans					
	Turnout	Carter	Kennedy	Brown[a]	Others	No preference	Turnout	Reagan	Bush[b]	Anderson[c]	Others	No preference
By Region												
East	5,326,985	42%	51%	2%	1%	4%	2,628,895	47%	38%	9%	6%	0%
South	5,176,905	65	20	3	1	11	2,198,868	62	28	4	5	1
Midwest	4,097,520	57	34	4	3	2	4,635,318	56	23	18	2	1
West	4,066,793	40	43	4	2	11	3,135,732	78	8	13	1	0
Territories	870,235	52	48	0	0	—[d]	186,371	—[d]	60	—[d]	40	—[d]
By System												
Closed	10,215,983	48	40	3	1	8	5,869,518	66	22	9	3	0
Open	9,322,455	55	35	3	2	5	6,915,666	55	25	15	4	1
By Phase												
First phase (2/17–4/5)	7,232,129	54	38	4	1	3	4,519,284	47	24	22	7	0
Second phase (4/22–5/27)	6,534,606	56	30	3	1	10	4,256,614	54	38	5	2	1
Third phase (6/3)	5,771,703	42	46	2	3	7	4,009,286	81	9	9	1	0
Grand Total	19,538,438	51	38	3	1	7	12,785,184	60	24	12	3	1

[a] Brown withdrew April 1. [b] Bush withdrew May 26. [c] Anderson withdrew April 24. [d] Not on ballot.

SOURCE: Cook, "Carter, Reagan Exhibit Similar Assets," pp. 1867–75, at p. 1869.

Appendix D

STATE SYSTEMS FOR CHOOSING
NATIONAL CONVENTION DELEGATES, 1968–1980

State, District, or Territory	1968	1972	1976	1980
Alabama	DP	DP	OP	OP
Alaska	CC	CC	CC	CC
Arizona	(D) CO (R) CC	CC	CC	CC
Arkansas	CO	CC	OP	(D) OP (R) CC
California	CP	CP	CP	CP
Colorado	CC	CC	CC	CC
Connecticut	CC	CC	CC	CP
Delaware	CC	CC	CC	CC
District of Columbia	CP	CP	CP	CP
Florida	CP	CP	CP	CP
Georgia	(D) CO (R) CC	CC	OP	OP
Hawaii	CC	CC	CC	CC
Idaho	CC	CC	OP	(D) CC (R) OP
Illinois	DP, CC	CP	OP	OP
Indiana	OP	OP	OP	OP
Iowa	CC	CC	CC	CC
Kansas	CC	CC	CC	CPI
Kentucky	CC	CC	CP	CP
Louisiana	CO	CC	CC	CP
Maine	CC	CC	CC	CC
Maryland	(D) CO (R) CC	CP	CP	CP
Massachusetts	CPI	CPI	CPI	CPI
Michigan	CC	OP	OP	(D) CC (R) OP

State, District, or Territory	1968	1972	1976	1980
Minnesota	CC	CC	CC	CC
Mississippi	CC	CC	CC	(D) CC
				(R) DP
Missouri	(D) CC, CO	CC	CC	CC
	(R) CC			
Montana	CC	CC	OP	OP
Nebraska	OP	OP	OP	OP
Nevada	CC	CC	CP	CP
New Hampshire	CPI	CPI	CPI	CPI
New Jersey	CPI	CPI	CPI	CPI
New Mexico	CC	CP	CC	CP
New York	DP, CO	DP, CO	DP	(D) CP
				(R) DP
North Carolina	CC	CP	CP	CP
North Dakota	CC	CC	CC	CC
Ohio	OP	OP	OP	OP
Oklahoma	CC	CC	CC	CC
Oregon	CP	CP	CP	CP
Pennsylvania	CP, CO	CP	CP	CP
Rhode Island	(D) CO	CPI	CPI	CPI
	(R) CC			
South Carolina	CC	CC	CC	(D) CC
				(R) OP
South Dakota	CP	CP	CP	CP
Tennessee	CC	OP	OP	OP
Texas	CC	CC	OP	CP
Utah	CC	CC	CC	CC
Vermont	CC	CC	X	X
Virginia	CC	CC	CC	CC
Washington	(D) CC, CO	CC	CC	CC
	(R) CC	CP	CP	CP
West Virginia	CP	CP	CP	CP
Wisconsin	OP	OP	OP	OP
Wyoming	CC	CC	CC	CC
Puerto Rico	(D) CO	CC	CC	OP
	(R) CC			

NOTES: CC = Delegates chosen by state and local caucuses and conventions. CO = Delegates chosen by state party committee. CP = Delegates chosen or bound by presidential preference primaries open only to voters preregistered as members of the particular parties. CPI = Delegates chosen or bound by presidential preference primaries open only to voters preregistered as members of the particular parties or as independents. D = Democrats. DP = Delegates chosen directly by voters in primaries; no presidential preference poll. OP = Delegates chosen or bound by presidential preference primaries open to all registered voters without regard to party preregistration. R = Republicans. X = Vermont, 1976 and 1980: both parties elected delegates in local caucuses; Democrats held a non-binding presidential preference primary; Republicans held a presidential preference primary binding on ten of nineteen delegates if one candidate received at least 40 percent of the votes.

SOURCES: The information for 1968 and 1972 is taken from descriptions of each state's delegate selection processes by *Congressional Quarterly Weekly Reports;* information for 1976 is taken from Austin Ranney, *Participation in American Presidential Nominations, 1976* (Washington, D.C.: American Enterprise Institute, 1977). Information for 1980 is taken from releases issued by the Democratic National Committee and the Republican National Committee.

Appendix E

Party and Coverage	1968	1972	1976	1980
PROLIFERATION OF PRESIDENTIAL PRIMARIES, 1968–1980				
Democratic party				
Number of states using a primary for selecting or binding national convention delegates	17	23	29[a]	31[a]
Number of votes cast by delegates chosen or bound by primaries	983	1,862	2,183	2,489
Percentage of all votes cast by delegates chosen or bound by primaries	37.5	60.5	72.6	74.7
Republican party				
Number of states using a primary for selecting or binding national convention delegates	16	22	28[a]	35
Number of votes cast by delegates chosen or bound by primaries	458	710	1,533	1,482
Percentage of all votes cast by delegates chosen or bound by primaries	34.3	52.7	67.9	74.3

[a] Does not include Vermont, which held a nonbinding presidential-preference poll but chose all delegates of both parties by caucuses and conventions.
SOURCE: The figures for 1968, 1972, and 1976 come from Austin Ranney, *Participation in American Presidential Nominations, 1976* (Washington, D.C.: American Enterprise Institute, 1977), table 1, p. 6. The figures for 1980 were compiled by Austin Ranney from materials distributed by the Democratic National Committee and the Republican National Committee.

Appendix F

Congressional Outcomes by State and Region, 1980

	Senate											
Region and State	Party lineup before election		No. of incumbents retired		No. of incumbents lost in primary		No. of incumbents lost in election		Party lineup after election		Net gain	
	D	R	D	R	D	R	D	R	D	R	D	R
Nation	59	41	2	3	3	1	9	0	47	53	0	12
New England												
Conn.	1	1	1	0	0	0	0	0	1	1	0	0
Maine	1	1	0	0	0	0	0	0	1	1	0	0
Mass.	2	0	0	0	0	0	0	0	2	0	0	0
N.H.	1	1	0	0	0	0	1	0	0	2	0	1
R.I.	1	1	0	0	0	0	0	0	1	1	0	0
Vt.	1	1	0	0	0	0	0	0	1	1	0	0
Total	7	5	1	0	0	0	1	0	6	6	0	1
Middle Atlantic												
Del.	1	1	0	0	0	0	0	0	1	1	0	0
Md.	1	1	0	0	0	0	0	0	1	1	0	0
N.J.	2	0	0	0	0	0	0	0	2	0	0	0
N.Y.	1	1	0	0	0	1	0	0	1	1	0	0
Pa.	0	2	0	1	0	0	0	0	0	2	0	0
Total	5	5	0	1	0	1	0	0	5	5	0	0
Deep South												
Ala.	2	0	0	0	1	0	0	0	1	1	0	1
Ark.	2	0	0	0	0	0	0	0	2	0	0	0
Ga.	2	0	0	0	0	0	1	0	1	1	0	1

					House of Representatives						
Party lineup before election		No. of incumbents retired		No. of incumbents lost in primary		No. of incumbents lost in election		Party lineup after election		Net gain	
D	R	D	R	D	R	D	R	D	R	D	R
273[a]	159	23	13	4	2	28	3	243	192	0	33
5	1	2	0	0	0	0	0	4	2	0	1
0	2	0	0	0	0	0	0	0	2	0	0
10	2	1	0	0	0	0	0	10	2	0	0
1	1	0	1	0	0	0	0	1	1	0	0
2	0	0	0	0	0	1	0	1	1	0	1
0	1	0	0	0	0	0	0	0	1	0	0
18	7	3	1	0	0	1	0	16	9	0	2
0	1	0	0	0	0	0	0	0	1	0	0
6	2	0	0	0	0	0	1	7	1	1	0
10	5	1	0	0	0	2	0	8	7	0	2
26	13	2	2	0	0	3	0	22	17	0	4
15	10	2	0	0	0	2	0	13	13	0	2
57	31	5	2	0	0	7	1	50	38	0	7
4	3	0	0	0	1	0	0	4	3	0	0
2	2	0	0	0	0	0	0	2	2	0	0
9	1	1	0	0	0	0	0	9	1	0	0

(Table continues)

Senate

Region and State	Party lineup before election		No. of incumbents retired		No. of incumbents lost in primary		No. of incumbents lost in election		Party lineup after election		Net gain	
	D	R	D	R	D	R	D	R	D	R	D	R
La.	2	0	0	0	0	0	0	0	2	0	0	0
Miss.	1	1	0	0	0	0	0	0	1	1	0	0
S.C.	1	1	0	0	0	0	0	0	1	1	0	0
Total	10	2	0	0	1	0	1	0	8	4	0	2
Outer South												
Fla.	2	0	0	0	1	0	0	0	1	1	0	1
N.C.	1	1	0	0	0	0	1	0	0	2	0	1
Tenn.	1	1	0	0	0	0	0	0	1	1	0	0
Tex.	1	1	0	0	0	0	0	0	1	1	0	0
Va.	1[b]	1	0	0	0	0	0	0	1	1	0	0
Total	6[b]	4	0	0	1	0	1	0	4	6	0	2
Border												
Ky.	2	0	0	0	0	0	0	0	2	0	0	0
Mo.	1	1	0	0	0	0	0	0	1	1	0	0
Okla.	1	1	0	1	0	0	0	0	1	1	0	0
W.Va.	2	0	0	0	0	0	0	0	2	0	0	0
Total	6	2	0	1	0	0	0	0	6	2	0	0
Great Lakes												
Ill.	1	1	1	0	0	0	0	0	1	1	0	0
Ind.	1	1	0	0	0	0	1	0	0	2	0	1
Mich.	2	0	0	0	0	0	0	0	2	0	0	0
Ohio	2	0	0	0	0	0	0	0	2	0	0	0
Wis.	2	0	0	0	0	0	1	0	1	1	0	1
Total	8	2	1	0	0	0	2	0	6	4	0	2
Farm Belt												
Iowa	1	1	0	0	0	0	1	0	0	2	0	1
Kans.	0	2	0	0	0	0	0	0	0	2	0	0
Minn.	0	2	0	0	0	0	0	0	0	2	0	0
Nebr.	2	0	0	0	0	0	0	0	2	0	0	0
N.Dak.	1	1	0	1	0	0	0	0	1	1	0	0
S.Dak.	1	1	0	0	0	0	1	0	0	2	0	1
Total	5	7	0	1	0	0	2	0	3	9	0	2

House of Representatives											
Party lineup before election		No. of incumbents retired		No. of incumbents lost in primary		No. of incumbents lost in election		Party lineup after election		Net gain	
D	R	D	R	D	R	D	R	D	R	D	R
6	2	0	0	1	0	0	0	6	2	0	0
3	2	0	0	0	0	0	0	3	2	0	0
4	2	1	0	0	0	1	0	2	4	0	2
28	12	2	0	1	1	1	0	26	14	0	2
12	3	0	0	0	1	0	0	11	4	0	1
9	2	0	0	0	0	2	0	7	4	0	2
5	3	0	0	0	0	0	0	5	3	0	0
20	4	2	0	0	0	1	0	19	5	0	1
4	6	1	0	0	0	2	0	1	9	0	3
50	18	3	0	0	1	5	0	43	25	0	7
4	3	1	0	0	0	0	0	4	3	0	0
8	2	1	0	0	0	1	0	6	4	0	2
5	1	1	0	0	0	0	0	5	1	0	0
4	0	1	0	0	0	1	0	2	2	0	2
21	6	4	0	0	0	2	0	17	10	0	4
10	14	1	1	1	0	0	0	10	14	0	0
7	4	0	1	0	0	1	0	6	5	0	1
13	6	2	0	0	0	1	0	12	7	0	1
10	13	1	1	0	0	1	1	10	13	0	0
6	3	0	0	0	0	1	0	5	4	0	1
46	40	4	3	1	0	4	1	43	43	0	3
3	3	0	1	0	0	0	0	3	3	0	0
1	4	0	1	0	0	0	0	1	4	0	0
4	4	1	0	0	0	0	0	3	5	0	1
1	2	1	0	0	0	0	0	0	3	0	1
0	1	0	1	0	0	0	0	1	0	1	0
1	1	0	1	0	0	0	0	1	1	0	0
10	15	2	4	0	0	0	0	9	16	0	1

(Table continues)

Senate

Region and State	Party lineup before election		No. of incumbents retired		No. of incumbents lost in primary		No. of incumbents lost in election		Party lineup after election		Net gain	
	D	R	D	R	D	R	D	R	D	R	D	R
Mountain												
Ariz.	1	1	0	0	0	0	0	0	1	1	0	0
Colo.	1	1	0	0	0	0	0	0	1	1	0	0
Ida.	1	1	0	0	0	0	1	0	0	2	0	1
Mont.	2	0	0	0	0	0	0	0	2	0	0	0
Nev.	1	1	0	0	0	0	0	0	1	1	0	0
N.Mex.	0	2	0	0	0	0	0	0	0	2	0	0
Utah	0	2	0	0	0	0	0	0	0	2	0	0
Wyo.	0	2	0	0	0	0	0	0	0	2	0	0
Total	6	10	0	0	0	0	1	0	5	11	0	1
Pacific												
Alas.	1	1	0	0	1	0	0	0	0	2	0	1
Calif.	1	1	0	0	0	0	0	0	1	1	0	0
Hawaii	2	0	0	0	0	0	0	0	2	0	0	0
Oreg.	0	2	0	0	0	0	0	0	0	2	0	0
Wash.	2	0	0	0	0	0	1	0	1	1	0	1
Total	6	4	0	0	1	0	1	0	4	6	0	2

NOTE: D indicates Democrats; R indicates Republicans.

[a] Total does not include three vacant seats last held by Democrats.

[b] Senator Harry Byrd was elected as an independent but participates in the Democratic caucus.

SOURCE: *Congressional Quarterly Weekly Report*, November 8, 1980, pp. 3338–45.

House of Representatives

Party lineup before election		No. of incumbents retired		No. of incumbents lost in primary		No. of incumbents lost in election		Party lineup after election		Net gain	
D	R	D	R	D	R	D	R	D	R	D	R
2	2	0	0	0	0	0	0	2	2	0	0
3	2	0	1	0	0	0	0	3	2	0	0
0	2	0	1	0	0	0	0	0	2	0	0
1	1	0	0	0	0	0	0	1	1	0	0
1	0	0	0	0	0	0	0	1	0	0	0
1	1	0	0	0	0	0	0	0	2	0	1
1	1	0	0	0	0	1	0	0	2	0	1
0	1	0	0	0	0	0	0	0	1	0	0
9	10	0	2	0	0	1	0	7	12	0	2
0	1	0	0	0	0	0	0	0	1	0	0
25	18	0	1	1	0	4	1	22	21	0	3
2	0	0	0	0	0	0	0	2	0	0	0
4	0	0	0	1	0	1	0	3	1	0	1
6	1	0	0	0	0	1	0	5	2	0	1
37	20	0	1	2	0	6	1	32	25	0	5

Appendix G

Gubernatorial Election Results, 1980

State	Candidates	Votes	Percent
Arkansas	Bill Clinton (D)[a]	397,262	48
	Frank D. White (R)	427,818	52
Delaware	William J. Gordy (D)	64,903	29
	Pierre S. du Pont (R)[a]	159,773	70
	R. Lawrence Levy (LIBERT)	1,903	1
Indiana	John A. Hillenbrand II (D)	900,433	42
	Robert D. Orr (R)	1,231,227	58
Missouri	Joseph P. Teasdale (D)[a]	967,757	47
	Christopher S. Bond (R)	1,079,454	53
Montana	Ted Schwinden (D)	185,060	55
	Jack Ramirez (R)	148,732	45
New Hampshire	Hugh Gallen (D)[a]	226,285	59
	Meldrim Thomson, Jr. (R)	155,717	41
	James E. Pinard (LIBERT)	1,309	0
North Carolina	James B. Hunt, Jr. (D)[a]	1,128,317	62
	I. Beverly Lake, Jr. (R)	686,973	38
	Bobb Yates Emory (LIBERT)	9,879	0
North Dakota	Arthur A. Link (D)[a]	127,034	47
	Allen I. Olson (R)	145,941	53
Rhode Island	J. Joseph Garrahy (D)[a]	284,418	74
	Vincent A. Cianci (R)	99,469	26
Utah	Scott M. Matheson (D)[a]	327,806	55
	Bob Wright (R)	264,523	45
Vermont	M. Jerome Diamond (D)	76,328	37
	Richard A. Snelling (R)[a]	121,985	59
	John Potthast (LU)	1,803	1

APPENDIX G (continued)

State	Candidates	Votes	Percent
	Bruce Cullen (I)	2,050	1
	Daniel Woodward (I)	5,136	2
Washington	James A. McDermott (D)	670,383	44
	John Spellman (R)	869,945	56
West Virginia	John D. Rockefeller IV (D)[a]	387,269	54
	Arch A. Moore, Jr. (R)	328,911	46
	Jack K. Kelley (LIBERT)	3,059	0

NOTE: D = Democrat; R = Republican; LIBERT = Libertarian; LU = Liberty Union; I = independent.

[a] Incumbent.

SOURCE: *Congressional Quarterly Weekly Report*, November 8, 1980, pp. 338–45.

Appendix H

Partisan Control of State Legislatures, 1968-1980

FIGURE H–1

NUMBER OF STATE LEGISLATORS BY PARTY

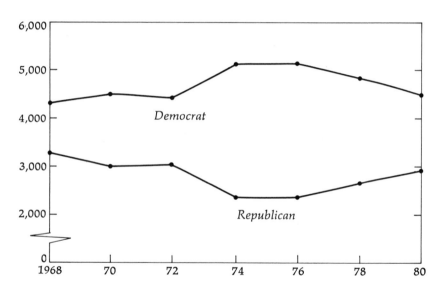

FIGURE H–2

NUMBER OF LEGISLATIVE CHAMBERS BY PARTY

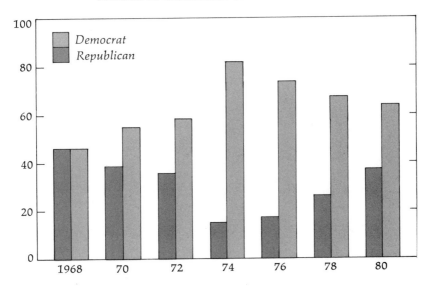

SOURCES: Figures for 1968, 1970, and 1972 are from *Statistical Abstract of the United States, 1973* (Washington, D.C.: Bureau of the Census, 1973), table 608, p. 377; figures for 1974, 1976, and 1978 are from *Statistical Abstract of the United States, 1979*, table 831, p. 511; figures for 1980 were compiled by Norman J. Ornstein.

Contributors

ALBERT R. HUNT is congressional and national political correspondent for the *Wall Street Journal* and a regular participant in public television's "Washington Week in Review."

CHARLES O. JONES, Maurice Falk Professor of Politics at the University of Pittsburgh, will become Robert Kent Gooch Professor of Government and Foreign Affairs at the University of Virginia in September 1981. The author of *Clean Air, An Introduction to the Study of Public Policy*, and the forthcoming *The United States Congress: People, Place, and Policy*, he served as managing editor of the *American Political Science Review* from 1977 to 1981.

ANTHONY KING, an adjunct scholar at the American Enterprise Institute, is editor of *The New American Political System*, author of *Britain Says Yes: The 1975 Referendum on the Common Market*, and a contributor to *Britain at the Polls, 1979: A Study of the General Election* and *Democracy at the Polls: A Comparative Study of Competitive National Elections*. He is professor of government at the University of Essex and comments on elections for the British Broadcasting Corporation and the London *Observer*.

MICHAEL J. MALBIN is a resident fellow at the American Enterprise Institute and a contributing editor to the *National Journal*. His books include *Unelected Representatives: Congressional Staff and the Future of Representative Government* and *Parties, Interest Groups, and Campaign Finance Laws*.

THOMAS E. MANN is executive director of the American Political Science Association and a visiting fellow at the American Enterprise Institute. He is the author of *Unsafe at Any Margin: Interpreting Congressional Elections*, coauthor of *Vital Statistics on Congress, 1980*, and coeditor of *The New Congress*.

NORMAN J. ORNSTEIN is associate professor of politics at Catholic University, adjunct scholar at the American Enterprise Institute, and political editor of "The Lawmakers" series on public television. His books include *Congress in Change, Interest Groups, Lobbying and Policymaking, Vital Statistics on Congress, 1980,* and *The New Congress.*

NELSON W. POLSBY, professor of political science at the University of California, Berkeley, was editor of the *American Political Science Review* from 1972 to 1977. His books include *British Government and Its Discontents, Community Power and Political Theory, Presidential Elections, Congress and the Presidency,* and *The New Congress.*

AUSTIN RANNEY, a former professor of political science at the University of Wisconsin–Madison and a former president of the American Political Science Association, is codirector of the program in Political and Social Processes at the American Enterprise Institute. His recent works include *Participation in American Presidential Nominations, The Federalization of Presidential Primaries,* and *Referendums: A Comparative Study of Practice and Theory.* He was coeditor of *Democracy at the Polls: A Comparative Study of Competitive National Elections.*

MICHAEL J. ROBINSON, on leave from the faculty of Catholic University, is director of the Media Analysis Project at George Washington University. Author of more than fifty articles dealing with the media and politics, he is completing two books on that topic: *Over the Wire and on TV,* with coauthor Margaret Sheehan, will be completed in 1981, and *National Media, Natitonal Politics* will appear in 1982.

WILLIAM SCHNEIDER, a senior research fellow at the Hoover Institution at Stanford University, is a political consultant to the *Los Angeles Times* and senior editor of *Opinion Outlook,* a Washington-based newsletter on public opinion. He is coauthor with Seymour Martin Lipset of *The Confidence Gap: How Americans View Their Institutions,* to be published in 1982. He has taught political science at Harvard University and recently held an International Affairs Fellowship from the Council on Foreign Relations.

AARON WILDAVSKY is professor of political science, Political Science Department, and principal investigator, Survey Research Center, at the University of California, Berkeley. His most recent books include *The Politics of Mistrust: Estimating American Oil and Gas Resources, How to Limit Government Spending,* and *Speaking Truth to Power.*

Index

AEI's *At the Polls* Studies

Australia at the Polls: The National Elections of 1975, Howard R. Penniman, ed.

The Australian National Elections of 1977, Howard R. Penniman, ed.

Britain at the Polls: The Parliamentary Elections of 1974, Howard R. Penniman, ed.

Britain Says Yes: The 1975 Referendum on the Common Market, Anthony King

Britain at the Polls, 1979: A Study of the General Election, Howard R. Penniman, ed.

Canada at the Polls: The General Elections of 1974, Howard R. Penniman, ed.

France at the Polls: The Presidential Elections of 1974, Howard R. Penniman, ed.

The French National Assembly Elections of 1978, Howard R. Penniman, ed.

Germany at the Polls: The Bundestag Election of 1976, Karl Cerny, ed.

India at the Polls: The Parliamentary Elections of 1977, Myron Weiner

Ireland at the Polls: The Dáil Elections of 1977, Howard R. Penniman, ed.

Israel at the Polls: The Knesset Elections of 1977, Howard R. Penniman, ed.

Italy at the Polls: The Parliamentary Elections of 1976, Howard R. Penniman, ed.

Japan at the Polls: The House of Councillors Election of 1974, Michael K. Blaker, ed.

A Season of Voting: The Japanese Elections of 1976 and 1977, Herbert Passin, ed.

New Zealand at the Polls: The General Elections of 1978, Howard R. Penniman, ed.

Scandinavia at the Polls: Recent Political Trends in Denmark, Norway, and Sweden, Karl H. Cerny, ed.

Venezuela at the Polls: The National Elections of 1978, Howard R. Penniman, ed.

Democracy at the Polls: A Comparative Study of Competitive National Elections, David Butler, Howard R. Penniman, and Austin Ranney, eds.

Referendums: A Comparative Study of Practice and Theory, David Butler and Austin Ranney, eds.

Studies are forthcoming on the latest national elections in Belgium, Canada, Denmark, France, Germany, Italy, India, Israel, Jamaica, Japan, the Netherlands, Norway, Portugal, Spain, Sweden, and Switzerland and on the first elections ot the European Parliament. Also *The American Elections of 1980*, edited by Austin Ranney.

A NOTE ON THE BOOK

*The typeface used for the text of this book is
Palatino, designed by Hermann Zapf.
The type was set by
Hendricks-Miller Typographic Company, of Washington, D.C.
Braun-Brumfield, Inc., of Ann Arbor, Michigan,
printed and bound the book, using
paper manufactured by the S. D. Warren Company.
The cover and format were designed by Pat Taylor,
and the figures were drawn by Hördur Karlsson.
The manuscript was edited by Joanne Ainsworth and
by Gertrude Kaplan, of the AEI Publications staff.*

SELECTED AEI PUBLICATIONS

AEI ASSOCIATES PROGRAM